RESPONSIBLE FREEDOM

RESPONSIBLE FREEDOM

Guidelines
to Christian Action

L. HAROLD DeWOLF

1817

HARPER & ROW, PUBLISHERS
New York, Evanston, and London

FIRST EDITION

LIBRARY OF CONGRESS CATALOG CARD NUMBER: 79-126034

To
Arline W. Marsh
with appreciation and affection

Contents

Preface

A comprehensive treatment of Christian ethics in a single volume cannot take the place of more specialized writings.

On the other hand, the full weight of appeal for a position on any one ethical issue can be evaluated only in a broad context. Basic theory must be seen in relation to concrete problems if it is to be understood, appreciated, and adequately tested. Likewise, proposals for dealing with particular issues need to be seen in relation to basic principles. Moreover, different social evils and also resources for good are so deeply interrelated that policies regarding some invariably affect others also.

Consequently, I believe there is still value for the experienced scholar, as well as for the beginner, in having an occasional inclusive volume like this one. Attention to the references in the text and footnotes with aid from the indices will provide the reader with a considerable list of authors and writings dealing more fully with the various topics.

Two kinds of incompleteness in this volume are intentional. I have not tried to include consideration of all important social problems or even all in which I have a keen interest. The reason should be obvious. I have not always made explicit the use of various principles and elements of method explicated in Part I, when treating the particular problems in Part II. To have made them invariably explicit would have introduced too much repetition and would have unduly prolonged the whole. However, even when the process of application has not been made explicit, I have endeavored, in thought, to adhere faithfully to the principles and method advocated. Anyone using the book may fill in details as he may wish, in order further to test the method and the proposals of policy.

There is here no chapter on race relations. Racial pride and prejudice penetrate deeply the church, the economic system, our use of technology, the state, and the international order. They cannot be usefully discussed apart from these subjects. There are, therefore, discussions of race in many places throughout the book, rather than combined in a single chapter.

I acknowledge with gratitude my indebtedness to many persons without assigning to them responsibility for my errors. R. Eugene Gilmore, my friend of many years and recent colleague, especially encouraged my embarking on this complex and difficult task. Three scholars with whom I have team-taught in Christian Social Ethics have contributed much to my knowledge and thought. They are Walter G. Muelder, Haskell M. Miller, and Philip Wogaman. I am similarly indebted to Charles E. Curran of Catholic University who joined me in teaching an interseminary course on Ethics of Natural Law in the spring semester of 1968. To the last three men named, to James C. Logan, and also to an unidentified reader engaged by the publisher, I am indebted for critical reading of the first draft.

This is the tenth book for the careful typing of which I am grateful to my wife, Madeleine. In fact this one, like some of its predecessors, was typed complete in two successive drafts and with many helpful observations.

My thoughts on medical ethics were considerably advanced by the opportunity to lecture, and subsequently participate in discussion with various specialists, in a section of the American Association for the Advancement of Science presented by Boston University in December, 1969. The discussion of ecology and conservation owes much to my naturalist son Daniel. Writing on this subject I have drawn considerably on material first presented in my lecture at the conference entitled "A Theology of Survival: Ecology in Theological Perspective," sponsored by the School of Theology at Claremont, California.

L. HAROLD DEWOLF

Wesley Theological Seminary
Washington, D.C.

part I

BASIC PRINCIPLES

chapter one

Preliminary Exploration

———————— •⟨◇⟩• ————————

A. INITIAL DEFINITIONS

The decade of the seventies is a period of fateful human decisions. As we choose what to do about race relations, technological unemployment, pressures of population, war, crime, poverty in the midst of affluence, the use of drugs, and the style of our daily living, we are often deciding technical issues. We are always deciding ethical issues. For when we make choices so freighted with significant and partially predictable consequences, we are making morally good or evil, better or worse decisions.

Ethics is the discipline concerned with the evaluation of human conduct, that is, with determining the goodness or evil properly ascribed to human choices.

Christian ethics is this discipline pursued in the perspective of Christian faith.

The present approach to Christian ethics will attempt an orderly study of the subject designed to establish norms and methods by which the serious reader may approach particular choices in a carefully planned way. This does not mean to promise computerized solutions for moral problems. Theoretical ethics cannot be worked like plane geometry nor can the right choices in practical ethics be reached even with the imperfect degree of precision and assurance of a design for a bridge. On the other hand, it is not necessary to attempt moral choices in the random, impressionistic, blindly traditional, or purely emotional ways which are all too common. The reader is invited into a common search for as valid, orderly, and reliable norms and methods as can be discovered for guiding human decisions.

Neither legalism nor irresponsibility characterizes authentic Christian living. Christian decisions are made in God-given freedom, true, but in *responsible freedom*. Hence this study will seek to build a structure of definable principles by which the conduct of human wills freed by God's grace can be reasonably and responsibly guided.

3

All this may look very general and abstract. Indeed, no small part of the study must inevitably be rather abstract theory. If we are to establish norms to guide all or even many decisions, they will have to be stated and defended, at least in part, in somewhat general terms.

However, we must keep in mind, from start to finish, that our concern is with real choices which real people must make, choices on which may depend the future of nations or of all mankind. Even the daily decisions of ordinary people may deeply influence their own destinies and the lives of others as well. Whatever other effects they have, they do certainly determine, as they are determined by the character of the persons making the choices, for the pattern of a man's choices is the man's character. Likewise, the choices made by a church, a community, or a nation determine its character and future.

B. The Human Stuff of Moral Decision

Let us now look at some dilemmas of choice which have confronted people in real life and see some of the characteristic elements in a practical moral problem.

Case 1.   The Price of a Teaching Position

Ruth Jameson looked forward with joy to graduation from a teachers' college. She hoped that in the fall she could teach in the high school near her parents so that she could live at home with them. They were growing old and needed her. Moreover, she knew how hard many people had worked to establish and build up a good high school in her home town, despite a corrupt government and other obstacles. She would be one of the better-trained teachers in the school and could make a solid contribution to the life of the community.

Soon Ruth heard a rumor that the school committee was leaning toward another applicant who was so poorly trained that rules would have to be suspended to elect her. She was also known as a young woman of careless habits who would not provide the kind of responsible teaching and example needed. It seemed incredible that such a person could be seriously considered. Yet the rumors grew and at times seemed intentionally directed to Ruth by a woman very closely related to the committee.

Finally the whole situation was made clear. The poorly trained applicant was ready to pay a corrupt majority of the school committee for the place. The other committee members did not want her to have it. Ruth Jameson was their choice. But they lacked one vote of a majority. Now one of the corrupt members agreed to vote for Ruth if he could receive five hundred dollars. Ruth was told, indirectly but reliably, that if she would put five hundred dollars in cash into a certain man's hand, she would be promptly appointed. Moreover, the committee would then suspend the rules and elect her immediately to life tenure. She asked her minister's advice.

Should she refuse to pay and leave her neighbors' children to the incompetent teaching and dubious moral example of the rival applicant while she herself left her parental home and sought a position elsewhere? Or should she perform this one evil act and compensate by years of generous and able service?

Oh yes, she had thought of taking a third course, paying with marked bills and then exposing the corruption of the committeeman. But she knew a girl who had attempted that in a neighboring town. The police, the town counsel, and the county government were such an intertwined network of corruption that the would-be reformer had succeeded only in getting herself maligned and blacklisted. Her teaching career was ruined and no good had come of it. Perhaps such a martyr's role would be the noble one, Ruth thought, but under the circumstances it would seem futile and pointless.

She paid; she was elected to life tenure; and she has taught for many years. Did she make the right choice?

This true story (only the name being fictitious) illustrates a number of characteristics which recur in many problems of practical ethics.

Circumstances have a way of complicating and blurring issues. Ruth Jameson would have had not the slightest difficulty in answering the question, "Is it right to bribe public officials?" It was the concrete situation which made the answer hard.

One trouble is that in particular circumstances good rules of conduct often come into conflict. On the one side, it is clear that a good citizen should refrain from bribing. On the other, it is also clear that a good citizen should try to improve education and seek the welfare of the youth in his community. To be a loyal daughter, helpful to one's aging parents, that, too, is good.

It is also worthy of notice that the weighing of such a moral problem raises questions of probable consequences to be expected from different courses of action.

Again, many a moral dilemma is too simply stated. There may be other possible courses of action beside the ones contemplated. A less obvious way may be much better than either of the distasteful choices under consideration.

Among other aspects of the example before us only one more will be indicated here. This is the way in which an individual may properly look to others to assist him in his more difficult and momentous decisions. Especially in a Christian church, a person may, like Ruth, look to a pastor or a lay Christian friend to talk things out from similar basic perspectives and so clarify the ethical issues.

It may not take high intelligence or great skill to choose with good intentions. But it does require both intelligence and skill, along with knowledge, personal sensitivity, and creative imagination, to do the morally best thing possible in many a situation. Goodness needs brains as well as upright motives.

Case 2. Pills for Single Girls

Should birth control pills be dispensed to unmarried women by public welfare agencies? The very question raises intense moral indignation. Such a policy would, it is said, make the government partner in a conspiracy to ruin the morals of our young women. It would represent official public acceptance of sex without marriage.

Not so, reply the advocates of the policy. "The pill" would be provided only for girls who requested it. Evidently, they would already have expected to engage in sexual intercourse, else they would not be seeking medical protection against pregnancy. Besides, how else is society to protect itself against the great numbers of illegitimate children continually added to the welfare rolls? Obviously, many indigent girls are indulging in sex, with or without birth control. Granting that such behavior is an evil, should we not at least try to avoid the additional evil of unwanted, homeless, illegitimate children?

The way to deal with such illegitimacy among the poor, the opponents retort, is by cleaning up the slums, abolishing poverty, providing significant jobs for everyone, and launching effective character education. It is conceded that some girls who would ask for the pill would be indulging in sex anyway, but others would not. Some would be near the borderline of surrender to temptation and for some of them the inhibiting fear of pregnancy would be of crucial importance. Hence to remove this fear would be to promote immorality. This would mean also the promoting of venereal disease, already spreading rapidly since the pill made sex easier and safer for those who knew about it and could afford to buy it.

At this mention of easy access by the affluent, the advocates of free protection are likely to point to a "double standard" of morality for upper and lower economic classes, as well as for men and women. Why, it is contended, should the poor girls be threatened with unwanted babies when those on upper-class allowances or earned incomes can indulge in the same behavior without fear? From discussion of class differences the argument may go into charges and countercharges with racist overtones.

This issue presents in some form every typical characteristic noted in connection with the earlier example. In addition, it conspicuously exhibits two other aspects of ethical issues.

One is the tendency of different social problems to interpenetrate. Standards of sexual behavior, relative responsibilities of men and women, justice in economic and race relations, and problems of public health are all interrelated. Further extension of the argument would probably introduce also the effects of military service and war, the question of proper functions of the law in relation to morality, and the relevance of religion to public and private morals.

A critically important need is barely beneath the surface during much of the discussion. This is the need for dependable information on such subjects as the following questions: How many illegitimate births are there per year in the population concerned? Are they increasing or decreasing? What is known about sex behavior of unmarried women among the poor and the affluent? What, precisely, are the trends in the spread of venereal disease and how are they statistically related to the availability of the pill? What can be known about the importance of fear of pregnancy as a deterrent to illicit sex?

Serious pursuit of the discussion would also raise questions about basic ethical presuppositions. Someone would ask whether we could properly assume "middle-class standards" of morality when discussing the conduct of the poor. Others would ask whether modern thought could justify the assumption that premarital sex was evil. They might question whether it was evil in itself or only socially undesirable when likely to produce children of uncertain or irresponsible paternity or without secure homes for their support and personal nurture. Why, it could be asked, should we assume that chastity of the unmarried and faithful monogamy of the married are morally required? Replies might appeal to religious scriptures and historic doctrines, to traditions of Western culture, or to more general considerations of superior social values claimed for strict monogamy as over against polygamy, promiscuity, and premarital sexual experimentation.

Other Cases

Many ethical questions concern choices confronting governments, corporations, universities, labor unions, or churches. All persons who can participate in the decision-making of such bodies have moral obligations relative to them. A few examples follow.

Ought the United States to take the initiative in nuclear disarmament? If so, by what steps? In a period of inflation what are the obligations of corporation management regarding wages, profits, and the pricing of products? What should a university do for the education of black young people who have graduated from inferior segregated high schools and so cannot compete on even terms for college admission? When a construction workers' union with exclusively white membership faces competition from unorganized members of minority groups working for lower wages, what should it do? What proportion of its budget ought a city church to spend on music, and what proportion on service to the poor?

These questions raise more general and basic ones regarding the kind of society or of individual life most worthy of cultivation. How essential is the family to the good life? What are the relative values of order and freedom? What kind of being is the human? Under what social conditions can he grow and flourish? What needs must be provided if he is to fulfill his own essential nature?

Such basic issues as these will be examined in the course of our study.

C. Relation of Ethics to Other Studies

1. Subject Matter Shared with Other Sciences of Man

As our original definition indicates, ethics is concerned with human choices. But so is psychology. So also are anthropology and sociology. What about economics, political science, and history?

Indeed, all the disciplines devoted to the study of human beings as living agents must describe, relate, and interpret at least some kinds of human choices. The historian may include in his preview any *past* choices which he regards as sufficiently significant in relation to his particular study. The political scientist examines such choices as affect the structure and operation of government. Economists are concerned with those choices which affect the production, distribution, or consumption of goods and services. Like ethics economics includes many references to values, although unlike ethics it looks upon values as material or in terms of material equivalents (such as prices or wages). Anthropology in the broadest sense, as "the science of man," could include descriptive generalizations on all human choices. Usually it seeks to describe rather the various groupings of men, together with their cultures and their ways of relating to each other and to their physical environments. Obviously, such study includes a very wide range of human choices; indeed, it may include any choice without exception, but only so far as the choice is seen in relation to the various human groupings.

Sociology, too, as the study of human groups, is concerned with choices by groups, or as affecting group structures and processes, or as affected by group influences. Since all human choices can be viewed from one or more of these perspectives, none are exempt from the sociologist's examination.

Psychology, as the study of the human mind or human behavior, has an immediate interest in any and every process of human choice, together with its causes or conditions and with its effects on the chooser and on other persons.

The field of ethics begins to look crowded! Indeed, the making of ethical decisions is the responsibility of every person and group without exception. Ethicists do not claim moral superiority to other people. They do specialize in seeking to identify proper norms and methods of making ethical decisions. The methods are bound to draw heavily on data contributed by other disciplines. For our decision-making we all need the most accurate and comprehensive possible knowledge of relevant facts. To gain such knowledge we must continually draw on the findings of various disciplines. But moral decision must always go beyond knowledge of the data to ethical judgment of relative value and obligation. The study of such judgment is ethics. These relationships must be further illustrated.

2. *Descriptive and Normative Interests*

The primary focus of most disciplines is on the description of data and their relationships.

History, for example, chronicles past events and displays their relationships to preceding and succeeding events. To be sure, many a historian is especially interested in history because it may warn men from repeating past mistakes or suggest by analogy useful solutions of present problems. Thus Thucydides wrote,

> I shall be content if those shall pronounce my History useful who desire to give a view of events as they did really happen, and as they are very likely, in accordance with human nature, to repeat themselves at some future time,—if not exactly the same, yet very similar.   [*History*, I:2:2]

However, when the historian draws analogies between past and present and then goes on to give advice regarding decisions which should be made now, he is stepping out of his role as historian to bring the products of his historical study to bear upon practical decision-making. This is not to complain of his doing so. On the contrary, without some knowledge of past events, it is hard to see how we could possibly hope to make decisions wisely in the present. We can be glad when the man who is a good historian is also a morally responsible citizen and even, on occasion, a moral philosopher as well.

Sociologists, too, are much given to saying what social policies we ought to adopt for solution or amelioration of such ills as poverty, social discord, or rising rates of crime. All of us are decision makers and all are affected by social decisions being made. The sociologist is no exception. Moreover, he, along with the economist and the political scientist, is especially competent to predict the probable consequences of proposed public policies. It is his business to interpret the interconnections of group structures and activities. But when he goes beyond such interpretation and prediction to say what consequences *ought* to be sought, then no matter how salutary his advice he is speaking as a moralist. Similarly, an economist can say that a certain policy will shift more economic activity to the public sector and away from the private sector. Whether this is good or bad may depend in part on other social data, but it will depend also on the answer to the question what form of community life ought to be preferred.

When the psychologist studies a process of human choices, he is asking how this process is related to previous conditioning experiences, to the social pressures upon the chooser, or the structure of his affective psyche.

For example, a psychological account of a young man's choosing to prepare for the ministry may describe his conditioning by his family's deference for one or more pastors, by his own useful and significant experience with a minister, or by his long-conditioned desires to help people with their personal problems. On the other hand, the psychologist may explain that the young man shrinks from the aggressive competition of business and industry and, being of rather passive personality, prefers the security of the pastoral office to the risks and opportunities of higher earnings in the marketplace. Very likely, the total motivation is a mixed affair. Knowing these things can be highly useful to the theological student and his adviser. However, these facts and interpretations, in themselves, do not tell whether his choice is the one he ought (ethically) to have made. The answer to that question will require placing with the facts certain judgments as to the standards or criteria by which one determines what are ethically sound choices in general and decisions for entering the ministry in particular.

Ethics is concerned with establishing norms and methods by which to evaluate choices as morally good or evil, better or worse. It must take careful account of what *is*. Hence it must draw information from many descriptive sciences. Its primary and distinctive focus of concern, however, is on what *ought* to *be*, and even more specifically on what human beings *ought* to *do*.

It is to be observed that some other disciplines are also normative, though their norms are concerned with categories other than the ethical. Logic is concerned with discovering the *value* of different kinds of thinking for the gaining and extending of knowledge. All its principles, whether axioms or other, imply a preceding conditional clause reading, "If thought is to be consistent, then . . ." or "If thought is to be of a kind reliably extending knowledge, then . . ."

Aesthetics is another normative study. Its task is to seek the meaning of beauty, in its many forms, and to define norms for the judgment of beauty. The aesthetic good, beauty, may not be good at all in other categories of value.

I once precipitated an argument in Africa when I commented on the beauty of the skin which my son had removed from a puff adder. With intense feeling an African teenager replied, "No! It is not beautiful. It is bad. It kills people!" Only after a long discussion of various pictures and designs he finally conceded, "Oh, I see. You mean it *looks* beautiful only to my *eyes*." Even then he added, "But it is not *really* beautiful because it is bad." His ingrained feeling of fear and hostility was so deep that he could not fully abstract an aesthetic judgment from the urgently practical attitudes which had long been necessary to survival.

From its own particular perspective ethics is interested in every kind of value, including economic, logical, and aesthetic values, and also the value of preserving life against the threat of poisonous snakes. But the interest of ethics in all these values is only ancillary to the concern with evaluation of human choices. In fact, it is even more specialized. For it may be conceded that a certain choice is logically sound, given the agent's presuppositions, or that it is economically productive and profitable, yet it may be insisted that it is ethically evil. For example, a man seeking a financially secure and rewarding investment may select stocks which are very attractive as far as these characteristics are concerned, but his choice may be ethically evil because the company which he is strengthening by his investment may produce socially destructive products or compete successfully by maintaining a particularly vicious labor policy. We must return soon to examination of the moral category with which ethical judgments have to do.

Logic answers the question how we ought to think, but this *logical ought* is not to be confused with the *moral ought* of ethical obligation. We need to think logically if we are to extend knowledge in any field. Logic is therefore important to ethics, even though the two disciplines must not be confused. As ethics needs to be in cooperative relations with sound psychology and sociology, so also ethical thinking must be logical; but ethics is not psychology, sociology, nor logic.

3. *Interdependence of Disciplines*

Probably few of the people now engaging their lives in the sciences of man, especially social studies, would be doing so if they did not expect that they or others could use the results of their research and instruction in the wise guidance of human decisions. Often they take for granted certain ethical assumptions that, together with the sociological facts and relationships which they discover or transmit, lead to the support of particular personal, organizational, or political decisions. Yet the ethical assumptions are there and without them the findings of sociology would not lead to any decisions other than the purely descriptive ones.

For example, statistical facts show that, in the United States, per 100,000 live births in 1965 four times as many nonwhite mothers died as white mothers. Most social scientists infer that more effort must be exerted to make adequate nutrition and medical services available to nonwhite mothers. The fact that the mortality rate of the nonwhite babies in the same year was nearly three times as high as that of white babies is taken as added argument for the same practical conclusion.[1] This conclusion is justified only if one makes some such ethical assumption as that the maternal and infant mortality rates of nonwhites *ought* to be reduced to a level comparable to those of whites. The ready acceptance of such assumptions by the reader does not alter the fact that they are ethically normative propositions and not descriptive ones.

In this, as in innumerable instances, social studies are dependent upon ethics for determination of their practical application. At the same time it is obvious also that ethics is dependent on social studies for the facts and the delineation of the causes necessary to move from general ethical propositions to decisions of policy. For example, with the aid of social statistics we can move from the assumption that the citizens of a country have rights to life and the means of life without regard to race to the decision that nutrition and maternal service available to nonwhites in the United States should be improved.

Indeed, the interdependence of ethics and social sciences goes even further. Ethical convictions, even moral outrage, often serve to direct social scientists to study one set of social data rather than another. Generally speaking, the direction of social research is determined by the need which some people, at least, feel for getting information to assist in making sound decisions. On the other hand, serious ethical study concentrates upon problems which facts, often as interpreted and disseminated by social scientists, show to be in especially urgent need of attention for action.

Psychology is in many ways closely related to ethics. The psychologist may, of course, describe the process of personal decision-making itself, together with certain influences affecting it and other influences exerted by it. Psychology can render great help to students of ethics and even more to thoughtful practitioners by disclosing devices of self-deception which frequently misguide us into wrong decisions and by enabling us to understand better how alternative courses of action are likely to affect other people.

1. Statistics from the Report of *The National Advisory Committee on Civil Disorders* (March 1, 1968), p. 136.

If we seek to base ethical theory in whole or in part upon the nature of man, as in ethics of natural law, then psychological knowledge concerning man is obviously essential.

4. Ethics and Philosophy

Ethics is generally regarded as a branch of philosophy. If philosophy be regarded as the disciplined study of first principles, then its various branches are concerned with first principles of different kinds of knowledge or of truth. So considered, ethics is the branch of philosophy concerned with first principles of good conduct, that is of moral choice.

Like all other thoughtful pursuits, ethics is bound by the basic canons of logic. If what I say is not understood to exclude the contradictory of my assertion, all seriousness and progress of thought are excluded. If in ethics I say that I ought to love my neighbor as myself, but I still agree with the proposition that I am under no obligation to love my neighbor as myself, I have contributed nothing but confusion to ethical discussion.

The relation between ethics and metaphysics is especially difficult to interpret clearly and with assurance. At first glance the two may seem so radically different as to be poles apart. Metaphysics is asking what is truly real. Ethics is asking not what is but what ought to be chosen.

Actually, the two are much more closely related than this. If we ought to choose certain ends or in a certain manner, then that *obligation* is one kind of reality needing to be taken into account by the metaphysician. He needs to observe that the whole reality of which we are a part is of such a nature that words like "obligation," "ought," and "duty" have meaning in that whole. Moreover, the more ethics enables us to understand about true obligation the more definitely known is the nature of this ethical reality which the metaphysician must consider.

On the other hand, ethical obligation does not occur in a vacuum of nothingness. It occurs in a real world. The goals we ought to seek are certainly related to the kind of reality we are and the nature of the whole reality in the midst of which we live and make decisions. Hence the kind of metaphysics to which one subscribes deeply affects the kind of ethics which one is entitled to hold.

Many people never heard of metaphysics. Marxians, some theologians, and various others reject it. Nevertheless, they, like all other people, have certain ideas about what is most basically real. However arrived at, those ideas provide the background or context in relation to which problems of obligation are confronted. This is especially evident among the very groups just mentioned. Believing in dialectical materialism and hence in economic determinism, Marxian moralizing stresses the virtues and vices which have especially to do with economic production, distribution, and consumption, and with loyalty to the socializing of means of production. Christian theologians, believing in God, speak of doing his will, of faith, and of Christian hope, all of which would be unintelligible in the senses intended, apart from the conception of reality as grounded in God.

D. THE MORAL CATEGORY

As previously noted, ethics is primarily concerned with a particular kind of goodness and evil in human choices. Not logical validity nor economic advantage nor aesthetic attraction, but moral good is its object. The corresponding evil in human decision is not logical fallacy nor economic blunder nor aesthetically offensive uncouthness, but moral evil.

How shall we define this moral category of judgment? We can say that it has to do with what we *ought* to do or, more ambiguously, what we are under *obligation* to do, or with human *duty*, or with *right* and *wrong*. But the words here emphasized, if understood as intended, simply represent the same category of valuation as the word "moral," and so do not take us far in definition.

There have been various efforts to define or explain the *moral* "ought" in terms of something else. For example, it is said that the sense of obligation is simply a conditioned fear of social disapproval.

To such a reductionist claim the moralist may reply that people occasionally feel and believe that they ought to choose and act directly contrary to social pressures from all their associates. When as a matter of conscience a man deliberately takes action which incurs the emphatic disapproval of his associates, his moral sense is on one side and his fear of social disapproval is directly contrary to it.

The psychologist may, however, respond with a more sophisticated version of the theory which would still reduce the meaning of moral obligation to a nonmoral psychological phenomenon. For example, Sigmund Freud explains what we commonly call the conscience as the *superego*, a whole structure of internal inhibitions resulting from the social approvals and disapprovals to which a person has been subjected in early childhood. The superego may cause an adult to feel that he ought to take actions which all his present associates disapprove but which were either approved by the mentors of his infancy or are logical or symbolic extensions of actions so approved. This is closely related to Freud's interpretation of mental illness.

If my present desires lead me to violate the strong inhibitions of my superego, the result is conflict which may become so intense as to produce not only anxiety but repressed memories, abnormal physical symptoms, and serious mental illness. Freud observes that the superego, having been nurtured in infancy and childhood, is likely to be ill-adapted to guide a vital, realistically flexible course of conduct in adulthood. When a person's deep-seated impulses (in the "id" or unconscious, affective self) clash hard with an unadapting, imperious superego, he becomes ill-fitted for effective living and may become conspicuously ill.

What does Freud propose to do about such situations? Through psychoanalysis he would seek to strengthen the confidence and aggressive vigor of the conscious, thinking self so that with an objective understanding of reality it can put both the id and the superego in their proper places.[2] But why? Why not let the superego and id fight it out? Or why not seek to break down the strength of the superego or of the id, to give complete victory to one or the other? As history and present practice abundantly show, there are many other ways to handle the mentally ill besides psychoanalytic treatment. Freud's desire to develop objective self-understanding and reasonable adaptation of the patient to his social environment may be worthy of all praise. The acceptance of this goal is a necessary premise for his whole program. The proposition that this goal ought to be chosen cannot, however, be established by any amount of psychological description of man. Its persuasive appeal clearly rests upon humane ethical assumptions nurtured in Western society by the Judeo-Christian heritage and the ideals of the Enlightenment.

There is no question that the specific content of an individual's moral conviction is due to his training and other experience. This is the reason why many people of India regard the killing of a cow as outrageously immoral, while some American tourists think that the veneration of cows is an immoral superstition which allows cattle to roam the streets of cities and villages, spreading filth and eating food where human beings are dying of hunger. Similarly, many people in the United States, especially among Roman Catholics, consider the pill and other birth control devices sinful, while the neighbors regard their failure to impose voluntary limitations on their families by such means

2. See Sigmund Freud, *New Introductory Lectures on Psychoanalysis* (New York: W. W. Norton & Company, 1933), pp. 108–12. Cf. the critical discussion of Freud's interpretation of ethics in Peter A. Bertocci and Richard M. Millard, *Personality and the Good* (New York: David McKay Company, 1963), pp. 24–46. I am especially indebted to Bertocci (who wrote that chapter) in the present section, and have profited much from the book as a whole, despite basic differences in purpose and substance.

as irresponsible and immoral. In the learning experiences which have produced such differences in moral conviction, social approval and disapproval have played very important parts.

Yet this is a far cry from saying that the whole *meaning* of moral belief or the sense of obligation is fear of social disapproval or hope of social approval or both. It is one thing to say that the steering of an automobile determines where it will go; it is another to infer from this that the steering powers the car or that the whole meaning of the journey is to be found in the process of steering. Experiences of approval and disapproval, pleasure and pain, successful and unsuccessful achievement of personal goals, all influence the *direction* of the moral sense. The *meaning* of this sense, as expressed by the ethical "ought," is something more than any specific direction it may take.

What, then, is this moral category which is thus capable of being variously directed? The whole of ethics may be regarded as an elaboration of that meaning. In a narrower sense it may correctly be said that it is impossible of any but circular definition. The moral category, capable of holding a great variety of diverse and even conflicting contents, is one of those ultimates, like space, time, cause, or quantity, which are capable of illustration but not capable of definition in other terms.

If a man wants to know what I mean by the moral category, I can recall or await an occasion when he makes charges of dishonesty, selfishness, tyrannical behavior, or cruelty against someone or when he praises another for generosity of spirit, courage, sensitive sympathy, or self-discipline. Then I can say, "There. That approval (or disapproval) you have expressed is of the moral kind. You have spoken of moral good (or evil)."

Occasionally, one finds a person who shows little or no moral inhibition in his own conduct within the limits of escape from punishment or vengeance. His only law seems to be the ability to "get away with it." Sometimes such a person will even declare openly that he has no regard for what other people call moral limits. But if he is watched, he will soon be observed angrily condemning an act of someone else and perhaps even self-righteously proclaiming his right to avenge the wrong. The Apostle Paul observed such phenomena long ago and wrote,

> Therefore, you have no excuse, O man, whoever you are, when you judge another; for in passing judgment upon him you condemn yourself, because you, the judge, are doing the very same things.　　[Rom. 2:1][3]

3. Here and elsewhere, unless otherwise stated, biblical quotations are from the Revised Standard Version.

the world retaliation and violence must be practiced, but that Christians must practice forgiveness and unlawfulness, then these objections, which have as their goal a double Christian morality, and which are very widespread, proceed from a false understanding of the word of God.[6]

In this matter, Bonhoeffer is representative of much contemporary Christian ethics. One may read the account of any assembly of the World Council of Churches to see how deeply the theologians of the Church are involved in the problems of the world. Or one may read from the Lutheran bishop, Gustaf Aulén—much more conservative than Bonhoeffer—that to be "a living conscience of justice is the Church's primary duty in relation to Society."[7] As Aulén develops this theme we see how far Lutheranism has come from Luther's division of Church and world. Few, if any, theologians today, whether Protestant, Eastern Orthodox, or Roman Catholic, radical, liberal, or conservative, would try to defend a division of labor which would assign one realm of life to secular ethics and another to Christian ethics. Certainly it is not proposed to suggest such division in this work.

The teachings of Jesus are full of admonitions concerning ordinary worldly human relations—of rich and poor, law courts and mortgages, soldiers and citizens. The hope to which we are called is of the day when "The kingdom of the world has become the kingdom of our Lord and of his Christ, and he shall reign for ever and ever" (Rev. 11:15). No earthly realm is free from the judgment or the love of Christ.

2. *Theories of Displacement*

Given this kind of apparent relationships, it is small occasion for wonder that many secular moralists and some Christian theologians have asserted that one kind of ethics or the other must be simply dismissed as invalid. General ethics should displace so-called Christian ethics altogether, say some, while others would have Christian ethics wholly displace all other ethical theory.

Men who have dismissed Christian faith as illusory wish, of course, to see Christian ethics supplanted by other approaches to all our problems of decision. In a way, Freud would represent such men, but, as we have seen, he would profess to have found a better alternative to all ethics.

A significant *ethical* attack on Christian ethics was mounted on the basis of the rational ethics of Immanuel Kant by Eduard von Hartmann.[8] Its importance is due chiefly to the fact that with or without

6. *Ethics* (New York: The Macmillan Company, 1962), p. 322.
7. *Church, Law and Society* (New York: Charles Scribner's Sons, 1948), p. 98.
8. In his *Phaenomenologie des sittlichen Bewusstseins* (1879), pp. 88, 92. Cited

the reference to Kant, essentially the same argument has been used often and continues current.

Kant maintained that truly ethical action is autonomous, that is, willed by a person because he himself believes he ought so to will; it is in accord with his own ideal. In contrast with such praiseworthy autonomy is heteronomy. A heteronomous choice is made because the chooser is motivated by social pressure, by fear of consequences, by hope of reward, or by some other force or consideration apart from his own moral reason.

Von Hartmann and others contend that so far as a Christian is influenced by his belief in God's will, or by hope or fear of divine judgment, his choices are heteronomous and so not ethically good. On the other hand, so far as the Christian acts simply from his own ideals, without reference to God or Christ or future Judgment, his religious beliefs are irrelevant to his ethics. In popular discourse the argument often takes the form of a boast by the critic of the church that he does not, like church people, need the threat or promise of divine sanctions in order to do what is right.

Such argument overlooks the fact that the genuine Christian's moral ideals are themselves part and parcel of his Christian faith. His faith is not a set of externally imposed sanctions, but the innermost core of his own life.[9] There are, however, professing Christians who do not see an essential goodness in the Christian life, but regard themselves as grimly enduring a rather unpleasant and stultified life on earth in order to receive a heavenly reward hereafter. Such persons have unfortunately fallen heir to a poor legalistic substitute for an authentic Christian faith.

The opposite kind of displacement theory, contending for the exclusive validity of Christian ethics, must have much attention in connection with the subjects of the next two chapters. It is presented here only in the most preliminary way.

Dietrich Bonhoeffer says, "We know of no relation of God to the world other than through Jesus Christ" (*Ethics*, p. 321). As he thus dismisses all natural theology, so he also dismisses any philosophical or natural-law ethics. He insists, "Whatever the Church's word to the world may be, it must always be *both* law *and* gospel" (*ibid*.). Then he continues,

---

by Albert C. Knudson, in *The Principles of Christian Ethics* (New York: Abingdon Press, 1943), p. 17n.

9. Kant himself believed that man's moral consciousness demanded that virtue should at least be rewarded with God-given happiness, and he did not regard the hope of such reward as defiling the true autonomy of action according to one's ideals. Cf. his *Metaphysik der Sitten* and *Die Religion innerhalb der Grenzen der blossen Vernunft*.

This implies a denial of the view that the Church can speak to the world on the basis of some particular rational or natural-law knowledge which she shares with the world, that is to say, with an occasional temporary disregard for the gospel.   [*Ibid.*]

Elsewhere in the same work Bonhoeffer describes the discrediting of natural law in Protestant ethics as "a disastrous mistake," and regrets that "the concept of the natural . . . was entirely abandoned to Catholic ethics" (p. 101). Yet he also says, "Faith in this Jesus Christ is the sole fountainhead of all good" (p. 78). Perhaps if Bonhoeffer had survived his imprisonment he would have put these contradictions in order. As it is, his writings speak on both sides of the issue.

Karl Barth is less equivocal, although his dialectical method does sometimes leave doubts. Generally, he roundly condemns both natural theology and ethics of natural law. In his view the Christian is solely under the gospel.

Emil Brunner enters into a careful critique of ethics without the gospel and wholly rejects it. He regards "natural ethics" as not only hopelessly involved in inescapable antinomies, but as being itself a sinful assertion of man's autonomy over against God. A life based on such ethics is not a step from sin, for "it is precisely morality which is evil."[10]

3. *Supplementary Theories*

In the long history of Christianity the great majority of thinkers have viewed both natural-law ethics and the guidance provided by the Christian gospel as having legitimate place. Christian philosophers and theologians have had various ways of relating the two, but have generally regarded Christian ethical teachings as supplementing the ethics of natural law.

Augustine's high regard for some philosophical ethics, particularly the teaching of the Stoics, was based on his personal experience and is important to the whole history of Christian ethics. In *The Confessions* he tells how, in his nineteenth year of age, he was reading for the improvement of his rhetoric when he came upon "a certain book of Cicero," widely admired for its language. Augustine found there something much more valuable than linguistic style. He continues,

This book of his contains an exhortation to philosophy, and is called *Hortensius*. This book, in truth, changed my affections, and turned my prayers to Thyself, O Lord, and made me have other hopes and desires. Worthless suddenly became every vain hope to me; and with an in-

10. *The Divine Imperative* (New York: The Macmillan Company, 1942), p. 71.

credible warmth of heart, I yearned for an immortality of wisdom, and
began now to arise that I might return to Thee.[11]

After his conversion, Augustine's use of moral philosophy changed
but did not end. The changed use is clearly displayed in *The Morals
of the Catholic Church*. Praising the four traditional virtues of the
Platonists and other Greek philosophers, he gives to them Christian
redefinition, so that

> temperance is love keeping itself entire and incorrupt for God; forti-
> tude is love bearing everything readily for the sake of God; justice is
> love serving God only, and therefore ruling well all else, as subject to
> man; prudence is love making a right distinction between what helps
> it towards God and what might hinder it.   [Chap. XV]

So interpreting the Greek cardinal virtues as aspects of the true Christian virtue of love as he understands that virtue, he not only supplements the pagan ethics, but in the process transforms it. Still it continues its usefulness and he soon returns to "the four virtues" as he
exhorts conformity of life with each in turn, as reinterpreted and
reinforced with the aid of Scripture (Chaps. XIX–XXIV).

In the teaching of Thomas Aquinas and in the medieval and modern
Roman Catholic Church generally, the relationship is conceived less
integrally. The natural law, discoverable without the aid of revelation,
is absolutely and always binding and is set forth as the main basis of
statute law and international relations, including just war. The "divine" or "revealed" or "ecclesiastical" law, on the other hand, is
essential to salvation and the life of the Church. The questions raised
by both the Augustinian and Thomistic views must be included in our
examination of natural law in Chapter Three.

F. CHRISTIAN ETHICS AND SYSTEMATIC THEOLOGY

Christian theology has the task of elucidating the meaning of the
Christian faith, whatever else the theologian may regard as also included within its task. As John MacQuarrie puts it,

> Theology may be defined as the study which, through participation
> in and reflection upon a religious faith, seeks to express the content of
> this faith in the clearest and most coherent language available.[12]

11. *The Confessions*, Book III, Chap. IV.
12. *Principles of Christian Theology* (New York: Charles Scribner's Sons, 1966),
p. 1.

Actually, the word "coherent," as MacQuarrie uses it, implies the significant relating of the religious faith studied, "so far as this is required, with all the other intellectual enterprises of the human mind" (p. 3). Most theological studies, regardless of initial definition, include similar basic tasks.[13]

Now "the content" of the Christian faith certainly includes whatever descriptions or obligations of Christian living are implied in that faith. Hence Christian theology must inevitably include, or at least deeply overlap, Christian ethics.

It is not strange, then, that works of systematic theology include discussions of God's goodness and his righteous law, man's sin, the question of man's freedom, the drawing together of Christian believers in the Church, the meaning of Christian love, forgiveness, justification, sanctification, and the Judgment. All these and more topics of theology are subjects also included in Christian ethics or deeply relevant to it. Indeed, some writers include all their systematic teachings on the discipline we are calling Christian ethics in their works on theology. Karl Barth is a particularly noteworthy example. There is good precedent for this, going back through the *Institutes* of John Calvin and the *Summa Theologica* of Thomas Aquinas.[14]

On the other hand, one cannot do everything at once. At the least there would be obvious justification for setting apart Christian ethics as a significant, complex, and important subject within systematic theology for specialized treatment.

We may, indeed, go further. Christian ethics, examined as a special discipline, draws us into careful consideration of subjects not usually included in systematic theology, even when a work in theology runs into many volumes. There are traditions of coverage in various disciplines of study. Neither philosophical metaphysics nor Christian theology customarily goes far into the issues of practical choice which man must make nor into the methods by which those choices are to be determined. If adequate attention is to be given the relation between the Christian faith and the way a man uses knowledge of the sciences in deciding what he should do about technological unemployment or nuclear bombs, then the issues of ethics need to be taken up in a discipline which will deal with them, not as incidental to other subjects, but in their own urgent importance and unique meanings.

When this is done, systematic theology and Christian ethics will still

13. For some other recent definitions, see Gustaf Aulén, *The Faith of the Christian Church* (Philadelphia: The Muhlenberg Press, 1948), p. 3; and L. Harold DeWolf, *A Theology of the Living Church*, 2nd rev. ed. (New York: Harper & Row, 1968), p. 18.

14. Cf. the recent book, *The Shaping of Modern Christian Thought. A Sourcebook on Faith and Ethics*, by Warren E. Groff and Donald E. Miller (Cleveland: World Publishing Company, 1968). See especially p. vii.

necessarily be closely related. If, in accord with our original definition, we are to study moral issues "in the perspective of Christian faith," we must have ideas about the meaning of that perspective. It is the business of theology to provide such ideas.

It is not always so readily appreciated that Christian ethics has much to contribute to the themes of systematic theology concerning our conceptions of God and of his relations with men.

If we face the issues of Christian ethics squarely in the terms demanded of us in the present time, we shall be better prepared to seek anew the truth of the Christian faith in God. In the past century both theoretical and applied Christian ethics, in interaction with other disciplines and institutions of modern culture, have influenced systematic theology especially conspicuously as regards the doctrine of the Judgment and the punishment of sinners hereafter. In the present and coming years such influences are especially likely in relation to doctrines of sanctification, the mission of the Church, and Christian understanding of our natural environment.

In short, systematic theology and Christian ethics deeply overlap and cannot be legitimately defined in such a way as to assign them separate fields of study. They must be distinguished in central focus, however, and when pursued in distinct specialization, they can interact in an essential and highly useful manner.

chapter two

The Revolt
Against Moral Norms

———————•⤫∞⤫•———————

We must place our systematic study of Christian ethics in its contemporary context of confrontation with both a practical and a theoretical tendency to reject the very idea of moral laws, or even principles or ethical norms of any kind. We shall be mainly concerned with the theoretical rejection and especially by Christian theologians. However, such rejection must be seen in the larger context of a broad trend in the life of contemporary society.

A. PREVALENCE OF THE REVOLT

1. Popular Practice and Talk

Each year Americans are informed of new, sharp increases in violent crime. Juvenile delinquency rises significantly in city and suburbs, among poor and rich. Riots in the cities, drug abuse, chronic vandalism in school buildings, wholesale violations of law by slum landlords, and assassinations of prominent Americans all produce alarm lest the whole fabric of social order may be breaking down.

Our traditional mores of sex and marriage are being challenged as never before. It is true that these standards have been frequently violated in all periods of our national life. But it is a new development when university student newspapers insist on the propriety of unmarried male and female students living together and some coeds defend in the public press their own living arrangements of this kind.

It is difficult to know with any precision how much increase in extramarital or premarital sex has occurred. However, it would appear to be very large. The great increase in availability of contraceptives and in public attention to them must decrease very substantially the proportion of sexual acts which result in pregnancy. Yet between 1940 and 1968 the number of illegitimate births per 1,000 unmarried women 15 to 44 years of age, in the United States, increased from 7.1 to 24.1, more than tripling, or increasing by ·239 per cent.[1]

Underneath these widespread violations of law and of traditional sex standards is a pattern of rapid technological and social change which has produced general moral confusion. Many assume that the mores of monogamy were socially needed only to establish paternity and secure responsibility for home care and support of children. If the peril can be reduced by the pill to the level of other dangers in modern living—like traffic accidents—then why not substitute the new safety devices for the old morality?

While technology makes its own immediate impact on moral custom, rapid social change accompanying it produces a deeper and a wider moral confusion. Most human societies have held their members under close control, not only by enforced laws, but much more by moral and religious ideas which prevailed throughout the society. The standards thus established were regarded as axiomatic. Even people who violated them recognized their validity and saw their own actions as wrong, or rationalized a defense of them on grounds of exceptional circumstances. Now the ease of travel, popular mass communications, and the mingling of people of different cultures expose more people to a variety of cultural systems. No one structure of religion or morals can be taken for granted today.

We have noted that some psychologists would reduce the very meaning of moral obligation to inhibitions and tensions adequately describable in altogether nonmoral terms. Such reductionism would make moral obligation as such altogether illusory. Similarly, we observed the claim that anthropology had eliminated ethics for the educated by showing the radical differences of mores among different peoples.

2. Anthropological Relativism

The anthropological argument has seemed especially decisive to many. If headhunting is required as a duty among the Ibans and is forbidden among other tribes, is it not evident that the sense of duty is purely relative to the customs of the society in which it occurs, so that the proper form of ethics is simply a description of mores in different societies? Should we not conclude also that obligation has no claim to respect beyond the sanctions of a particular society? If, then, I can escape the sanctions, am I not free to disregard what are called obligations?

It will be replied by some that although moral obligations are wholly

1. U.S. Bureau of the Census, *Statistical Abstract of the United States: 1970* (91st ed., Washnigton, D.C., 1970, p. 50. The figures before 1960 exclude Alaska and Hawaii.

relative to the society which sanctions them, they are genuinely valid in that society. A young male of a tribe which requires its young men to bring back heads from neighboring longhouses is truly under obligation to do so. We are not atomistic individuals but members of social wholes. Individuals are not free to live on their own personal terms. The society as a whole may come under new conditions which will lead to changes in the whole structure of tribal customs and institutions —even as the Ibans are now giving up the headhunting as they come into the larger structure of the Malaysian economy, education, and government. But the individual is not free to write his own law. He ought to be faithful to the particular society of which he is a part.

We must take note, then, of two kinds of moral relativism inferred from the observation of differing and changing mores. If we use the ancient saying of Protagoras, "Man is the measure of all things," we may note two possible meanings of "man." One may say that man in the person of the individual is free to write his own moral law or to acknowledge none at all. He is "the measure of all things" in ethics. On the other hand, one may take "man" as represented by a particular society—a nation, religious community, or tribe—and make all ethics relative to the measure of that collective "man."

When we make these observations, we are on the verge of a third interpretation which would consider "man" as universal man, or human nature itself, as "measure of all things" in ethics. But then we should be leaving moral relativism and introducing the ethics of natural law which is to be examined in Chapter Three.

There are two other types of relativistic revolt against moral law, however, which must be introduced now.

3. Moral Skepticism in Philosophy

The principal contemporary philosophical form of the revolt is launched by analytical philosophy.

The method of analysis is directed to an effort to find out what ethical language means. The analyst would say that if it is intended to describe some aspect of the real world, then it must be subject to empirical verification. Ethical statements, however, seem quite incapable of such verification. If I make the statement, "It is raining outside," I am saying that I could step out and feel drops of water falling upon me, see wet grass and walks, talk with neighbors about the rain, and so on.

But what experience will verify the statement, "I ought to seek reconciliation with my angry neighbor"? This is clearly not a prediction that he will welcome my effort. If it is understood as a prediction that other people whose opinion I respect will praise my attempt, then the statement must be taken to imply also that I must let those people know about it. However strongly inclined I may be to do so, it will hardly be conceded that this is the *meaning* of the original ethical statement. Moreover, if the ethical statement means a social approval, then it is reduced to a social descriptive meaning and no longer implies anything distinctively obligatory.

Instead, the philosopher may suggest, ethical statements should be considered not to attempt or mean to affirm any knowledge, but rather to express an attitude or an assertion of will, like an exclamation or a command. In this case ethics is not cognitive at all, but expresses a subjective feeling or volition of the person speaking. It is an act rather than a proposition. Thus my statement, "I ought to seek reconciliation with my angry neighbor," may be an expression of a certain affective tension within me. Some motivations are inclining me to go to him and others are holding me back. As a cat which wants the liver in her master's hand, but fears the noise of the power mower beside him, advances, retreats, and finally yowls, so I utter my ethical statement. Other statements including the specifically moral signals—such as "ought," "obligation," "good," "righteous," "sinful," "evil," and the like—are actions springing from other subjective conditions.[2]

Obviously, if the meaning of ethical statements is exhausted in such analysis, then the idea of a moral law or of any binding obligation is illusory.[3]

4. *Theological Attacks on Moral Law*

Joseph Fletcher and John Robinson are agreed that the tide of modern feeling is against moral law. So far few observers of the present scene would be likely to disagree. But Fletcher and Robinson agree further that for this reason a Christian ethics without law "is the only ethic for 'man come of age.' "[4] Robinson continues, "To resist it in the name of religious sanctions will not stop it; it will only ensure that the form it takes will be anti-Christian" (*ibid.*).

I have no doubt that he and Fletcher are correct in their appraisal of the popular mood as strongly opposed to moral law. However, it may not follow that we should all join this anti-law "new morality" in the name of Christian ethics. Authentic Christianity, from the beginning, has often opposed the popular mood and may need to do so now. Of course the theological writers named would agree that they

2. Cf. C. L. Stevenson, *Ethics and Language* (New Haven: Yale University Press, 1944).
3. Cf. the critique of the emotive theory by A. C. Ewing, entitled "The Nature of Ethical Judgment" in *A Modern Introduction to Ethics*, ed. by Milton K. Munitz (Glencoe, Ill.: The Free Press, 1958), pp. 553–68.
4. Quoted by Fletcher, with approval, in *Situational Ethics: The New Morality* (Philadelphia: Westminster Press,, 1966), p. 153, from Robinson, *Honest to God*.

must seek to support their "allergy towards any kind of law"[5] by considerations drawn from within traditions of ethics and Christian ethics.

It is exceedingly difficult to define precisely the position which Fletcher is defending. At times he contrasts his view with both legalism and antinomianism.

Few if any Christian ethicists would suggest a different placement of their own views. Who wants to be known as either legalistic or antinomian (that is to say lawless or unprincipled)? More specifically, Fletcher says,

> We might say, from the situationist's perspective, that it is possible to derive general "principles" from whatever is the one and only universal law (*agape* for Christians, something else for others), but not laws or rules. [*Ibid.*, p. 27]

Now we need to know precisely how principles and laws are intended to be distinguished, but Fletcher does not say. He does add, "We cannot milk universals from a universal" (*ibid.*). This suggests that "principles" are not universals, but if they are not, what are they? A principle must be applicable at least to a number of particulars, and if so, it assuredly is a universal. Moreover, it would be strange news to any logician that "We cannot milk [which presumably means deduce] universals from a universal."

We come nearer to understanding what he is meaning when, two paragraphs later, he quotes with approval Dietrich Bonhoeffer's statement, "Principles are only tools in God's hands, soon to be thrown away as unserviceable."[6] Fletcher complains that classical moral theology has instructed us

> to follow laws but do it *as much as possible* according to love and according to reason. . . . Situation ethics, on the other hand, calls upon us to keep law in a subservient place, so that *only* love and reason really count when the chips are down! [P. 31]

Here we have two absolutes, love and reason, or as the situationist might say, one law which is love, and then reason as means to figure out how love should be applied in the concrete situations. Such a view has much to commend it.

This reason, however, appears to be purely subjective, and no man's decision is to be held to account by himself or anyone else before any bar of universal reason. This pure individualistic subjectivism is

5. The phrase is quoted from Urban Voll by Fletcher, in *Situation Ethics*, p. 153. Although saying that "allergy" is an "inexact" term, Fletcher accepts the description of his view.

6. *Ibid.*, p. 28. Quoted from *Ethics*, p. 8.

made explicit when Fletcher quotes Kenneth Kirk as follows, adding his own comment:

> "Every man must decide for himself according to his own estimate of conditions and consequences; and no one can decide for him or impugn the decision to which he comes. Perhaps this is the end of the matter after all." *This is precisely what this book is intended to show.*[7]

The difference between this and antinomianism is at most small and uncertain.

Readers of *Situation Ethics* readily observe that the main weight of the book is against "legalism," not against antinomianism. Most mentions of belief in moral laws are of badly formulated law often poorly applied. Most illustrations introduced are chosen with an eye to making a case against premarital chastity or marital faithfulness, or to justify adultery, dishonesty, or lying. The reader finds extremely rarely illustrations of special circumstances which dictate obligation to extraordinary abstinence from sex, food, drink, or comfort.

If one wants to understand the popular excitement and glee over "the new morality" which Fletcher advocates, one needs to imagine reading through the eyes of a man looking for escape from responsibility a passage like the following:

> Is adultery wrong? . . . One can only respond, "I don't know. Maybe. Give me a case. Describe a real situation." Or perhaps somebody will ask if a man should ever lie to his wife, or desert his family, or spy on a business rival's design or market plans, or fail to report some income in his tax return. Again the answer cannot be an answer, it can only be another question.   [Pp. 142–43]

A quite different expression of the revolt against moral laws, understandably much less popular, occurs in the writings of Karl Barth. Many discussions of ethical issues in Barth's *Church Dogmatics* had major part in preparing the intellectual climate for the more radical rebellion represented by some passages of Bonhoeffer and more popularly by Robinson and Fletcher.

Karl Barth's strictures against moral law are the expressions of two main themes in his theology. First is his rejection of natural law on the ground that all our valid knowledge of God and his purpose for us is through Jesus Christ. Any supposed religious knowledge about God apart from Christ is idolatrous and false. Along with natural theology, natural law must go into discard because sin has corrupted both the will

7. *Ibid.*, pp. 36–37. The quotation from Kirk is from that author's *Conscience and Its Problems* (London: Longmans, Green and Co., 1927), p. 331. The italics of Fletcher's comment are his own.

and the reason of man. Soundness in relationships and understanding is restored only in Christ. Hence a true ethical wisdom must begin with Christ. Second is Barth's distrust of system. He drew from Kierkegaard and never lost the view that system is an idolatrous and futile work of man's pride. On each and every subject and occasion a man must sit under the Word of God, regardless of what the man has said or done at another time.

Barth therefore opposed an ethics of natural law and likewise the effort to build a rationally structured system of Christian ethics. This did not prevent his discussing at great length the various vocations and circles of special relationships and responsibilities in which God places us. Much less did Barth maintain with Fletcher the individual unaccountability of each person as he decides for himself what to do in his situation. At the same time, Barth's manner of declaring himself without rationally structured argument on great moral issues calling for rational decision has further encouraged the rebellion against law.

Emil Brunner also accentuated the trend away from the effort to construct a systematic ethics. Brunner sought to derive the whole of Christian ethics from justification by faith alone. This effort proved to be by no means as antinomian as it sounded, for eventually Brunner carefully delineated the "orders of creation" and the responsibilities which God lays upon us by the orders (i.e., forms of social structure) in which he places us.[8] Yet he made many statements of a kind greatly to encourage the revolt even against generalizations which Christian ethics might formulate before the event, for the purpose of guiding our decisions. For example, he wrote,

> All the "Commandments" point towards the one "Command"; "Love God—and your neighbor." But that also is law, the supreme law, and I can only learn what it means at the moment at which God calls me; I can never know it beforehand.[9]

In passages like this, Brunner is writing with moral earnestness, although he is speaking also in a way dear to the heart of any rebel against moral law. Perhaps he is saying something which needs to be said. There is, indeed, much of truth—exceedingly important truth—in the whole movement we have been describing. To that truth we must now turn.

8. Cf. the very title of his principal ethical work in the original German, *Das Gebot und die Ordnungen* (The Command and the Orders); translated as *The Divine Imperative*. Perhaps it is well that the title of the English translation is radically changed. Otherwise, readers might confuse it with ideas of "law and order." Cf. also the title of another of his books, *Gerechtigkeit: Eine Lehre von den Grundgesetzen der Gesellschaftsordnung* (Justice: a Doctrine of the Fundamental Laws of the Social Order).

9. *The Divine Imperative*, p. 112.

B. ELEMENTS OF TRUTH IN MORAL RELATIVISM

No one can go far in ethical reflection without observing that circumstances alter the very meanings of our actions. A mother may be in the habit of offering sweet cookies to her children's friends when they come in from play, and this may be a normal expression of kind hospitality. But if one of the neighbor children is diabetic, the meaning of the offer is radically changed. If I am entertaining Jewish or Hindu guests for dinner, hospitality demands that I make inquiries about dietary restrictions not ordinarily needed if I am host to a group of Christian friends. Again, if I am guest in a Japanese home, I must remember to take off my shoes at the door.

These matters go far beyond etiquette. They concern the genuineness of my loving-kindness as well.

Legalism encounters much difficulty in such matters. In a particular physical and cultural setting men may carefully draw up many moral prescriptions of conduct which would properly express loving-kindness. Then new cultures flow in, the technical situation changes, and the literal following of the old precepts will lead to the most unkind acts.

The legitimate concerns of situation ethics are especially prominent in this age of rapid change. An age of population explosion, of worldwide interdependence, of nuclear bombs, and of polluted air and water offers many situations demanding moral choice without precedent and covered by no prescriptive rule. The various essential elements in moral computation are always turning up in new combinations. A person who forms a number of particular rules for his conduct and then routinely follows them will in many circumstances be acting like an absent-minded professor of the worst kind, mechanically going on his irrelevant way, sadly out of touch with the realities around him.

As Fletcher points out, it is precisely for the sake of dealing adequately with all these situations, so many of which are in some respects exceptional, that casuistries are elaborated.[10] Casuistry is an attempt to foresee and prescribe in advance for all possible kinds of circumstances. It can, as it develops, come nearer and nearer to its goal as it provides for more and more varieties of situation. Its exceptions become so numerous that casuistry may seem to specialize in developing ways of breaking moral law morally, much as civil law, as elaborated by court decisions, often seems to provide lawyers with ways of breaking the law legally. But no matter how detailed and elaborate casuistry be-

10. Cf. *Situation Ethics*, pp. 18–20, 29, 67.

comes, it can never provide a net fine enough to hold the complex and subtle particularities of single situations of moral choice.

A situation of moral decision involves at least one unique individual and usually several or many such individuals. Moreover, the ways in which the one (the agent himself) is related to the others is also unique. In a very real sense, then, the particular situation, while *accurately* describable by many universals, is *adequately* describable by no combination of propositions definable in advance—nor at the time nor afterward. There is something *sui generis* about every moral situation. The existentialists frequently dwell on this theme. The concrete particulars of human existence, they insist, are never captured by universal concepts, whether in metaphysics or in ethics.

Sören Kierkegaard stressed this truth to the point of requiring that we leave ethics behind for a life of faith, sensitive to God and neighbor in each new situation, untrammeled by previous choices or generalizations.[11]

It may seem now that situation ethics has fully won the day! But we must examine the matter further. There are critically important flaws in that position when taken alone. We must look at them carefully. Then we must seek a way of adopting the situationist's truths without the defects of his position.

C. Criticisms of the Revolt

1. Loose Thinking

Situation Ethics: The New Morality is vivid, exciting, and, on the face of it, persuasive. But when one begins to read with more attention to detail, serious stumbling blocks appear.

a. Love Poorly Defined. Since the one and only law which Fletcher recognizes is love, everything in his position depends on its meaning. He knows that the word is ambiguous (p. 15). But he does not take account of the extreme differences in understanding even of *agape*-love among Christian theologians and ethicists.

His nearest approach to full definition of love is in a statement putting some key phrases into italics for emphasis:

> Jesus and Paul replaced the precepts of Torah with the living principle of *agape*—agape being *goodwill at work in partnership with reason*. It seeks the neighbor's best interest with a careful eye to all the factors in the situation.   [P. 69]

11. Cf. *Concluding Unscientific Postscript*, tr. by David F. Swenson and Walter Lowrie (Princeton: Princeton University Press, 1944), pp. 105, 315 ff.

We must still ask whether this is exclusive of all interest in the virtue or other good of the self, as Anders Nygren insists it must be to be Christian, or whether it is compatible with due self-interest and even requires it, as Joseph Butler contends. Does this love seek a sharing, communal fellowship with the neighbor, or is it permitted to prefer separation, as in the "separate-but-equal" goal, so long as one seeks the "best interest" of the neighbor there in his separateness?

Fletcher must know of these serious questions which have been raised regarding the meaning of *agape*-love. It might be answered that one does not need to know a good definition if one has been divinely given this love and the definition will do no good if one has not received the gift. But this answer clearly will not do in Fletcher's case for he believes, correctly, that in the time of choice the Christian needs to reason clearly as he thinks what love requires.

b. Definition and Scaling of Value Excluded.   In his most careful definition of love Fletcher tells us, "It seeks the neighbor's best interest with a careful eye to all the factors in the situation." But what is that best interest? Will love put higher the neighbor's comfort or character, religion or long life?

Not only are we not given a definition of best interest or a method for determining priorities of value; such considerations are excluded. We are told that "Love is the Only Norm," and that "*The ruling norm of Christian decision is love: nothing else*" (p. 69).

c. These Weaknesses Inherent in the Theory.   Love without an accompanying distinction or method of distinction between value and disvalue, and between higher and lower values, is empty sentiment. To give love positive concrete meaning in real life, a person must be able to distinguish between neighbor experiences which would be good and others which would be evil, also between some good experiences and others which are better.

The lack of any such value theory is not a mere personal oversight or foible in Fletcher's writing. If value theory were to be constructed, then the central theme of *Situation Ethics* and "the new morality" would be abandoned. For the theme is that the Christian needs to know only love and the situation.

2. *Encouraging of Slack Responsibility*

One of Fletcher's minor themes is his criticism of "pietism," "moralism," and the stress of some churches on petty matters while neglecting great social issues. The great issues are mostly unspecified, but explicit support is given to racial integration. I heartily applaud this support and also vigorously endorse his criticism of the churches' tardiness and inadequacy of witness to interracial brotherhood. But I must protest when, in this context, Fletcher says that there has been in the churches, of late, "a decline of moral concern" (p. 162). The illustration he uses to support the charge actually exemplifies the painful growth of the churches in the opposite direction when one takes note of the true facts instead of the distorted version used in *Situation Ethics*. Fletcher says,

> When Father [Jerome A.] Drolet of the Roman Catholic Church and Mr. [Rev. Lloyd] Foreman of The Methodist Church stood together in front of a picket line of their own people (who were trying to prevent integration of a New Orleans school), . . . to shame their people into going back to their homes, *nobody saw any connection between Christ, the Scriptures, and racial justice and loving-kindness.* [P. 26]

Before the integration of New Orleans schools began, the District Superintendent and all but one of the pastors in the New Orleans District of The Methodist Church joined Foreman in signing a statement published in the newspapers urging wholehearted compliance with the court-ordered integration. When school opened and the going became rough, day after day different neighboring pastors took turns in driving their cars to take Foreman and his child to the school, while Bishop Aubrey G. Walton gave them solid administrative support during the crisis. None of the pickets were members of Drolet's or Foreman's congregations, so far as Foreman has been able to discover. Moreover, most of Foreman's people were loyal and enough other local church people rallied to his support so that even in the common statistics of attendance and financial giving his local church wrote a success story for the year.[12]

This correction takes nothing away from the courageous witness of Foreman and those who joined him, but it adds testimony to his wise foresightedness and to the understanding churchmanship of the other ministers who with him seized the initiative and united ranks beforehand. It also indicates that while The Methodist Church leaders and people of the New Orleans District and Area were not ceasing to support the religion and the morals of a conventional or customary kind (p. 162), they did not restrict themselves to that support.

Casual acquaintance with the story as it came through the mass media could easily have given the impression which Fletcher conveys. But did he not have an obligation to be more careful in reporting an affair which could so deeply affect many lives? This question led to a more fundamental one.

According to the "new morality," why should a situationist take care to report accurately in this or other instances? An ethics which

12. My own sources include several pastors involved and Bishop Walton, in personal accounts in Louisiana soon after the events, later confirmed in writing by Lloyd Foreman himself.

acknowledges no principled obligation to keep contracts or report honestly for income tax (p. 143) would recognize, presumably, no general obligations to make sure of the facts in an illustration to be published, particularly if the story as it stood were especially effective in making a desired point.

The handling of the New Orleans story exposes a serious defect to which situation ethics is peculiarly liable. By emphasizing only the particular time and place of the decision and laying exclusive weight on the chooser's own appraisal at that time, for which he is not further accountable, the situationist gives all the advantage of consideration to the neighbor who is there in view. All the other neighbors who have a stake in the full truth of reporting, in the institutions of loyal, confident marriage, in the strength of the church, and the like, are too easily lost to view.

3. Inadequacies Even in More Moderate Forms

Karl Barth, Emil Brunner, and Dietrich Bonhoeffer all protect their views from the worst of Fletcher's weaknesses by inconsistently introducing much of biblically based law along with their decrying of law. We have already observed this in the work of Barth and Brunner.

Bonhoeffer is far from the "new morality" of a situationism without moral laws, despite some statements which point in that direction. He presents each of "the three uses of the law" defined by Lutheran tradition and critically discusses their relationships. He advocates not their being dropped but rather their being more effectively preached, in their intimate interconnection (*Ethics*, pp. 271–73). In regard to secular institutions, Bonhoeffer says that there are four divinely mandated institutions, namely, "marriage and family, labour, government, and Church" (p. 295). The word of the Church, he says, must place all "the secular institutions under the dominion of Christ and under the decalogue" (*ibid.*). Thus he affirms the Decalogue, rather than denying it.

Early in his essay, "What Is Meant By 'Telling the Truth'?" Bonhoeffer makes a statement which would look altogether congenial to situationism: "From this it emerges that 'telling the truth' means something different according to the particular situation in which one stands" (*ibid.*, p. 326). But he discusses the orders of priority to which a person is subject and in relation to which he holds the truth, and he proposes principles by which, in different situations, a person should be guided in his speaking of the truth (pp. 333–34).

In fact, even his exclusively Christocentric position does not prevent him from moving close to an acceptance of natural-law ethics. For he writes that through Christ we understand the status of life as "creaturehood" and as "participation in the kingdom of God" (p. 107). He then goes on to speak of man's rights given him *in creation* and of his consequent duties.[13]

Bonhoeffer, then, represents the revolt against moral law only in certain moods and passages, emphatically countered by other themes in his tragically incomplete writing.

The declamations of Karl Barth against moral law and ethical system, despite his dialectical modifications, have had two unfortunate effects. One is to encourage a movement which, in its extreme forms, has moved far over toward the moral anarchy and irresponsibility of anti-nomianism. The second is to reduce the contribution which Barth might have made to international reconciliation and peace after World War II. Because he had no defined method for moving from his theological presuppositions to his political conclusions regarding East and West, his voice could be and was easily written off in the West as representing simply unsupported and irrational bias.

This instance reveals a grave underlying weakness of all efforts to free individual choices from accountability before the minds of men through a structure of ethical system. In an increasingly crowded world with many serious causes of disagreement and tension we deeply need structures of thought which can be tested in public written and oral debate and within which particular policies can be similarly tested. The alternative is simply shouting or writing our exclamations of disagreement until political or economic or military power decides the issue.

It is tragic that in this momentous period since World War II Protestant ethics has been largely unfitted for effective debate of issues because it has been so largely deprived of structure through the direct and indirect influence of Karl Barth. Meanwhile, traditional Roman Catholic ethics had become all too dependent on natural-law ethics alone, as far as issues of public policy were concerned. It had also developed a structure of casuistry so cumbersome, rigid, and outmoded as to be falling by its own weight.

One of the most significant recent books in Christian ethics is Paul L. Lehmann, *Ethics in a Christian Context*.[14] Lehmann carefully examines many competing positions and presents a highly instructive study to which all of us now at work in Christian ethics must be deeply indebted. Nevertheless, in whatever moderate, scholarly, and responsible terms, he does participate in the rejection of natural law and also of a systematically structured Christian ethics of a type which would provide method and principles in advance for the guidance of moral decisions.

Lehmann defines our subject as follows:

13. See especially pp. 108 and 110.
14. New York: Harper & Row, 1963.

*Christian ethics, as a theological discipline, is the reflection upon the
question and its answer: What am I, as a believer in Jesus Christ and as
a member of his church, to do?* [P. 25]

Two characteristic emphases appear here, in the initial definition.
First, Lehmann stresses that Christian ethics is concerned with defining, "not 'What *ought* I to do?' but 'What *am* I to do?' " (p. 131).
This may look like a distinction without a difference. The explanation
of it points to the second emphasis which is that the Christian lives
and chooses, not alone, as a solitary individual, but in the *koinonia*,
the Church. The grave failures of the church are acknowledged.

Nevertheless, the empirical church points, despite its ambiguity, to the
fact that there is in the world a *laboratory of the living word*, or, to
change the metaphor, a *bridgehead of maturity*, namely the Christian
koinonia. [P. 131]

Here "in the *koinonia* one is always fundamentally in an *indicative*
rather than in an *imperative* situation" (*ibid.*). This does not mean
that there is no " 'ought' factor." It does mean that "the 'ought' factor
is not the primary reality." The primary reality is the human situation
in the *koinonia* created by what God is doing in the world. God is
"bestowing the enabling power of maturity" (*ibid.*). One may then
ask what the Christian does in this power, as a member of the *koinonia*.
One is then moved beyond the "ought" of Kantian autonomy and the
"must" of heteronomy to the indicative actuality of Christian the-
onomy.

Lehmann agrees with Erich Fromm's stress, in his humanistic work,
Man for Himself, on man's need to be human and to grow toward
maturity.[15] But in fact, he contends, man is made fully human and
grows to true maturity only in the *koinonia* of Christian faith. Here
we participate in what God himself is doing in the world.

One of our perplexities arises from the fact that in the empirical
church, even among people who take their Christian faith seriously,
men are doing radically contrary things, as, for example, proclaiming
and seeking to realize full human brotherhood regardless of race and
also resisting such effort with utmost strenuousness. Do we not need,
by study of Scripture, of humanity, and of history, to form some
general principles to guide our judgments on such matters? May we
not seek to learn what is the trend and purpose of God's action in the
world and so formulate guiding generalizations for our participation
with him? Lehmann answers,

15. *Ibid.*, p. 219. Cf. p. 54.

There is no formal principle of Christian behavior because Christian behavior cannot be generalized. And Christian behavior cannot be generalized because the will of God cannot be generalized.   [P. 77]

This last statement seems no less than shocking from a biblically oriented writer. In another connection Lehmann affirms as biblical doctrine "the behavioral dependability or faithfulness of God" (p. 160). To say that God is faithful (Heb. *'âman;* Gr. *pistos*) is to say that he is dependable, steadfast, trustworthy. If he is so utterly unpredictable that one cannot make any generalization concerning his will, then it is only nonsense to say that he is faithful in this biblical sense.

Not only are such generalizations possible; it is also necessary that they be formulated if "doing the will of God" is to have any useful meaning for our own lives. If there are no generalizations by reference to which we can distinguish between the activity of God in the world and the sinful activity of man, then we are left, not in Christian freedom, but in an utterly gray confusion.

Lehmann is rightly concerned with avoiding the bondage of legalistic casuistry and the aridity of general abstractions which have the most uncertain relevance to concrete situations. He is especially helpful in stressing the *koinonia* as the rightful context for Christian decision concerning action in the world.

But unless the Christian ethicist is to be a blind leader of the blind he must have better answers to the ethical questions of our time than the description of utterly unpredictable actions of Christians in obedience to a will of God about which no generalization is possible.

D.   Need for Ethics of Responsible Freedom

The whole truth of Christian ethics would seem to lie in some kind of dynamic tension between freedom and obedience to the generalizations we commonly call ethical principles or moral laws. In obedience to God there is perfect freedom, but it is a freedom of lawful responsibility, a *responsible freedom.*

In order to understand what would be an authentic Christian ethics of responsible freedom, we must examine the ethical resources of the Bible and of Christian tradition.

chapter three

Ethics of the Old Testament
and the Gospels

A. Hebrew Ethics

1. The Covenant

The peculiar relation between Yahweh and the people Israel, known as "the Covenant," provides the context out of which came Jesus and the Christian faith. Hence the Jews' tradition of the Covenant is the tradition of Christians as well.

The tradition of this sacred compact was forged in the desperate flight from Egypt and the struggle for life in the Sinaitic wastelands. We are told again and again how Moses related to his people God's promise to deliver them, to give them the Promised Land, and to make them a great people. But they, on their part, must worship him and him alone and must keep his commandments.

The people of the Covenant then saw how God had, long before the flight from Egypt or even the going into Egypt for food, taken an earlier initiative, to bring Abraham out into the desert to form his own people. God had renewed the promise to Abraham's son Isaac and to Isaac's son Jacob or Israel, the common ancestors of the Hebrew people. Then the idea of the Covenant initiated by Yahweh was read back, far back, into the very beginnings of human life. For in the very creation of the first man and woman God had intended the founding on earth of a holy people to live in faithfulness to him and his commandments.

2. The Torah

When the earliest codes of law contained in the Pentateuch, especially the Ten Commandments (Exod. 20:1-17) and the Covenant Code (Exod. 20:23-23:19), are compared with other codes of Canaan and more distant lands of the ancient Near East, striking similarities appear. Since many regulations in the Covenant Code pertain to agriculture and not nomadic conditions, it is doubtful that more than a core of this material dates back to Moses and the wanderings in the wilderness. However, even Moses lived about 1200 B.C. and the similar Babylonian Code of Hammurabi dates back to about 1800 B.C. Other codes of the kind date back one or more centuries before Moses. We need not doubt the agency of God in the learning of the law by Israel in order to grant the evident fact that much of the learning was mediated by other peoples of the Near East.

All notions of good and evil, duty and law, justice and nationhood, are, in Israel's law, or Torah, related to the Covenant. Moses is represented in Deuteronomy as having given out the many requirements of the legal code. Then he recounts the wonderful things which God has done for the Israelites, bringing them miraculously out of Egypt, enabling them to overcome many foes and trials in the wilderness, and now bringing them near the entrance to the Promised Land. Soon they will go over and possess it, by the power of God, even though Moses is about to die on the east side of the Jordan. Then Moses declares,

> See, I have set before you this day life and good, death and evil. If you obey the commandments of the Lord your God which I command you this day, by loving the Lord your God, by walking in his ways, and by keeping his commandments and his statutes and his ordinances, then you shall live and multiply, and the Lord your God will bless you in the land which you are entering to take possession of it. But if your heart turns away, and you will not hear, but are drawn away to worship other gods and serve them, I declare to you this day, that you shall perish; you shall not live long in the land which you are going over the Jordan to enter and possess. I call heaven and earth to witness against you this day, that I have set before you life and death, blessing and curse; therefore choose life, that you and your descendants may live. . . .
> [Deut. 30:15–19]

The commandments of the Covenant take different forms, with different emphases, in different periods and different kinds of writing. In the early and best-known form of the Decalogue (Exod. 20:1–17), it is simple and terse, four of the ten laws concerning relations with Yahweh and six governing relations with other Israelite people. The nearest approach to religious ceremonial requirement is the fourth: "Remember the Sabbath day, to keep it holy." In Deuteronomy there is much provision for complicated relationships of a settled society, including both cities and farms, employers and employees, as well as masters and slaves. In the Priestly Code of Leviticus and the Chronicles there is further refinement of law on human relations, but the most conspicuous feature is the dominant stress on intricate requirements of ceremonial religious observance.

There are two distinguishable forms of statement in which the laws are given. On the one hand are the conditional laws, or "Ordinances," with prescribed penalties. These are similar to the laws of states generally. If a specified offense is committed, then a specified penalty is to be inflicted. For example, "Whoever strikes his father or his mother shall be put to death. Whoever steals a man, whether he sells him or is found in possession of him, shall be put to death."[1]

On the other hand, we find unconditional commands, or "Words,"[2] which are simple imperatives, like "Thou shalt not kill" or "Love the sojourner therefore; for you were sojourners in the land of Egypt" (Deut. 10:19).

However, the covenantal context provides a kind of implied condition for even the tersest Words. Implied throughout the laws of every kind is the teaching that *if* you are to keep your side of the Covenant with Yahweh you must obey this law; if you disobey it you will be violating the Covenant and you risk being cut off from Yahweh's favor and consequently losing all the promises and even life itself.

Since Yahweh has made Israel a people and all Israelites owe their identity to him, all have unlimited, absolute obligations to him. His prescribed laws cover all aspects of life, since all belong to him. Hence there can be no distinctions between religious and secular, legal and ethical. We who now read the ancient codes may classify the various laws in these different categories, but the writers and especially the priests, who recorded them, did not.

In content, the Old Testament Law is notable for its concern with protection of the weak and the poor. E. Clinton Gardner goes too far when he speaks unequivocally of its "equalitarianism."[3] The Torah takes for granted differences between the rights and powers of slaveholder and slave, man and woman, rich and poor, first-born and later-born. Yet, in its historical context, it does exert much pressure in the *direction* of human equality. There are many provisions for protection of slaves, employees, wives, concubines, widows, and orphans. The Word in Leviticus, later quoted by Jesus as the second greatest commandment, would, it is true, imply equality if pressed all the way to its logical conclusion and without any limiting law of any kind. If you truly "love your neighbor as yourself,"[4] it would seem that there was little room left for discrimination against him. However, in the

1. Exod. 21:15–16. These particular statements, in Hebrew, are in participial form and are similar to laws of other peoples living as desert nomads. Hence they are thought to be likely remnants of forms prescribed by Moses in the wilderness.

2. Cf. Exod. 24:3, and see the discussion in E. Clinton Gardner, *Biblical Faith and Social Ethics* (New York: Harper & Row, 1960), p. 29.

3. *Op. cit.*, pp. 27 and 31–32. Gardner is speaking of "biblical ethics" and some of his more convincing illustrations are from the prophets and the New Testament; but he includes the Torah and draws most of his illustrations from it.

4. Lev. 19:18. Cf. Mark 12:31.

second verse following that command there is explicit provision for discriminatory practice regarding a woman who is a slave.

The laws of ancient Israel seem to us barbarously cruel, with their many provisions for the death penalty. But again one must consider the historical context. Life was rough and difficult. Our modern provision for prisons in which convicted criminals are kept at public expense would have been impossible in a society the members of which were often called upon to struggle desperately to keep themselves alive. Israel's prescribed penalties in ancient times were more severe than those of many primitive peoples, but were characteristic of the Near East and were probably affected by peculiar social conditions of life in the desert.

The *lex talionis*, on the other hand, as seen in historical context, is relatively a law of mercy. To punish by taking "life for life, eye for eye, tooth for tooth, hand for hand, foot for foot, burn for burn, wound for wound, stripe for stripe" (Exod. 21:23–25) is to *limit* vengeance which otherwise is likely to follow "the law of the jungle," taking a life for an eye and a life for a tooth. The direction of movement and pressure is on the side of mercy. This development would continue, with the later assessing of fines in place of bodily injury, until Jesus was finally to denounce the whole system of human retributory justice (Matt. 5:38–41).

3. The Prophets

The growing edge of ancient Hebrew ethics was embodied largely in the marvelous succession of prophets. There have been remarkable prophets among many peoples, but no succession of them in such towering greatness or cumulative continuity of tradition as in ancient Israel.

Although there are sporadic references to prophet or prophetess living in the time of Moses (Exod. 7:1; 15:20) and even Abraham is called a prophet (Gen. 20:7), the line of prophetic succession begins properly with Nathan.[5] It continues with Elijah, Elisha, and Micaiah.

The grand prophetic tradition, however, is only anticipated by these men. It bursts forth in its splendor in the first of the literary prophets, Amos, in the eighth century B.C.

This shepherd of Tekoa was sent by God on the dangerous mission of prophesying in the Northern Kingdom on the sins of the prosperous leaders of that land and their impending punishment. Their ceremonial religion, he tells them, is offensive. Speaking for God, he cries out, "I hate, I despise your feasts. . . . But let justice roll down

---

5. Samuel might have best prior claim, but he is rather a kind of inspired ruler or "judge."

like waters" (5:21–27). Amos does not deal in abstractions, but explicitly charges that the people of Israel sell and oppress the poor (2:6–7, etc.), commit specified sexual offenses (2:7), indulge in sensuous luxuries based upon exploitation of the poor (3:15–4:1), are proud and ungrateful to God (6:13), and are dishonest in trade practices (8:5–6). Amos does not spare his own kingdom of Judah (see 2:4–5).

Although Yahweh is the God of Israel and Judah, his Law is not limited to these people of the Covenant. He judges other nations, too. Most of their offenses which Amos condemns are offenses against the people of the Covenant, or are indicted without mention of the victims, but there is one notable exception. Says Amos,

> Thus says the Lord:
> "For three transgressions of Moab, and for four,
>   I will not revoke the punishment;
> because he burned to lime
>   the bones of the king of Edom."
>   [2:1]

Amos appears to be deliberately making clear that Yahweh's rule is universal. He judges among the nations in equity. This emphasis prepares for Amos' denunciation of Judah and Israel and his warning of divine punishment to come upon them. Yahweh is no mere partisan, as other gods are reputed to be. Even the peoples in Covenant with him may not presume on his favor, for he judges all the nations in righteousness.[6]

Hosea, the younger contemporary of Amos, but himself a native of the Northern Kingdom, dwells more on the idolatry of Israel, but he, too, condemns dishonest trading, oppression, pride, and luxury.[7] He makes two notable further ethical contributions.

When denouncing sexual immorality he goes out of his way to stress that one norm must apply to men and women alike. The passage, a truly remarkable one to have appeared in the eighth century B.C., is as follows:

> I will not punish your daughters
>   when they play the harlot,
>   nor your brides when they commit adultery;
> for the men themselves go aside with harlots,
>   and sacrifice with cult prostitutes. . . .
>   [4:14]

6. Cf. the thoughtful discussion of this matter by Norman K. Gottwald, in *All the Kingdoms of the Earth* (New York: Harper & Row, 1964), pp. 109–12.
7. E.g., see 12:7–8.

The other, and most prominent contribution, has to do with the very purpose of God, which lies at the heart of all Hebrew prophecy. Like Amos, Hosea warns of terrible punishment which God will inflict upon the people Israel. But Hosea represents the punishment as itself a stratagem of divine love. Israel is like a beloved wife gone into harlotry. God is determined that through depriving her of wealth and even of necessary food, he will turn her from her present dissolute, idolatrous ways. Then he will tenderly invite her return to him and when she returns he will lavish upon her the gifts of his love (chap. 2). Such a teaching about God cannot fail to reflect also upon ideas of human vengeance and retributive punishment, and, in general, upon harsh insensitiveness in human relations.

The great southern contemporary of Amos and Hosea, the prophet Isaiah, includes in his powerful writing all of the main ethical themes of Amos, excepting that his concern with the pagan nations seems limited to their relations with Judah. Perhaps the most significant ethical ideas not found in Amos have to do with the relation between justice and peace. When the nations come under the rule of Yahweh from Jerusalem, then

> they shall beat their swords into plowshares,
> and their spears into pruning hooks;
> nation shall not lift up sword against nation,
> neither shall they learn war any more.[8]

Despite the focus on Judah as the center of all God's concerns with other nations, Isaiah holds an international philosophy of history closely related to ethics. As he warns of the dread punishment to come upon Judah, he identifies Assyria as the instrument God will use for this purpose. Yet this does not imply an overlooking of Assyria's pagan pride and cruelty. The conscious intent of the Assyrians will be for proud, selfish plunder. But God rules over the scene with a different aim (10:5-14). In turn God will deal with Assyria, and in the end a reformed remnant of Judah will be divinely empowered to overcome that presently great power (10:20-27).

Well worthy of mention also is Isaiah's image of the good king who is to rule "in steadfast love . . . one who judges and seeks justice and is swift to do righteousness" (16:5). The suggestion that an ideal king's justice is an expression of "steadfast love" is worthy of special note (16:15).

Jeremiah, in the seventh century B.C., true to the well-established tradition of the genuine prophets, denounces idolatry, oppression of

8. 2:4. Isa. 2:2-4 is very nearly identical with Mic. 4:1-3.

the poor, adultery, and deceit. He especially condemns the smooth-tongued prophets who say what people want to hear and do not declare the judgments of God.

A distinctive ethical idea of Jeremiah is his declaration that in the days of God's holy reign, family and descendants will not be punished for a man's sin, but the sinner himself alone must bear the consequence of his wrongdoing (31:29–30).

This doctrine of individual responsibility is more extensively and emphatically stated by Ezekiel in the early sixth century. He stresses also that a man must not trust his past righteousness to bring him God's favor, nor is he to despair on account of past sins. The present is all-important (33:10–20).

The later writings added to the Book of Isaiah as Chapters 40–66 had an important part in preparation for the understanding of Jesus as the Christ, both by Jesus himself and by the few of his contemporaries who accepted him. The principal ethical significance of these writings is to be found in the image of the Suffering Servant in the Servant Songs.[9]

The question whether the writer of these passages was thinking of his nation Judah or of an unexpected kind of gentle messiah who would conquer by suffering rather than by violent strength is of little ethical importance. In either case there is here a vision of innocent suffering as a mighty instrument of God's own power, leading to an era of true brotherhood. This vision both prepared for Jesus as the Christ and for the acceptance of other innocent suffering as effectively redemptive.

Many ethical insights of the prophets enter finally into the later versions of the Law. The Deuteronomic Law (c. 621 B.C.), especially, incorporates many of the more humane concerns of the eighth- and seventh-century prophets.

Much of prophetic ethical teaching is included also in the finer Psalms and other liturgical materials of the Old Testament. These, too, provided invaluable instructional media which popularized and made respectable ideas which were generally rejected when they were first declared by the prophets.

Jonah marks in one respect a high-water mark of Old Testament prophecy. He represents Yahweh as having sent his prophet on a mission to warn the people of Nineveh that because of their sins their great city was about to be destroyed. The prophet was as reluctant as one would expect any good Jew of his time to be. Why should he care about giving a warning to such a hostile, cruel, pagan city? After the famous encounter with the storm at sea and the big fish, however, he went and proclaimed his message. To his dismay, the people re-

9. Isa. 42:1–4; 49:1–6; 50:4–9; 52:13–53:12.

pented, and God did not destroy the city. Jonah sulked angrily. The final verse gives the central message in a word of Yahweh:

> And should not I pity Nineveh, that great city, in which there are more than one hundred and twenty thousand persons who do not know their right hand from their left, and also much cattle?

Nowhere else in the Old Testament is it taught so clearly that God loves all the peoples of the earth, even the worst enemies of the Covenant people. It is implied that he has an especially tender concern for the innocent children of pagan wrongdoers and even has some regard for their cattle! This is a far cry from the wars of total extermination described earlier as commanded by God.[10]

The prophets often reflect the moral standards of their times, cruel and base as well as merciful and lofty. But again and again their utterances break through the level of established law and custom to new moral insights. While there is no such reliable trend as would guarantee that a later prophet will express loftier moral standards than an earlier one, nevertheless there is a cumulative series, moving like the successive waves of an incoming tide, from Elijah to Second Isaiah and Jonah. Many of the prophetic teachings were incorporated in Law and Psalter, but the most exalted and exacting of all their ethical visions remained theirs alone until the coming of Jesus.

The latest period of the Old Testament canon, the third and second centuries B.C., was a period of fierce nationalism which produced some of the most extreme doctrines of ethnic superiority and exclusiveness ever to find human expression. Not only was intermarriage with non-Jews forbidden, but under Ezra's instruction, it is said, the people were required to put away all foreign wives whom they had previously married, and all the children of these marriages as well. (See Ezra, chap. 10.) The resultant cruelty and suffering may hardly be imagined.

In the Books of the Chronicles, coming from the same period, hatred of the Samaritans comes to full expression. In both Ezra and the Chronicles the laws of religious ceremony reach such emphasis and detail as would surely have provoked the utmost indignation from the great prophets.

4. Law and Mercy

Christians often exaggerate the contrast between Law and gospel. There is, in truth, difference enough. But it is not of the kind or degree sometimes supposed.

---

10. E.g., see Deut. 20:16–18.

The Law, it is said, is hard, impersonal, and burdensome. It points to vengeful, merciless retribution. People under the Torah, it is said, joylessly try to obey its minimal requirements in fear of its penalties.

The gospel, on the other hand, stands for mercy, love, joy, concern for persons above abstract, standard concepts, and effort for redemption rather than judgment. We must put the gospel in proper perspective later, but now misconceptions of the Law need correction.

The Law is, indeed, *law*, and hence prescribes standards of righteousness or justice, often with specified penalties for violations. Moreover, as we have noted, the penalties are often harsh and seem to us altogether out of proportion to the offenses. Especially is this true of some early Ordinances believed to have originated during nomadic life in the desert.

But conceptions of the Old Testament Law as harsh, impersonal, and loveless must be modified by taking adequately into account several important considerations.

a. Historical Context. As already observed, many prescriptions of the Torah, while looking harsh from our present perspective, were, in their historical setting, moderating common practice and pressing hard on the side of mercy. Moreover, some provisions of the Law were obviously motivated by generous consideration for the poor. For example, in both the Deuteronomic and Priestly Codes, it is required that the wages of a hired servant be paid on the very day of his earning (Deut. 24:15; Lev. 19:13). Likewise, there are provisions in the same two codes, forbidding thorough harvesting of crops, a residue to be left, rather, for alien travelers and for the poor (Deut. 24:19–21; Lev. 19:9–10).

b. Law as Guiding Work of Divine Love. The Torah is a peculiar kind of law, looked upon by the pious Israelite, not as an externally imposed set of arbitrary rules, but rather as the kindly instruction of Yahweh. God loves his people and wants them to prosper, so he gives the Law to guide them aright.

The Hebrew word Torah is, indeed, properly translated as "precept" or "teaching," as well as "law." This teaching is a gift of God's love.[11]

c. The Law Accepted with Grateful Joy. If the Torah was sometimes regarded as an onerous burden, quite a different attitude is reflected in many passages. In the Psalms, especially, there are many expressions of gratitude and pleasure in the receiving of the Law. The righteous man is not one who grudgingly tries to carry out its minimal demands. Rather,

11. Cf. Deut. 33:3–4.

> . . . his delight is in the law of the Lord,
> and on his law he meditates day and night.
>
> [Ps. 1:2]

Israel is especially fortunate in having the Law which other nations do not know. Hence thankful praise is due to Yahweh (Ps. 147:19–20).

The writer of Psalm 119 has so written that every one of the one hundred seventy-six verses speaks in some way of the Law, usually in praise of it. Despite the studied artificiality of the acrostic composition in the Hebrew, and the gloating over the inferior peoples who lack the Law, this Psalm is an impressive refutation of the notion that the Torah was a grimly borne burden. Characteristic of Hebrew piety are the following lines:

> If thy law had not been my delight,
> I should have perished in my affliction.
> I will never forget thy precepts;
> for by them thou hast given me life. . . .
> Oh, how I love thy law!
>
> [Ps. 119:92–93, 97]

d. Law of Steadfast Love (Hesed). In a famous word study,[12] the Jewish scholar Nelson Glueck has laid open the rich meaning of the Hebrew word *hesed*, which appears very frequently throughout the Old Testament and is variously translated, according to context and translator's preference, as "mercy" (commonly in KJV), "steadfast love" (favored in RSV), "love," "steadfastness," "loyalty," or "faithfulness."

The word is especially important to our understanding of the Law because the Law is at once an expression of God's *hesed* and a detailed injunction to human *hesed* toward God.

Glueck tells us that this word is not used of mercy or kindness shown toward casual acquaintances or anyone with whom one is not in some kind of binding or obligating relationship. God's *hesed* toward Israel is, of course, an expression of the covenanted relationship. Likewise, every Israelite is obligated by the covenantal relationship to show *hesed* to God and to every other Israelite.

Christian readers should note especially the significance of Glueck's conclusion on the relation of *hesed* and grace:

12. *Hesed in the Bible*, tr. by Alfred Gottschalk (Cincinnati: Hebrew Union College Press, 1967). First published in German as a doctoral dissertation in 1927.

The *hesed* of God, while it is not to be identified with His grace, is still based upon the latter, insofar as the relationship between God and people, structured by Him as a covenantal relationship, was effected by electing Israel through an act of grace.   [*Ibid.*, p. 102]

The prophets stress that the *hesed* owed to God must be shown, not only by worship and loyalty directed to him alone, but also by stead-fast love directed to other human beings. Most, at least, of the pro-phetic passages cited by Glueck fail to make clear any transcending of Israel's limits, so perhaps he stretches a point beyond justification when he says that *hesed* is required toward "all men" (*ibid.*, p. 56), rather than "all Israelites" or "all people of the Covenant." It is true that Jonah (not cited by Glueck) portrays the mercy of God toward Nineveh, and teaches that a Jew should have a similar attitude, but the word *hesed* is not used in this connection. Moreover, Jonah's teaching is regrettably far from the dominant narrow nationalism of Judaism in the late centuries before Christ.

5. Casuistry

As the life of the Jews, both in Judea and in other lands, became increasingly complex and often fell under dominance by alien law and culture, it became increasingly difficult to fulfill the literal require-ments of the Torah. When it was impossible to carry on the prescribed rites in the temple at Jerusalem, when trade and industry in pagan cities required new relationships between trader and customer and be-tween employer and employee, the old precepts could not be literally followed. Hence rabbis whose authority was widely recognized gave carefully phrased interpretations of the Torah for application to speci-fied kinds of situations. For centuries these authoritative legal opinions were passed along orally from teachers to disciples and disciples to the people coming to the synagogues. Therefore, this body of opinion was sometimes known as "oral Torah," even though there were doubtless many personal notes in use by the rabbis. In the third century A.D. an authoritative written compilation of such opinions was edited and is known as the Mishnah. Thereafter the process continued and in the fifth century later interpretations of the Mishnah were published in separate compilations in Jerusalem and Babylon. The later materials are known as the Gemarah. Mishnah and Gemarah together constitute the Talmud, finally canonized as authoritative revelation among the Jews.

The development of the interpretations later collected in the Mish-nah was, of course, in process and already far advanced at the time of Jesus. It is to portions of this growing legal cauistry that Jesus refers when, after examples, he says, "So, for the sake of your tradition, you have made void the word of God" (Matt. 15:6).

Often the casuistry of the Mishnah lightens the burden of the Torah as literally read, or as rigorously interpreted in earlier times. On the other hand, there are many provisions in the Mishnah for especially cruel punishments, specified in detail, including many requirements of death by torture.[13]

When there is a basic law and social change makes it difficult or unreasonable to enforce it literally, there are two possible directions for judicial tradition to take, without simply repealing or abandoning the original law. One is for each case to be decided by direct appeal to the general spirit or intent of the original law at the time of its enactment, but with due regard for the new circumstances. The other is the construction, decision by decision, of a body of judicial precedent which itself becomes law. The latter, the development of casuistry, is the direction principally taken by Jewish Law.

The result was the amassing of an exceedingly formidable body of law which no one but a full-time specialist could hope to know and which even a specialist could know less than perfectly. It must be borne in mind that the Jewish casuistry was law, both in the sense of human civil law, with material penalties attached, and also religious law believed to determine the relations between an individual and God.

Whether the Mishnah moderates or intensifies a particular requirement of the ancient Law, it almost invariably[14] adds to the technical complexity of law and so puts the poor, untrained man at a disadvantage, and in general gives to the lawyers great advantages of power (cf. Matt. 23:2–4). In the Mishnah as finally compiled two centuries later, we do not find the precise legal traditions to which Jesus made reference, but there are many other examples of similar overloading of the law with technicalities. It will be worthwhile to cite some examples since they not only make more concrete our understanding of the context and meaning of Jesus' teaching, but also illustrate the ethical problems of casuistry in general.

The provision for doubling one's legal Sabbath journey is a case in point. The reader must bear in mind that the Sabbath begins with nightfall Friday evening and ends at the same time Saturday. The liberalizing passage is as follows:

> If a man was on a journey and darkness overtook him, and he recognized a tree or a fence and said, "Let my Sabbath resting-place be

13. See, e.g., the Mishnah, Nezekin, Sanhedrin. 7:2; 9:4, 5; 11:1.
14. The exceptions are a few provisions for partial or complete remission of penalties because the offender was ignorant of certain Mishnaic provisions.

under it," he has said nothing; [but if he said,] "Let my Sabbath resting-place be at its roots," he may walk from where he stands to its root [up to a distance of] two thousand cubits, and from its root to his house [up to a distance of] two thousand cubits. Thus he can travel four thousand cubits after it has become dark.[15]

Woe be to the poor fellow who, in his ignorance of the legal niceties, expresses his intent to rest under the designated tree instead of "at its root"! He will be subject to the penalties of Sabbath violation from which his more sophisticated brother escapes scot-free.

Again, it is a punishable offense for a man to carry food from his house on the Sabbath. But it is all right if he lays it on the threshold in one act and then, in another act, later in the same day, takes it farther.[16]

6. Concluding Observations

Ancient Hebrew ethics, then, presents some remarkable paradoxes. The prophets uttered loftier moral injunctions than had ever been heard and many of their teachings were codified into religious and civil law. Yet life-degrading cruelty and harshness typical of ancient desert peoples were fixed in the law and carried over into the Christian Era. There is much remarkable practical concern shown toward the poor and friendless. Yet the elaboration of Law in the oral tradition, while moderating some requirements, excludes by its technical complexity the poor and ignorant from many of its advantages. The Law is received with joy as the gift of God's steadfast love. Yet, through the centuries, it is so overlaid with technical interpretations having also the force of law that it becomes a burden impossible to carry out with full success. The Old Testament prophets cut through the niceties of ceremonial law to exalt the very heart of a godly, compassionate, and responsible life. Yet after the prophets the process of legalistic and ceremonial elaboration continued on to new absurd and stifling extremes. In places both prophecy and Law show a far-sighted sense of divine love toward people of all nations. Yet as the Old Testament canon comes to a close in Ezra and the Books of Chronicles, the dominant perspective is one of extremely narrow and exclusive nationalism.

All of these antinomies were fed into the context and subject matter of the New Testament. Much of the teaching in the Gospels and Letters has to do with the resultant religious and moral teachings. This is inevitable because Jesus and his apostles were Jews. It is also a great blessing to Christians, both because the loftiest teachings of the Old

15. Moed. Erubin. 4:7. *The Mishnah,* by Hervert Danby (London: Oxford University Press, 1933), pp. 126–27.
16. *Ibid.,* Moed. Shabbath. 10:2.

Testament were thus made part of their heritage and also because these paradoxes and tensions placed before Jesus, the New Testament writers, and subsequent generations supremely important issues for an ethical religion and a religious ethics.

B. Ethical Teachings of Jesus

1. Apocalypticism and Jesus' Ethics

It is known that apocalyptic expectation of a spectacular divine intervention in behalf of the Jews was high among the Palestinian Jews of Jesus' time. It is also evident that some passages in the Gospels represent Jesus as participating fully in such expectation.

If the only evidence we had was of the kind which we find in Mark 13, there would be little question about Jesus being himself an apocalyptist. However, there is other evidence of precisely contrary character. Mark 13:1-23 describes, with some symbolism, events which subsequently did occur within fifty years of Jesus' teachings in Jerusalem. The next four verses (24-27) are, as they stand, clearly apocalyptic predictions of God's final intervention by the agency of the "Son of man"—whether we take that phrase to indicate, in this passage, Jesus himself or a heavenly figure yet to come (cf. Matt. 24:27). But over against that must be placed the most explicit repudiations of apocalyptic expectations.[17] Other passages describe the coming of God's reign in ways which seem clearly to indicate a gradual, quiet spread from one understanding and obedient life to others.[18]

The fact that apocalyptic expectations were so prevalent in Jesus' time cuts both ways. It is argued by Albert Schweitzer and others that because of the prevalence of these views Jesus must have shared in them. But it is obvious that Jesus did not conform to the prevalent attitudes and ideas of his people. The Sanhedrin plot which led to his crucifixion by the Romans is proof enough of that. The very prevalence of the apocalyptic teachings might have led the more readily to the distortion, in oral reporting, of the very few words which, in the record, appear to declare apocalyptic expectations.

I have discussed this problem further elsewhere,[19] and need not dwell on it here. It is important to know whether Jesus' ethical teaching represents only an "interim ethic," valid for the short time before the expected consummation of the age. However, the answer to that does not necessarily depend on our determining whether Jesus was apocalyptic

---

17. See especially Luke 17:20-21. Cf. Matt. 12:39 and 16:4.
18. See Matt. 13:33; Luke 13:20-21. Cf. Matt. 5:13-16.
19. See *A Theology of the Living Church*, pp. 306-17.

in his expectations. Even if he was not so, it is evident that some writers of the Gospel material have represented him as holding such views and the report of his ethical teachings might be influenced in places by the same misunderstanding of his position. On the other hand, even if he did hold such expectations he might believe that human conduct in the interim should conform to divine commands and purposes which were valid for all times and not only for the period now facing faithful believers.

In short, the presence of apocalyptic material in the Gospels requires us to look carefully at the various ethical teachings attributed to Jesus to see whether their nature or the arguments cited by Jesus in their support would indicate that they represented an interim or a permanent ethics.

Most of the ethical teachings attributed to Jesus in the Gospels are of such nature as to indicate his belief in their permanent validity. Most of them are deeply rooted in the Old Testament, especially the great prophets and Psalms of nonapocalyptic character. This fact is attested both by the similarity of the teachings to the ancient writings and also by the literally hundreds of allusions to them.

Jesus represents his ethical teachings as based on the nature and purpose of God the Father. God's nature and purpose are not thought of as being about to change.

If there is any important aspect of Jesus' teaching, as reported in the Gospels, which we should expect to be influenced by the idea of an interim ethic, it would be the extreme rigor and perfectionism of it. But precisely in the heart of such teaching the Gospel illustrates the timeless bases of the ethical demands. Note these words from the Sermon on the Mount:

> You have heard that it was said, "You shall love your neighbor and hate your enemy." But I say to you, Love your enemies and pray for those who persecute you, so that you may be sons of your Father who is in heaven; for he makes his sun rise on the evil and on the good, and sends rain on the just and on the unjust.[20]

When did God start making "his sun rise on the evil and on the good," and how long has he been sending "rain on the just and on the unjust" alike? These activities of God are expressions of his lasting concerns for all people and have been going on throughout all the ages of human life on earth.

20. Matt. 5:43–45. I am not assuming that these or other passages quoted are the very words of the Jesus who lived in ancient Palestine. The writer of the Gospel so represented them and they formed an ethical resource of the ancient church, much prized both within and outside the tradition of apocalyptic expectation.

After continuing in similar vein, the chapter closes with the most exacting and difficult of all Jesus' teachings—the command to be "perfect." Why be perfect? He does not say it is because the Son of man is about to come from the clouds and inaugurate the reign of God. Rather, he says, "You, therefore, must be perfect, as your heavenly Father is perfect" (Matt. 5:48). Understanding that the Greek word (*teleioi*) here translated "perfect" means mature or complete in relation to the goal of being, we must ask now how long Jesus or the writer who attributed these words to him believed God had been perfect. Here there could be no doubt. The very question would border on blasphemy. God had been perfect from everlasting and would be so to everlasting. Hence the injunction to be perfect is applicable to any age or place.

Some highly specific injunctions may have reference to a short time remaining before the end of the age, as, for example, instructions to the Twelve about their mission in Israel on which they were to carry no provisions and to spend little time in each place (Matt. 10:5–15). But most such instructions are so specifically related to one place and time, in any case, that they would hardly bear transfer to other circumstances without change, regardless of our thought about apocalypticism. Not that such passages are without usefulness to us. They do, after all, help to put temporal values into the perspective of eternal values, regardless of Jesus' relation to first-century apocalypticism.

2. Forms of Ethical Teachings by Jesus

Most of our knowledge concerning Jesus' verbal ethical instruction must come from the reports in the Synoptic Gospels. In those reports four main forms of moral guidance may be distinguished.[21]

a. Direct Commands.   The Gospels report many straightforward imperatives, both positive and negative. Some are directions for a particular situation, often followed by generalization.[22] Others are without any such reference. Thus:

"Love your enemies and pray for those who persecute you."[23]

b. Blessings and Woes.   Sometimes Jesus says that persons of certain attitudes or conduct are or will be blessed or rewarded or that others are or will be under condemnation, without directly commanding or forbidding either type of attitude or conduct. In some instances

21. This classification, of course, has little to do with the categories used by the various schools of "form criticism."

22. E.g., see Mark 9:38–41 and parallel in Luke 9:49–50; Mark 10:21 and parallels in Matt. 19:21 and Luke 18:22; and Luke 18:23–24.

23. Matt. 5:44 and parallel in Luke 6:27. Other instances are found in the following and parallel passages: Matt. 5:39, 6:6, 7:1; and indirect commands in Luke 14:33, 16:18, etc.

there are immediate implications concerning conduct. Examples are the Beatitudes pronouncing blessings on the merciful (Matt. 5:7) and the peacemakers (5:9). Similar in direct moral implication are various woes.[24]

c. Parables. Some of Jesus' parables are important sources of ethical ideas. Such is the story of the Good Samaritan, teaching practical compassion to any and every person in need, regardless of class, nation, or customary barriers of hostility (Luke 10:25–37). Another example is the parable of Dives and Lazarus, with its strong condemnation of failure to care for the poor (Luke 16:19–31).

The parable of the Prodigal Son is most commonly thought of as a teaching concerning God's love toward lost sinners. So it is; but the context provided by Luke and the concluding section of the story emphasize strongly an ethical teaching regarding human relations also. The parable is a clear warning against proud, self-righteous scorn or cold indifference toward any outcast, however sinful or disreputable he may be (Luke 15:1–2, 11–32).

As one more illustration of ethical teaching by parable, we may observe the parable of the Judgment, with its memorable line, "as you did it to one of the least of these my brethren, you did it to me" (Matt. 25:31–46).

d. Sayings Concerning Relative Values. Many of Jesus' teachings do not immediately direct or imply one kind of conduct rather than another, but are nevertheless of great ethical importance. In our moral problems we are continually forced to choose between one goal and another, not only as good or bad, but also as good or better. All-important in determining moral decision are the priorities of valuation which underlie it. Much that Jesus has to say bears on such priorities.

One of the clearest instances is the saying,

> Therefore do not be anxious, saying, "What shall we eat?" or "What shall we drink?" or "What shall we wear?" For the Gentiles seek all these things; and your heavenly Father knows that you need them all. But seek first his kingdom and his righteousness, and all these things shall be yours as well.   [Matt. 6:31–33.]

The main point of the parable of the Unjust Steward has to do with priorities as between the values of earthly wealth, on the one hand, and the eternal values of personal relations with God and his people on the other, as declared in the concluding words, "And I tell you, make friends for yourselves by means of unrighteous mammon, so that when it fails they may receive you into the eternal habitations" (Luke 16:1–9).

24. E.g., see Matt. 23:23 and Luke 6:26.

e. Personal Example. The final and supreme form of ethical instruction by Jesus is his personal example. Whether we think of courage, of generous kindness, of compassion on the friendless, of forgiving mercy, of willingness to sacrifice one's very life for a cause, of prayer for one's enemies, of single-minded response to God's call, indeed of any kind of conduct which his words enjoined, there leap to our minds memories of acts which he performed, sublimely exemplifying his teachings.[25]

His going to Jerusalem in the face of impending personal disaster and, in that tense situation, cleansing the temple and carrying on his ministry at its very gates speak more eloquently of courage than could any words.[26] His prayer for the forgiveness of his torturers at whose hands he was in mortal agony is a mightier influence for a forgiving spirit than any exhortation could be (Luke 23:34). His eating with sinners and tax collectors strikes a heavier blow at spiritual pride and exclusiveness than any verbal instruction on these matters.[27]

3. Vignettes of a Style of Life

If a reader tries to take the various specific ethical teachings of the Gospels as constituting a system of rules, he will soon be in serious moral confusion.

"Give to him who begs from you" (Matt. 5:42). What? Even if the beggar wants a knife with which to commit murder or suicide? Even if the gift which he asks is needed by me to save someone else's life? If I give always to beggars I shall soon be continually besieged, and finally have nothing for my family or even to get to my work to earn more to give. Is there to be no selection of recipients at all? No giving to one and withholding from another?

Or what shall we make of the saying, "Do not resist one who is evil" (Matt. 5:39)? If that is treated as a rule, then what shall we make of Jesus' driving the tradesmen out of the temple and overturning the tables of the money-changers? Was that not resisting some who were evil? When a crazed man in a tower of a Texas campus was shooting to death person after person on the walks below, was it wrong for the police and civilian volunteers to stop him, let alone killing him in the process? No resistance at all to evil people?

There are basically two ways of designating good conduct. It may

25. Here, again, I leave to the specialists the arguments concerning the accuracy of the various accounts of Jesus' acts. The living faith in which Christians participate is rooted in belief that such accounts as are here mentioned do represent well the true character of Jesus, whatever the precise details of this or that event. We are concerned here with the ethical resources of that faith.

26. Luke 9:51; Matt. 16:21; Mark 11:15–18; etc.

27. Luke 5:29–32; 15:1–2; 19:1–7.

be accomplished by means of carefully defined principles—the way used, for example, by the Thomists. Another way is to use concrete examples. Jesus employed the latter method in the parable of the Good Samaritan. In the short commands, "Give to him who begs from you, and do not refuse him who would borrow from you," to be sure, he is not describing one particular event, but he is, nevertheless, illustrating a spirit and style of life, as he is in the story of the Good Samaritan. In the parable he is not telling the exact way one should always care for a wounded and robbed wayfarer—a way which must make use of donkey and innkeeper—but is making clear the properly unbounded nature of neighborly love fully pleasing to God. So in the command, "Give to him who begs from you," he is urging a generous caring for others in need, as also in the further saying, "and do not refuse him who would borrow from you."

How do we know that Jesus is, by such vignettes, teaching a spirit and style of life rather than laying down rules to be followed literally in all circumstances?

Jesus protests again and again the efforts to produce good conduct by means of casuistry. He is not starting a new casuistry. While denouncing the casuistry of the oral rabbinical tradition, he follows the way of those rabbis who would move rather in the direction of simplicity, subordinating all other law to the commandments of wholehearted love for God and neighbor (Matt. 22:35–40; Mark 12:28–34; Luke 10:25–28). When giving to the beggar or lending to the one who asks a loan is in accord with wholehearted love to God and to every neighbor, then I should plainly give or lend. But by Jesus' teaching, love to God and man must be dominant. The words about giving and lending are vignettes which illustrate the love of neighbor.

4. *Characteristic Ethical Emphases of Jesus*

When we examine all the forms of Jesus' moral teaching, we find certain emphatic themes predominating.

a. Repentance. John the Baptizer stressed above all else the requirement of repentance and new beginning.[28] Jesus began with that message. When he came out of the wilderness and began his public ministry, we read, "From that time Jesus began to preach, saying, 'Repent, for the kingdom of heaven is at hand'" (Matt. 4:17). As the Greek words *metanoia* and *metanoeo* make abundantly clear, the repentance demanded by both John and Jesus is much more than the feeling or expression of regret or contrition for past sin, or even the pleading for forgiveness. It is a change of mind and heart, a turning away from sin to live a new life.

28. See Mark 1:4; Matt. 3:2, 8; Luke 3:3, 8; Acts 19:4.

Neither John the Baptizer nor Jesus suggested a minor or gradual alteration of the world's ways. They both called for so radical a change of personal identity as to make baptism a fitting celebration of it.

Baptism had been, and is to this day, a rite by which Gentiles are inducted into the Jewish community. Males are first circumcised, but male babies born of Jewish parents are circumcised, also. The rite of baptism is the one universal rite signifying the transforming of both male and female Gentiles into Jews. John the Baptizer told the Jewish people that God's Reign was about to be inaugurated and that because of their sins which violated the Covenant they were no more God's people now than the Gentiles. Their ancestry would not save them. They must repent and be baptized into the true Israel, as if they were Gentiles. By repentance and baptism their very identity was to be changed and they were to live accordingly (Matt. 3:7–9).

In Christian use baptism was to change its character by becoming a celebration of induction into the community of the New Covenant, the community of which Jesus Christ is head. But Jesus' message began with John's emphasis on the necessity of repentance, and this continued to be a basic Christian theme.[29]

b. Faith. A second major theme of Jesus, according to the Synoptic record, is faith, faith in God and in Jesus himself.

The meaning of faith in the Synoptic Gospels is most often trust in the power of God to provide, to heal, or to save from danger. Jesus enjoins his hearers not to be anxious about their physical needs. They are not to be "of little faith," but to trust God for their food, drink, and clothing, while devoting their main attention to God's "kingdom and his righteousness."[30]

The trust for which Jesus calls is a personal entrusting of self to God in an enduring relationship. The original meaning of the Greek word for faith (*pistis*) is faithfulness or reliability, and we can see the continuing sense of reliable endurance in Jesus' words, ". . . when the Son of man comes, will he find faith on earth?" (Luke 18:8).

Yet in the Synoptic record the dominant meaning of faith is clearly trust or belief in God and in Jesus as provider, healer, or protecting savior from peril.

c. Obedience. Jesus is not content, however, with enjoining people to trust him or to trust God for everything. There was work to do and active obedience to his command was required. He warns, "Not every one who says to me, 'Lord, Lord,' shall enter the kingdom of heaven, but he who does the will of my Father who is in heaven" (Matt. 7:21). Again, he asks, "Why do you call me 'Lord, Lord,'

29. E.g., see Acts 26:19–20.
30. Matt. 6:25–33. Cf. Matt. 9:28–29 and Mark 4:40.

and not do what I tell you?" and follows his question by comparing
the person who acts according to Jesus' words to a man who builds
his house on rock so that a flooding storm "could not shake it" (Luke
6:46–49).

The emphasis on obedience comes also in various indirect ways, as
when he calls his disciples with the commanding invitation, "Follow
me" (Mark 1:16–20); or when he rebukes the unnamed man in Samaria
who offers to follow him but wishes first to attend to certain traditional home responsibilities and when he concludes, "No one who puts
his hand to the plow and looks back is fit for the kingdom of God"
(Luke 9:57–62). In his healings he sometimes tests and cultivates
obedience, as well as faith by commanding an action. Thus, the man
with the withered hand is first told, "Come here," then commanded,
"Stretch out your hand" (Mark 3:1–5).

Obedience is closely related to faith, for to trust Jesus as Lord is to
entrust oneself to the way in which he leads. This more inclusive and
active meaning of faith comes to much fuller expression in the work
of the Apostle Paul.

d. Love.   Undoubtedly, the supreme ethical teaching of Jesus concerns love, love of God and love of man. This is so central to all else
that a more analytic and complete study of it must be presented in
Chapter Five, in the light of the whole New Testament and of later
Christian tradition.

Here it will suffice to remind the reader of grounds for speaking of
love as central in Jesus' moral instruction, according to the Synoptic
Gospels.

We have, of course, the reported word of Jesus as to the commands
which are not only most important, but according to the version in
Matthew, are basic to all others. The teaching reads:

> You shall love the Lord your God with all your heart, and with all
> your soul, and with all your mind. This is the great and first command-
> ment. And a second is like it, You shall love your neighbor as yourself.
> On these two commandments depend all the law and the prophets.
> [Matt. 22:37–40.]

When he gives his parable of the Judgment, the only requirement he
names for God's approval is providing for various forms of human
need (Matt. 25:31–46), that is, for practical expression of loving-kindness.

Every form of Jesus' ethical teaching emphasizes love, including
commands, blessings and woes, parables, and comparisons of values.
His example is most impressive of all as he devotes attention to the
poor and friendless, despite the necessity of meeting much hostility to

such concern. Even as he suffers an agonizing death in behalf of others, in his agony he comforts a dying thief beside him (Luke 23:43).

5. The Perfectionism of Jesus

A striking feature, but also a serious stumbling block, in the ethics of Jesus is the perfection of conduct and life on which he insists.

a. Motive Independent of Social Approval or Disapproval. Non-Christian, especially Jewish, commentators on the teachings of Jesus often object to what they describe as his lack of realism. He seems to leave no room for personal adaptation to the desires, even the weaknesses of family, friends, or nation. Both by precept and by example he enjoins a lonely life of austere self-denial and disregard for the good or bad opinions of others. He sees that such a life will lead to his own death at the instigation of those whom he has offended. So far from regret is he that he bids his disciples to welcome persecution, knowing that their "reward is great in heaven" (Matt. 5:10–12; Luke 6:22–23). As for the cross which he must accept, he demands quite ruthlessly of his followers the willingness to accept similar and continual resignation of life.[31]

b. Supremely Exacting Norms. Not only is a disciple called on to be continually ready to face persecution or to lay down his life; he is commanded also to adopt standards of life above those ordinarily regarded as human. "Love your enemies"? Return good for evil and pray for the forgiveness of those who are killing you? How much further into superhuman levels of life would Jesus have us go?

According to Matthew he would have us go all the way to godlikeness. He bids us to be true sons of the "Father who is in heaven" and who gives good gifts to "good and evil," "just and unjust" men alike. But, we protest, we are only human. Does he expect us to be perfect? As if anticipating our protest, he says, "You, therefore, must be perfect, as your heavenly Father is perfect" (Matt. 5:48). No other norm is adequate for us but the norm of God's own moral perfection. The problems and meanings of this for our decisions we must examine in appropriate context. But nothing can take away the absoluteness of Jesus' teaching.

c. Inwardness—But Also Deeds. One aspect of the Lord's perfectionist instructions is his demand for inward purity. As if it were not enough to require godly acts of superhuman character, he requires that even our inner life be cleansed. He tells us that as before God we are guilty if we kill, so also if we are angry at a brother we are answerable

31. Luke 9:23–24. Cf. Matt. 16:24–25; Mark 8:34–35; Matt. 10:38–39; Luke 14:27, 17:33.

according to the various degrees to which the anger gains the ascendancy (Matt. 5:21–22). Adultery is committed not only with a physical act, but, says Jesus, "I say to you that everyone who looks at a woman lustfully has already committed adultery with her in his heart" (Matt. 5:28).

This does not mean that Jesus is preoccupied with subjectivity, so that he is not concerned about deeds. As we have already observed, according to his teaching it is only those who *do* the Father's will and who actually perform acts to help the needy who receive heavenly favor.

Moreover, on the negative side, the Jesus of the Synoptic Gospels does not think of *sin* as primarily a subjective *condition* such as an unsaved human nature or a lack of faith. Simple evidence of this is in the fact that in the three Synoptic Gospels together sin is spoken of in the singular only once and even then in a plural sense,[32] while Jesus is quoted as speaking of "sins" seventeen times.

6. *Jesus and the Torah*

Much as later prophets built on the teachings of their predecessors, Jesus based his own teaching on the Old Testament. The relation of Jesus' teachings, as well as of his person and mission, to the Old Testament Law has never been more concisely stated than in Jesus' own words, "Think not that I have come to abolish the law and the prophets; I have come not to abolish them but to fulfill them" (Matt. 5:17). His own ethical teaching fulfills the Torah by supporting the main prophetic center and thrust of it and carrying it out to its consummation.

At the same time, as his teaching completes the Law, it also transcends and supplants it, as is abundantly illustrated in the thirty-one verses immediately following his statement about not abolishing but fulfilling. By the reinterpretation of all requirements in relation to the demands of love, by stripping down the many hundreds of casuistical rules into the stark simplicity of absolutely new life of repentant faith and obedient love, he inaugurates a new ethics. Even if every element in his ethical teaching could be traced to an earlier Old Testament or Rabbinical teaching—which is doubtful—it would still remain true that his ethics is recast in a new *Gestalt*, a structure with a new center in his own relation with the Father and with the community of Christian faith.

It is only in the context of new life in this new community of faith

32. Matt. 12:31. Contrast Paul's usage which employs the singular more than forty times in the Letter to the Romans alone. Of course this should not be taken to indicate that Jesus, unlike Paul, is unconcerned about evil in human nature or about lack of faith.

that the full meaning and possibility of Jesus' ethical teachings can be understood. Hence we must turn our attention next to the record and teachings of that community in its first, formative years.

The Synoptic Gospels are themselves witnesses from that community and contain much from church life as well as from Jesus himself. Nevertheless, without trying to argue the many critical points which could be raised, we have sought to give primary weight to ethical teachings which I believe authentically represent Jesus' own style of thought and life. Now we shall be examining other writings in which the authors are not seeking to recall or discover and record the words of Jesus himself, but rather to speak out of their own experience and the experience of the Church their witness to the new life which they have received and now partially and imperfectly, yet joyfully live.

chapter four

Pauline and Subsequent Christian Ethics

A. THE ETHICS OF ST. PAUL

Writing earlier than the final editing of any of the Gospels, the Apostle Paul gave to Christian doctrine and some aspects of Christian ethics certain directions which bear the indelible imprint of his own intense personality and life-changing experience through the power of Jesus Christ and the Holy Spirit.

1. *Salvation by Grace Through Faith*

For Paul a radically new life began with his conversion on the Damascus road when he gave up his hostility to the Christians, resigned his effort to win God's favor by obedience to the law, and surrendered to the risen Christ as Lord of life.

It is impossible to satisfy all the requirements of the law, Paul believes from his own vain experience. We can be in favor with God only by his free gift of grace given through Christ and received by faith.

> Therefore, since we are justified [*dikaiōthentes:* set right, made just or righteous, vindicated, or treated as righteous] by faith, we have peace with God through our Lord Jesus Christ. Through him we have obtained access to this grace in which we stand, and we rejoice in our hope of sharing the glory of God.   [Rom. 5:1]

For the Christian any notion of earning his life privileges and the eternal favor of God is out of the question. "For no human being will be justified in his sight by works of the law . . ." (Rom. 3:20). Jews who have been trying to keep the Law and others who have not even known the Torah, but who do know that they have sinned, are on the same footing before God. All alike must depend upon the goodness of God.[1]

Paul is grateful for the Torah, however, through which sin was "shown to be sin" (Rom. 7:13) so that he was prepared for his surrender to Christ.

a. Forgiveness. The justification which Paul says has come by God's grace through faith is far from the common present-day meaning of the English word. We speak of a man as being justified when his conduct is defensible as right, often contrary to first appearance. Thus we commonly say that a man was justified when he has shot another if it is proved that he did so in self-defense. Paul is speaking of our being justified despite a sinful life for which there is no possible defense. Rather, however wretched may be our guilt, when, convicted by the righteousness of Christ and, at the same time, encouraged by God's love seen in Christ, we throw ourselves on God's mercy, we receive his forgiveness. When God has forgiven me he treats me as if I were a righteous man. I am justified in the sense that I am made just or righteous (*dikaios*) in the sight of God, that is in his dealings with me. Justification, then, means, first of all, forgiveness by God.

b. Empowering for Righteous Living. We are forgiven, however, not in order that we may sink back into the death of sin but in order to live a new life in Christ. The divine stratagem of love is to turn us to Jesus Christ by the power of his sacrificial death, then, forgiving us and treating us as righteous, to make us truly righteous. Thus Paul writes,

> I have been crucified with Christ; it is no longer I who live, but Christ who lives in me; and the life I now live in the flesh I live by faith in the Son of God, who loved me and gave himself for me. I do not nullify the grace of God; for if righteousness were through the law, then Christ died to no purpose.   [Gal. 2:20, 21]

In this passage where I have used the word "righteousness," I have followed the King James Version and the American Standard Version which are clearly correct. The Revised Standard Version has apparently permitted some doctrinal prejudice to get in the way, for it places "righteousness" in the margin and carries "justification" in the text, thus cutting the heart out of the meaning. There is a good, common Greek word which Paul uses elsewhere for justification, the word *dikaiōsis;* but he does not use it here. Instead, he uses the plain, clear

---

1. The whole Letter to the Romans is saturated with this theme, and it is expressed in a large number of passages elsewhere, especially in Galatians and Ephesians.

word *dikaiosunē*. The Arndt-Gingrich lexicon of New Testament
Greek devotes two columns to elaborating the usages of this word in
various phrases. It gives the basic translation as "righteousness, upright-
ness." Applying it as "a characteristic of a judge," we are told, it may
mean "justice," but nowhere is it suggested that it may have any such
meaning as justification, vindication, or treating as righteous.

This aspect of justification, the actual empowering of a man by divine grace to live a righteous life, is known also, in theological literature, as sanctification. No such distinctive meaning of the *term* can be
supported in Pauline usage, but the *idea* is thoroughly Pauline, despite
much contrary theological teaching, as I shall be demonstrating further. The human life which Paul wishes to see established in his hearers by the power of God is not a trusting faith in Jesus' righteousness
which leaves the believer as sinful in reality as ever. It is "the *obedience*
of faith."[2]

2. Christian Liberty

After his grim and frustrating struggle with intricate legal casuistry,
Paul rejoices that he and other Christians have been delivered from
bondage.

a. Freedom from a Fearful Conscience.   The new liberty is first of
all freedom from the burden of feeling that the only hope of salvation
is a perfect keeping of the law. It was a rabbinical teaching that to
disobey any of the hundreds of laws given by the Torah and its authoritative interpretation is to be in violation of all and so to be lost.
As a true Jew, Paul had delighted in the law. Yet he had found it impossible to obey it all. He expresses his former dilemma and his gratitude for the new liberty he enjoys, in this dramatic passage:

> So I find it to be a law that when I want to do right, evil lies close at
> hand. For I delight in the law of God, in my inmost self, but I see in my
> members another law at war with the law of my mind and making me
> captive to the law of sin which dwells in my members. Wretched man
> that I am! Who will deliver me from this body of death? Thanks be to
> God through Jesus Christ our Lord!   [Rom. 7:21–25]

As Paul describes his wretched bondage to sin in this passage, I believe he is using a dramatic present tense to speak primarily of the
past. This interpretation is supported by his statement two verses later,
"For the law of the Spirit of life in Christ Jesus has set me free from
the law of sin and death" (Rom. 8:2). However, Paul knows he has
not been made perfect, as he confesses explicitly (Phil. 3:12). He now

2. Rom. 16:26. Emphasis mine.

knows the love of God who by grace accepts his commitment of faith. He is not now, as in the old days, frozen with fear lest by transgressing some commandment even unknowingly, he will lose his eternal salvation. The forgiveness and renewal of justification by faith is not something which operated once, at his conversion, and then was left behind. It continues on and is a present source of strength.

This is a doctrine of great moral significance to all men who live with the most sensitive conscience and a determination to do right and yet face such uncertainties of decision that very often they cannot be sure they are choosing the best way. Knowledge that we are justified by faith gives us release, both from protection of the ego by the dulling of conscience and from paralysis of will for fear we may be doing wrong. We thus enjoy a creative freedom now in anticipation of the final "glorious liberty of the children of God" (Rom. 8:21).

b. Freedom from Ceremonial Law. Paul rejoices also in freedom from the necessity of observing the rites and restrictions to which he had been subject as a Jew. He does not worry now about circumcising converts, about observing the ancient dietary rules, about eating with Gentiles, or even about eating meat offered to pagan idols. Devoted to Christ he can now do what love requires in such things, and this may vary with circumstances.³

c. Responsible Freedom. The Apostle Paul is very far from being an antinomian or a situationist who cannot tell whether adultery is wrong until he is told all the circumstances and even then believes that the individual should not be held accountable excepting to himself. Nowhere does Paul dwell more dramatically on Christian liberty than in Galatians. He devotes the first half of Chapter 5 to expanding on the opening words, "For freedom Christ has set us free." Then, after the transitional 13th verse, he enjoins against the "works of the flesh" and lifts up "the fruit of the Spirit." He is not vague about the sins. He writes,

> Now the works of the flesh are plain: immorality [*porneia:* fornication, adultery, or other illicit sexual conduct], impurity, licentiousness, idolatry, sorcery, enmity, strife, jealousy, anger, selfishness, dissension, party spirit, envy, drunkenness, carousing, and the like. I warn you, as I warned you before, that those who do such things shall not inherit the kingdom of God.⁴

3. See 1 Cor. 8:10–13. Cf. Gal. 2 and 5.
4. Gal. 5:19–21. Again I am puzzled by the RSV translation. Do the translators shrink from a clear translation of *porneia* which unambiguously refers to *sexual* immorality? Or do they think that there is no immorality other than sexual misconduct? There is no textual problem. The only significant textual deviation is the inclusion, in some ancient texts, of the additional word *moicheia* which refers solely to adultery. Cf. KJV.

Could anything be plainer? It is to be noted that only those who belong to Christ possess the freedom in which Paul rejoices. It is especially significant, then, when he says that "those who belong to Christ Jesus have crucified the flesh with its passions and desires" (Gal. 5:24).

He is somewhat less specific, but still clear when he turns to the positive virtues: "But the fruit of the Spirit is love, joy, peace, patience, kindness, goodness, faithfulness, gentleness, self-control" (Gal. 5:22–23).

The freedom in which Paul glories, then, is a responsible freedom which is found through a commitment of faith to live in active loyalty to Jesus Christ. The character of a Christian life is determined, not by a long list of legalistically defined rules, but by Christ himself. His purpose and character, through the power of the Holy Spirit, rule over the life of the disciple. People who do live under the power of the Spirit will not be ruled by passion or pride but by a humble, faithful, serving love. The resultant life is not lawless; it is under Christ's exacting but glorious and liberating control. Paul can even speak of this, too, as "law," as when he says, "Bear one another's burdens, and so fulfil the law of Christ" (Gal. 6:2). Similarly, he writes, "For the whole law is fulfilled in one word, 'You shall love your neighbor as yourself.'"[5] Paul rejoices in being under "the law of the Spirit of life in Christ Jesus" by which he has been set "free from the law of sin and death" (Rom. 8:2). So also he speaks of himself as "not being without law toward God but under the law of Christ" (1 Cor. 9:21).

3. Social Conservatism and Radicalism

Paul is never a man for half measures. When he is making a point he usually pulls out all the stops in sounding that emphasis. Balance is restored by similar stress on a different point on another occasion. It is not strange, then, that he has been quoted both by social conservatives and by social radicals in support of their positions.

a. Paul's Social Concern Focused on the Church.   Although both a Jew and a Roman citizen, after his conversion Paul was not able to exert much direct influence on the development of Jewish institutions, and certainly there was not much he could do to exercise his Roman citizenship for the improvement of Roman imperial law. There was, however, one institution in which he produced the most profound influence and into which he poured the intense energy of his ministry. That institution was the Christian church. Through his incalculably great influence upon the structure, policies, and growth of the churches, he exercised an eventually profound influence upon the Roman Empire and upon Judaism, too. Yet the issues which he discusses in his

5. Gal. 5:14. Cf. Rom. 13:8–10.

letters concern the life of the Church and the individual Christian. Only as these issues or others raised by interference with his work compel attention to Jewish or Roman government does he discuss political affairs.

This preoccupation with church policy tends to give Paul's writings a conservative cast when they are read in the context of a modern country under popularly elected government, where the churches have a numerous membership. In our present situation when we are silent about issues of political or economic injustice or about dangerous national adventures abroad, the effect is a tacit stamp of approval on present public policies. To cite the preoccupation of Paul with the church and his relative silence on Judean and Roman politics as normative for modern Christians is to do violence to historical context.

b. Political Conservatism. One passage in Paul's writing, when taken alone, comes near to canonizing the authority of the state as the authority of God himself. The passage begins as follows:

> Let every person be subject to the governing authorities. For there is no authority except from God. . . . Therefore he who resists the authorities resists what God has appointed, and those who resist will incur judgment.   [Rom. 13:1–2]

Speaking further of the ruler in authority, Paul says that "he does not bear the sword in vain; he is the servant of God to execute his wrath on the wrongdoer" (Rom. 13:4).

These words and others in the passage have been used to defend the most outrageous injustice against efforts by some citizens to resist or to overthrow evil law or government. Martin Luther used them to condemn the desperate peasants' revolt. In our century they were used by many German churchmen to condemn German resistance to Adolf Hitler.

A brief glance at Paul's personal history shows that there is something dubious about such literal use of this passage, standing alone. Was Paul "subject to the governing authorities"? Was it his invariable experience that, as he says in the passage under study, "rulers are not a terror to good conduct, but to bad" (Rom. 13:3)? Did Paul find always that when he would "do what is good" he would "receive [the ruling authority's] approval" (Rom. 13:3)? Hardly! Speaking of other people who may try to undermine his authority and boast that they are "servants of Christ," he says, "I am a better one." He proceeds to give proofs, and one is that he has experienced "far more imprisonments"! He continues on to tell of other punishments he has received from the governments—both from the Jewish authorities who exercised considerable autonomous rule under imperial Rome and from the Romans themselves (2 Cor. 11:23–25). Not only, then, did Paul suffer from his violations of orders from legally constituted authorities, but he also counted such sufferings as evidence of his faithful Christian service.

Is there any way to harmonize the contradiction? Not completely. It is altogether incredible that Paul would have meant to say that anyone who, like Peter and John, was legally commanded to speak or teach no more of Jesus should obey such orders. And certainly, if he had intended to promote invariable awe of human government, he would not have boasted to the Corinthians of his many imprisonments and other legal penalties.

The intent of Romans 13 seems to be to instruct the Christians about their obligation to be orderly, law-abiding citizens. There may have been some enthusiasts who claimed such superiority to all earthly affairs as to warrant their refusing taxes and other ordinary obligations of life in an orderly society. The fact that he speaks of taxes in verses 6 and 7 would support this understanding. He then goes on to warn against going into debt. He is giving sound counsel to Christian people, not only to meet the common obligations of civilized life but also to avoid needless creating of bad reputation and confusion. If they followed his example they would save their clashes with authorities for occasions when there were important issues of conscience worthy of their trouble and risk.

There is also an old tradition in ethics which interprets Paul as maintaining divine source and authority for governmental dominion as such, which we may distinguish from particular governors and laws. This seems doubtful exegesis of Paul, but the idea in itself has considerable merit.

Of course some of Paul's ethical ideas, when torn from historical context and read in the present time, are offensively conservative. An example is the way in which he takes the institution of human slavery for granted.[6] It is true that when he declares that as between slave and master "there is no partiality" with God (Col. 3:25; Eph. 6:9), and when he sends Onesimus back to Philemon "no longer as a slave but more than a slave, as a beloved brother" (Philem., 16), he is stating and illustrating a principle and spirit which could not be accepted generally in society without condemning slavery to an early end. Yet he has not thought this matter through to such conclusions himself. In this, as in regard to woman's place in church and her relation to her husband, he had not escaped bondage to the world of his time.

c. Social Radicalism. The Jewish Law was for the Jewish com-

6. See Col. 3:22–4:1. Cf. Eph. 6:5–9.

munity of the first century enforceable civil law, as well as religious law.

This was one of the main sources of Paul's many sufferings at the hands of his Jewish fellow citizens. In most cities to which he went he first appeared as a Jew, making a local synagogue his base of operations. He angered many by declaring that Jesus, who had been hounded to death by the Jewish legal authorities in Jerusalem, was the long-awaited Jewish Messiah, the Christ.

As if this were not enough to put Paul into legal and popular jeopardy, he associated in religious observance and fellowship at table with Gentiles, in flagrant violation of strictly separatist Jewish laws. According to Acts, he was finally arrested and ultimately sent to Rome on the false charge of having taken Greeks into the temple at Jerusalem (Acts 21:17-33). But even if he was innocent of that particular offense, it was true that he had violated and encouraged other Jews to violate the law—including its requirements concerning diet, the circumcision of their sons, and personal relations with Gentiles.

There were other teachings of Paul which had more far-reaching radical implications for political systems generally. When a man maintains such passionate religious convictions as lead him to undergo mob attacks, arrests, imprisonments, and other punishments again and again, continuing until his execution, he becomes highly disruptive of law and order. According to Paul's teaching and example, this kind of passionate devotion was the very meaning of faith, by which alone God would save a person. Such religious absolutism becomes politically revolutionary whenever it comes into direct collision with the demands of government.

Radical change in the policies of governments would be required if even the spirit of Paul's injunction to return good for evil were to come into general acceptance. Clearly echoing Jesus' radical ethics of love toward enemies, Paul writes,

> Bless those who persecute you; bless and do not curse them. . . . Repay no one evil for evil. . . . Do not be overcome by evil, but overcome evil with good.[7]

Even if such teachings be regarded as meant literally for personal relations only, their adoption in such relations would so alter the spirit of a people as to make it impossible for them to support a government's pursuit of international relations or domestic penal policies of the kinds long traditional in most countries.

7. Rom. 12:14-21. Cf. 1 Thess. 5:15.

4. Special Pauline Contributions

Paul's formative influence in Christian theology is accompanied by a major impact on Christian ethics as well as his direct ethical teachings.

a. The Problem of Predestination and Free Will.   Much more than any other biblical writer, Paul was responsible for the centuries-long disputes in Christendom concerning divine predestination and human free will. In places he seems to leave no room at all for human freedom or responsibility as he dwells on God's all-controlling predestination.[8] Man becomes only the clay in the hands of the divine potter. God does with him whatever he chooses, and man has no right even to question his fate (Rom. 9:19–24). These statements occur in the long section of Romans dwelling on the philosophy of history pertaining to God's dealings with Jews and Gentiles. Paul is defending God's giving to Gentiles through his own missionary work the privilege of being the people chosen as recipients and instruments of salvation. With the reckless rhetoric to which he is prone he makes it appear that both Jews and Gentiles are mere pawns in God's hands.

Yet in Chapter 11 he addresses the Gentiles and warns them not to presume on God's present selection of them over the Jews. "They were broken off because of their unbelief," he says, "but you stand fast only through faith." You Gentiles, he insists, receive God's favor only "provided you continue in his kindness; otherwise you too will be cut off." The Jews will be restored to God's favor "if they do not persist in their unbelief" (Rom. 11:13–24). So Paul first stresses very one-sidedly the overruling purpose of God, but then, in characteristic fashion, turns about to warn of the responsibility of men.

In later centuries, when the relation between responsibility and freedom of choice came to be observed and examined, this Pauline dialectic would underlie much acrimonious debate relevant to the very possibility of ethical responsibility.

b. Inadequacy of Legalism.   A foremost theme throughout Paul's writings is the powerlessness of law to save any man from sin and death. Law can define the distinction between good and evil, but it is impotent to produce goodness or true life in communion with God. Law can be helpful in defining good and evil and so it may give guidance in decision. But it is utterly powerless to make an evil will good.

c. Ethics of Redemption.   According to Paul, our redemption is accomplished, not by adherence to a system of laws, but by giving ourselves to the person, Jesus Christ. He is not a concept, but a living

8. See especially Rom. 8:29–30; 9:14–18.

reality, the Christ who has given himself in love for us and to whom the Holy Spirit enables us to respond with a similar self-giving (Rom. 6:5–8).

This response of faith is symbolized by our being "buried . . . with him by baptism into death" (Rom. 6:4). But it is no mere verbal assent or ceremonial rite. It is a subordinating of all other attachments, and even of life itself, to the one relationship to Christ. Christ had said that anyone who would come after him must "take up his cross daily and follow" him (Luke 9:23). Paul responds by laying his life on the line day after day. When he says he dies "every day" (1 Cor. 15:31), he is not speaking of some conceptual or ritual act but of letting go his life, treating it as expendable for Christ's sake. This is the very essence of the way of the cross, the way of faith, as Paul understands and lives it.

d. Imitation of Christ. In this willingness to accept death as the cost of his discipleship, Paul is consciously imitating Christ's own acceptance of his crucifixion. In the laying of his life on the altar of Christ, he lets the living Christ take over his very existence. Hence he testifies,

> I have been crucified with Christ; it is no longer I who live, but Christ who lives in me; and the life I now live in the flesh I live by faith in the Son of God, who loved me and gave himself for me. [Gal. 2:20]

This is more than a kind of external and conceptual effort to "do what Jesus would do" or to walk "in his steps." It is a sense of being veritably possessed by Christ, so that all springs of life's meaning and decisions come from him. Paul himself grossly understates it when he says, "Be imitators of me, as I am of Christ" (1 Cor. 11:1). Yet there is a real imitation involved in the deep relationship which is his faith in Christ or his "Christ-mysticism," and it was destined to have an important, ever-recurring role in Christian life and ethics through the ages.

e. Christian Life as Church Life. The Old Testament doctrine of salvation always relates the future to Israel as the community of the Covenant. Individuals may hope to participate in the benefits of God's purpose only as they are related to God's people, Israel. Indeed, there will be only a faithful remnant of Israel which will be God's instrument and the nucleus of an obedient people in whom God's promises will be fulfilled. The notion of purely individual salvation, involving solely a relation between an individual and God, is alien to the Old Testament and equally so to the New.

During Paul's ministry many in the Church assumed that the Christian community was the true remnant of Israel, called to participate in the new Messianic age. Hence, they reasoned, if any man not a Jew wished to participate he must first be initiated into the Jewish community by circumcision and acceptance of the other Jewish obligations. Paul, on the other hand, insisted that the community of the New Covenant in Christ[9] was free of any dependence upon membership in the old Israel. The new community of salvation was formed solely by faith in Jesus Christ. Eventually, Paul's views were to prevail, so that Christianity became, not a Jewish sect, but an independent movement.[10]

In the letters of Paul there is much of teaching concerning the nature of the Church, and this teaching has profound ethical significance. The Church, according to Paul, is the living body of Christ, Christ being the head, and all Christians, with their various special gifts and functions, being members of this body.[11] It is no accident that Paul's most exalted teachings of Christian love are included within or immediately follow his description of the Church in these terms.

If concentration upon the Church means development of an ingrown institutionalism, certainly this means ethical loss and not gain. But if it means, rather, joining together in mission of service to the world, then there could hardly be a teaching needed more by Christian people today, especially in American Protestantism. In its most heroic achievements—such as the evangelization of the Roman Empire, the illumination of the Dark Ages, the elevating of the British masses in the eighteenth century, or the establishment of popular education throughout Africa in the twentieth—the close-knit, corporate fellowship and united action of the Church or of a Church community within Christendom, has been a major secret of Christian strength. If the new world of the late twentieth century is to be ensouled and redirected toward life rather than catastrophe, this will not be done by individuals acting alone but by community of purpose and action.

Paul did not invent the idea of the Church as community of salvation, nor did he found the Church itself. But he did more than anyone else to formulate and record doctrine concerning the nature of the Church and to show the ethical implications of this doctrine—about which much more must be said later.

9. Cf. Mark 14:24; Matt. 26:28; Luke 22:20.

10. Unfortunately, the process of breaking free was accompanied by much ill feeling, as we know from the accounts of Jewish persecutions of Christians in the New Testament and Christian utterances which assumed that "the Jews" were enemies of Christian faith, even though Jesus, Paul, and most of the earliest Christians were themselves Jews. When these utterances were read in later centuries, they were interpreted to encourage the anti-Semitism which has been and is such a horrible blot on the pages of Christian history.

11. See 1 Cor. 12:12–31. Cf Rom. 12:3–8; 1 Cor. 10:17.

B. JOHANNINE TEACHING

Interpreting the theology of the Gospel and the Letters of John, Rudolf Bultmann says, "Jesus as the Revealer of God *reveals nothing but that he is the Revealer.*"[12] A reader who searches through the Johannine writings may be surprised to find how much justification there is for this extreme statement. It is, nevertheless, a gross exaggeration.

The Gospel of John teaches that God loves all people ("the world") and sent his Son to offer the gift of eternal life. The First Letter teaches that this love of God for us is the source of all our loving. "We love, because he first loved us" (4:19). Both the Gospel and the First Letter teach again and again that we are to "love one another."[13]

There is not, in the Johannine literature, much elaboration of the meaning of love, despite the frequent reiteration of the command. However, there is considerably more elucidation of the meaning than might at first appear.

The command to "love one another" and some of the contexts in which it is set emphasize the bonds of fellowship within the community of faith. The same emphasis appears in John 17. Nevertheless, Bultmann himself, despite his exaggerated statement about the circularity of John's testimony concerning Christ's revealing work, points out the thrust of the love commandment into the world beyond the circle of believers. The love is generated by God within this circle, it is true.

> But this is no closed group. On the contrary, it is the eschatological Congregation whose vocation it is to "bear witness" (15:27). Therefore, the world constantly has the possibility of being drawn into this circle of mutual love. Furthermore, the statements of 1 John about brother-love seem not at all to be restricted to one's Christian brother (e.g., 1 Jn. 3:17). [*Op. cit.*, p. 82]

There is further evidence that Bultmann is correct here. The biblical author assumes in this passage that we should follow the example of Jesus who "laid down his life for us" (1 John 3:16). Obviously, Jesus was not giving his life for people already in the community of faith.

There are other ways, too, in which the Johannine literature makes the meaning of love more definite. The very passage to which Bultmann has called our attention makes clear that the writer is not speaking of a mere sentiment. He says,

12. *Theology of the New Testament*, tr. by Kendrick Grobel, Vol. II (New York: Charles Scribner's Sons, 1955), p. 66. Emphasis Bultmann's.
13. John 13:34. Cf. 13:35; 15:12–14, 17; 1 John 1:7, 2:9–11, 3:11, 14, 4:7–8, 11, 12, 20–21; 2 John 5.

> But if any one has the world's goods and sees his brother in need, yet closes his heart against him, how does God's love abide in him? Little children, let us not love in word or speech but in deed and in truth.
> [1 John 3:17–18]

Moreover, in the narratives of the Gospel, Jesus' healing ministry is illustrated. It is evident that the writer is especially concerned with showing Jesus' divine *power*. Nevertheless, the ways in which he illustrates the *use* of that power are significant. The power is used in the service of love, making a blind man see, restoring a dead man to life, and healing a sick man even when that requires violating the law of the Sabbath (John 7:22–23).

By his washing of the disciples' feet, narrated in John's Gospel only, the virtue of humble service is taught the more impressively because the writer, even in this very passage, so strongly emphasizes the other-worldly prerogatives of Jesus (John 13:3–5).

The Gospel and Letters of John, with their preponderant stress on the relation between God and man, nevertheless declare with powerful emphasis the command that we love our brother men. To express such love effectively in action we require much further appraisal of the values which love seeks for the brother and of the strategies through which these values are to be won. Yet, with all the value theory and with all the strategic planning, if love is not made central, then all is in vain. The Johannine writings have given relatively little ethical instruction. What they have given is not found exclusively in them. Yet they do accentuate the main center of all Christian ethics—love.

C. Other New Testament Teachings

1. The Acts

The most significant ethical contribution of The Acts is further light on the meaning and implications of Christian love. As the account is given of some major victories of the primitive Church, it appears that all of them may be regarded as victories of faith and love by the empowering of the Holy Spirit. Faith is, as depicted in the Synoptic Gospels and Pauline Letters, the trusting and active commitment of self to God as known through Jesus Christ. An added element is the greater emphasis on the work of the Holy Spirit in all this. In the narratives of Christian love at work, The Acts emphasizes strongly three characteristics of this love.

a. Love Includes All Kinds of People. This theme is established in Chapter 2, where the author—presumably Luke—describes the launching of the church in power on the Day of Pentecost. Much is made of the many nations in Europe, Asia, and Africa from which Jews of the Dispersion had gathered for the harvest festival in Jerusalem when they were caught up in the coming of the Holy Spirit. In the dramatic and picturesque language about "tongues as of fire" and about people of many lands testifying that "we hear them . . . in our own tongues," the writer describes the way in which Christian communication embraced people from all the known continents and races of the earth (Acts 2:1–12).

The theme of ethnic inclusiveness is carried further in many other passages which must be studied in our treatment of the Church.

b. Brings All into Profound Community.   The Acts shows also the deep unity of fellowship into which authentic Christian love brought this highly diverse collection of people. The love was not unvarying and the traditional hostilities among the people of various nations doubtless accentuated the tensions inevitable in the forming of such an extremely dynamic movement. But Acts is mainly concerned with the achievements and victories. It is highly significant that these are represented, not as defeats for any factions, but rather as reunions on higher ground after disputes and new agreements. In Paul's Letters we learn more of the sharpness, persistence, and hurtfulness of the disputes, but Luke in the Acts and Paul in his Letters are agreed that when people are being truly Christian their common bonds of faith and love hold them in too close a fellowship to permit lasting disruption.

c. Includes All Aspects of Life.   Not only does Christian love include in intimate unity all kinds of people. It is inclusive also in embracing all of life and not merely the aspects which many of us might think of as "spiritual" or "religious." In The Acts, the spiritual life is all of life controlled by the Holy Spirit. This includes all social relationships and all economic needs. The economic life, which is especially resistant to the love ethic in modern times, was explicitly and emphatically included in the accounts of Acts. Examples are the original sharing of goods,[14] the appointment of deacons to make the daily distribution to the needy (Acts 6:1–6), and the sending of relief from the Christians at Antioch to the famine-stricken "brethren who lived in Judea."[15]

2. Hebrews

The Letter to the Hebrews includes, of course, the great chapter in praise of faith and the ensuing exhortation to the imitation of Christ (11 and 12:1–3).

14. Acts 2:44–46; 4:32–5:5.
15. Acts 11:27–30. Cf. Rom. 15:25–28; and 1 Cor. 16:1–3.

It has also much to say of Christ's great sacrifice for his human brethren. It speaks of God's observing "the love which you showed for his sake in serving the saints" (6:10). The author exhorts his readers, "Let brotherly love continue" (13:1), and he says, "Do not neglect to do good and to share what you have, for such sacrifices are pleasing to God" (13:16). An interesting and useful exhortation is the injunction, "let us consider how to stir up one another to love and good works" (10:24).

The principal ethical teaching of the Letter to the Hebrews, then, concerns the centrality of faith and love, inextricably joined.

3. The General Epistles

a. James. Most of the Letter of James is devoted to exhortations to Christian living and it is rich in ethical content, much of it clearly reflecting the influence of Jesus' teachings as we have them in the Synoptic Gospels.

Many virtues are praised. They include steadfastness (1:4, 7, 7; 5:7–11), wisdom (1:5; 3:13, 17), endurance (1:12), listening well and restraint in speech (1:19), control of anger (1:19), and meekness (1:21; 3:13). The author is especially eloquent as he writes about the need to work in the active expression of our faith. With biting sarcasm he describes a mere verbal piety which says to the poor, " 'Go in peace, be warmed and filled,' without giving them the things needed for the body." He adds, "So faith by itself, if it has no works, is dead."[16]

Other virtues praised in this plain-speaking little book include impartiality in church affairs (2:1–7, 9), peace making (3:18), humility (4:6, 10, 16), acknowledged dependence on God (4:13–15), and mercy to poor laborers (5:4–6). James teaches that a man should not blame God for his temptations. It is a person's own desire which tempts him, not the circumstances in which he is placed (1:14). Especially dangerous is one's own tongue, an organ prone to all kinds of evil doing.[17] The injunction which Jesus called the "second" commandment, James named "the royal law" (2:8).

Especially memorable is the famous definition of religion at the end of the first chapter, as follows:

16. 2:16, 17. Such passages are often regarded as putting James into flat contradiction of Paul's teaching that we are saved by faith and not by works. But Morton S. Enslin is surely right when he says that "what Paul stigmatized 'works of the law' are by no means the same as the works which James demands, while the sort of faith which James calls 'dead' would never have been classed as faith at all by Paul." *The Ethics of Paul* (New York: Abingdon Press 1957), p. 68.

17. 3:2–12. Cf. 4:11–12; 1:26.

Religion that is pure and undefiled before God and the Father is this: to visit orphans and widows in their affliction, and to keep oneself unstained from the world.

The Church is described as rightly a community of mutual aid, correction, and forgiveness (5:13–20).

Many a modern writer has blamed greed as a prime cause of war. But this is hardly a new idea. We read from James:

> What causes wars, and what causes fightings among you? Is it not your passions that are at war in your members? You desire and do not have; so you kill. And you covet and cannot obtain; so you fight and wage war.   [4:1–2]

James gives a good definition of *formal* sin when he says, "Whoever knows what is right to do and fails to do it, for him it is sin" (4:17).

b. 1 Peter. The reader is reminded of Romans 13 as he reads injunctions to obey "every human institution," and finds the emperor and governors explicitly mentioned as "sent by [the Lord] to punish those who do wrong and to praise those who do right" (1 Pet. 2:13–14). It is good to read, "Honor all men. Love the brotherhood. Fear God." But it is rather startling to read on, "Honor the emperor" (2:17). For this was a time of persecution. Indeed, Christians are told to submit meekly to injustice.[18] However, this whole matter of obedience to civil law is put in the best balance to be found in any one statement of the New Testament, as follows:

> But let none of you suffer as a murderer, or a thief, or a wrongdoer, or a mischief-maker; yet if one suffers as a Christian, let him not be ashamed, but under that name let him glorify God.   [4:15–16]

Wives are to be submissive, and not indulge in luxurious self-adornment, while husbands must be considerate and respectful.

Christians are to seek mutual love and unity (3:8), serving one another "as good stewards of God's varied grace" (4:8–11). Here we are reminded of Paul's descriptions of the Church with its various specialized members. Reminiscent of Paul also is a vigorous warning against the indulgence of sensual passions and idolatry (4:1–5).

c. 2 Peter. In the Second Letter of Peter, some of the virtues now familiar are listed (1:5–7), and the writer dwells at length on the need to remain faithful under persecution by wicked men of power (2:4–22). This being a time of stress and confusion, he enjoins his

18. 2:18–23; 3:14–17; 4:12–14.

readers also against the compromising of the true faith or following teachers of "destructive heresies" (1:16–2:3). All must be faithful and watchful to the end, which is awaited with eagerness for the fulfillment of God's promise or "new heavens and a new earth in which righteousness dwells" (3:1–13).

d. Jude. In the tiny Letter of Jude, more than anywhere else in the New Testament, the stress is on orthodoxy. In this book is the one passage where the word faith (*pistis*) is used to mean plainly the body of orthodox doctrine. This is "the faith which was once for all delivered to the saints," and is to be held inviolate despite the efforts of evil infiltrators (3–23).

4. The Revelation

The Revelation was written, it is believed, in the reign of the emperor Domitian (c. 81–96 A.D.), perhaps about 93 A.D. It was a time of fierce persecution, and the dominant purpose of the writer was to strengthen the determination of the Christians, in the churches addressed, to hold fast uncompromisingly to the faith. His method includes exhortation, but consists mainly of predicting the terrible defeat and sufferings which God will bring upon the enemies of the Church and the rewards in store for the faithful who endure to the end.

The most frequently praised virtue in the Revelation is patient endurance.[19] Closely akin to patient endurance is faithfulness to death. The book is intended to prepare readers for martyrdom, if that must be faced as the cost of unmoved loyalty to Christ.[20]

However, a faith which endures to the very death is not alone enough. An endurance which is passive is inacceptable. There must be a positive love which produces acceptable works (2:3–6). Little is said about the kinds of works which are required, but clearly they are to include positive efforts to keep idolatry and heresy out of the Church.[21] Sexual immorality is condemned, for even if references to it are symbolic denunciations of idolatrous practices, their symbolism would fail unless fornication and adultery were also condemned.

When the writer turns to his favorite theme, he devotes much attention to the terrible fate in store for "Babylon the great," that is, Rome, the "mother of harlots," sitting on her "seven hills."[22] But all who have betrayed or helped to persecute the Christians have awful punishments awaiting them and so do all who forsake the faith under the temptations and persecutions of an evil time.[23] The imagery of hellfire com-

19. E.g., see 2:2–3. Cf. 1:9; 2:19; 3:10; 14:12.
20. Rev. 2:10. Cf. 2:13; 14:13.
21. E.g., see 2:14–16.
22. 17:3–18. Cf. 18:1–24.
23. 6:10–11; 9:4; 11:5–13; 15:5–19:21.

mon in the history and present life of Christendom is derived largely from Revelation and especially from this passage:

> But as for the cowardly, the faithless, the polluted, as for murderers, fornicators, sorcerers, idolaters, and all liars, their lot shall be in the lake that burns with fire and brimstone, which is the second death. [21:8]

On the other hand, the faithful, in their purity, cleansed by the death of Christ, will be rewarded by everlasting joy in heaven (21: 1–22:5).

These accounts of vindictive torture in store for the wicked, along with the rewards for the righteous, are plainly intended to strengthen faithful endurance through persecutions. But there is also implied in such themes an acceptance of the basic principle of the sub-Christian *lex talionis*. In Revelation God's mercy and grace freely given through Christ are still implied but have fallen far into the background, while reward and punishment according to works have come back into the prominent foreground.

D. SOME HISTORICAL TRENDS

In this primarily systematic study it is impossible to include even a brief history of Christian ethics. The attempt will be made only to mention a few of the disparate emphases which have come into prominence at different periods.

1. Early Strenuous Legalism

In the Christian literature of the second century there are many attempts to codify requirements of Christian conduct. This is not so surprising. Even the Apostle Paul, with all his stress on salvation by grace through faith, had found it necessary to rebuke and warn members of the churches concerning conduct unbecoming to Christians and inconsistent with faith in Christ. In doing so he was led, as we have seen, to specify conduct appropriate and inappropriate to faith, "fruit of the spirit" and "works of the flesh" (Gal. 5:16–22).

When the Christian message comes into a new area of the world and Christian converts are formed into a Church set in a sea of paganism, invariably, it seems, the Church is quickly compromised and swallowed up unless some defining limits of Christian conduct are established. This early legalistic stage can be observed in contemporary new churches of Africa, Malaysia, and other lands recently evangelized. Later, when a Christian style of life has become more generally known in its apparent forms, more attention can be effectively directed to its inner spirit. For Paul and other earliest Christians this preparation had been made by the Torah. When the gospel began reaching many Gentiles who had not been trained under the law as *paidagōgos*,[24] it became necessary to spell out the new law of Christ more carefully. The need became urgent when the first ardor of conversion cooled.

In any event, such writings of the second century as *The Shepherd of Hermas*, the *Didache*, and *The Instructor* by Clement of Alexandria, all illustrate a legalistic turn of the ancient Church and, to different degrees, a rigorous standard.

The Shepherd of Hermas (c. 140 A.D. or earlier) makes much of inner chastity and the sin of a man's sexual desire for any woman not his wife, and idealizes the notion of Christians so pure that men and women could live and sleep together promiscuously with no impurity even of thought, but only with constant devotion to prayer. The main theme of the work, however, is a call for immediate repentance by all Christians who have committed any sin since baptism, for never again will such opportunity be open. Here is little of detailed law, but the extreme limitation of forgiveness breathes the spirit of legalism.

The *Didache*, well described by Kirsopp Lake as "a manual of church instruction,"[25] consists almost entirely of commands and exhortations. So much of the earlier part, on the "two ways," seems to echo the Torah or its rabbinical interpretations, that some critics believe it to be an adaptation of a Jewish manual of the first century or even a somewhat earlier time. As it stands it is a law for individual churchmen, as the Torah is directed to individual Israelites. However, much concerns the maintenance of a committed, mutually helpful, and severely disciplining fellowship.

Clement of Alexandria, writing late in the second or early in the third century, does not expect the Christian to be perfectly free from all sin nor teach that one sin after baptism will irrevocably condemn him to death. Christ, "the Instructor," is able to judge us "because He alone is sinless."[26] To us he gives this instruction:

> As far, however, as we can, let us try to sin as little as possible. . . .
> It is best, therefore, not to sin at all in any way, which we assert to be

---

24. Gal. 3:24–26. *A paidagōgos* was an attendant who accompanied a boy to school and supervised his conduct in a way to prepare him for his teacher.

25. *The Apostolic Fathers* with an English translation by Kirsopp Lake (Cambridge, Mass.: Harvard University Press, 1959), Vol. I, p. 305.

26. *The Instructor*, Book I, Chap. 2. The text quoted is from *The Ante-Nicene Fathers*, Vol. II (New York: Charles Scribner's Sons, 1925).

the prerogative of God alone; next to keep clear of voluntary trans-
gressions, which is characteristic of the wise man; thirdly, not to fall
into many involuntary offenses, which is peculiar to those who have
been excellently trained. Not to continue long in sins, let that be ranked
last.   [*Ibid.*]

Clement is accordingly described by some modern writers as having
given up the rigorous demands of the gospel for a compromised and
"practical" law. Waldo Beach even says,

Whether Clement's composite ideal of the good life is more like that
of a Greek gentleman or of a disciple of Christ is a question which
deserves discussion, after the study is made of Clement's own words.[27]

It would appear that after the study no such question could reasonably
remain. Clement himself contrasts sharply the ways of the pagan world
with the commands of Christ the Instructor. He is glad to find all the
reason he can, in Greek philosophy or elsewhere, to support his argument, but the way of Christ is constantly portrayed by biblical references and is full of requirements of chastity, humility, generous loving-
kindness, trust in God, and meditations on him by day and night.

Clement gives many instructions on matters which we should generally assign to etiquette; but he has a sound purpose as he seeks to
make concrete his description of a Christian style of life in contrast
to the pagan customs pressing upon the believer from every side.

Characteristic of Clement's work is his conception of the Christian
life as a process of learning under the tutelage of Christ. Beginning
with the first hearing of Law and gospel the disciple accepts the Word
by faith, then moves on from minimal and simple rules of life toward
the perfection which Christ enjoins. The higher levels of this development Clement describes as the true Gnosis (Knowledge), sharply contrasted to the false claims of esoteric knowledge put forth by the he-
retical Gnostics. The learning not only moves from more superficial
commands to the most difficult requirements of self-sacrifice, but also
from exterior acts to the cleansing and sanctifying of the innermost
motives. From instructions about temperate, even abstemious habits
at table, he moves to the praise of martyrdom, not because the body
is despised, but rather because the body, purified and put to holy use
in life, is gladly given up as an offering to God. We may question
whether Clement sometimes quotes the pagan philosophers and poets
in support of his Christian teaching when he would better omit refer-

27. Waldo Beach and H. Richard Niebuhr, editors with introductions, *Christian
Ethics. Sources of the Living Tradition* (New York: Ronald Press Company,
1955), p. 80.

ence to them, as in the closing paragraphs of the *Stromata*. For here he both distorts their meanings by quoting in his Christian context instead of their own quite different one, and weakens his Christian intent by the connotations of the learned pagans' words. But the demands of his ethics still remain too rigorous for any pagans excepting some of the Stoics, and too completely centered upon love and upon the person of Christ for anyone but a person whose will and affection have been captured by Christ.

Clement of Alexandria, then, does teach a distinctively Christian ethics, but his teaching is done with a quantity of rules in striking contrast to most of the New Testament.

2. *Accommodation to the Empire*

If one remembers the contempt and condemnation heaped upon imperial Rome in the Book of Revelation, one finds shocking contrasts in the Christian literature of the fourth century. Instead of regarding the imperial power as "the beast" and the emperors as a series of "beasts" (Rev. 13 and 14), Eusebius describes the Emperor Constantine as "one, image of the all-imperial God."[28] Eusebius says that "two roots of blessing, the Roman Empire and the doctrine of Christian piety, sprang up together for the benefit of men" (*ibid.*).

Athanasius called Emperor Constantine "a lover of God by descent," and addressed him with such titles as "your worship," "most worshipful Augustus," "your Piety," and "your Grace."[29]

Of course the change in Christian attitudes of church leaders from hostility to praise is due to the imperial throne having changed from the persecution of Christians to the profession of Christian faith and the making of Christianity the official religion of the Roman Empire. The charge seemed an answer to anguished prayers among their tortured people.

However, a price had been paid and much more was yet to be paid for the close partnership of church and empire. At the beginning the Apostles said, "We must obey God rather than men" (Acts 5:29). The way of Christ was contrasted with the ways of "the world." In the second century Justin Martyr had said that Christians could not serve in the army (which was also the police force). We "now refrain from making war upon our enemies," he said (*First Apology*, Chap. 39). Tertullian knows that there are Christians in the Roman legions (*Apology*, Chaps. 1, 6, 42), but when he discusses directly the question whether a Christian may properly be a soldier, he gives an emphatic

28. Quoted by Kenneth M. Setton in *Christian Attitude Towards the Emperor in the Fourth Century* (New York: Columbia University Press, 1941), p. 48.

29. *Ibid.*, pp. 74 and 75. Setton adds, "These terms stand in sad contrast to what he had to say about the Emperor a little over a year later."

negative answer, even if the soldier be of inferior rank not required to participate in pagan rites or in capital punishment.

> But how will *a Christian man* war, nay, how will he serve even in peace, without a sword, which the Lord has taken away? For . . . the Lord . . . , in disarming Peter, unbelted every soldier.   [*On Idolatry*, Chap. 19]

As Tertullian acknowledged, even in the second century there were Christians in the Roman legions, despite protests like his. But when Constantine placed the cross on military banners, identifying Roman conquest with the cause of Christ, a radically different atmosphere pervaded the church as well as the empire. It was now popular and politically advantageous to be a Christian. The standards of Christian life were rapidly compromised with the prevailing customs of a pagan society.

The course of relations between church and empire was not smooth. There were times of persecution of Christians generally or of adherents to one or another party during the great doctrinal disputes. Some individuals and movements within the church protested vigorously the prevailing laxity. But the predominant ethical pattern from the fourth through the fifteenth centuries was mutual accommodation between church and empire, both in the East and in the West.

3. Natural Law and Counsels of Perfection

As the ethical teachings of the Western Church were codified, they were based mainly on natural law, and not on the Bible or on distinctively Christian doctrines. Indeed, the moral instruction of the Roman Catholic Church, including much of the canon law, was and is today drawn largely from the imperial code of the emperor Justinian.

From at least as early as the second century some churchmen distinguished between ordinary Christians and certain ones who aspired to more rigorous standards of life in an effort to be fully faithful to Christ's own example.

Before the rise of Christianity there had existed such monastic sects among the Jews as the Essenes and the Qumran Community. The earliest monastic movement among Christians, of which we have record, was in Egypt in the third century. It seems to have spread into Syria in the fourth century and soon the various monastic orders became an important feature of Christian life.

While Christian laymen might live a life of coarse sensuality and selfish materialism without much if any criticism from the Church, the men and women of the religious orders sought to live by "counsels of perfection," under strict community discipline. Celibacy, personal poverty, and much time devoted to prayer were prominent demands of most monastic orders. The monasteries were not immune to changes in the Church at large, and in such periods of general religious division and degradation as the late thirteenth and early fourteenth centuries, many of the orders lost most of their discipline and ethical significance. However, they recovered in the late fourteenth and fifteenth centuries.

In general, through the ages of Christian history the monastic orders have been a reminder that Jesus' teachings were very exacting and that the true Christian cannot live in easy conformity with the world around him. Critics of monasticism raise the question whether it does not degrade marriage and family life by exalting celibacy as essential to the life of "the religious." Those orders which separate their members from the larger community are also criticized for substituting separation from the world for service in and to the world exemplified and taught by Christ and the Apostles.

4. *Protestant Rigor and Freedom*

The Protestant Reformers rejected the dual system of moral standards. All are called, they insisted, all have the responsibilities of ministry to one another and to the world, and all are under the same requirements of faithful obedience to Christ. At the same time, the Reformers stressed the Pauline doctrine of salvation by grace through faith and denounced the whole system of penances, works of supererogation, the doctrine of purgatory, and all else which seemed to imply salvation by merits.

Within these broad outlines there were many differences among Protestants from the beginning. Luther's emphasis on the priesthood of all believers, while not the individualistic doctrine many Americans suppose it to have been, nevertheless weakened the authority of the clergy and opened the way for further divisions within the Church. Calvinists sought to establish, at Geneva and at Plymouth, Massachusetts, a close union of church and state under a rule based on Scripture. Some emphasized an ascetic simplicity of personal and family life, protesting against the luxury, militarism, and worldly compromises of the larger society including most professing Christians. Such groups, exemplified by the Friends and various bodies of Brethren, are much like the monastic orders of Roman Catholicism, excepting that they reject celibacy and seek to live under exacting disciplines of obedience in family life and often in daily relations with larger communities.

In general, Protestants have sought to establish more exacting demands upon the main body of Christians than were characteristic of the medieval Church, while denouncing the legalism, celibacy, and, with some exceptions, asceticism characteristic of the monastic orders. Yet, with the passage of time, Protestants have become more and more adapted to the common culture around them, which they have deeply affected but by no means made completely Christian.

5. H. Richard Niebuhr's Typology

In his book *Christ and Culture*[30] H. Richard Niebuhr has classified the principal ways in which Christian theologians have interpreted the relation between Christian faith and life, on the one hand, and the culture of the world on the other. The typology suggested delineates usefully a number of important issues concerning philosophical and theological ethics, and concerning the practical relation between the church and the world.

a. Christ Against Culture. As Niebuhr indicates, the most unambiguous New Testament demands for the outright rejection of the whole non-Christian culture, with all its thought and works, is in the First Letter of John. For example, we read, "Do not love the world or the things in the world. If any one loves the world, love for the Father is not in him" (2:15). Continuing on, we learn that the writer thinks the world is full of "the lust of the flesh and the lust of the eyes and the pride of life." This entire pagan world which surrounds the Christian community is doomed, "but he who does the will of God abides for ever" (2:16–17). Hence the Christian is simply to reject this whole doomed culture, and live in the fellowship of which Christ is head.

On the whole, this mood seems to have dominated Christian thought through the second century and to have continued with much strength until Constantine. Tertullian was especially outspoken in his condemnations, not only of pagan sensuality and idolatry, but also of all Greek philosophy. His position, however, was more radical than most Christian thought and practice of his time. Moreover, his own tendency was itself so extreme as to lead him into the Montanist heresy.

However, the separatist tendency toward all-out hostility to secular or pagan culture has recurred again and again throughout Christian history. The early Friends, for example, protested not only against war but also against worldly deference for rank, customary clothing, and church ritual.

Such movements always run into two embarrassments. First, they find that some aspects of the culture have gone along in the heart of

30. New York: Harper & Row, 1951. Cf. also the famous distinction of "church" and "sect" and acute analysis of interactions between Christian teaching and culture in Ernst Troeltsch, *The Social Teaching of the Christian Churches,* tr. by Olive Wyon (London: George Allen and Unwin, 1931).

the rebel, with or even within the most world-rejecting thoughts and decisions. Thus Tertullian, while rebelling against pagan philosophy and law, formulated Christian doctrine in ways which only a man trained in Greek philosophy and in Roman law could have employed. Second, the Christian individual or group, despite every contrary effort, remains at some points dependent on the larger society and unable to shake off some responsibility for its condition. Indeed, such considerations and others are now giving rise to much new thinking within the Catholic monastic orders themselves regarding the location and responsibilities of monasteries.

Nevertheless, the separatist type of Christian thought and action serves to warn all Christians that no state or society yet produced on earth has been in full harmony with Christ, and if Christ is to be Lord of our lives, we must always keep somewhat detached from the world, however deeply God may also bid us to be involved in service to the world. In some respects, at least, Christ has always been, and is today, against the culture of the world.

b. The Christ of Culture. Some theologians of many generations have seen intimations of Christ in the cultures of the world not touched by the Church and knowing nothing about Jesus of Nazareth. There is a suggestion, at least, of such thought in some passages of the New Testament. Thus John speaks of "the light" which was incarnate in Jesus as "the true light that enlightens every man."[31]

In the second century, while Tertullian was denouncing the Greek philosophers, other defenders of the faith whom we commonly call "the Greek Apologists" were finding in the Greek philosophies testimony to the same truth which was in Christ. One of them, Justin Martyr, even wrote of Christ,

> He is the Word of whom every race of men were partakers; and those who lived reasonably [*meta logon:* with reason, or according to the word] are Christians, even though they have been thought atheists; as among the Greeks, Socrates and Heraclitus, and men like them.[32]

In modern times especially clear illustrations of such teaching are in the philosophies of John Locke, Immanuel Kant, and Georg W. F. Hegel.[33] The theologian Friedrich Schleiermacher exhibits the same trend of accommodations to culture in a more characteristically Chris-

---

31. John 1:9. Cf. Acts 14:16–17, 17:26–28.
32. *First Apology*, Chap. 46. Niebuhr speaks of Justin as a representative of the motif Christ above Culture. However, in the passage cited here and in many others he seems to represent well the theme we are now discussing.
33. See Locke, *The Reasonableness of Christianity;* Kant, *Religion Within the Limits of Reason;* and Hegel, *Philosophy of Religion.*

tian way. In popular church ethics and practice today, this motif is very prominent, indeed.

The motif of the Christ of culture is in constant danger of so compromising the meaning and power of Christian faith that professing Christians become the "salt which lost its savor," people who have no prophetic impact upon society. Indeed, they are often a part of the problem, rather than of its solution, that is, part of the world's resistance to Christ, not members of the body of Christ.

On the other hand, seeking Christ within the culture has the merit of reminding all men that the principal place of Christian service is in the world, the world where Jesus talked with adulterers and tax collectors, championed the cause of the poor, and suffered death on the cross. It reminds us also that God is still *there*, at work in the world, where he calls us to join him in his task of reconciling the world to himself and all men to their brothers and sisters.

c. Christ above Culture. Niebuhr says rightly that both the motifs we have examined have represented minority movements in the history of the Church.

In the "great majority . . . the church of the center" (*Christ and Culture*, p. 117) are embraced three motifs more complex than the first two. The first of these three is the motif of synthesis, placing Christ above culture, yet in intimate relation to it.

Representatives of this motif recognize the great difference between Christ and the world. But this does not lead them to seek escape into cave or monastery nor to adopt a loveless, undiscriminating scorn for everything in the world. Its typical representatives are Clement of Alexandria, whose thought we examined earlier, and Thomas Aquinas, whose great medieval synthesis has dominated Roman Catholic thought since the thirteenth century.

Thomas Aquinas found in Aristotle sound philosophical reasons for believing in the existence of God. Likewise, he found in the ethics of Aristotle true and useful instruction concerning the cardinal virtues of temperance, courage, prudence, and justice, and also concerning various other matters such as the relations between habit formation and both temptation and virtue. However, Aristotle could not give us the glorious knowledge of God's redemptive love nor concerning the heavenly reward which we owe to revelation. Similarly, we are called upon to move from the cardinal virtues on to the Christian virtues, faith, hope, and love, with the beatific vision of God as supreme goal.

Thomas bids us follow "the Philosopher" as far as he can take us. Then he bids us continue the upward way, both of thought and of life, by faithful apprehension of God's holy revelation.

There is much to commend in such a program. By such means, it is hoped, a persuasive appeal for faith may be made in the world and the world penetrated deeply by Christian ideas and purposes, while the unique beliefs, resources, and responsibilities of Christian faith are affirmed.

There are two main difficulties with this motif as it appears historically. Sometimes the synthesis fails to relate effectively so that we are left with two bodies of teaching and two forms of life between which the seams are so open as to give the whole structure an unconvincing character. The other peril appears more conspicuously and is evident in the system of Thomas Aquinas.

Since the categories of thought are adopted from pagan philosophy, the Christian doctrines of God and of the Christian life tend to be seriously distorted. Thomas' doctrine of God never quite escapes the impersonal abstractness of Aristotle's Pure Form, and most Thomistic ethics owes more to the natural law of the Stoics and Roman jurists than to the gospel. This is true despite Thomas' explicit treatment of such subjects as the "theological virtues," drawing mainly on the New Testament as basic source.[34]

Seeing this, some theologians, especially in the tradition of Martin Luther, have rejected synthesis while not rejecting culture. Their determination to affirm much in culture in its own proper setting, while maintaining not only distinction but sharp contrast between culture and faith, has led to a fourth motif.

d. Christ and Culture in Paradox. The paradoxes of the Pauline Letters are often cited in support of this motif, and the paradox of Law and grace especially lends itself to this treatment, as does the closely related paradox of Christian freedom and obedience. When Paul describes the Law as "our custodian until Christ came" (Gal. 3:24), his thought seems to fit rather Niebuhr's motif of "Christ Above Culture." But when he writes of the part which the Law has taken in making him a sinner, even though he insists that the Law is God's law and is good,[35] he exposes a high degree of tension in his thought of the Law from his present standpoint in faith. Similarly, after he exults in Christian freedom and exhorts the Galatian Christians not to return to bondage, he is soon speaking of the requirement that Christians be disciplined and obedient (Gal. 5:1, 13–24). The life according to moral law is not abandoned, but retained in a new relationship, a position of constant tension with the forgiving, liberating grace of Christ.

Martin Luther sees a much more intense contrast of the law in secular society and the life of love and grace in Christ. Yet he affirms both as under God.

34. See especially *Summa Theologiae*, 1a2ae. 62.
35. E.g., see Rom. 5:20; 7:5, 7–12.

The Christian is to live by faith, with generous, forgiving love, and eager helpfulness.[36]

On the other hand, in his polemic *Against the Robbing and Murdering Hordes of Peasants* Luther calls upon the civil authority for ruthless suppression and says that

> a prince or lord must remember in this case that he is God's minister and the servant of his wrath to whom the sword is committed for use upon such fellows. . . . Here there is no time for sleeping; no place for patience or mercy. It is the time of the sword, not the day of grace.[37]

The tension of paradox between society and Christian faith has been renewed again and again since Luther. One form of it is seen in the life and work of Sören Kierkegaard, which has influenced so much of theology and ethics a century later. In recent thought it is particularly prominent in the work of Reinhold Niebuhr.

Niebuhr is not comforting to the many easygoing Christians who keep their religion in a closed compartment for Sunday profession, prayer, and some personal relations not affecting their decisions on political and economic problems. On the other hand, he has poured scorn upon those Christians who attempt to give direct expression to Christian love in civil law and especially in international relations. Against the idealism of Christian pacifism he places a "Christian realism." The proper law of political and economic relations is not love but justice. The effort to express Christian love in public policy results in self-deception and the strengthening of the most violent and unjust forces. Yet the love ethic of Christ must be held in tension with social justice, restraining national self-interest, and tempering the stern justice of the courts with mercy.

Reinhold Niebuhr and other "Christian realists" have been merciless and useful in their exposure of the self-deceptions and outright hypocrisies all too prevalent in the church and its teachers. They will not permit Christian idealists to claim without protest that they have a right to an easy conscience about war just because they choose the conscientious objector's release from military service. They protest usefully against easy simplifications of complex social problems and any identification of a political policy with the kingdom of God.

On the other hand, to describe the tension between the real and the ideal and to say that we cannot hope here and now to fulfill all the

---

36. *Christian Liberty*, in *Works of Martin Luther* (Philadelphia: 1915–1932), Vol. II, p. 338. Quoted in Niebuhr, *Christ and Culture*, pp. 170–71.

37. *Works of Martin Luther*, Vol. IV. pp. 251–52. Quoted in Niebuhr, *op. cit.*, p. 171.

norms of the consummated reign of God will not tell us much about what we can and ought to do. Often the motif of paradox becomes a defense of the status quo. If the best we can do is still sin in the sight of God, a worldly work and not truly a Christian work, then the nerve of passion for reformation is likely to be cut. Where the best we can do is still darkness in the sight of God, incentive to try to do the best is at least reduced. Even when, as in the case of Reinhold Niebuhr, the ethical dualist is concerned with practical reform, many of his readers find themselves encouraged to make unnecessary "realistic" compromises with evil. The forward movements with which Niebuhr is associated owe much of their dynamic to more hopeful and idealistic prophets of a new age.

e. Christ the Transformer of Culture. Like the dualists of ethical paradox, the churchmen whom H. Richard Niebuhr calls "conversionists" recognize the great disparity between the realm of grace and the kingdoms of this world. Also, like them, they refuse to separate themselves from the world. Sometimes they think theologically in terms of a synthesis which acknowledges Christ as above culture fulfilling all the deepest needs and best promise of the world. But in ethical demands, at least, they are not synthesists, nor can they rest in a continuing paradoxical position acknowledging at once the contrary claims of world and gospel.

"What distinguishes conversionists from dualists is their more positive and hopeful attitude toward culture."[38] Not only did God create the world and man; despite human sin he continues to be active in history, and by his power working in us and beside us the course of history can be turned in the direction of his purpose.

This motif is found in widely distributed passages throughout the New Testament. It is especially clear in the Fourth Gospel. "God sent the Son into the world, not to condemn the world, but that the world might be saved through him" (John 3:17). Here is a positive and hopeful view of the world and the possibilities of its being turned to God.

Niebuhr names John Wesley as a representative of Christ the Transformer of Culture. Wesley teaches that the world is fallen and corrupt. However, God by his prevenient grace restores enough of the divine image so that men have the possibility of responding to the gospel with faith. Moreover, the grace of Christ is not only sufficient to effect the justification of man in his sin; it also enables the converted individual to "go on to perfection" in love. Christian perfection is not absolute perfection of deed, because a man remains limited in knowledge

38. H. Richard Niebuhr, *Christ and Culture,* p. 191.

and skill. It is perfection of intent, the perfection of a loving purpose to serve God in serving other persons. Wesley is convinced that the work of God is social to the core. Says he,

> "Holy solitaries" is a phrase no more consistent with the Gospel than holy adulterers. The Gospel of Christ knows no religion, but social; no holiness, but social holiness.[39]

This teaching led Wesley to give much attention to drawing converts together in religious societies and class meetings for mutual assistance —not only "spiritual," but also educational and economic. It led him also into some active interest in the abolition of slavery and the correcting of other social injustice. These wider applications of the conversionist theme, however, were not so much developed in Wesley's own work as in writings and actions by many of his followers.

A particularly interesting and suggestive more recent development of this motif occurs in the writing of Frederick D. Maurice. Maurice recognized and stressed heavily the vast distance between contemporary society and the kingdom of God. This did not lead him to suggest separating the Church from the world. Indeed, such separation would not help, because the Church, like the rest of the world, is divided against itself and disobedient to God. But Christ died for all men and all now belong to him. Writes Maurice: "The truth is that every man is in Christ; . . . except he were joined in Christ, he could not think, breathe, live a single hour."[40] The task of professing Christians is to share this good news and call all men to live accordingly in communal relationships with Christ and with each other. These relationships are to embrace all of life, economic and political, as well as ecclesiastical. They are opposed to the divisions of the Church and the destructive competitiveness of the economic order alike. In economics Maurice was a socialist, but his primary concern was the working out from the innermost human spirits the reconciliation and unity in all things which we have in Christ.

We have examined some types of thought in the rich historical heritage of Christian ethics, from the Bible to modern times. It is now our task to begin formulating basic presuppositions and principles to guide Christian action in the present day. This is neither an easy nor a popular undertaking.

39. Preface to *Hymns and Sacred Poems*. Published by John Wesley and Charles Wesley in London, 1739.
40. *The Life of Frederick Denison Maurice Chiefly Told in His Letters*, ed. by his son Frederick Maurice (New York: Charles Scribner's Sons, 1884), Vol. I, p. 155.

However, some must seek to draw the evidence together, and dare to attempt a systematic statement of the premises and methods by which choices ought to be made by Christians in contemporary society. The reader is invited to join critically in this task.

chapter five

Assumptions and Principles
of Christian Ethics

———•⟨∞⟩•———

A. Human Nature

No amount of describing what human nature is and telling how human beings behave can answer the ethical questions what human beings *ought* to be and how they *ought* to act. On the other hand, it would be absurd to attempt an answer to the ethical questions without taking serious account of actual human nature and human behavior. We are concerned with the ethics of human nature, not of angels nor of porpoises. While some attention has already been given to various psychological, anthropological, and philosophical ideas of human nature, we must now speak of specifically Christian teachings concerning man.

1. Imago Dei

The most basic and important biblical teaching on the subject in hand is that God created man in his own image. What is the image of God in man? The source of the doctrine is, of course, Genesis 1:26–27. There we read,

> Then God said, "Let us make man in our image, after our likeness; . . ." So God created man in his own image, in the image of God he created him; male and female he created them.

Again, in the fifth chapter, we read, "When God created man, he made him in the likeness of God" (5:1). Some light is thrown on the author's meaning when the same words are used in the next verse to say that he "became the father of a son in his own likeness, after his image, and named him Seth." Comparison of the two passages suggests that men and women are thought of as having some kind of similarity to God, a likeness based on a personal kinship. Perhaps Luke had this in mind when, in his genealogy of Jesus, he described Adam as "the son of God" (Luke 3:38).

It may be asked whether it is not the biblical view that man lost this likeness in the Fall. No Old Testament writer supports such a view. There are, to be sure, passages of extreme self-deprecation, like the Psalmist's lament,

> Behold, I was brought forth in iniquity,
> and in sin did my mother conceive me.
> [Ps. 51:5]

There are also extreme denunciations of wicked men, as when it is written,

> The wicked go astray from the womb,
> they err from their birth, speaking lies.
> [Ps. 58:3]

But the mood of self-condemnation is not a doctrine of absolute and universal human depravity, while excoriations of "the wicked" are usually, as in the passage quoted, set in explicit contrast to references to "the righteous."

What of the passage cited by Paul when he charges that "all men, both Jews and Greeks, are under the power of sin"?[1] It is true that the Psalmist, speaking of "the children of men," says,

> They have all gone astray, they are all alike corrupt;
> there is none that does good,
> no, not one.
> [Ps. 14:2, 3]

Yet even here the context contrasts all these evildoers with "my people," who are being devoured by the wicked, so the hyperbole is evident. Moreover, it would be one thing to say, even in solemn literalness, that no man ever does anything good, but quite another to say that men were in no respect like God. Important as is God's goodness, other attributes are ascribed to him as well.

In the New Testament, and especially in the Pauline Letters, a doctrine of human depravity is emphatically stated and at times the divine image or likeness is attributed to Jesus Christ alone.[2] However, neither the acknowledgment of a unique likeness in Jesus nor the doctrine of universal human sinfulness is equivalent to the teaching

---

1. Rom. 3:9. Cf. vv. 10–12.
2. E.g., see 2 Cor. 4:4, 2 Cor. 3:18, and Col. 1:15.

that man has no likeness of any kind or degree to God. In fact, Paul argues that in prayer and prophecy "a man ought not to cover his head, since he is the image and glory of God."[3] James significantly denounces men's inconsistent and evil use of the tongue as he confesses, "With it we bless the Lord and Father, and with it we curse men, who are made in the likeness of God" (Jas. 3:9). The wide moral significance of this demand for respect to all human beings as "in the likeness of God" is evident and must be further treated later.

Thomas Aquinas writes,

> Man is made to God's image, and since this implies, so Damascene tells us, that he is intelligent and free to judge (*arbitrio liberum*) and master of himself, so then, . . . we go on to look at this image, that is to say, at man as the source of actions which are his own and fall under his responsibility and control.[4]

This teaching was basic to Thomas' conception of natural law ethics.

Many Christian writers would lay less emphasis on man's intellect than does Thomas while yet agreeing that the doctrine of God's image in man affirmed the spiritual nature and moral dimension of man's being.

2. Freedom of the Will

The freedom of will which any man possesses is extremely limited. He has little strength compared with the vast forces which surround him. He is only one individual among the billions on earth, and the tides of history are too powerful for him to control. The numbers of acts which a given individual cannot perform at a given moment are infinitely larger than those which he can perform.

Even when a person thinks he is choosing with complete freedom, for thoughtful reasons of which he is conscious, he is often so deeply affected by subconscious forces that much of his claimed freedom is illusory. Sigmund Freud and many subsequent depth psychologists have made this clear.

If there is no freedom of choice whatever, then the moral life is an illusion and ethics at most a science of what *would* be obligatory for a nonexistent responsible creature. To speak of what a man ought to do would then be as pointless as to talk about the duties of rocks or the responsibilities of hollyhocks.

3. 1 Cor. 11:17. The faulty exegesis by which Paul excludes woman from the likeness taught in Gen. 1:27, and so reflects the social bias of his time, does not affect the argument here.

4. Foreword to *Summa Theologiae*, 1a2ae. Blackfriars edition (New York: McGraw-Hill Book Company, 1963), Vol. 16, p. 1.

There are two lines of argument by which even the slightest margin of freedom has been denied in Western thought. One is a theological argument from the Bible, the other a philosophical inference from the natural sciences.

a. Biblical Argument Against Freedom.   Most of the argument by biblical citation against belief in human freedom of will is drawn from the Letter to the Romans. As Paul emphasizes our dependence upon God's mercy and God's assigning of peoples to their special roles in history, he provides texts which seem to leave no room for human freedom of choice. His demeaning of man's autonomy comes to a climax as he writes,

> So then he has mercy upon whomever he wills, and he hardens the heart of whomever he wills.
> You will say to me then, "Why does he still find fault? For who can resist his will?" But, who are you, a man, to answer back to God? Will what is molded say to its molder, "Why have you made me thus?" Has the potter no right over the clay, to make out of the same lump one vessel for beauty and another for menial use?   [9:18–21]

Nevertheless, Paul seems not to have intended the denial of responsible human freedom. Within the next two chapters of Romans he calls upon his readers to make the decisions which will place them among the favored people who receive God's mercy. Here he appears to make all depend upon men's free choice (11:19–23).

We may regard Paul's position as substantially self-contradictory. On the other hand, we may think the paradox more rhetorical than substantial. In any event, it is not strange that in his time and place he was not aware of metaphysical debates concerning freedom of will and so did not shrink from affirming the free responsibility of man's will directly after emphasizing God's sovereignty with such exclusive absoluteness as seemingly to leave no place for any choices save those of God.

Similarly, the Gospel of John describes the events of the gospel story as if all the persons involved were puppets manipulated by unseen divine fingers.[5] Yet the Fourth Evangelist, too, represents every person's relation to God and his salvation as depending finally on the person's own choice (3:16–21).

Precisely what we are to believe, metaphysically, about God's will and the relation between that will and human freedom is a subject which must be more precisely defined in systematic theology.[6] For our purposes just now it suffices to point out that the biblical testimony

5. Cf. John 6:64–65; 8:20; 13:21–27; 17:2, 4, 6, 9. 11, 12; 19:31–37.
6 Cf. my treatment in *A Theology of the Living Church*, Chaps. 21 and 22.

does not exclude the human freedom of will essential to moral responsibility.

b. Science-based Determinism. Since the rise and growth of modern science, the assertion of human free will has come into serious question because of the apparently universal reign of causal law. If every event, without exception, is in principle absolutely predictable from previous events, no room is left for genuine human choice. When we affirm that a man's decision is on some occasions, at least in certain aspects, made by free choice at the time, are we not affirming the unscientific notion that some events occur without a cause?

We may reply at once that we who affirm some freedom of will are not saying that the person's free choice and the acts which he chooses to form are without cause; we are saying that one of their causes is the person in his act of willing. This particular point in the series of events, we believe, is a pivotal point from which the causal series may move in any one of several directions. It is precisely the nature of human willing to be just such an unpredictable cause.

The modern physics of relative indeterminacy makes this affirmation more plausible than it seemed in the nineteenth century. For it is now recognized as probable that all events are both actually and in principle predictable only within limits. One of the few great physicists to disagree, Max Planck, still believes that an act of human will is this kind of indeterminate event.[7]

While the biblical and scientific arguments *against* belief in freedom of will can be refuted, we cannot give a decisive *positive proof* of freedom. We can, however, postulate freedom as necessary to moral obligation.

If someone responds that it is so much the worse for moral obligation—and for ethics—we must point out that ethics will not go down the drain alone. Along with it will go the sciences and all organized human knowledge. For if there is no obligation to be consistent, honest, cooperative, and self-disciplined, then we may as well accept as of equal worth the ideas of the Flat Earth Society and the most careful astronomer, the claims of an outrageous promoter of bottled witches' brew as the prescriptions of a trained and experienced physician. The acceptance of moral obligation underlies commerce, industry, friendship, science, and every other meaningful endeavor of man. When Immanuel Kant proclaimed "the primacy of the practical

7. For the doctrine of indeterminacy and its relevance to human freedom of will, as viewed by some physicists, see Albert Einstein and Leopold Infeld, *The Evolution of Physics* (Cambridge: Cambridge University Press, 1938), especially p. 313. Cf. Planck's view in his book *Where Is Science Going?* (New York: W. W. Norton & Company, 1932), pp. 221 and 161. See also my treatment of this subject, with citation of other scientists, in *A Theology of the Living Church*, pp. 167–72.

[i.e., moral] reason" he put his finger on a great truth of life. Moral reason requires belief in the validity of the category of obligation. Because all meaningful human endeavor rests on the prior assumption of moral reason, all such endeavor requires genuine freedom of will—however limited in extent. We have no alternative, then, to the postulate that freedom of will is real, unless it be simply to give up all effort to think or live meaningfully. Faced with that alternative, few human beings will hesitate. Certainly no Christian who understands what the issues are can fail to believe in obligation, responsibility, and hence some margin of real freedom.

Freedom is, however, a highly variable commodity. The alcoholic in the throes of his awful compulsion has less freedom than the trained and sober pastoral counselor who is seeking to decide on love's best counseling strategy. Freedom is a variable and every time we use it we increase or decrease it by the choice made. Every one of us is limited today by missed opportunities for learning and habits of self-centeredness, self-indulgence, or self-deception developed by previous choices. On the other hand, our present freedom is enhanced by previous choices of far-ranging personal concern, courageous honesty, and self-disciplined purpose.

As Christians we regard our own freedom as God's gift from his own infinitely greater freedom, a sharing of his own nature, a part of the divine image, a breathing of his own creativity into ourselves. This gift is enhanced by being held close to its Author's own will in prayerful obedience. It withers in the self-centered estrangement from him which we know as sin.

B. HUMAN SINFULNESS

Sin does not belong to our essential nature. If it did we could not affirm that the Christ was truly man. But we cannot escape the fact that all other actual human beings are sinful. Thus Paul Tillich speaks of sin as the universal estrangement of our existence from our essence. Our task as human beings is to become and enable our neighbors to become truly human.

Not only must we all confess that we have sinned; we find in ourselves both the limiting consequences of our sins and also the proneness to sin again. God does not cease to make our true humanity cry out in judgment and protest, but our sinful condition continues to draw us away from him and from our true selves. So the battle is perpetually joined.

What is true of the individual is true also of society. A society utterly without moral restraint, communal concern, and noble aspiration would disintegrate and die.[8] Yet every society seems constantly threatened by internal forces which tend to tear it apart. The struggle between the ordering and aspiring forces and the threatening disorders ebbs and flows. The stakes of this struggle in the late twentieth century can hardly be overstated.

C. Justification by Grace Through Faith

If the moral soundness of our lives could be restored only by the decisions of our own wills, our condition would be hopeless. It is precisely our wills which are infected with evil. But God continually renews his creative work in us by his grace, that is, his own free gift. For this we are no more dependent on our merit to receive it than we were created because we merited existence before existing. Creation is a gift of God's grace. So also is the renewal of a healthy condition and relation with God.

God's prevenient grace, that is his gift of life and ability to will rightly before we consciously respond to him by faith, is given even to people who never heard of Christ or of God. This is "the true light that enlightens every man" (John 1:9).

However, in order to have a right relationship to God and full possession of moral and spiritual health, we must turn to God in faith. Faith is the response by which we acknowledge and welcome God's forgiving, life-giving grace, submitting ourselves gratefully to his reign in our lives.

Hence, in every condition we acknowledge that we have no occasion to boast. All of the life and good in us we have by God's gift. The dominant moods of authentic Christian life are gratitude, charitable forgiveness, and overflowing love for all people, in the knowledge that God loves all and all are, like ourselves, in need of forgiveness.

D. Law and Grace

As we observed earlier, the Apostle Paul sometimes wrote, with characteristic one-sidedness, as if all law were set aside for the Christian. Consequently, many writers in Christian history have set law and gospel in absolute contrast. Yet, as we also observed, Paul continued to lay down the law in no uncertain terms (as in Galatians 5). When faith is genuine the faithful person is willingly obedient to God's law. Disobedience is thus seen as a faltering or lapse of faith. The Christian seeks to know and obey God's will, not to earn marks of merit to

8. Cf. Calvin's "second office of the law." See *Institutes*, II, vii. x.

balance his heavenly books and so win eternal life, but in order to live for God who has given life, and to let God work through him in extending love and life to all men.

E.   Christian Love

There is nearly unanimous agreement among Christian ethicists that the central, dominant principle of Christian ethics is love, in the full New Testament sense. Even those who balk at calling it a principle regard love as central to Christian living. Here Augustine, Thomas Aquinas, Luther, Calvin, Wesley, and such different recent writers as Anders Nygren, Johannes Messner,[9] Paul Tillich, and Joseph Fletcher are agreed.

However, as soon as we begin to define the meaning of love, the agreement comes to an end. Does this matter? Many a person has truly loved without being troubled about definitions of love. Is not the reality much more important than correct definition of it?

Undoubtedly this is so. However, if we are to seek or aspire to love, as Paul bade the Corinthians to do, then we need to know what it is we seek. Moreover, so many moods, attitudes, and activities go by the name of love that we are likely to be badly misled if we do not take some care to understand.

The proper understanding of love in the Christian sense is especially important when we begin the task of ethical problem-solving in the complex field of social issues. For here the best of personal motivations will often go astray if we do not know with fair accuracy what basic, purposive principle we ought to consider in relation to data provided by the social sciences. It will make decisive differences, as we confront some problems, for example, whether we think of love in primarily affective or volitional, individual or collective terms.

1. Historic Interpretations

We shall not consider here interpretations unrelated to Christian tradition or those which, like the doctrine of Bernard of Clairvaux, relate almost wholly to the mystical relations with God. We will examine only a few historic ethical teachings which typify important trends of thought still influential today.

9. Messner writes so voluminously without *explicit* reference to love that one might doubt the centrality in his case. Indeed, his work might be much stronger by more explicit use of this principle. However, he writes unequivocally, "The fundamental principle of this social order is charity." *Social Ethics: Natural Law in the Western World*, tr. by J. J. Doherty, rev. ed. (St. Louis: B. Herder Book Co., 1965), p. 334. Cf. the footnote on the same page.

a. *Caritas:* Augustine.   The great Bishop of Hippo sought to define Christian love in terms of the *object* admired and desired.

Among men of the world the great desire is for perishable things of this world, such as wealth, comfort, popularity, and pleasure. Such desire he called *cupiditas* or cupidity.

On the other hand, *caritas* or charity—in a sense now uncommon—is directed toward God. Augustine thought it obvious that a base and unworthy desire is directed toward low objects, while a worthy desire must be seeking the truly valuable. The highest of all beings is God. Therefore the worthiest of all desires must be the desire for God himself. Such desire is true Christian love or *caritas.*

We must remember that Augustine was a Platonist who saw every particular instance of a quality, such as beauty or honesty, as participating in the ideal of that quality. Augustine thought of all such ideals as subsisting from eternity in God himself. Hence by every good quality he possesses a person participates in God. To love God, then, means both to love him in all his perfect fullness of being and also to be drawn to every good quality found in any human being. Thus the Christian loves God both directly, as we might say, and also in the neighbor, but only so far as truth, beauty, and goodness are to be found and cultivated in the neighbor. Likewise, we must seek to embody every good in ourselves.[10]

In such ways we love God in our neighbors and in ourselves, as well as in himself. So also God loves. We must not suppose that God desires anything less worthy than the best. Hence God loves himself only. However, he loves himself in men, as he desires and rejoices in their embodiment of good. Our love, if it be genuine, will be no more feeling, or thought. To seek or truly desire is to be in active quest. Love, then, requires the service of self and neighbor earnestly cultivating all that good which is truly God in humanity.

Thoughtful and suggestive as it is, Augustine's definition leaves some questions unanswered and raises others. Why seek a neighbor's good if the same good is also in myself? Again, why seek and rejoice in imperfect human manifestations of God's good when one can give oneself to desire for the perfect good in God himself? This latter question has occurred to many Christians and is one root of mystical monasticism.

Why should God or a godly man concern himself with a particularly base sinner? If love is directed to the ideal good, then the higher and purer be the good observed the more it should be loved. Augustine wrote eloquently on God's grace to sinners, but his doctrine of grace was in serious tension with his definition of love.

10. *The Morals of the Catholic Church*, Chap. vii.

b. Benevolence: Joseph Butler. Over thirteen centuries in time and a vast difference in perspective separate Augustine from Joseph Butler. His *Analogy of Religion* manifests a cool, rational mind arguing the superior claims of revealed Christian faith against its deistic opponents and reductionists. Likewise, in other writings he seeks to commend Christian virtues and duties to reasonable men.

Happiness is the good which all men seek and this is natural and right, though there are, of course, right and wrong ways to seek happiness. Moreover, to seek only one's own happiness is excluded by Christ's teachings. The command, "Thou shalt love thy neighbor as thyself," requires that one seek happiness for one's neighbor as for oneself.

This means, says Butler, not that we must have the same quantity, degree, or continuous preoccupation with the happiness of every neighbor as for ourselves—which would be both impossible to achieve and undesirable to attempt. It means, rather, that we must have

> the same kind of affection to our fellow creatures, as to ourselves; that, as every man has the principle of self-love, which disposes him to avoid misery, and consult his own happiness; so we should cultivate the affection of goodwill to our neighbor, and that it should influence us to have the same kind of regard to him.   [Sermon XII]

Such goodwill is eminently reasonable, for happiness is good in every human life. Hence I should seek it in all whom my own action clearly affects. The command does not bid me to love everyone as myself, for that would be impossible. It requires love toward my neighbor, that is, everyone obviously affected by my action (*ibid.*). What could be more reasonable?

Yet the uneasy question arises whether Butler's benevolence is all that the New Testament means when speaking of love. In such benevolence what is the basis for the utter self-sacrifice of Christ or the self-expending devotion of Paul? Butler seems to have reduced the way of the cross to a pleasant and kindly life concerned about others but only those conveniently near and not becoming so generous as to threaten loss of one's own happy existence.

c. Absolutely Selfless *Agape:* Anders Nygren. A view radically different from Butler's is that of Anders Nygren in his well-known work *Agape and Eros.*[11] Nygren contrasts Plato's idea of love as a yearning for ideal good, an aspiring quest for self-realization, with the utterly selfless devotion to the good of another person which he believes to be the New Testament conception. He interprets "Love thy

11. *Agape and Eros; a Study of the Christian Idea of Love,* tr. by A. C. Hebert, 3 vols. (New York: The Macmillan Company, 1932–38).

neighbor as thyself" to mean that I ought to love my neighbor as I do love, but ought not to love, myself. Concern for the other person is thus to supplant altogether the concern for self. Even a desire to develop my own personal virtue, whether of industry, humility, or generosity, is a pagan *eros*, not Christian *agape*. As God's redeeming grace is given from his absolutely selfless purpose to save a sinful man, so the forgiven man is divinely empowered to serve another without thought of any good to accrue to himself. If the Christian has, in his generous act, any thought of the other's desert, or of becoming more virtuous by this act, or of winning God's favor by it, then to that degree his motivation is polluted by *eros* and is not true *agape*.

The emphasis of Nygren on disregarding the desert of the recipient and on reckless self-giving sounds authentic Christian notes and must be welcomed as an important corrective of both Augustine and Butler. However, it raises new critical questions.

Nygren concedes that *agape*, as he interprets it, is bound to be regarded as psychologically impossible. But he responds by insisting that it is a miracle of grace. However, unless we can find a person who in actuality is, at least at times, absolutely devoid of any self-concern, even of the desire to be kind or Christlike, or to win a friend, in his absolute preoccupation with the good of one or more others, the psychological objection remains serious.

It is doubtful that Nygren's *agape* is descriptive of any human being. Certainly the Jesus of the Gospels is fully aware of the self-reference of his acts and is concerned to be obedient to the Father.

Even if it were possible to love another human being in the way Nygren describes, other critical questions would remain. Could we love God in this way and thus fulfill the commandment which Jesus identified as the first and greatest? Would love of this kind toward another human being be good? Is this the kind of love depicted in the New Testament?

When a believer performs an act for the service of God, the believer is spiritually enriched, and would be so enriched whether he sought to be or not. Thereafter it would be impossible to perform such an act for God's sake again without expecting the enrichment and making this expectation a part of his choice.

If Christian A continually chooses good for Christian B, while disclaiming all good for himself, where does that leave B? As a Christian of the kind Nygren idealizes, he will be refusing to accept the good and insisting on its going to A or to a third person C. It would be conceivable, even though psychologically impossible, for every believer to display Nygren's *agape* consistently only if there were enough unloving unbelievers for all Christians to make the recipients of their self-sacrificial giving, while the Christians who tried to love each other would be continually frustrated. Surely a part of Christian grace is grateful receiving as well as generous giving! *Agape* as Nygren describes it is an aristocratically one-sided, even patronizing attitude. There has already been too much of such "charity," even though never unmixed.

But is this kind of utterly selfless *agape* actually commended to us in the New Testament? Paul both approaches and follows his great chapter on *agape* with exhortations to seek the "higher" or "spiritual gifts"—as clear a demonstration of Nygren's "*eros*" as could be found (1 Cor. 12:31; 14:1). Again and again, as Jesus exhorts his disciples to love and forgiveness, he proposes motivation by desires having self-reference, such as to be true children of the Father, or to receive his forgiveness.[12]

2. *All These Views Highly Individualistic*

Each of the historic views examined defines love in terms of the object loved. Augustine enjoins desire only for the *best*, that is, God. Butler advocates concern for the good of *every* person affected, whether the self or another. Nygren describes *agape* as concern for the *other* person to the exclusion of all self-interest.

Despite the plausibility or attraction of each view on its own terms, each is in striking contrast with the New Testament in this respect, that all are purely individualistic. Although Augustine has great thoughts on the City of God, his understanding of love is in terms of the value which an individual wants for himself. Butler writes about family and nation, but only to distinguish the individuals who should have priority of active attention and concern. Nygren believes that we ought to choose the individual other in place of the individual self.

In actuality no human being can discover himself as a person in such individual isolation. We discover ourselves in community, beginning with child and mother. In time the individual learns to affirm himself in some degree or other of independence from the various groups to which he belongs. But even the most individualistic "loner," so long as he remains sane, identifies himself as a member of a group, whether other members are near or far.[13] However, different persons have greatly varying degrees of such social identification, and identify themselves with different sizes and types of groups.

---

12. See, e.g., Matt. 5:45; 6:14–15; 6:3–4, 16–21.

13. On the development and importance of self-conscious personal identity in relation to groups, see Gordon W. Allport, *Personality: A Psychological Interpretation* (New York: Henry Holt and Co., 1937), pp. 159–65; and Peter A. Bertocci and Richard M. Millard, *Personality and the Good* pp. 595–96. Cf. Erich Fromm, *The Art of Loving* (New York: Harper & Row, 1956), and Martin Buber, *I and Thou* (various publishers and editions, tr. from *Ich und Du*).

3. Love as Active Quest for Koinonia

Love in the high New Testament sense, whether named *agape* or *phile*, is a deeply communal word. It designates a relationship in which the separation of "I" and "Thou" is overcome in a sense of "We." To be sure, the one who loves another in this way may be unappreciated and rejected by the person loved. But the loving one still seeks to eliminate the barrier which isolates them and identifies his interest and purpose, rather his very self, with the other so that already he thinks "We," even while rejected.

It is no accident that the gospel of God's love gave rise to the Church which is an organic community, the body of Christ. It is significant that Paul's great poetic chapter on love stands between two chapters on the Church. An illuminating commentary on love is The Acts, where we read about the great accomplishments of the Holy Spirit in creating and empowering the Church with its many works of love.

This communal meaning of love has been nearly all lost to view in Western thought, especially in modern times. We so idealize individual independence and achievement that we can even talk absurdly of a "self-made man."

In contrast, the Old Testament always relates salvation to the nation Israel. In the New Testament it is invariably related to the community of faith in Christ. The idea of a single individual being saved and then loving other individuals while all remain "separate but equal" in their individuality never appears. Thus Paul speaks of people as being "cut off" from or "grafted into" the "olive tree," the community of salvation (Rom. 11:17, 19, 22–24).

Whenever genuine love for other people is experienced, it brings more than an active willing and working for their well-being. It involves also a desire to share some of life's values with them. This is better understood in some "primitive" cultures than by most people in our technological societies.

Thus, in various African tribes, when one man congratulates another on the birth of a son or on some signal achievement or honor, he replies by a phrase which means approximately "All of us." By such a reply he indicates that his good fortune is due to the whole community and he shares his pleasure with all. Because of its limitation to larger family, village, or tribe, this acknowledgment falls far short of the creative and universal love discovered in the primitive Christian community. Yet it is a foretaste and an aid to understanding.

Although a teenager may never tell his parents that he loves them, he may still rush home with the account of an athletic victory, or the narrative of some social excitement, or with a new joke. As he thus shares his own treasure with his parents, they can be reassured that he does love them in a very important way.

So, too, when a man who loves his wife enjoys reading an article which he knows would give her special pleasure, he wants not merely to leave it where she will be sure to see it, but to talk about it and perhaps to read some paragraphs aloud so that they can enjoy them *together*.

Where there is not any such desire for *shared* experience—even if it is possible only by letter or by imagination—there may be general goodwill, and even kindness, but there is little love.

Love as taught and exemplified in the New Testament has a further dimension. The treasure shared is known to be God's own gift and God himself is unseen participant in the relation.

"We love because he first loved us" (1 John 4:19). God created us because it is his own nature to love and he sought to share his own good, his freedom, his creative power, his spirit, the beauty of his holiness, his eternal joy. Because he loved he sought, not only to give life and good things, but also to draw his human creatures into a relationship of sharing with him. Because human beings were alienated from him and did not acknowledge the source of their good nor draw near to him, he gave his love to us in the form of the man Jesus, so that this visible incarnation of his love might draw us to him.

The greatest commandment is said to be the command to love God, that is, to seek to share his treasure with him in gratitude, praise, and the faithful obedience which further unites us with him in purpose. This cannot be separated from the command to love our neighbors, for God is loving them. In the story of the Prodigal Son, the elder brother cannot share life with his father while sulkily refusing to accept his brother, because the father is loving the brother and celebrating his return.

To love a human neighbor is to seek a relationship of sharing God's bounty with him in a common thanksgiving and rejoicing. Love in the full New Testament sense, as represented by the Pauline Letters, Luke, and the Johannine writings, is characterized both by a particular kind of active desire, namely, the desire to participate with another in a community of shared experience, and also by a special content of experience to be shared, namely, those treasures which God himself seeks to share with human beings. The Christian believes that all things which are truly of value, from daily food to the most sublime vision of God, are included among these gifts of God's sharing love. Accepting and sharing them with this understanding and in this mood adds to all a special dimension of sacred value.

Such *koinonia* love is especially well described in Acts 2:42–47:

> And they devoted themselves to the apostles' teaching and fellowship, to the breaking of bread and the prayers. . . . And all who believed were together and had all things in common; and they sold their possessions and goods and distributed them to all, as any had need. And day by day, attending the temple together and breaking bread in their homes, they partook of food with glad and generous hearts, praising God and having favor with all the people.

The sharing included food, money, homes, teachings, prayers, thanksgiving, and gladness.

The *koinonia* sought by Christian love is a holding in common not only of things and ideas, but even of selves, so that all become truly one body with Christ. So the Fourth Gospel represents Jesus as praying concerning his disciples and others who will later believe "that they may be one, even as we are one," and again "that they may all be one; even as thou, Father, art in me, and I in thee, that they also may be in us."[14]

This is not that easygoing, good-natured affability in which people of similar interests, class, and prejudices do things for each other in common expectation of reciprocity. It is such an indomitable eagerness to share as led Jesus to Calvary and sent Paul through perils, persecution, and never-ceasing toil, to martyrdom, in order to share with the Gentiles "the unsearchable riches of Christ" (Eph. 3:8). So far from restricting itself to the most admirable and pleasantly lovable persons as objects of attention, this love is especially drawn to the most unlovely, wretched, and lonely, even as water rushes with greatest rapidity into the lowest places.[15]

This love is not inconsistent with anger. Indeed, anger may accompany it. A good example is the anger of Jesus at the men who were waiting to report his violation of the sabbath law if he healed the man with the withered hand (Mark 3:1–6).

Love is less a matter of feeling than of intention, less of glandular activity than of purpose. It is a "set" or state of dominant eagerness to share God's gratefully received gifts with God himself and with other persons in a community of experience.

While a person loves another in such *koinonia* love, he may experience a wide variety of transient feelings and their accompanying glandular changes, depending on other circumstances. Such changes do not imply fluctuation or ambivalence of the love itself. Love that is constant and unequivocal still includes many and diverse affective moods and attitudes.

Paul is showing neither ambivalence nor some barely repressed hostil-

14. John 17:11, 21. Cf. vv. 22–23.
15. Cf. Matt. 9:9–13; Mark 2:13–17; Luke 5:27–32; 1 Tim. 1:15–16.

ity when he writes, "Let love be genuine; hate what is evil, hold fast to what is good" (Rom. 12:9). No more is there any confusion in his thought when, as he continues to elaborate on the proper manifestations of love, he says, "Rejoice with those who rejoice, weep with those who weep" (Rom. 12:15).

It is important that these complex and variable relations between Christian love and the emotions be properly understood, for two reasons. Psychological analysis which correctly shows the great complexity of affective tones which may accompany supposedly loving acts often produces misguided cynicism regarding the very possibility of Christian love. A similar misunderstanding among church people leads many to suppose that love requires them always to avoid controversy and situations of conflict, so that a mood of sweet agreeability may be maintained without interruption. Such saccharine evasion of hard issues frequently hides a most unloving selfish acquiescence in social injustice. For this reason many a church congregation which fancies itself the very embodiment of Christian love and fellowship is instead an incarnation of cowardice, pride, and selfish complacency.

Christian love, properly understood, is not any one feeling but an outward-turned attitude of sharing many feelings, ideas, and material goods in a community of experience with God and all persons. Such a quest requires aggressive struggle, risk, and hard thinking, as well as praise, thanksgiving, and forgiving kindness. It begins with the grateful acceptance of God's love, is nurtured in the opening of human affections and wills to God in prayer, and is expressed both in public and private prayer and in generous sharing with people of all kinds and conditions.

F.   Perfection and Compromise

The New Testament speaks many times of perfection, and the idea of perfection has had a significant place in the development of Christian ethical thought.

1.   Perfection in History of Christian Ethics

The ideal of perfection has led many earnest Christian men and women to withdraw from the common world into monastic seclusion. To be in the world requires participation in communities and institutions which are shot through with evil. To eat one must buy; to buy is to contribute money to an unjust economy and taxes to an unjust, often cruel state. To marry is to take on obligations which require sustaining a family other members of which may be doing what one believes to be sinful. To be in a family makes it more difficult also to keep free from other ambiguous involvements. Thus a man who, if without dependents, might take a bold stand despite possible penalties of poverty, imprisonment, or death must, when responsible for support of a family, think again. He may then decide that compromise with social injustice which injures others is better than to inflict severe hardship on his family.

Monastics may grant that in the world only minimal standards of conduct can be required by the church. But for themselves they choose withdrawal into a monastic order where, without personal dependents or property, they may obey "counsels of perfection" apart from an evil world.

One important feature of the great present changes in Roman Catholic thought and practice is the growing stress on the apostolate of the laity. There is much recent teaching that not only "the religious" but *all* Christians are called to holiness and perfection of life.[16]

Various Protestant groups have insisted that perfection was to be sought in the world by all Christians. Some have assumed that serious Christians would always be a minority and hence have not felt bound to explain how a whole social order could operate on their own exacting principles. Yet in accepting family responsibilities and in some types of participation in the economic order of the world, they have differed from the monastics. For example, the early Quakers practiced a selective withdrawal, rejecting many customs which they regarded as idolatrous and above all refusing military service, yet marrying and engaging in commerce.

John Wesley, on the other hand, believed that God intended a life of Christian perfection for all men, without withdrawal. His thought, therefore, poses especially serious issues for Christian ethics. Perfection, according to his understanding, is

> purity of intention, dedicating all the life to God. It is the giving God all our heart; it is one desire and design ruling all our tempers. It is the devoting not a part, but all, our soul, body, and substance to God.[17]

In his thought of perfection, Wesley was influenced more by the Eastern than by the Western tradition. The primary meaning he gave to the term was to indicate, not an absence of sin, but rather a fullness of faith and love.[18] He believed that when a Christian was made perfect it was "generally" at "the instant of death, the moment before the soul leaves the body," and "usually many years after justification."

16. See especially the *Second Vatican Council, Constitution of the Church*, Chap. 5.
17. *A Plain Account of Christian Perfection*, 27.
18. He wrote, "I do not contend for the term *sinless*, though I do not object to it." *Brief Thoughts on Christian Perfection* (Jan. 27, 1767).

Though occurring in an instant "by a simple act of faith," yet it was in the midst of "a gradual work, both preceding and following that instant" (*Plain Account*, 26). It does not imply an end of all growth or effort. "It is not absolute. Absolute perfection belongs not to man, nor to angels, but to God alone" (*ibid.*). More explicitly Wesley writes,

> It is improvable. . . . It is amissible, capable of being lost; of which we have numerous instances.   [*Ibid.*]

Some who have been made perfect have experienced this in an instant, reports Wesley, but others do not know when this gift was given; it appears to have been gradual. Wesley theorizes that when it occurs it must always be instantaneous, even though the time is unknown.

This doctrine obviously leaves many matters imprecise and questions unanswered. Wesley's chief interest in it was evidently not in the exactness of theoretical statement. It was rather the very practical interest in stirring professing Christians out of easygoing acquiescence in a formal and largely loveless religion into active, eager striving for complete Christian living. If a person was to make maximum effort, he must have some hope of attaining the goal. Wesley intended, however, that all he said on the subject should be defensible on grounds of biblical teaching. It is to the New Testament we must now turn.

2. Perfection in the New Testament

There are several Greek expressions rendered "perfect" in the various English translations, but one is of special ethical importance, namely *teleios*. This is an adjective closely related to *telos, end* or *goal*. To be *teleios* is to have attained the goal or to be *complete*. Hence it is ofen used simply to signify that a person is *mature*, an *adult*. When Jesus says, "You, therefore, must be perfect" (Matt. 5:48), the primary meaning is not to be without sin, but to be complete in righteousness. The emphasis is positive, not negative. Exhortations to be perfect, then, urge the maturing of Christian discipleship into moral and spiritual completeness. There is a similar connotation in the verbs *toleioō* (*accomplish* or *be perfected*) and *epiteleō* (*finish up*). Wesley is on good ground, then, when he interprets perfection in the New Testament sense as fullness of love and grace. If he had always been as guarded and hesitant about equating such fullness with sinlessness as he was on some occasions, his doctrine would be less vulnerable to criticism than it is today.

On the other hand, Jesus is held up to us as the model of righteous humanity and he is described as without sin.[19] Undoubtedly, the ideal to which we are called is a life so full of love for God and neighbor, and so informed by the Spirit, that pride and selfishness have no room.[20]

3. Perfectionism in Practice

Such quest for personal sinlessness frequently works in favor of growth in effective life. The agonizing efforts to attain personal purity were important in the development of such mighty Christian servants as Augustine, Luther, and John Wesley. On the other hand, the desire to be personally perfect, especially in the sense of being free from all taint of sin, often impedes true righteousness.

In such men as the three just mentioned, the good fruits of the quest for personal purity were produced when the seeker came so to trust in God's forgiving grace as to be relieved of anxiety about himself and enabled to forget himself in service to the community. This is true in part because preoccupation with self—even with the self's aspiration to sanctity—preempts attention needed by others. But there is more than this involved.

The Christian is called to "seek first," not his own purity, but the total reign of God. He who places his own perfection above all other considerations is likely to settle for a mere individual piety in which he is guilty of unconcern—or at least inactivity—in weightier matters affecting many or all his human brothers. If he is to be actively concerned about poverty, war, and materialistic exploitation of life, he must plunge into alliance with imperfect, sometimes vulgar and profane people of mixed motives and do things which will predictably have some evil consequences. To refuse such alliances is to refuse loving concern in the true sense of active, effective concern for true community.

In the sinful world even Jesus performed acts of which some predictable consequences were evil. By his own rigorous and concrete denunciations of hypocrisy he provoked resentment, hate, and killing —not only the killing of himself but also of many faithful disciples. Loving all people as he did, and particularly his faithful followers, he surely did not approve such consequences. Moreover, he clearly foresaw such results of his work.[21] Yet he acted as he did for the sake of other results. He chose the conduct which he believed, under all the

19. E.g., see 2 Cor. 5:21; Heb. 4:15; 1 John 3:5.
20. Cf. 1 John 3:2–3.
21. See Matt. 10:34–36.

circumstances, offered best promise of good, on the whole. His own purpose, I believe, was pure, but in pursuit of his goals he had to perform actions which were far from perfect in predictable effects. Certainly we are unable to escape similar necessity.

chapter six

Ethics of Natural Law

A. Relevance to Our Place and Time

Americans often discuss the question whether the Christian religion provides the foundation of their liberty. No document can settle such a question, for apart from documents the character and presuppositions of the people which are so important to democratic freedom are to a large extent formed by their religious beliefs and practices.

However, as far as explicit historical statement is concerned, the fact is unequivocal. The claim to freedom by all the thirteen United States of America was based, not on Christian, Jewish, or biblical presuppositions, but on an ethics of natural law. Let the reader note precisely the presuppositions on which the claim to independent liberty is based in the Declaration of Independence. The text is as follows, with appeals to natural law here placed in italics:

> When in the Course of human Events, it becomes necessary for one People . . . to assume among the Powers of the Earth, the separate and equal Station to which *the Laws of Nature and of Nature's God* entitle them, a decent Respect to the Opinions of Mankind requires that they should declare the causes which impel them to the Separation. *We hold these Truths to be self-evident,* that all Men are created equal,[1] that they are *endowed by their Creator with certain unalienable Rights.* . . .

The historical rootage of this appeal to "the Laws of Nature and of Nature's God" is the deistic thought of the personal author Thomas Jefferson, largely shared by Benjamin Franklin, John Adams, and other signers. The majority were nominal Anglicans, but church life in the Colonies was in a low state and few of the signers were active church members. Jefferson himself wrote,

1. Unfortunately, the Congress struck out Jefferson's caustic denunciation of slavery which would have given more convincing integrity to this statement.

I am a Christian in the only sense in which he [Christ] wished anyone to be; sincerely attached to his doctrines, in preference to all others;
ascribing to himself every *human* excellence; and believing he never
claimed any other.[2]

Jefferson was a serious student of the Bible and especially of the
Greek New Testament; but he read through the eyes of a rationalistic
son of the Enlightenment rather than those of a churchman.

What did Jefferson and his colleagues mean by the statement that
men under colonial oppression were entitled to "separate and equal
station" by the "Laws of Nature and of Nature's God"? How do laws
of nature apply to the political arrangements of men?

In common parlance the term "laws of nature" means *causal* laws
like "the law of gravity" or "laws of learning." From such a standpoint
it may seem strange to regard any laws of ethics as laws of nature or
natural laws. Yet there is a relationship much more than verbal.

The general notion of natural law is that as the nature of things
imposes upon their motions certain invariable laws which they *necessarily* follow, as a released stone falls to earth, so the nature of man
and his world imposes upon human beings laws of conduct which they
ought to follow.

There are many theories of natural law which differ widely. Indeed,
proponents of some theories would already have reservations, even
concerning the above simple definition. A. P. d'Entrèves goes so far as
to say, "Except for the name, the medieval and the modern notions
of natural law have little in common."[3]

The question whether a sound ethics of natural law can be discovered and formulated is especially relevant to the present world
situation. In an age of nuclear fission it is evident that the nations, and
especially the great powers, cannot afford to submit their differences
to the arbitrament of war. It is necessary, if humanity is to survive,
that representatives of the nations be able to reason together about
issues in dispute and that there be developed a community of nations
with a firm structure of international law. If two parties are to reason
together there must be some common ground of assumptions on which
the reasoning can proceed. Among nations now existing what can
serve as this common ground?

Bonhoeffer says, "Faith in Jesus Christ is the sole fountainhead of all
good."[4] If this is literally and finally true, then it is vain to look for

2. Letter to Dr. Benjamin Rush, quoted in Thomas C. Hall, *The Religious Background of American Culture* (Boston: Little, Brown, and Co., 1930), p. 172.
3. *Natural Law: An Historical Survey* (New York: Harper & Row, 1965),
p. 9.
4. *Ethics*, p. 78. Although this statement is unrelieved by context and ends a

any good where there is not Christian faith. Surely knowledge of what is good is itself a good, and hence according to this particular dictum of Bonhoeffer we shall look in vain for any such knowledge among Communists, Hindus, Buddhists, animists, or men of other faiths. Such a situation would place beyond all possibility the meaningful discussion of justice or the fair resolution of any conflict between representatives of the United States and the Soviet Union or India or Israel or Morocco. Indeed, at a time when the American diplomat may be a secular humanist or an earnest Jew, the impossibility of starting from specifically Christian premises arises not solely from the presence of non-Christian representatives of nations other than the United States.

Actually, diplomatic discussions between nations usually appeal to certain general needs, rights, or interests which are regarded as universally *human*, such as the right to live and so the right of access to the means of life which all people need, and the interest in opportunity for economic and cultural self-development. So well-established are these and other similar appeals in diplomatic tradition that even when an international dispute is between nations the majority of whose citizens are of the same faith the common religious assumptions are often unmentioned.

If there is a true basis for such moral appeals to a common humanity, then it would be obviously helpful to formulate its principles, to enter into intercultural discussion of them, and to work assiduously at the task of promulgating and using them as a basis for international and intercultural community. They would also serve as a basis for mutual understanding in the recommendation of one's own faith to people of other faiths.

We have observed that there are radically different theories of natural law. In order to understand and see both their relative strengths and weaknesses, we must examine briefly some of the most important, beginning with ancient Greek philosophy.

This must not be taken to imply that the idea of natural law arose in ancient times in the Western world only, for the basic idea was known in ancient China as well. J. C. H. Wu quotes the opening sentence of "the Confucian classic, *The Unvarying Mean*," as follows:

"What is ordained of Heaven is called the essential nature of man; the following of this essential nature is called the natural law."[5]

In this present study we must be limited, however, to surveying briefly

chapter, it is not Bonhoeffer's last word on the subject. Other teachings of his are radically different, as we have seen.

5. "Natural Law," in *New Catholic Encyclopedia* (New York: McGraw-Hill Book Company, 1967).

highlights of the principal tradition which has affected Christian ethical thought and the civil laws of the Western world.

B. Ancient Philosophy and Law

1. Socrates

Socrates sought to uncover and define precisely ideas of the good which he was confident were present, in however confused or ignored form, in every man. His method was to seize every opportunity to ask for the definition of good—justice, love, holiness, beauty—and then give examples which either the questioned man would want to include but could not without changing his definition or would have to include under the definition as stated but would wish to reject. While on the surface this was a method only for prodding people to define precisely the meaning of their words, actually it served to disclose common beliefs about moral goodness and about other values which men *ought* to seek.

The Socratic method was intended to learn and teach one form of what we may call natural law. A moral law of nature in this sense is simply a universal good which any man can recognize as good when his thoughts are clarified and his implicit knowledge is made explicit. We might speak of this conception of natural law as the theory of a *common moral sense* or *innate ethical knowledge*.

2. Plato

Plato carries his teacher's method further and in the process begins the development of a different notion of natural law. This is best seen in *The Republic*.

Plato believes that man is composed of three "souls" or aspects of personal life. All three are conceived dynamically. One is the sensory, perceiving, appetitive self, seeking always the pleasure of filling the self's needs for food, drink, and all else which may be *received* and so added to the life of the self. In general, the "appetitive soul" is the self as seeking the pleasures of sensory satisfaction. The second is "spirited soul" (*thumoeides*), sometimes called "the spirit," but with the consequence of likely misunderstanding. The "spirited soul" is the capacity of a person to be angry and brave, aggressively taking risks and willingly spending himself.

The third aspect of the individual is the "rational soul," the truth-seeking or wisdom-seeking self. Animals and plants, as well as men, have appetitive souls and many animals have spirited souls, as evident in spirited horses and brave dogs. But the crown of man's being is his reason.

Now what is a just, righteous, or virtuous man? A good saw is obviously one which performs well the function of a saw, that is cutting. Similarly, a good man is one whose functions are well-developed and operating at their best. Such a man is one whose appetitive soul is directed to wholesome pleasures in right proportion, so that they truly build up the person. This virtue is *temperance*. Likewise his aggressive, self-risking tendencies are strong and well-directed, that is, he has *courage*. So also his reason is effective in its quest so that he exemplifies the virtue of *wisdom* or *prudence*. Finally, the whole man is well-coordinated so that his wise reason directs his temperate enjoyments and brave adventures in harmonious action toward good ends. Such a man is just or righteous. He has, then, a fourth virtue, that of justice or righteousness (*dikaiosunē*).

In a way which many critics believe is illegitimate, Plato transfers this analysis from the individual to the state. Indeed, he has early shifted the discussion to the city-state, on the ground that it will be easier to delineate justice in the large than in the small expression of it in an individual. However, all the attention devoted to the state does not change the logic of argument from the nature of man to the definition of the good. Note that it is the various seeking functions of the *individual*, as Plato conceives him, which determine what are the true virtues. Since these four virtues, known as the cardinal virtues, have had a prominent influence in the ethical thought of every age since Plato's time, with or without the psychological theory on which Plato established them, it is apparent that his theory of natural law has been of first-rate importance.

The type of approach in which formulations of natural law are derived from analysis of the dynamics (or "drives") which are universally found in fully developed men may be called the theory or method of *psychological dynamic analysis*.

In *The Laws* Plato used considerable observation of the nature of human social and political relations, as well as the individual psychology already observed. This movement into social empiricism was developed much further in the thought of Aristotle.

3. *Aristotle*

Aristotle's principal ethical writing is in two parts which have come to us under the titles *The Nicomachean Ethics* and *The Politics*. The former is the effort to delineate the character or style of life in which a man finds his true happiness or well-being (*eudaimonia*). The sequel seeks to describe the form of political and social life in which such a personal life can best be cultivated.

He seeks to discover the character in which is true well-being by two methods, often confusingly joined. First he analyzes the individual soul or life, believing that the good life will actualize the potentials of these various psychological forces. The second method is to inquire widely concerning the pursuits in which people do in fact find most satisfaction.

Nature, in Aristotle's natural law ethics, is the humanity of man, including his instinctive desires, his inherently social interdependence, and his reason—but especially such aspects of his being as distinguish man from animals and other things.[6]

His psychological analysis finds two main parts or aspects of the soul (*psuchē*) or life, one the irrational, the other the rational. The irrational is, in turn, divided. One division "appears to be common to all living things, and of a vegetative nature: I refer to the part that causes nutrition and growth."[7] This nutritive part is a matter of no further relevance to ethics, Aristotle believes, "since it exhibits no specifically human excellence" (*ibid.*, I, xiii, 14).

In the irrational part there is another division which is active, conscious desire or will. It is more or less amenable to control by reason and needs training to bring conduct under rational guidance. It is also subject to the forming of habits. Good habits constitute good character, while evil habits constitute bad character and offer resistance to efforts to do good, even when a person clearly sees the desirability of the good.

The rational part of the soul is also divided, one division being practically oriented to quest for the best courses of action of the active will, while the other division is devoted to purely intellectual quest for truth.

Aristotle sees virtue as such habitual operations of the various aspects of the soul (or life) as best to secure happiness or well-being (*eudaimonia*). While he sometimes speaks of the four cardinal virtues defined by Plato, he redefines them and he introduces a number of others.

There are various forces or tendencies in man which are in opposition. Each one, if active without inhibition, goes to excess. To be in proper harmonious balance, needed for total well-being, a person must learn to develop habits which represent a "golden mean" between extremes. This mean is not a mathematically calculable mid-point between extremes, but as a degree of moderation requiring to be wisely

---

6. See *Nicomachean Ethics*, I. Cf. Johannes Messner, *Social Ethics*, pp. 15–17.
7. *Nicomachean Ethics*, I, xiii, 11.

chosen and learned in each instance, with due consideration of all the relevant factors.[8]

Thus the virtue of temperance is neither indulgence nor ascetic self-abuse, but prudential control of eating, drinking, and other pleasures. Courage is neither foolhardiness nor cowardice but willingness to take risks proportionate to purposes to be achieved and the necessities of the occasion.

The principle of the mean is not applicable to all actions or dispositions. Aristotle uses as illustrations "malice, shamelessness, envy [all dispositions] and, of actions, adultery, theft, murder." Regarding these, he says,

> It is impossible . . . ever to go right in regard to them—one must always be wrong; nor does right or wrong in their cases depend on the circumstances, for instance, whether one commits adultery with the right woman, at the right time, and in the right manner; the mere commission of any of them is wrong.   [*Ibid.*, II, vi, 18]

Moreover, it must not be supposed that Aristotle is content with a moderate amount of virtue. Moral virtues can be described as themselves means between certain extremes, but when one identifies a virtue one is not to avoid the excess of its achievement. For

> while in respect of its substance and the definition that states what it really is in essence virtue is the observance of the mean, in point of excellence and rightness it is an extreme.   [*Ibid.*, II, vi, 17]

For similar reason, the principle of the mean does not pertain to the virtues of reason, whether the moral virtues of practical wisdom or the dianoetic virtues of the pure intellect. Wisdom and truth are not means.

In the second part of his ethical work, *The Politics*, Aristotle studies the actual constitutions of existing city-states, of which he had caused one hundred fifty-eight to be compiled for this purpose.[9] He criticizes various existing constitutions and some proposed schemes, like the one set forth in Plato's *Republic*, and out of his critical comparisons seeks to bring sound instructions for good government and society. There is much emphasis on empirical observation, and Aristotle rejects the

8. This is true despite Aristotle's contrary introductory account of the meaning of a mean (*ibid.*, II, vi, 4–7). Note II, vi, 7–15 and II, viii, 6–8.

9. See editorial comment in Aristotle, *The Nicomachean Ethics with an English Translation* by H. Rackham (Cambridge: Harvard University Press, 1934), p. 642, footnote b. Unfortunately, only one, the constitution of Athens, is now known to us, that one discovered in 1890.

notion that a single constitution or even a certain type of constitution would be most desirable in every city. Much depends on the relative proportions, education, and power of different classes.

This kind of natural law ethics is so characteristic of its famous author and so complex in its various phases that it may, perhaps, be best designated as the Aristotelian theory. We might also speak of it as a *pragmatic, empirical, psychosocial* theory. At the same time we must remember that the inclination to frequent pragmatic adaptability did not prevent Aristotle from believing in some absolute ethical laws. Some of these are as general as the principle that good government serves the happiness (or well-being) of its citizens, and some are as specific as the law that adultery is wrong under all circumstances.

4. The Stoics

The form in which ancient Greek natural law ethics most deeply influenced early Christian tradition was developed by the Stoics, though later Aristotle's views assumed larger place.

Founded by Zeno of Citium about 308 B.C., Stoicism was a philosophical movement mainly concerned with ethics. The various writers differed considerably in their metaphysical doctrines and in the details of ethics, but were in general agreement on certain broad outlines of emphasis. The movement came to its full flower between the first century B.C. and the second century A.D., among the Romans, through the writings of the Greek slave Epictetus, and the Romans Cicero, Seneca, and Emperor Marcus Aurelius. Some of its basic ideas and of its specific teachings were congenial to some of the Church Fathers, and so it readily penetrated Christian thinking.

One of the best statements concerning natural law to be found in Stoic literature is by Cicero:

> True law is right reason in agreement with Nature; it is of universal application, unchanging and everlasting; it summons to duty by its commands, and averts from wrong-doing by its prohibitions. . . . We cannot be freed from its obligations by Senate or People, and we need not look outside ourselves for an expounder or interpreter of it. . . . One eternal and unchangeable law will be valid for all nations and for all times, and there will be one master and one ruler, that is, God, for He is the author of this law, its promulgator, and its enforcing judge.[10]

Natural law, so conceived, is not grounded simply in the nature of man or of human society, but rather in the whole of "Nature," conceived as an all-inclusive, rational divine Being, or as ruled throughout by the divine reason.

10. *De Republica*, III, xxii, 33; quoted by d'Entrèves, *Natural Law*, p. 21.

A common Stoic injunction is to "follow Nature." This does not mean to do "what comes naturally," that is to follow impulse. Far from it! It means to do what reason requires, regardless of inclination or consequences. The supreme virtue of the Stoic is *ataraxia*, a calm, unperturbed, passionless frame of mind. This is to be attained by rigorously trained self-discipline and meditation on the divine, rational order of all being. Thus Marcus Aurelius speaks of

> One Universe made up of all that is; and one God in it all, and one principle of Being, and one Law, the Reason, shared by all thinking creatures, and one Truth.   [*Meditations*, VII, 9]

Because all that one confronts is under control of God who is supreme reason and good, I must learn to accept all that happens to me as good. There is then no room for peevishness, discouragement, or anger. Moreover, since every man is intended by God for a rational and happy life, I must respect every man. If he is evil, he is to be pitied and instructed, not hated nor injured.[11]

The same author expresses a foremost principle of Stoicism when he says that "there is nothing good or evil save in the will."[12]

The Stoic theory of natural law, then, is characterized by the quest for calmness of mind, to be obtained by self-disciplined obedience to Nature, conceived as universal, all-encompassing Reason. Moreover, it is less concerned with the particular acts which a person may perform than with the rational, independent intent of his will. This is to say that it is a formal ethics.

In distinction from the other views examined, we may describe the Stoic approach to natural law ethics as a mainly *formal, pantheistic,* and *rationalistic* theory.

However, the most important entry of natural law as understood by the Stoics into later Christian and legal tradition was through the *Corpus Iuris Civilis* (Body of Civil Law) compiled under the Christian emperor Justinian I in the sixth century. The countries which live under Roman or Roman-Dutch law today, especially on the Continent of Europe and in southern Africa, are subject to many of the laws formulated by Justinian or under his orders. Even more important to the modern world is the idea of a universal law which is at the heart of the important part of the *Corpus* which was to be applied, not only to Roman citizens (who were subject to the *Ius Civile*), but also to all other persons whom trade or conquest brought within Roman jurisdiction. Such law, applicable to all concerning whose actions or af-

11. See Epictetus, *That We Ought Not to be Affected by Things Not in Our Own Power*, 24.

12. *In What Manner We Ought to Bear Sickness*, III, 10.

fairs Roman judges had to decide, was called *Ius Gentium* (Law of Nations).

It seemed reasonable to expect anyone to obey the relatively simple requirements of the *Ius Gentium*. The idea of such universal law was a heritage from Greek and Roman Stoic thought. Certainly in the commending of the Law of Nations to later generations, the appeal to natural law ideas was often explicit and clear.

C. ROMAN CATHOLIC THOUGHT

1. Before Thomas Aquinas

Augustine is an unequivocal advocate of a natural law doctrine. One of his clearest statements on the subject is as follows:

> Sin, then, is any transgression in deed, or word, or desire, of the eternal law. And the eternal law is the divine order or will of God, which requires the preservation of natural order, and forbids the breach of it. But what is this natural order in man?[13]

He goes on to answer, and concludes,

> Therefore, as the soul is superior to the body, so in the soul itself the reason is superior by the law of nature to the other parts which are found also in beasts; and in reason itself, which is partly contemplation and partly action, contemplation is unquestionably the superior part. [*Ibid.*]

Augustine appeals to this doctrine of natural law to support his teaching that we are created for the contemplation and love of God. He does not elaborate natural law ethics into a system. He uses it, not to give moral instruction, but rather as an apologetic device to point to man's need for God's grace to complete the natural order of his own being, that is, as Lehmann would say, to make human life human and mature.

Natural law was made the basis, however, of the earliest codification of law by the Church, the *Decretum Gratiani* (mid-twelfth century). In that work natural law is described as absolutely binding and above all other laws. This is because it represents the decrees of God himself and "came into existence with the very creation of man as a rational being," and "remains unchangeable."[14]

13. *Reply to Faustus the Manichean* (about 400 A.D.), XXII, 27.
14. *Decretum Gratiani*, P.I, dist. v, I, 1. Quoted in d'Entrèves, *Natural Law*, p. 34.

In Justinian's *Corpus*, while Roman law had been commended to the public as the work of reason, that is, natural law in the Stoic sense, there had been no suggestion that any Roman law should be disobeyed or was nullified if found in violation of natural law. In contrast to the *Corpus* is the explicit declaration of the *Decretum Gratiani* in which we read:

> Natural law absolutely prevails in dignity over customs and constitutions. Whatever has been recognized by usage, or laid down in writing, if it contradicts natural law, must be considered null and void.[15]

Such doctrine can be and has been used as ground both for revolution (as in the *American Declaration of Independence*) and for support of civil disobedience, as by Henry David Thoreau during the Mexican War, by James Russell Lowell in his poem "On the Capture of some Fugitive Slaves Near Washington," and by Martin Luther King, Jr., in various speeches and writings of the 1960's. Lowell expressed this theme especially vividly when he wrote,

> Man is more than Constitutions; better rot beneath the sod,
> Than be true to Church and State while we are doubly false
>   to God!

> We owe allegiance to the State; but deeper, truer, more,
> To the sympathies that God hath set within our spirit's core;
> Our country claims our fealty; we grant it so, but then,
> Before Man made us citizens, great Nature made us men.

The idea of natural law as supreme and eternal, rightly determining both the content of positive law and even, in some conditions, the individual's decision whether to obey positive law, was brought to new heights of development in the work of St. Thomas Aquinas. His formulation has dominated subsequent Roman Catholic thought. It is under intense critical reexamination by Catholic theologians today.

2. Thomas Aquinas

Natural law in the broad sense is defined by Thomas as follows:

> Granted that the world is ruled by divine Providence . . . it is evident that the whole community of the universe is governed by God's mind. Therefore the ruling idea of things which exists in God as the effective sovereign of them all has the nature of law.[16]

15. *Decretum Gratiani*, I, viii, 2. Quoted by d'Entrèves, *loc. cit.*
16. *Summa Theologiae*, 1a2ae, 91, 1. Blackfriars, Vol. 28, p. 19.

The law of nature, so understood, governs all things, but in different ways suited to their natures. Thus we must take note of "non-rational creatures, which act for an end solely through a driving determinism, unlike man who reasons and wills how to act for an end" (1a2ae. 91, 2. Blackfriars Vol. 28, p. 21).

Strictly speaking, natural law is, for Thomas, one kind within the more inclusive Eternal Law or Eternal Reason. The Eternal Law is the whole of God's purposive plan for all his creatures. As far as human beings are concerned it is God's all-encompassing purpose for men, including the plan of redemption and the promise of eternal bliss. Within the Eternal Law, the natural law directs men "only to an end not beyond their natural abilities" (p. 29. 1a2ae. 91.4). This law, therefore, is innate in man's own nature, as he is, and is knowable by every normal adult, through the proper development of his understanding, even though his immaturity, sin, or bad instruction may keep him from this knowledge.

God wills that men should, for the governance of their societies and the moral education of all men, enact positive, or human, law, with provisions for its enforcement. Human law must be solidly based upon natural law. If it opposes natural law it is invalid.

Neither human law nor natural law would give a human being knowledge of that part of Eternal Law which directs him to his eternal goal. For men

> are set towards an eternal happiness out of proportion to their natural resources, . . . and therefore must needs be directed by a divinely given law above natural and human law.   [1a2ae. 91, 4. Vol. 28, p. 29]

This divine law is given by revelation. It is never contrary to natural law, but reinforces and supplements it.

As man seeks to formulate natural law, he must depend, not only on his reason, but also on observation of human nature. What does he find? The answer given by Thomas is momentous for subsequent history, having much to do with some of the teachings and omissions of Catholic instruction which are most offensive to many Protestants and also most criticized by contemporary Catholic thinkers. Thomas Aquinas writes as follows:

> The order in which commands of the law of nature are ranged corresponds to that of our natural tendencies. Here there are three stages. There is in man, first, a tendency towards the good of the nature he has in common with all substances; each has an appetite to preserve its own natural being. Natural law here plays a corresponding part, and is engaged at this stage to maintain and defend the elementary requirements of human life.
>
> Secondly, there is in man a bent towards things which accord with

his nature considered more specifically, that is, in terms of what he has in common with other animals; correspondingly those matters are said to be of natural law which nature teaches all animals, for instance the coupling of male and female, the bringing up of the young, and so forth.

Thirdly, there is in man an appetite for the good of his nature as rational, and this is proper for him, for instance, that he should know truths about God and about living in society.   [1a2ae. 94, 2. Vol. 28, pp. 81–83]

It might be expected that Thomas and all who have followed in his tradition would make the third "stage" of man's "natural tendencies" decisive in natural law ethics. Would not the needs or tendencies of reason, and knowledge about God and society, be regarded as superior to instinctive animal behavior?

The historical fact is not so simple. According to Thomas, the one primary precept is simply "that good is to be sought and done, evil to be avoided" (1a2ae. 94, 2. Vol. 28, p. 83).

But what is the good to be sought and the evil to be avoided? In answering this question for the positive law of states, the Thomists rely on natural law, and especially that based on the second stage, that is the instinctive drives which man "has in common with other animals." Even canon law has been much influenced by this emphasis, especially in regulations concerning marriage.

The stress on man's animal nature as basis of natural law and hence of legislation by the state is in accord with the teachings of Ulpian, a Roman jurist who lived in the third century A.D. and whose writings bulk larger than those of any other man in the *Digest* (or juridical comment) included in Justinian's *Corpus Iuris Civilis*. Ulpian had written,

Natural law is that which nature has taught all animals; this law indeed is not peculiar to the human race, but belongs to all animals. . . .[17]

Ulpian makes the animality of man basic for natural law, hence for Roman law; then he adds man's rationality.

This is the main explanation for the traditional Catholic teaching that the purpose of sexual intercourse, in the law of nature, is reproduction and hence birth control is sin. In this teaching the significance of sex in the development and expression of full personal love between a man and his wife is ignored because that significance is not observed as a universal law of animal nature.

This stress on man's biological nature, rather than on his rational

17. *Digest*, I,i,1. Quoted by d'Entrèves, *op. cit.*, pp. 24–25.

and spiritual nature, is also the ground of the distinction, in Roman Catholic teaching, between sins contrary to nature and sins according to nature. Sins against nature are regarded as generally worse than sins according to nature. Hence homosexuality or sodomy of any kind is a sin "against nature," while adultery or even rape is "according to nature," because the physical relations in the latter conform to common animal practice, although in these instances the meanings of these relations as understood by the *rational* animal man are contrary to proper social order.[18]

3. Recent Roman Catholic Thought

In Vatican Council II, many critical doubts about long-standing moral teachings of the Church and traditional Thomistic theory of natural law came to new expression and were given authoritative standing among Roman Catholics.

The pronouncements of the Council did not cast doubt on the reality of a sound ethics accessible to both Christian and non-Christian. Indeed, the belief in such moral truth was reaffirmed. One thing modified is the cocksure assumption that the truth about all moral problems is already known to the Church in her long-established formulas which await only acceptance and application. Both the reaffirmation and the new humility are well represented in such statements as the following:

> Through loyalty to conscience Christians are joined to other men in search for truth and for the right solution to so many moral problems which arise both in the life of individuals and from social relationships.[19]

Another highly important change is in the concept of law itself and its relation to Christian love. We have observed that the moral instruction and even much of the canon law of the Roman Catholic Church are formed largely from elements of ancient Roman law. Specifically Christian teachings had not so much altered its substance and juridical spirit as added to its prohibitions and penalties, as in designating the

18. I am especially indebted to Charles E. Curran, of Catholic University School of Sacred Theology, for calling attention to the rationale of these teachings as influenced by Ulpian and Roman law, in lectures at Wesley Theological Seminary in the spring semester of 1968. Cf. Curran's criticism of traditional frequent exclusive concern with "the physical structure of the act," in his recent book, *Contemporary Problems in Moral Theology* (Notre Dame: Fides Publishers, 1970), pp. 142–48.

19. *Schema 13, The Pastoral Constitution on the Church in the Modern World*, Art. 16. Quoted by W. H. M. Van der Marck, *Toward a Christian Ethic: A Renewal in Moral Theology* (New York: Newman Press, c. 1967), p. 20.

awful penalties for missing Sunday Mass or for any of many faults a priest might commit in the liturgy. Vatican Council II opened the way to see these things in a new light.

Bernard Häring, one of the consultants who helped produce the liberating effect of the Council, continues to stress the need for change in approach. He protests, for example, the practice of moralists in the last century, whereby they treated the sacraments after the Decalogue. He continues,

> Nolding and Prummer together find about 200 laws of the Church ruling the reception and administration of the Sacraments and the liturgical vestments that have the sanctions of eternal ruin attached to their violation. . . . This, of course, is not the Christian approach to the Sacraments. . . .
>
> It seems that many priests administer the Sacraments with great anxiety because they fear all the sins they could commit while administering them.[20]

It is not that Catholic teaching has had nothing to say about love. Häring goes to the heart of the matter when he writes,

> When one concentrates on casuistry on a juridical plane without the guiding light of love, it is of little help to preface it or to add a postscript to the effect that love is the primary consideration and should mould the Christian life. [*Ibid.*, p. 76]

Häring and other Roman Catholics who are taking such liberalizing positions are not renouncing natural law or canon law. They are seeking to free the teaching of both from the rigid structures given to the tradition under the influence of the ancient law of the Roman Empire, and so to eliminate from tradition the substantial contradiction between law and Christian love.

Currently, many Catholic moralists are trying to work out a more dynamic conception of natural law. Thus, Charles E. Curran writes, "Too often in the past Catholic writings have implied that the natural law consists in detailed norms and exact rules for human conduct. Such is not the case."[21]

As Curran points out, there are in the writings of Thomas Aquinas more provisions for flexibility and dynamism in legal theory than most Thomist teachers have recognized until recently.

Thomas Aquinas distinguished at times between primary and sec-

---

20. *Toward a Christian Moral Theology* (Notre Dame: Notre Dame Press, 1966), p. 71.
21. *Christian Morality Today* (Notre Dame: Fides Publishers, 1966), p. 79.

ondary precepts of natural law. Primary precepts, when accurately formulated and understood, are general, universal, and unchanging. Secondary precepts are less general, are nearer to the particular choice, and more dependent on a concrete historical social condition and situation. He says,

> Some human actions need a great deal of consideration of all the various circumstances, of which not everyone is capable, but only those endowed with wisdom.   [*Summa Theologiae*, 1a2ae, 100, 1. Vol. 29, p. 59]

R. A. Armstrong believes that Thomistic principles even justify the belief that some kinds of acts which were right at one stage in human history may be made quite wrong by changes in human society. As an example he speaks of changes which the invention of the hydrogen bomb makes necessary in just war theory.[22]

In view of all the past pronouncements of the Roman Catholic Church on innumerable matters of prescriptive moral law, what do such teachings do to the idea that the Church's moral teaching is infallible and unchanging? Some, like Häring, would stress the changing of scholarly interpretation, "the inventions of the moralists," as distinguished from "the teachings of the church."[23] Others, like Curran himself, speak more boldly and candidly. Thus, Curran writes that

> the traditional teaching of the Church on some points in the past has changed; for example, religious liberty, usury, cooperation with other religions, the love-union value of marriage and marital sexuality, the concept of servile work as a violation of the meaning of Sunday. Why the change? . . . In all the examples mentioned above the experience of Christian people seems to have been the primary factor in the change of the traditional teaching. The Holy Spirit is the primary teacher in the Church, but the Spirit does teach in the lives of the faithful in whom she dwells.   [*Op. cit.*, p. 90]

This is the new mood of Roman Catholic teaching on moral law, and it is found reflected in every discussion where the younger learned scholars are grappling with current issues.

In this mood natural law is still vigorously defended, if one understands "natural law" to mean ethical truth to be discovered by human beings through rational reflection on experience. But modest claims are made regarding knowledge of such truth, and concerning the precise

22. *Primary and Secondary Precepts in Thomistic Natural Law Teaching* (The Hague: Martinus Nijhoff, 1966), pp. 178–79. Cf. Michael Cronin, *The Science of Ethics*, p. 611; A. D. Sertillanges, *La philosophie morale de Saint Thomas d'Aquinas* (9th ed., Pains, 1961), pp. 110–22. Cf. *Summa Theologiae*, 1a2ae, 95, 2, 2, and Messner's comment on it in *Social Ethics*, p. 275, n. 16.

23. *Toward a Christian Moral Theology*, p. 87.

accuracy of its formulation. There is much doubt expressed, in these circles, concerning the wisdom of stating specific prescriptive rules on a wide variety of concrete actions.

Even such revised and limited concepts of natural law and of rational ethics, however, would be rejected by many Protestant writers.

D. CRITICAL REJECTION OF NATURAL LAW ETHICS

Protestants have not invariably rejected the belief in natural law. Indeed, John Calvin was quite explicit in his affirmation of it. Commenting on Romans 2:14, 15, he writes,

> If the Gentiles have naturally the righteousness of the law engraven on their minds, we certainly cannot say that they are altogether ignorant how they ought to live. And no sentiment is more commonly admitted, than that man is sufficiently instructed in the right rule of life by that natural law of which the Apostle there speaks.   [*Institutes*, Book II, Chap. II, xxii]

But alas! this knowledge of natural law does not guide men into the good life and so to their salvation. "The end of the law of nature, therefore, is, that man may be rendered inexcusable" (*ibid.*).

After Calvin has spoken of the law given through Moses, he defines the famous threefold "use of what is called the moral law" (*ibid.*, Book II, Chap. VII, vi). In this connection he does not explicitly refer to natural knowledge of the law, but the uses would seem to refer to moral law known by nature as well as by Old Testament revelation.

The first use is to convict man of sin, and so, through his fearful sense of guilt, turn him to Christ, in whom alone is salvation (*ibid.*, vi–ix). The second is to restrain men from the more extreme expressions of their sinful nature which, without restraint, would altogether disrupt society and destroy "public tranquility" (*ibid.*, x–xi). The third use is to assist "the faithful," who, although devoted to Christ and seeking to please God, profit by the instruction of the law concerning the life and conduct which do in fact please him (*ibid.*, xii–xvii).

Even Martin Luther, although generally suspicious or hostile toward rational philosophy and ethics, yet had left a place for natural law. Usually he treated both moral law and civil law as useful only for showing a man his inescapable evil, so bringing him in desperation to God's grace.

Yet Luther appeals to observations of nature to support his teachings of Christian conduct also. Thus, he says "Nature teaches" the need for a weekly day of rest.[24] From observation of the means by which the wealth of humanity can be truly increased, he argues against usury and commercial wealth,[25] and by observing the sexual nature of men and women he argues against the deprecation of marriage by the Roman Church.[26] The three uses taught by Calvin can all be found illustrated in the writings of Luther.

Nevertheless, the main movement of thought in the Reformers is away from natural law theory and toward an exclusive reliance upon Scripture for ethical truth. Without formulating codes of moral law, both Reformers write much on the life and conduct which God requires. In such moral instruction both men rely mostly on the Bible, especially the Decalogue as interpreted and supplemented by other passages of Scripture.

The principal motif of their ethical emphasis is the necessity of giving up all trust in man, his reason, his conduct, his desires, and his will, and putting all hope in God's righteousness and mercy as given in Jesus Christ. Fallen man is so utterly depraved and lost in sin that neither his reason nor his will has any soundness to serve as base for a holy life.

According to Thomas Aquinas, sinful man's knowledge of the law is imperfect, but it is still partially sound and partially effective (*Summa Theologiae*, 1a2ae. 93, 6).

Calvin, on the other hand, maintains that "the early fathers" gave too much credit to the power of fallen man to reason correctly, to exercise free choice, and so, to some extent, to do good. They made these concessions to the philosophers at the expense of the biblical teaching, he said, in order to avoid too great offense to the philosophers and to avoid influencing sinful men to be even more sinful (*Institutes*, Book II, Chap. II, iv). By the teaching of Scriptures men are totally corrupt so that no aspect of human nature is left in a sound condition.

Even though God in his mercy has given to all men some ability to discriminate between good and evil, he has given unsaved men only such moral knowledge as to convict them of sin. Man's reason is at best far from being able to know unaided "the principal points in the first table" of the Decalogue, while even the laws of the second table are known inadequately (*ibid.*, xxiv). Certainly Calvin would not dream of building an ethical system of knowledge of natural law gained by the wretched, corrupt reason of fallen man. Much less would he consent to erection of canon law even partly on such a base when the Bible is available.

24. *The Larger Catechism*, Exposition of the Third Commandment.
25. *Open Letter to the Christian Nobility*.
26. A sermon of 1545, on marriage, given in part by George W. Forell in *Christian Social Teachings* (Garden City, N.Y.: Doubleday & Company, 1966), p. 169.

The leaders of the Crisis Theology in this century, Karl Barth and Emil Brunner, as they revived the main themes of the Reformation, went beyond both Calvin and Luther in stressing the corruption of man's reason. Impressed by the terrible events in Central Europe during the World Wars, and influenced by Sören Kierkegaard, they denied that fallen man had any sound knowledge of God or any true knowledge of moral law.

Brunner has given with special care reasons for rejecting all ethics of natural law. He points out that different philosophers have presented differing and even contrary ethical ideas. He contends that "natural ethics" leads inevitably into antinomies which man's reason is unable to resolve—the need to base ethics on the idea of duty but also on the idea of the good; to believe in freedom but also in necessity; to accept individualism but also universalism; to center attention on what is but also on what ought to be. Moreover, natural or rational ethical life is a form of man's idolatrous faith in himself rather than in God. Hence philosophical or natural law ethics cannot be a partner of Christian ethics, but must be wholly rejected.

Of course the contextualists and the situationists or champions of "the new morality," discussed in Chapter Two, likewise generally reject natural law theory.

On the other hand, there has been much modern systematic philosophical effort to discover moral law independent of the Roman natural law tradition. Much of it has not used the term "natural law" in describing itself. More commonly it has been called philosophical ethics, theoretical ethics, rational ethics, or simply ethics, in distinction from Christian, revealed, or theological ethics. Many Protestants have participated in such thought and some do so today. Now that many Roman Catholic scholars are freeing themselves from commitment to Thomistic tradition, they, too, are showing increasing interest in these various types of modern ethics. Indeed, substantial work on philosophical ethics independent of natural law tradition is being done by such Catholic scholars as Karl Rahner, O. P. Van der Marck, and Robert O. Johann.

We must here review some modern types of philosophical ethics and then, against the background of that review, I will sketch out what appears to me a particularly promising ethical approach.

E.   Modern Philosophical Ethics Before 1900

Ethical theories may be classified as *formal* or *material*. A formal ethics judges the moral quality of a choice according to the subjective rational structure of a person's intent. A material ethics is concerned with the act performed or intended and its relations to the world outside the structure of subjective thought behind the intent. Typically, a formal ethicist wants to know whether my present choice is consistent with my ideals and with other choices I am making. The material ethicist inquires what will be the consequences of my choice, what it will do to my health, my relations with other people, the structure of the community, and the lives of all the people affected by it.

1. Kantian Formalism. Immanuel Kant (1724–1804) teaches that there is nothing "which can be called good without qualification, except a good will."[27] Skill, knowledge, beauty, and anything else anyone can name, he contends, can be misused and so be made evil. A good will alone is intrinsically and invariably good. The goodness of an act does not depend, then, upon its consequences, even upon its success in achieving its intended end, but solely on the intent of the will itself. The intent is not to be confused with the motive or emotional drive supporting the choice. The intent is not feeling or emotion, but the meaning of the choice in the mind of the person willing.

If we are to have a science of the good will (ethics), then we must, as in every other science, be guided by reason. The good will must be rational, that is, consistent. Hence the ruling principle of ethics must be a complete inner consistency of choice. Kant states this principle as "the categorical imperative": *"Act only on that maxim whereby thou canst at the same time will that it should become a universal law"* (*ibid.*, Section Two).

From the categorical imperative Kant deduces various corollaries of which we may here mention three.

Duty is always autonomous, never heteronomous, that is, a person is bound to choose according to a maxim which he himself—not someone else—is willing to see made universal in the action of all people. To make a certain choice against one's own reason, thus introducing self-contradiction into one's own intent, because someone else begs or commands that choice, is to act heteronomously—that is, as ruled by another—and is to disobey the categorical imperative. This is moral evil.

Since every person is similarly under a law of moral autonomy, both a subject and a legislator of moral law, he must be accorded proper respect as a possessor of dignity. "So act as to treat humanity, whether in thine own person or in that of any other, in every case as an end withal, never as a means only" (*ibid.*).

Not all of Kant's deductions are in such general or abstract terms.

27. Opening words of Section One in *Foundation of the Metaphysic of Ethics.*

One of his most famous ventures into specific moral prescription is his inference that a person must always, regardless of circumstances, tell the truth. This follows, he maintains, from the categorical imperative. To lie is to introduce contradiction between one's own inner and outer affirmations and so to do evil.

Kant's ethics is often charged with being self-centered and idolatrous because of the emphasis on autonomy. This charge seems unjust. Kant does not hold that a man may do whatever he pleases, but that he must be subject to the requirements of rational consistency. Arbitrary thinking about his conduct is as false as arbitrary thinking about mathematics.

A more serious criticism is that formal ethics is not enough. The paranoiac may have a highly systematized set of delusions, all quite consistent internally, but in conflict with reality. Only the relating of his system to data of experience can disclose the untruth.

In Christian context, even if a man is doing the best he knows how, when he lives or acts in opposition to God's will, he is committing sin —even though he "sins unwittingly" (Num. 15:27-29) and this is a less grave moral offense than when he sins "with a high hand" (Num. 15:30). When a person is seeking to know his duty in a difficult situation, it is not enough to consult his own thought; he must know how to bring the facts of experience to bear on his problem. A logic of internal consistency alone is as inadequate for ethics as for natural science.

Despite the defects, Kantian ethics offers positive and important values.

Although consistency of willing is not enough, it is essential to any responsible life. No principle or theme or motif of conduct has positive moral value if I assume freedom to regard and disregard it at will. Sincerity is far from being the only important moral virtue, but without the accompaniment of sincerity how seriously could any other virtue be taken? Sincerity is another name for internal consistency of intent.

Kant's interpretation of this rational consistency as implying the willingness to subject one's self to the same standard one applies to others parallels the Golden Rule: "Whatever you wish that men would do to you, do so to them" (Matt. 7:12), and also various other New Testament teachings (e.g. Matt. 7:2; Rom. 2:1, 21-23).

2. Hedonism. The theory that we ought to seek happiness, understood as maximum of pleasure and minimum of pain, is obviously a material, not a formal theory. Such a view, in various forms, has been philosophically formulated by many thinkers in ancient and modern times.

Hedonistic theories divide on the question whose pleasure I am obliged to seek. The two most famous ancient Greek hedonists agreed in answering, "Mine!"

Aristippus (c. 435–356 B.C.) favored a person's seeking the most intense pleasure in the greatest quantity he could get, without much concern for later consequences, since the future is uncertain at best.

Epicurus (c. 342–270 B.C.) believed that such recklessness as Aristippus had recommended was not wise. It would keep one from enjoyment of some especially satisfying pleasure and would cause too much unrest and pain of mind and body. It is better, he thought, to enjoy pleasures of the body in moderation, and to prefer generally the pleasures of knowledge, friendship, art, and the like, which do not lead quickly to satiety and even pain or disgust. However, the life is still to be centered on pleasure of the self. Hence if a friend who has given me much pleasure becomes ill, I must soon appraise his chances of recovery. If he is probably to recover in time, I should be loyal in attending him so that he will be drawn to me in gratitude and give me renewed and even increased pleasure in the future. If he is doomed to slow fading away in misery, then my visiting him will only make me unhappy, so I should drop him.

We might ask whether "friendship" on such terms as Epicurus prescribes would be true friendship at all and so doubt that a true Epicurean could ever know the higher joys which friendship can bring. Moreover, if every person seeks his own pleasure, as Epicurus advocates, there will be no one to bear the heavy responsibilities of community leadership (and Epicurus specifically advises against office holding in government). In the anarchy and economic chaos which will follow, few if any will long be able to find much pleasure.

Jeremy Bentham (1748–1832) revived hedonistic theory more than two thousand years after Epicurus. As a government official, he advocated laws calculated to produce "the greatest happiness for the greatest number." In such calculation, he maintained, one should take account of the number of pleasures, the certainty, intensity, duration, purity (without admixture of pain), number of persons enjoying them, and productiveness of further pleasure.

John Stuart Mill (1806–1873) brought to a climax the thought of the hedonistic school of thought which Bentham had launched and which is commonly known as utilitarianism. He sought to root the altruistic aspect of this theory in psychological observations of man's social nature. Personal happiness is to be found only by the right kinds of social involvements. The duty of a man is to seek his pleasure, but to seek it through serving the pleasure of all persons affected by his action.

Our duty, however, is not only to seek the *most* pleasure and least pain for all. It is also important that we give preference to the higher *types* of pleasure. A man who has experienced both the pleasures of sense and the higher pleasures of the spirit knows that the latter are to be preferred. In fact,

> It is better to be a human being dissatisfied than a pig satisfied; better to be Socrates dissatisfied than a fool satisfied. And if the fool, or the pig, are of a different opinion, it is because they only know their own side of the question. The other party to the comparison knows both sides. [*Utilitarianism*, Chap. 2]

In this contention, as in some others, while Mill makes hedonism more persuasive, he significantly modifies it. If some kinds of pleasure are preferable, not because *as pleasure* they are more intense, enduring, or productive, but because of their quality, then something besides pleasure *per se* is being considered. As hedonism reaches a climax in the thought of J. S. Mill, it also begins to pass over into a more inclusive kind of ethical theory.

What remains is a strong empirical emphasis, a concern for personal and social consequences as appraised in actual experience. These elements must reappear in any ethical theory which is to be acceptable.

3. Hegel. In ethics as in other divisions of his philosophy, Hegel uses his famous dialectical method. The right, of which ethics is in search, has to do with action and action flows from impulse. However, impulse is chaotic, frequently contradictory, and often destroys man's freedom of choice. Hence the search must turn from impulse to reason, which is needed to control and direct the otherwise impulsive and irrational will. The right, then, must be the rational impulse of an individual. But the individual is not sufficient to himself. It is impossible for him to direct his will rationally or even to be a real person without involvement in external relations with other people. Such relations can be rationally ordered only in a social group.

The family answers this need and so the right must be found in an ordered family. But the family, again, is inadequate in itself. It realizes its own rational ends only in relation to other families and other social institutions. Thus we move from family, through civil society, to state government. Unfortunately states, however orderly in themselves, produce international disorder. So, we read,

> This actual and organic mind (σ) of a single nation (β) reveals and actualizes itself through the inter-relation of the particular national

minds until (γ) in the process of world-history it reveals and actualizes itself as the universal world-mind whose right is supreme.[28]

Hegel's ethics is, then, at the same time, a philosophy of history. This fact became especially important to mankind when Karl Marx adopted Hegel's method for his own philosophy of history, while inverting the dialectic so that the materialistic and economic factors would be regarded as all-controlling, instead of the "World Spirit" as in Hegel's thought.

In specifying the particulars of his ethics and philosophy of history at all stages, Hegel is concerned with social order which involves also maximum real participation of individuals in the organic whole of the society. This requires monogamy (*ibid.*, Sec. 167), obedience to the law (Sec. 221), provision for overcoming all poverty—mostly by laissez-faire economy (Sec. 245), and a kind of superstate which looks too totalitarian for comfort, even though he says that it holds the loyalty of its citizens "in the fact that individuals have duties to the state in proportion as they have rights against it" (Sec. 261).

Hegel's triadic dialectic becomes at times a Procustean bed, forcing on history and on human nature grand generalizations which his data —and ours—do not support.

Perhaps his most valuable and permanent contribution to ethics is his insistence that to determine the right one must take into account the widest possible range of data. Truth is distinguished from falsehood by being consistent with all known facts and by being most positively and meaningfully related to a great variety of data. So, in ethics, a right course of action is distinguished from wrong by introducing a minimum of conflict between different objectives desired and a maximum of support for fulfillment of a wide range of desires of individual and community. Such a search for coherence in ethical consideration will be further discussed in the chapter which follows.

F.   RECENT PHILOSOPHICAL VIEWS

In the present century many philosophers have continued to develop constructive philosophical ethics in continuity with the thought of Hegel and other thinkers of the nineteenth century. Among these should be named such men as Wilbur M. Urban, Brand Blanshard, and Paul Weiss, while others, like David Baumgardt and Max Carl Otto, in their different ways gave modern versions of the Epicurean ethics of

---

28. *Philosophy of Right*, Section 33. Tr. by T. M. Knox in *Great Books of the Western World*, Robert M. Hutchins, ed. (Chicago: Encyclopaedia Britannica, Inc., 1952), Vol. 46, p. 20. The rest of the book spells this out in detail.

pleasure or the ethics of quest for happiness in the more elevated and critical sense of Aristotle.

There have also been some characteristic new approaches, and we must look briefly at three of these.

1. Analytic Theory of Ethical Language.   The moral skepticism of C. L. Stevenson and other analytic thinkers was mentioned earlier. Although there were anticipations of such views in the thought of the ancient Sophists, this recent moral skepticism is usually traced to the "emotive theory" of Alfred Jules Ayer. In his now famous work, *Language, Truth and Logic,* first published in 1936, Ayer wrote that

> in every case in which one would commonly be said to be making an ethical judgment, the function of the relevant ethical word is purely "emotive." It is used to express feeling about certain objects, but not to make any assertion about them.[29]

Hence ethical judgments "have no objective validity whatsoever" (*ibid.*).

R. M. Hare, much like Ayer, conceives of ethics as being "the logical study of the language of morals."[30] Moreover, he agrees with Ayer that moral judgments are not to be regarded logically as in the class of indicatives. But there ends the agreement. Hare objects to Ayer's assumption that indicatives hold a place of superior meaningfulness. Moral language is a special type of the class called "Prescriptive Language." Prescriptive language includes imperatives and value judgments. The latter, in turn, include nonmoral and moral value judgments.

A moral judgment, Hare contends, is always an appeal to a general prescriptive principle of a particular kind expressing moral compunction. Often this principle, or another principle from which it is derived, is generally accepted, and may have been accepted by many generations of people. This fact, he says, "is quite sufficient to account for the feeling we have that, when we appeal to a moral principle, we are appealing to something that is there already" (*ibid.*, p. 195). However, if the moral judgment is made in earnest, the maker must himself have adopted it as his own as Kant rightly understood (*ibid.*, p. 196).

The analysis of ethical language has led some but not all its practitioners to the moral skepticism of the emotive theory or even the degree of relativism represented by Hare. Frederick Ferré is a good example.[31] Although Ferré acknowledges the force of the analysts' argu-

---

29. Paperback edition (New York: Dover Publications, c. 1947), p. 108.
30. *The Language of Morals* (New York: Oxford University Press, 1964), Preface.
31. See his *Language, Logic and God* (New York: Harper & Row, 1961).

ments against the assertive validity of religious and ethical language, he does not rest in an emotive theory. He rejects Christian theism, but he believes in a religion of commitment to "integrity-in-community" concerning which he says, "In the Christian tradition it is called love."[32] That there is an objective obligation to such commitment cannot be proved. Yet one can show what is at stake in making such a commitment and so make it persuasively meaningful (*ibid.*, pp. 350–451).

John Hick addresses his attention primarily to the question of the *meanings* both of ethical judgments and of affirmations of Christian faith. While neither can be validated by the sense perceptions favored by logical positivists nor even by mystical or intuitive inner experiences, both are deeply meaningful. Ethical judgments—which are our main concern here—are, according to Hick, like other cognitive judgments, assertions of particular ways of apprehending our environment. Moral significance is a kind of meaning superimposed upon natural or causative meaning by an irreducible kind of volitional insight.[33]

Hick's emphasis on the voluntary and deeply personal character of moral affirmation and also of faith moves at times close to an existentialist point of view. This, too, must be briefly mentioned, for various forms of existentialism have exercised great influence in recent years. Before leaving analytic philosophy, however, we must observe that it does not provide means for determining or for helping us determine what we ought to do in any situation, beyond the exercise of care for precise and clear articulation of our meanings. When analytic philosophers do define norms for making ethical judgments, it is by appeal to criteria developed by other methods. For example, Ferré appeals to the "criteria of practical reason: valuational adequacy, valuational coherence, and valuational effectiveness" (*op. cit.*, p. 357). Hick, on the other hand, would rest ethical obligation on Christian faith (*Faith and Knowledge*, pp. 216–17).

2. Existentialism.   Sören Kierkegaard believed that any attempt to impose a system of concepts on personal decision-making so far reduces a man to a thing. As compared with an irresponsible life of selfishness and sensuality, disciplined thought and attempt at obedience to high ethical standards are good. Nevertheless, Kierkegaard maintained, the ethical level of life is finally self-defeating.

There are many reasons why this is so.[34] One of the chief is that

32. *Basic Modern Philosophy of Religion* (New York: Charles Scribner's Sons, 1967), p. 451.
33. See *Faith and Knowledge* (Ithaca, N.Y.: Cornell University Press, 1957), pp. 125–27 and 164–65.
34. Arguments by Kierkegaard against dependence upon rational concepts for determining the meaning or course of our existence are summarized and critically examined in my book *The Religious Revolt Against Reason* (New York: Harper & Brothers, 1949; republished in New York by Greenwood Press, 1968).

when I try to assume the air of detached objectivity to seek the truth about my duty or the proper goal of my existence, I falsify my position. I am not and cannot be such a dispassionate spectator. My problems are the questions of Harold DeWolf at a particular time and place, a sinful, erring individual confronting the issues of eternity and therefore infinitely involved in any answers I may propose.

Moreover, every moral decision I have to make in the real world is in a particular setting different from any other. No moral prescriptions established for man in general or for some type of situation will guide me in my individual confrontation with this particular situation.

To undergird a decision on which a man's eternal happiness depends, nothing less than certainty will do. Rational knowledge can never gain certainty, whether based on sense perception, historical data, or inclusive, coherent evidence. Hence for serious ethical decision rational knowledge is inadequate for any man.

> He moves constantly in a sphere of approximation-knowledge, in his supposed positivity deluding himself with the semblance of certainty; but certainty can be had only in the infinite, where he cannot as an existing subject remain, but only repeatedly arrive.[35]

Kierkegaard insists a man's only salvation is in making a passionate decision of faith in Christ, a decision to be repeatedly renewed by particular choices every day. The Christian faces each problem of choice without the attempt to reason from concepts, but rather in loyalty to a Person, the Person of Christ. This loyalty, held with "purity of heart," controls him in the depths of his existence.

When Kierkegaard makes his free decision ungoverned by guiding evidence or reasons, he decides for Christian faith. Other existentialists make different decisions. Moreover, Kirkegaard gives us no basis for deciding social issues, offering, instead, a purely individualistic faith. Both Christian and non-Christian forms of existentialism tend strongly to a subjective individualism, from the thought of Jean Paul Sartre or Martin Heidegger to a contemporary theologian like Gerhard Ebeling.[36]

H. Richard Niebuhr, however, represented important strands of existentialist thinking, while he rejected emphatically the individual subjectivism which has been more characteristic of the existentialist move-

35. *Concluding Unscientific Postscript* (Princeton: Princeton University Press, 1944), p. 75.

36. See Ebeling, *The Nature of Faith* (Philadelphia: Muhlenberg Press, 1961), and cf. the criticism of Ebeling's perspective on ethics by S. Paul Schilling in his *Contemporary Continental Theologians* (Nashville: Abingdon Press, 1966), pp. 139–40.

ment. Warning against the belief that particular Christian formulas were adequate for all time and all occasions, he nevertheless approved and defined formulations of ethical principle for the present age.[37]

3. Process Philosophy. Deeply influenced by Alfred North Whitehead, Charles Hartshorne has developed a philosophy which is in turn serving as a basis for some of the most interesting new theological systems-in-the-making, such as the work of John B. Cobb, Jr. and Schubert Ogden.

In contrast to the depreciation of rational concepts characteristic of existentialism, Hartshorne emphasizes the importance of concepts meticulously denied, by the use of logical analysis and constant reference to empirical data. In contrast to the individualism of Kierkegaard and Ebeling, he lays heavy stress on every person's deep dependence on the community and responsibility to the community.

One especially interesting characteristic of Hartshorne's ethical thought arises in connection with his "psychicalism" as applied to the nonhuman and even inorganic parts of the universe.[38] According to this view

"mind" and "matter" are not ultimately different sorts of entity but, rather, two ways of describing a reality that has many levels of organization. The "mind" way I take to be more final and inclusive, so that my position is the opposite of materialism.   [*Ibid.*]

This view leads Hartshorne to affirm that there are values in the natural order altogether independent of man's use or appreciation. Poets have often attributed to nonhuman creatures enjoyments and desires much like ours.

Science is eliminating the fanciful details. What it is not doing and cannot do is to establish a dualistic materialism in which the sentiment and intelligent arise out of mere bits of dead matter, human evaluations out of a nature devoid of values. *Human* values emerge, sure enough, but are there not simian values, amoebic values—and who dares to assign a first level of values?

If the foregoing is at all correct, then the social point of view is the final point of view. All creatures are fellow creatures.   [*Ibid.*, pp. 309–10]

Hartshorne explains that he does not mean to say that all fellow

37. See especially *Radical Monotheism and Western Culture* (New York: Harper & Row, 1960).

38. He uses the term "psychicalism" in *The Logic of Perfection and Other Essays in Neoclassical Metaphysics* (La Salle, Ill.: Open Court Publishing Company, 1962), p. 217.

creatures are equal. Far from it! Some insects, for example, must be killed for the sake of higher creatures. But his conception of nonhuman values and universal community does have importance for the ethics of ecology now coming into long overdue recognition. That is, it has importance if the ontology on which it is based can be accepted. Certainly that is at least worthy of thoughtful consideration.

General Principles
of Moral Decision

·•·~⟨∞⟩·•··

INTRODUCTION

Many moral philosophers have contended that by reason concerning our common human experience universal moral laws could be established, despite all the modern arguments to the contrary. But among recent philosophers outside the Roman Catholic tradition few have been willing to say what these laws were. Edgar S. Brightman, in his book *Moral Laws*,[1] not only defends the belief that there are discoverable, rationally defensible, universally valid moral laws, but by his rational empiricism he formulates and defends a system of such laws. These laws were later set forth with much more elaboration, in the context of a long psychological study of human nature, by Peter A. Bertocci and Richard M. Millard, in their useful book *Personality and the Good: Psychological and Ethical Perspectives*.[2] These authors speak of the formulas as "principles" rather than laws, and the change is a salutary one. They are far from being prescriptive rules or commands. They do not so much say what we should and should not do, as tell how we are to decide.[3] After the Brightman principles concerning personal conduct and character, Bertocci and Millard add a chapter on the character of a good society. More recently, Walter G. Muelder has commended the moral laws to his readers much as Brightman had formulated them and added two further classes of laws which I had proposed in unpublished lectures.[4]

Here I propose to present these "laws" as "ethical principles," in the

1. New York: Abingdon Press, 1933.
2. New York: David McKay Company, 1963.
3. Edward L. Long properly classifies Brightman under the "deliberative motif," rather than the "prescriptive motif." See his comprehensive and helpful book *A Survey of Christian Ethics* (New York: Oxford University Press, 1967), p. 53. Brightman is further from the prescriptive motif than some other thinkers classified under the deliberative, especially Thomas Aquinas.
4. See Muelder, *Moral Law in Christian Social Ethics* (Richmond: John Knox Press, 1966).

revised form in which I would commend them. They constitute by no means my whole ethical system, nor the center of it. They represent an attempt at improved formulating of a system which, though partial and inadequate when taken alone, seems to me, nevertheless, to be the most defensible set of natural law principles of comparable generality thus far set forth in our time.

In studying this system of principles, it is important to understand that this *is a system.* There is a genuine interdependence among all the principles. Every principle after the first is rationally inferred, directly or indirectly, from the Principle of Consistency combined with observations of experience. On the other hand, every principle excepting the last is elaborated and interpreted by those which follow. The first takes account of the least empirical data. The last is the most comprehensively inclusive of human experience and makes the most inclusive moral demands.

Every one of these principles must be understood in accord with the demands of every other.

1. Synthesis of Philosophical and Theological Ethics

As these Principles are presented some relations between them and biblical teachings will be indicated. The purpose will not be to give prooftexts in support of them. Even if a sound hermeneutics permitted such a procedure, it would be contrary to the present purpose.

The General Principles are established by rational reflection on the common experience of mankind, not by appeal to special revelation, biblical or other. They belong to philosophical ethics rather than Christian ethics. Why, then, should they be introduced here? And why should we inquire about relations between these Principles and Christian teachings?

Protestants have often charged all attempts at theological and rational synthesis with being "neo-Thomist." Such cries are still heard occasionally, but in this ecumenical age they are usually muted and mellowed by recognition that Thomas Aquinas was not all bad, just as Roman Catholic theologians are now occasionally paying tribute to Martin Luther. Actually, I have no intention of defending the Thomistic synthesis, for my philosophical ethics is not his and my understanding of gospel ethics also differs from his. However, Thomas was right in insisting that reason can lead to much truth and that since truth does not contradict itself the truth found by philosophical reason must be in harmony with truth revealed in Scripture or tradition. Where there is conflict, one or both, or at least our apprehension of one or both, must be in error.

There are different ways of looking at the relation between our

General Principles of Moral Decision and the demands or perspectives of Christian ethics, depending on the direction of approach. If we approach from the side of natural law or philosophical ethics, we shall then see Christian teachings as fulfilling and specifying the demands of the philosophical principles. If we approach from the side of Christian ethics, we shall find the General Principles useful instruments of thought in defense and application of Christian teachings, as well as in critique of initial moral skepticism.

2. Theological Ethics as Completing and Specifying Philosophical Principles

In no case do our General Principles specify an act which must or must not be committed. They are abstract and regulative, rather than concrete and creative. They bear a relation to a good life much like the relation of principles of art criticism to art. An observer may appeal to critical aesthetic principles to support a positive or negative judgment of a painting, but the principles alone will not give him much help in the art of painting. On the other hand, a manual for painters, particularly if well illustrated with art, may help very considerably, indeed, a person with some modicum of talent. Christian ethics is more like the manual and points to the concrete teachings, decisions, and lives of prophets, saints, and above all of Jesus.

A consumers' organization published certain requirements of a needed can opener, including modest price, durable construction, ease of operation, and minimal deposit of metal particles inside cans being opened. The would-be inventor was not told what material to use nor was the design specified. As various models were proposed the advertised requirements were used to evaluate them for acceptance or rejection. The formulated requirements, in short, were not creative or constitutive, but critical and regulative. Similarly, our General Principles do not describe or depict the style of life which will be coherent, but they are principles of criticism by which we can evaluate any proposed set of ideals or injunctions, or a particular individual or community, to see whether it is rationally defensible as ethically sound.

If the General Principles are valid, as here contended, and if Christian ethical teaching is also sound, then life lived according to Christian teaching will in fact measure up well according to the General Principles. Moreover, it will in that case be found possible to employ the General Principles along with Christian ethics coherently and in a way to illuminate the character of both. It is proposed to assume tentatively that this is so and to put the hypothesis to the test of relating the two sets of teaching and of using both in application to various problems requiring decision in our time.

3. Theological Ethics as Primary

While philosophical or natural law ethics may need to come logically and pedagogically first to the moral skeptic, to most believing Christians the teachings of Scripture and Christian tradition come first, both in time and in importance. Indeed, many faithful Christians never learn philosophical ethics, as such, at all.

Important as I believe the General Principles to be for theoretical purposes which deeply affect practice, the more concrete teachings of Christian ethics, especially as they point to Jesus Christ and the reign of God, are of far greater importance to life and in this sense primary. Fortunately, we can have the General Principles as aids to ethical evaluation, while also having the teachings of Scripture and tradition interpreted and organized in Christian ethics, teachings which point both to the masterpieces of godly living in history and to a present worthy life for ourselves and our contemporaries.

4. Values of General Principles to Christian Ethics

Three main contributions are offered by our rational General Principles of Moral Decision to specifically Christian ethics.

a. Internal Critique of Rational Relativism. Many thoughtful people doubt that there are any norms or obligations of moral conduct beyond the purely relative preferences of individuals, special interests of social classes, or mores of particular societies. Such moral skepticism closes minds to the claims of Christian ethics as to every other ethical system or tradition which claims universal validity. Assertions of Christian doctrine and quotations of biblical passages are regarded by the skeptical relativists as mere examples of mores limited to particular societies. A reasonable answer is provided by this system of philosophically defensible norms.

b. Apologetic Support for Christian Ethics. If it can be shown that Christian ethics, properly formulated and employed, will guide to decisions fulfilling the requirements of the rationally coherent system of General Principles, this demonstration will support the contention that Christian ethics, so formulated and used, is universally valid.

c. Instrumental Use in Problem Solving. Accepting Christian ethics as guide to conduct, it will be found that the General Principles will serve usefully for supplemental illumination of meaning and guidance in application.

5. The General Principles Given Flesh in
Christian Scripture and Tradition

If Christian ethics and the General Principles are coherently related, one would expect to find in Christian teaching many ideas parallel to the Principles or making more concrete specification of them. Such relationships are, in fact, readily discoverable by comparing the General Principles with biblical teaching, special attention being paid to the New Testament.

As the Principles are related to biblical teachings it will usually be unnecessary to examine explicitly the critical questions about authorship and precise situation of the utterances. The citations of biblical passages are not appeals to authority to prove the validity of the Principles, but simply efforts to call to mind ideas imbedded deep in Christian tradition and memory which are similar to the Principles or provide concrete illustrations of them. Care has been taken not to tear the passages out of literary or historical context in such a way as to do violence to their meaning. Beyond that it is needful only to remind the reader that the passages cited do belong to the resources of living faith. They are introduced here to show that such ideas as the Principles introduce are not alien, much less contrary, to the historic teachings in which Christian life is nurtured, but rather quite coherent with such teachings. Introducing them here will also serve frequently to illustrate the difference between the abstractness of philosophical ethics and the concreteness of ethical teachings in the biblical tradition.

A. FORMAL PRINCIPLES

1. The Principle of Consistency

Every person ought to will to be free from self-contradiction, that is, to be consistent in his intentions.

a. Validation and Exposition. No argued proof of this Principle can be given without reasoning in a circle, because every argument and every proof (on any subject) presuppose the obligation to be consistent, without which there can be no proceeding from premises to a conclusion. This is true even if one premise is the stated or unstated affirmation of a most dramatic special revelation. If it is revealed to me that God is love, and I accept that, I may still go on believing that God is not love but hate unless I recognize the obligation to avoid self-contradiction.

About all that one can do in support of this Principle is to point out that the whole of science, indeed all meaningful knowledge, all mutual trust, all sincerity, all moral and religious seriousness, depend upon it. So far as we violate the principle of consistency, so far our lives are invaded by meaninglessness, irrationality, and chaos.

The Principle of Consistency does not imply a static, changeless existence. Ralph Waldo Emerson's famous reference, in his essay "Self-Reliance," to "a foolish consistency" as "the hobgoblin of little minds," is speaking, as his preceding lines make clear, of the fear that in speaking what one sees as truth today one may contradict what one believed and said at some time in the past. When new facts or new insights convince me that I should choose differently than formerly, very well, but now I must not go on repeating the former choice which contradicts the new conviction.

b. Biblical Parallels. When Jesus enjoins his disciples against oath-taking, he says positively, "Let what you say be simply 'Yes' or 'No.' "[5] Oaths, lie detectors, and other devices for guaranteeing truth-telling—and pledge-keeping too—are made necessary by the discrepancy between men's different words and deeds.

The religions of Israel and of Christ are both rooted in obedience to the command, "You shall have no other gods before me [or besides me]" (Exod. 20:3). To have more than one god is to pollute the purity or singleness of heart and will; it is to introduce self-contradiction. The Hebrew principle of worshiping only the one God and the Greek principle of logical consistency happily joined in the early history of Christian thought to give moral seriousness and intellectual integrity to the Christian faith. Just so far as one is willing to accept self-contradiction in his own intentions, he becomes an unpredictable and irresponsible person who will not hesitate to worship "other gods," notwithstanding his declarations of undying loyalty to the one only God.

2. The Principle of Personal Conscience

Every person ought to choose in accordance with the ideals which he acknowledges.

a. Validation and Exposition. This Principle is derived from the first one plus the observation in experience that human beings choose *types* of conduct as well as particular acts. Such a type is an ideal. When an individual has chosen a kind of conduct, such as honesty, kindness, control of anger, or the like, then until he honestly repudiates that ideal, he is morally obligated to make particular choices accordingly. If he makes choices which contradict one of his own ideals, for example, kindness, then he violates the Principle of Consistency, for while approving kindness, he also approves unkindness in his own act of choosing to act unkindly.

This is another way of stating the fundamental obligation which Kant formulated as the Categorical Imperative. Kant's formula, however, would obligate me to form an ideal (which he here calls a "maxim") covering every fully conscious, voluntary choice I make. The categorical imperative seems to me to be too inclusive in that re-

5. Matt. 5:37. Cf. Jas. 5:12.

spect. Many of our choices, even deliberate, conscious choices, are not discernibly significant ethically. When a man goes out for an evening walk in his rather homogeneous neighborhood, he may pause at several intersections, deciding which way to turn. Must he form a maxim or ideal to include each such choice, or one to include all, and must he will that this ideal should be followed invariably by him and by every person in existence? Kant would probably answer affirmatively, for he did choose to walk along the same route at the same time every day. I do not object to his having done so. Personally, I have chosen neither an ideal of invariable sameness of route nor an ideal of maximum variation. I see no reason why I should.

On the other hand, when an act is *formally* of moral significance it is precisely because it does conform to or contradict an ideal of the person choosing. It may be significant materially even when the person has not formed a relevant ideal, but principles having to do with material ethics are yet to be presented.

b. Parallels and Applications in the Bible.   Paul implies the Principle of Personal Conscience when he writes,

> Therefore you have no excuse, O man, whoever you are, when you judge another; for in passing judgment upon him you condemn yourself, because you, the judge, are doing the very same things.   [Rom. 2:1]

The same Principle is invoked when it is written, "Whoever knows what is right to do and fails to do it, for him it is sin" (Jas. 4:17; 3:10–12). Note that in the former quotation, from Paul, the Principle is applied to condemn acts contrary to one's own judgment, as applied to others, whereas in the passage from James it is failure to act in accord with one's own judgment which is condemned. Hence, the latter passage requires positive performance, not mere refraining from evil. So it is also with the Golden Rule, as given in the Gospels: "So whatever you wish that men would do to you, do so to them," but here the form, too, is affirmative (Matt. 7:12; Luke 6:31).

If the positive character in this injunction were more widely emphasized, fewer people would fall into the serious error of supposing that morality consists mainly of refraining from evil, whereas nearly all serious philosophical and theological moralists acknowledge that morality consists mainly of doing good. A man cannot be a good man by being innocuous and good for nothing.

But whether positively or negatively, the Principle is applied again and again in the Scriptures, and especially in the New Testament.[6]

6. E.g., see Matt. 5:43–45, 7:3–5, 23:29–35; Rom. 2:12, 23.

B. Principles of Valuation

Anything which I desire or in which I find satisfaction is laying claim to be regarded as a value. Any such object of desire or of liking we will call a "claimed value." To determine whether a claimed value is a true value, a critical test must be applied. The principles rightly governing the process of testing to see what claimed values are real values and to determine what real values ought to be chosen are called by Brightman "Axiological Laws." A revised set will here be called "Principles of Valuation."

1. The Principle of Coherent Valuation

Every person ought to choose values which are consistent and coherent, not values which are contradictory or incoherent one with another.

a. Validation and Exposition. All people do in fact choose experiences which they desire, that is, claimed values. If such experiences contradict each other, then to choose them is to violate the Formal Principles and so is unethical. As I write, it is August. I desire to complete a quota of writing which I have assigned myself for this month. I should like also to take a good vacation. I find that the two claimed values are incompatible. To choose both is to be on collision course with myself. The sooner I face the reality and choose consistently, the better.

To choose coherently means more. Values which are not contradictory are consistent. To be coherent they must not contradict each other but must also be positively related.

Actually, if values chosen are not directly or indirectly supportive, one of another, they will be in opposition. Our time for realizing the various values we wish to choose is limited. To choose an afternoon of tennis is to choose against study of Hebrew grammar that afternoon. We all fill our days with quest for certain values and thereby exclude others.

The only way to prevent my values being in such conflict that realization of one reduces or eliminates another is to choose such values that realization of one assists me in realizing another. Thus, seeking the recreational values of a week or two at the seashore some time during the summer may enable me to write better the rest of the time and so augment the quality and quantity of my work in the summer as a whole.

Efforts to avoid subjective conflict by isolating one's different interests always produce conflict of choices. Thus, a businesswoman who intends to be deeply religious, but who isolates her business activities from religious examination, truncates her religion and prevents her business from achieving goals which some other religious business people find especially satisfying and useful.

b. Some Valuations in Scripture. In the Letter to the Ephesians the author exhorts his readers, "Put on the whole armor of God," and using the symbolism of armor he enumerates some of the values to be selected and actualized—truth, righteousness, "the gospel of peace," faith, salvation, and "the sword of the Spirit, which is the word of God." Dropping the symbolism, he continues to urge prayer, alertness, and persevering intercession (Eph. 6:11–18). Here there is not a general, abstract injunction to choose values which are coherent, but a concrete naming of examples, some of which—especially the word of God and prayer—generate and nurture others. Similarly, Paul contrasts with "works of the flesh" various virtues which constitute "the fruit of the Spirit," namely, "love, joy, peace, patience, kindness, goodness, faithfulness, gentleness, self-control" (Gal. 5:19, 22–23). The attentive reader will observe that Paul uses the plural "works" (*ta erga*) when he enumerates evils of the flesh, while he employs the singular "fruit" (*ho karpos*) when speaking of virtues which the spirit generates. The "works of the flesh" are indeed plural, for they are divisive, incoherent, impossible to integrate into one harmonious life or community, being such things as "immorality, impurity, licentiousness, idolatry, sorcery, enmity, strife, jealousy, anger, selfishness, dissension . . . and the like" (Gal. 5:19–21). On the other hand, the virtues can constitute one harmonious life in individual and community.

2. The Principle of Foresight

Every person ought to look ahead to the consequences of alternative choices before him and choose so that on the whole he approves the foreseeable consequences of his choice.[7]

a. Validation and Exposition. It is also known, even among generally ignorant people, that not to consider consequences is often to defeat one's purpose and perhaps to cause much additional damage as well. "Look before you leap," people say.

One must consider consequences to choose values which are coherent. A large proportion of the conflicts and also the supportive connections among values are discoverable in advance only by the foreseeing of consequences. Some people say we should choose the right with no regard for consequences. However, they never mean consistently what they say. They know well, and assume all the while, the consequences of wiggling a finger when it is on the trigger of a cocked gun or the button of a readied nuclear missile system. They advocate

7. Cf. Edward L. Long's account of "The Deliberative Motif" in *A Survey of Christian Ethics*.

ignoring *some* consequences but not others. We cannot choose the right in disregard of consequences, for we do not know what the right is, in a particular situation, without considering consequences. Usually, as in the case of the finger on the trigger, it is precisely foreseeable consequences which give an act all or most of its moral significance.

This, of course, is not to say that considerations of one's own comfort or life are not to be overridden for the sake of foreseen benefits to others. Every genuinely generous act and especially every act of personal courage or self-sacrifice are examples of such overriding concern for others.

We must say further that in matters of social policy and especially of political decision nearly every choice offered entails some foreseeable consequences which every thoughtful person will deplore. It is for this reason that the Principle must be stated to require, not that a person ought to choose so as to approve all the foreseeable consequences, but only so that "*on the whole* he approves the foreseeable consequences."

b. Scriptural Injunctions to Exercise Foresight. Jesus urges his hearers to "count the cost" of discipleship as would a prudent man "count the cost" of the whole undertaking before starting to build a tower or engage in a war (Luke 14:28–33). He warns that whoever will be his disciple will find that it will cost everything in the end. Hence this cost should be taken into account from the outset, and the man who is to be a disciple must "renounce all."

Warning that "a man's life does not consist in the abundance of his possessions," Jesus describes a man who accumulates material goods only to be brought up short by God's word, " 'Fool! This night your soul is required of you; and the things you have prepared, whose will they be?' So," concludes Jesus, "is he who lays up treasure for himself, and is not rich toward God" (Luke 12:15–20). His teaching of foresight is not contrary to the teaching not to be anxious about food, clothing, and the like. For both teachings proclaim that in the long view it is obedient faith in God which is secure and lasting, while material goods seem important only in the present.

Similar, but even more pointedly illustrating our Principle of Foresight, is the Parable of the Unjust Steward (Luke 16:1–9). Just as the unscrupulous but clever steward about to lose his job and hence his power used his doomed authority to put his master's debtors under obligation to him for the future, so we should look and plan ahead. Our earthly life and goods are doomed. While they last we are to use them to make friends who will endure. Then when the "unrighteous mammon . . . fails they may receive you into the eternal habitations."

Whereas the General Principle bids us to look ahead and choose with a view to long-range consequences, but does not tell what values to choose for the sake of the long future, the biblical injunctions point out the kinds of values which are only good for the short run and direct us to the lasting values of obedient faith in God, loving-kindness, and fellowship with his people.

3. The Principle of the Best Possible

Every person ought, on every occasion, to will the best possible values in the total situation; hence, if possible, to improve the situation.[8]

a. Validation and Exposition. As we approach a general election, most conscientious and well-informed citizens have some unhappy choices to make. If the voter likes senatorial candidate A's views on foreign policy, he may be scandalized by his relations with a corrupt political machine. A's opponent may be above reproach in honesty, but his views on foreign policy are more ambiguous and his past votes on civil rights are highly unsatisfactory. Only the two candidates' names will be on the ballot. To write in some other or to refrain from voting may be noted as a protest, but it may go unnoticed and simply leave the decision to others, thus abdicating the privilege and responsibility of voting. What ought the voter to decide?

The Principle of the Best Possible limits the moral responsibility of every person to the possible. If he votes for the candidate whose election would, on the whole, be the best, he is not to blame for not helping at the ballot box to elect a senator whose election would bring good and only good results. Most of the decisions we have to make in complex social situations offer no alternatives which we can approve totally in both present meaning and foreseeable consequences. We ought to do the best we can.

There is another side to this Principle. While it *limits* responsibility to the *possible*, it *elevates* responsibility to choose the *best*. Traditional Roman Catholic instruction is preoccupied with prescriptive commands to do a particular thing (for example, confess and receive absolution before taking Communion) or to refrain from doing something else (for example, telling a lie). The Principle of the Best Possible indicates that it is not enough to refrain from forbidden acts and to perform good acts. To do a good thing when one could do a better is to fail in one's duty.

The proof is that if one wills less than the best he introduces internal contradiction into his willing. He subjectively approves choice of value K as the best in the situation, but by his decision he prefers choice of value J.

8. Note that Fletcher, too, would seek "the most good possible in every situation" (*Situation Ethics*, p. 82). I could only wish that he would give attention to the question what is truly good rather than excluding this question, and would view the situation in much larger context.

It may be objected that the proof shows only that a person ought to choose what he *believes* to be best, not necessarily what actually *is* best. But if one does not *will* to do the actual best possible, one is willingly accepting less than the best in one's own subjective willing. Let us illustrate.

In an election with four candidates, I study the record; then I vote for C as the one I think is best. So far my obedience to the Principle appears to be impeccable. But suppose I am, in fact, mistaken. B would actually have served better; or suppose the result would have been better had I joined those who protested the sorry choice by refusing to vote at all! Have I disobeyed the Law of the Best Possible?

It must be replied here that moral responsibility goes only so far as a person's ability to know and his freedom to choose. Hence in the illustration cited I have thus far fulfilled the requirement of the Principle of the Best Possible within the limits of moral responsibility.

There is yet another requirement, namely, the concluding clause—"hence, if possible, to improve the situation." In politics this implies the need to explore possibilities of getting better candidates to be nominated next time. It may also mean that I should help secure and disseminate more adequate information concerning candidates. Indeed, every situation offering only rather unsatisfactory choices cries out for improving the situation itself so that better choices will be available later.

One warning is in order concerning a likely abuse of this Principle. We often claim that even though we did not do very well we did the best we could. We readily excuse ourselves for poor choices by saying we are "only human," or by blaming the times and circumstances.

Many achievements thought impossible by nearly everyone have been realized by bold and creative individuals who possessed rare determination to defy the odds. It is not easy to know the outside limits of the possible. To be faithful to the Principle of the Best Possible we must press very hard for those limits.

b. Exhortations to the Best Possible in Scripture. The Christian is not to be content simply with good deeds or talents, but will "earnestly desire the higher gifts" (1 Cor. 12:31). When Paul has given this exhortation he calls his readers on to "a still more excellent way," the way of love. Only the best is sufficient. The perfectionism of Jesus points in the same direction.

However, Paul, at least, recognizes that in a world of much wickedness we cannot choose to have everything actually be in accordance with the Christian ideal. He urges that the Roman Christians—and all of us—"live in harmony with one another," and indicates the humility, forbearance, and high purpose which will help toward that end. But realistically he adds, "If possible, so far as it depends upon you, live peaceably with all" (Rom. 12:16–18). No easygoing acceptance of custom or present trends will suffice; we are to seek the best that is possible.

Jesus' approval of the widow's mite as contrasted with the larger gifts of more affluent visitors to the temple well illustrates the Principle of the Best Possible. It was not the person who gave the largest gift, but the woman who did the *best she could* who was singled out for praise (Luke 21:1–4).

4. The Principle of Situational Relevance

Every person ought, in any given situation, to seek one or more of his approved values especially related to that situation and most readily attained in that situation.

a. Validation and Exposition.   This is a warning to absent-minded professors who wander off in their scholarly routine, oblivious to people around them; to students who study Greek through the lecture in ethics, and plan their lessons for church school during the class in Greek.

The proof is that if a person does not seize the most relevant opportunities to achieve his various approved values, he will not achieve the best possible values in the whole situation which constitutes his life. The danger in a conscientiously planned life is that we become so programmed that we cannot respond appropriately to the special opportunity which comes our way.

Actually, planning can help us with this problem if only we plan with margins for completion of tasks well before deadlines, so that we can have freedom to pay attention to the environment and seize the opportunity at hand without imperiling our long-range goals. But if we hold inflexibly to schedules and habits, we shall be daily missing opportunities for realizing most readily and well many of our approved value goals. Then they will either go unrealized or we shall have to seek them at other times and places where more effort and time will be required and often with inferior results.

b. Biblical Illustration.   While not in the mainstream of biblical revelation, and when taken alone giving too much credibility to an easygoing kind of situational ethics, a famous passage in Ecclesiastes illustrates well the special emphasis of situational relevance. It begins:

> For everything there is a season, and a time for every matter under heaven:
> a time to be born, and a time to die;
> a time to plant, and a time to pluck up what is planted;
> a time to kill, and a time to heal;
> a time to break down, and a time to build up. . . .

So the passage continues, through ten more pairs of opposites (Eccles. 3:1–8).

If all this is put into the setting of the General Principles and of Christian ethics, it will have to be modified. In such setting there is not a time "for *everything*," but only for everything which is in accord with other General Principles and with faith in Christ.

The biblical conception of *kairos* in the special sense of the right time, opportune time, or time chosen by God has an especially significant and interesting relation to the Principle of Situational Relevance. Sometimes the reference is simply to the carrying out of tasks at the appropriate time, as "the faithful and wise servant" serves food to the household *en kairō*, that is, "at the proper time" (Matt. 24:45). Similarly, the landlord sent a servant to collect his rent *kairō*, that is "when the time came" (Luke 20:10). However, there is here an eschatalogical analogy and in that connection a reference to God's chosen time. The coming and the suffering of Jesus are thought of as in the fullness of time (Gal. 4:4) or as John represents Jesus as saying, in "my time" (John 7:8. Cf. 2:4).

The *kairos* may appear to be a time arbitrarily set by God. However, on closer view it will be seen that the coming and death of Jesus are not unrelated to the events of history. Far from it! Previous events, especially the work of the prophets, had prepared the way. Then, "when the time had fully come, God sent forth his Son, . . . to redeem those who were under the law . . ." (Gal. 4:4).

Christians are to judge what is relevant to the situation, not by a mere superficially empirical view of the particular immediate events, but by seeing these events in the context of God's whole revealed purpose. We must seek to discern what God is doing in our time and act in relevance to his action in the world.[9]

In determining our action we are to take notice, however, not only of God's purpose, but also of evil forces around us, not to succumb to those forces, but taking account of them to do God's will. Similarly, Jesus warns his disciples, "Behold, I send you out as sheep in the midst of wolves; so be wise as serpents and innocent as doves" (Matt. 10:16).

An especially good example of this high Christian opportunism is given by Paul when he is in the Roman prison under death sentence. Instead of spending his time lamenting his unhappy fate or moaning over his inability to continue his itinerant church work, he spreads his good news in the prison itself. Even while he is there, uncertain of his earthly fate, he writes that

9. For an excellent answer to the question "Where Is God at Work in the World?" see the article under that title by Albert C. Winn, in *Lexington Theological Quarterly*, Vol. IV, No. 4 (Oct., 1969), pp. 116–21.

what has happened to me has really served to advance the gospel, so that it has become known throughout the whole praetorian guard and to all the rest that my imprisonment is for Christ.   [Phil. 1:12–14]

5. *The Principle of Variety and Depth*

Every person ought to choose the greatest possible amount of coherent value; hence to choose variety and depth in combination suited to his aptitudes and situation.

a. Validation and Exposition. If a person does not seek variety of appreciations, creativity, and achievements, he will find himself in many situations where he is helpless to realize values of which circumstances fairly cry aloud. Such instances would include the passerby with no knowledge of first aid, hence no ability to assist the child whom an accident throws injured at his very feet; or the minister who wishes to influence youth, but loses opportunities for effective communication because he has no appreciation nor understanding of contemporary youth interests. To fulfill the Principle of the Best Possible and Situational Relevance, we need to be seeking a variety of approved values.

But variety may threaten quality and depth. To spread attention over too many interests may be to make no significant contributions at any point. We are obligated to seek the right balance of variety and depth in order most significantly to achieve coherent value. If by such balance one does not choose the greatest possible amount of value, one is not conforming to the Principle of the Best Possible in the situation which is one's whole life.

b. Biblical Parallels. According to the Gospel, Jesus does not come to bring men into a narrowly confined, joyless life of negation, but rather "that they may have life, and have it abundantly" (John 10:10). The Greek word here translated "abundantly" (*perisson*) is a strong expression connoting an extraordinary quantity going beyond all that is usual or necessary.

Paul rejoices in his calling "to preach to the Gentiles the unsearchable riches of Christ . . ." (Eph. 3:8). Even more directly he exhorts his readers to nurture a rich diversity of values in their very thoughts, as he says,

Finally, brethren, whatever is true, whatever is honorable, whatever is just, whatever is pure, whatever is lovely, whatever is gracious, if there is any excellence, if there is anything worthy of praise, think about these things.   [Phil. 4:8]

It is not everything that is to be sought, but everything that is excellent and worthy, that is, in accord with Christ.

6. The Principle of Ideal Control

Every person ought to choose particular values in accordance with his ideal values.

a. Validation and Exposition. When popular pseudopsychiatry was at its height, there were many misguided warnings that it was dangerous to mental health to inhibit any desire. A motion picture of the time was issued under the alluring title, *Obey That Impulse!*

It requires little experience and thought to know that if we did this, both personal and social chaos would quickly result. Plato observed how unruly were human emotions, and innumerable philosophers, psychologists, dramatists, and other writers have commented on the same theme in the intervening centuries.

If we are to choose values which are coherent, as the Principle of Coherent Valuation requires, we must think carefully about the various types of claimed values and select the types which can be harmoniously related in the pattern of a single life. Then we must make our specific choices of value from day to day according to this selection of types. These types of approved value are ideal values.

If a man approves the value of calm self-control in the face of provocation, then when another makes an insulting remark he inhibits the impulse to hit him or otherwise achieve vengeance. Thus he controls his choice of particular values to conform with his ideal. Similarly, if he approves generous kindness, then as he receives many appeals for direct or indirect assistance to needy persons he chooses the positive value of giving such assistance on some, at least, of these occasions.

The Principle of Ideal Control serves the same function in regard to selection of *values* which the Principle of Personal Conscience serves in relation to choices generally. The Principle of Personal Conscience will be violated by any violation of the Principle of Ideal Control.

b. New Testament Parallels. As the Principle of Variety and Depth requires maximal quantity of value, the Principle of Ideal Control especially requires selected quality. Paul's injunction to feed the mind on all things excellent and worthy illustrates both.

Paul points out that there are many gifts among the company of people in the Church. We are not to look down on any who have the lesser ones. "But," he says, "earnestly desire the higher gifts. And I will show you a still more excellent way."[10]

It is no good to know what is truly good if we do not act accord-

10. 1 Cor. 12:31. Cf. 1 Cor. 13:13–14:1.

ingly. "For it is not the hearers of the law who are righteous before God, but the doers of the law who will be justified."[11] Both the state and the church are long on ideals but short on performing in accordance with them. When we speak much in declaration of faith but still choose unworthy values from selfish desire, we are among those "holding the form of religion but denying the power of it" (2 Tim. 3:5).

In the General Principles, the controlling guide to choice of values is simply the chooser's ideal values. We are given no further positive description of those ideal values. They must be coherent, else values chosen in deference to them could not be coherent and the Principle of Coherent Valuation would be violated. But what kinds of values should be controlling and what kinds subordinated or omitted altogether? The General Principles do not say.

The New Testament does indicate the kinds of values ("ideal values") which should be preferred. Hence it goes beyond the statement that a person is to choose values according to his ideals. Jesus instructs his disciples to place life itself above material possessions, friends above self, and the lasting treasures of the spirit above the perishing values of this earthly life.[12]

If Christian ethical teaching is basically sound, it will point to a coherent value system, coherent in thought and in practice, leading to a life of increasing harmony in individual and society. This I believe is true.

C. Principles for Choice of Beneficiary

The Formal Principles answered abstractly the question, *how* a person ought to choose. The gist of the answer was that he ought to choose consistently. The Principles of Valuation answered the question, *what values* a person ought to choose. The answer, in brief, was that he ought to choose maximum values capable of coherent organization in one life, with due regard to the particular facts of the situation.

The Principles for Choice of Beneficiary are concerned with the question *for whom* a person ought to choose values. Noting that values are desired experiences *of persons*, we must ask, "In what person or persons ought one to seek the realization of values?" Who is to be the beneficiary of the values I seek to create or achieve? All that we have said up to this point has been neutral on this question. We have said much about the person choosing, but nothing about the person or persons for whose benefit he ought to choose. This is the issue which must now be faced.

11. Rom. 2:13. Cf. Jas. 1:22 and Matt. 7:21.
12. See Luke 12:15, 23, 30, 33; Matt. 5:6–12.

1. The Principle of Self-Realization

Every person ought to seek realization in his own experience of the maximum possible value.

a. Exposition and Validation. The key phrase here is, of course, "in his own experience." If a person places a high value on courage he should seek to be himself courageous, not only applaud and seek to inspire courage in others. If he approves health he should safeguard and cultivate his own health. If he believes in generous, even sacrificial love, he ought to seek for development and expression of such love in his own thought and action. Is not this seeking of value in oneself regrettably selfish? Is it really virtuous or is it a vice?

If everyone were to seek for values in others but not in himself, there would be no one in whom the values would be welcomed. Most values cannot be much developed in any person without his positive desire for them. In fact, an experience thrust upon a man and not desired nor welcomed by him would not be in him an intrinsic value. That is, even though it might be an instrumental value, a means for producing some valued experience, it would not possess for him value in itself.

If a mother coerces and cajoles her teenage son into attending church while he himself is indifferent or hostile to the experience he has there, he does not experience worship as a positive value. The churchgoing may or may not be useful as a means to some other good, as to meet a girl who will later be his good wife. But any such usefulness as an instrumental value does not imply that the experience has any intrinsic value at all in him. It does not until he himself desires or welcomes it.

Food has no value as food until eaten, and then its intrinsic value as food is to the eater who enjoys it. Truth has intrinsic value only to him who seizes upon it, beauty to him who enjoys it. In short, if value is not sought in and for oneself, it will not be realized at all.

Finally, even to cultivate value in others requires much nurture of value in oneself. To impart knowledge a person must possess knowledge. To teach art appreciation one needs to appreciate art. To do the most for other people a person himself needs to enjoy a fair amount of health, education, patience, courage, and love—all values which require seeking and cultivation.

The requirement to seek "the maximum possible value" is clearly based upon the Principle of Variety and Depth. But should one seek so much in and for himself? Only so far as possible in harmony with the other Principles. We must note especially the limiting effect of the Principle of Altruism and the Principle of Social Devotion, yet to be defined.

b. New Testament Exhortations to Self-Realization. Some misguided Christians have supposed that they should seek the good of other persons only. But the New Testament, though it is often claimed to support such a view, actually urges serious concern for completing or perfecting our own lives. We have already observed Paul's injunctions to "desire the higher gifts." Jesus is quoted a number of times in support of self-realization. Consider the following passages:

> You, therefore, must be perfect [or complete], as your heavenly Father is perfect.   [Matt. 5:48]
> Ask, and it will be given you; seek and you will find; knock, and it will be opened to you.   [Matt. 7:7]

Jesus turns the attention of the self-righteous critic of others back to his own need for self-improvement, saying,

> You hypocrite, first take the log out of your own eye, and then you will see clearly to take the speck out of your brother's eye.   [Matt. 7:5]

2. The Principle of Altruism

Every person ought to assist in the realization of maximum value in other persons, with due respect for their dignity as autonomous centers of value appraisal and experience.

a. Validation and Exposition. While a person cannot give much to others if he does not cultivate virtues, talents, and other resources in himself which are worth sharing, it is also true that he cannot realize much value in himself without attention to the needs and capacities of others. Man is a social being.

Some values highly prized, even supremely prized, by many persons can be realized in oneself only by assistance to the value fulfillment of others. This is especially evident concerning the virtue love. To a lesser degree, it is true also of such virtues as humility, friendship, and trustworthiness.

Our sharing of ideas and information with others in school, market, industrial coffee break, sidewalk chat, or house party clarifies our thoughts and broadens both knowledge and attitudes.

A very large part of our currently available economic goods, aesthetic values, knowledge, religious values, and much else is produced, enhanced, or made accessible to us by a vast network of mutual assistance which builds a community of value.

Again, every person can greatly increase his contribution to the total realization of value by assisting the value experience of others. He himself is but one. Others to whom he can contribute value are many. Only by seeking to bring values to realization both in himself and in others can he achieve "the greatest possible amount of coherent value" called for in the Principle of Variety and Depth.

In his relations with others every person ought to take care lest he violate "their dignity as autonomous centers of value appraisal and experience." Each has his own ideals and the obligation to be true to his own conscience. Even in my effort to fulfill my duty by increasing the values of others, I must take care that I respect everyone "as an end withal and never as a means only."[13] I shall inevitably, in a sense, be using other people as means to my ends, but I must not use them as "means only." Whether they are my customers, employees, parishioners, parents, or friends, while they are useful in my quest for value, I must always seek to be useful also in their similar quest. Otherwise a maximum of coherent value cannot be realized or assisted to realization either in me or in others.

b. Biblical Teachings of Altruism.   Jesus knows well that the human inclination is to serve the self in preference to others. We may prefer that others possess whatever value there be in the more difficult virtues, but other values we tend easily to seek mostly for ourselves. Hence, while Jesus clearly admonishes self-realization, he gives more emphasis to seeking the well-being of others, even the most unattractive and hostile.

The first law of relations between human beings, according to Jesus, is "You shall love your neighbor as yourself" (Mark 12:31). James calls this "the royal law, according to the scripture" (Jas. 2:8). Similarly, Paul writes, "Bear one another's burdens, and so fulfil the law of Christ" (Gal. 6:2), and even says, "For the whole law is fulfilled in one word, 'You shall love your neighbor as yourself.' "[14]

So far is this deference to the other person to go that we are commanded even to love our enemies and do good to those who heap evil upon us.[15]

It will be observed that these commands go well beyond the Principle of Altruism. In fact, they involve a kind of purpose and of relationship transcending any moral principle contained in a philosophical ethics. As observed previously, the Christian is called to *love,* and in a quite special sense of the word. Yet, while going beyond the Principle of Altruism, love in the New Testament sense *includes* the respect and concern for the other which the Principle of Altruism requires.

13. Kant, *Foundation of the Metaphysics of Morals,* Section Two.
14. Gal. 5:14. Cf. Rom. 13:8–10.
15. Matt. 5:43–45; Rom. 12:17–21.

3. The Principle of the Ideal of Personhood

Every person ought to judge and guide all of his acts by his ideal conception of what the whole human being ought to become.

a. Exposition and Validation.   Every person has an image of greater or lesser clarity representing the kind of person he intends to be. Also in his relations with other people he takes with him a conception of what he thinks a human being ought to be. One will not advance his own development or the development of others in the direction of his ideal of humanity unless he works at it. Just as our choices need subjection to our ideals, and our value-seeking needs control by our ideal values, so our personal development requires direction by our ideal conception of true human personhood.

This Principle requires that I seek to become the kind of person I should like every other human being to be. If I want others to be patient, generous, honest, mature, and responsible people, then I must seek also to be true to this ideal. At the same time, we have specialized roles to take as fathers, mothers, merchants, farmers, or diplomats, and different specialized skills and character traits are required for best fulfillment of these roles. One does not, therefore, want all people to be the same. Yet we ought to form carefully our ideals of the human person in general and to subject our choices of value for ourselves and for other persons to that ideal.

Fair enough, someone may say, as far as choices for myself are concerned. But what business have I to be forming ideal conceptions of the person a neighbor ought to become? Does that properly respect his dignity as an autonomous valuer?

We are here dealing with a delicate matter in which great care must be taken, both in basic thought and also in action. On the one hand, I do not act according to the Principle of Altruism if I help a neighbor to realize chosen values which I believe will undermine and destroy more values in the neighbor and community. On the other hand, I do not properly respect the neighbor's dignity if I try to manipulate and control his life.

When a man who is already staggering asks me for lunch money and I have reason to suspect he actually wants it to buy more hard liquor, I do well to offer him a meal instead of cash. When does such critical appraisal of another's value choices become a disrespectful and wrong effort to impose my ideals upon him?

If a man's own choices are seriously injuring or threatening to injure others in the community, then it may be right even to use the police power of the state to prevent him by arrest and confinement. Here the dignity of other persons is also at stake. If his choices are only impoverishing his own life and appear not to be significantly affecting others, then much depends on the relationship I have or can cultivate with him. If the relationship is such that I can seek to persuade or win him to a more coherent personal ideal, without threatening his dominion over his own life, then the Principle of Altruism and the Ideal of Personhood would require my doing so. To decide aright requires knowledge and sensitive skill, as well as good intentions.

b. The Personal Ideal in the New Testament. The General Principle indicates that beyond our various values there needs to be formed or chosen an ideal of the whole human person. We are not told, however, what, concretely, would be the character of such a person. We know from the Principles defined earlier that the ideal person must be of such a kind as to bring the values of self and of others as chosen by him into harmony, not only in abstract theory, but in actual practice and consequence.

Many kinds of persons can be quickly rejected. A Hitler, both in theory and practice, pits person against person and nation against nation. The limited organic national unity he gains is at the expense of the most extreme violation of the Principle of Altruism and inevitably brings on self-destructive conflict.

An easygoing, self-indulgent playboy finds his values diminishing with the vigor of his bodily life and health, while his self-centered interests lead him to violation of the Principle of Altruism and choosing often trivial values for self rather than far greater values for others, so violating the Principles of the Best Possible and Situational Relevance. In the end the fact that human life is social to the core and cannot be fully lived for self alone catches up with him, and his quest for his own happiness defeats itself.

The Christian looks to Christ as his ideal of personality. The individual may look to certain faithful followers of Christ as more concretely known, for more direct clues to living in particular modern situations, and for more immediacy of impact. So many a young person today looks to Martin Luther King, Jr., or Albert Schweitzer, or Barbara Ward. Some may hold a particular ideal person in mind for a special compartment of life, as many idealistic young people in politics speak of John F. Kennedy.

However, there are always flaws to be found upon sufficiently detailed study of such recent heroes. The Christian looks beyond them to Jesus of Nazareth or to the Christ of his faith.

Many psychologists have pointed out that every person carries in his mind a certain "gallery," a select person or group of persons whom he would like to please. They may be personal acquaintances or men or women of the past. If an individual in the midst of any difficult effort to choose the right course of action can observe introspectively his own mental process, he will find that he matches proposed actions against the actions, ideals, approvals and disapprovals, real or imaginary, of people in his gallery. Not only people of conformist type do this. So also do nonconformists, even, or rather especially, extreme bohemians or hippies. When we choose the persons for our mental "gallery" of imaginary spectators of whose approval we seek to be worthy, we go far toward determining the course of our lives.

The Letter to the Hebrews, in the eleventh chapter, proposes to the reader a great list of men and women, all heroes of faith, who have prepared the way for us. Then the passage comes to its climax with these words:

> Therefore, since we are surrounded by so great a cloud of witnesses, let us also lay aside every weight, and sin which clings so closely, and let us run with perseverance the race that is set before us, looking to Jesus the pioneer and perfecter of our faith. . . .[16]

D. PRINCIPLES OF COMMUNITY

As already observed, human beings are social in their deepest nature. One cannot be a person without interaction with others. Interaction gives rise to communities. It also makes possible the very personhood of an individual. The structure and activities of a community deeply affect the lives of its members and often of other communities as well. The possibilities for realization of value and of personhood are very different in an Iban longhouse, a prosperous American suburb, an Israeli kibbutz, an urban slum, and a Maoist-controlled village.

Every one of us carries in himself relations with other persons. The language in which an individual thinks, the symbols he imagines, the emotions he feels, all exhibit the social context in which he has become a person. All persons are persons-in-relationships. In turn each affects the community.

Our General Principles of Moral Decision, then, must include some directions for choosing our relations to the community and the kind of community to be developed. As we have identified certain Principles for Choice of Beneficiary, directed to answering the question for whom values should be chosen, we must now ask how we are to choose our relations to communities and how we are to determine the right kind of community to form.

16. Heb. 12:1–2. Cf. 1 John 3:2–3 and Gal. 2:20.

1. The Principle of Cooperation

Every person ought, when possible, to cooperate with others in the production and enjoyment of shared values.

a. Validation. Many values can be much enhanced by sharing in a cooperative relationship. When four people form a quartet and sing together, each one of the four may have much more enjoyment than he could have had in singing alone. This is partly because by cooperation new forms of the values shared can be produced—in this instance combinations of solo and harmony of two, three, and four parts. Added to that great increase is the value of the social relationships themselves.

Most values are capable of enhancement by sharing in cooperation although often alternation with solitary cultivation or preparation is needed. Consequently, if a person is to contribute maximally to the realization of values, he must seek to cooperate with others in the production and enjoyment of shared values, ranging from economic to religious.

b. From Cooperation to the Body of Christ. The General Principle does not state what the shared values are to be nor say anything about the method for securing cooperation or the form it is to take. In the New Testament, on the other hand, we read of the actual formation of a profoundly cooperative body, the Church.

The account in Acts 2 undoubtedly idealizes the primitive Church. We can read elsewhere in Acts of the dissensions, and more detail is to be found in the earlier documents, the Letters of Paul. However, even if we discount as symbolic or exaggerated the stories of apostolic miracles, the long list of nationalities represented, and the numbers of converts on the first day, the account is still impressive. We must go further, however. The exceedingly rapid spread of Christianity and the founding of churches throughout the Roman Empire, which are facts of known history, indicate that there must have been some such exciting and contagious fellowship as is here described.

According to the account in Acts the primitive Church was formed by the power of the Holy Spirit, and included the most diverse nationalities, races, and classes of people who shared their new spiritual riches and also their food, and, as needed, their wealth. All this sharing is pictured as a grateful, glad, and spontaneous outpouring which was understandably contagious (Acts 2:41–47).

It is generally assumed in the New Testament that this kind of cooperation in organic unity can be experienced only among believers. Since Christ is the very center of life to them, all their purposes and values are united in him. People who do not participate in this faith could hardly cooperate in "the production and enjoyment" of *this* system of "shared values." In the primitive Church the intensive cultivation of the close-knit Christian fellowship was of prime importance.

Yet by its very nature this fellowship reached out beyond itself. Its passion was the sharing of its supremely valued spiritual treasure with others. The Church sought to extend the circle of Christian cooperation and sharing throughout the world.

While the Church remained a small minority body within the empire, even though suspected and often persecuted by the government, its members were exhorted to be cooperative, law-abiding citizens, as we have noted. Only when they received commands from the government which contradicted commands of God were they to refuse cooperation.

If we are to follow the same Principle today, this will mean that as Christians we must cooperate especially closely with fellow Christians in the sharing of all the values we associate with Christ. At the same time, as we seek the production of values to which Christ calls us— such as economic justice or world peace—we are to cooperate with all who will work with us toward those ends. In fact the boundaries of the body of Christ are now ill-defined. Many people professedly in the Church know little of historic Christian faith and are little concerned about many of its values. On the other hand, both from centuries of Christian teaching and also influenced from other sources, many people outside the churches labor diligently for some of the goals approved by the most sensitive Christian conscience. We have every reason to cooperate with them for the purpose of seeking to achieve those goals.[17]

2. The Principle of Social Devotion

Every person ought to devote himself to serving the best interests of the group and to subordinate personal gain to social gain.[18]

a. Explanation and Validation. It is often said that a person ought to subordinate his own interests to his neighbor's. We have examined critically Nygren's call for a complete *denial* of self-interest. But even the call for invariable *subordination* of self-interest to the interests of another encounters insuperable objections, despite an initial favorable response from idealistic impulse.

The first objection is that the demand would be impossible for the

17. Cf. Matt. 21:28–31; Mark 9:38–40.
18. Cf. Muelder, *op. cit.*, pp. 117–19, where an earlier and slightly different version of my formulation is quoted and expounded. The idea of principles (or "laws") of community was proposed in one of my classes by Rev. Glen W. Trimble, then a graduate student, and the formulation of them owes much to him. Muelder uses all, with thoughtful exposition.

people of any community to fulfill, even if everyone were perfectly desirous of this fulfillment. If Mr. Smith is subordinating all his interests to Mr. Brown's, then how does Mr. Brown give priority to Mr. Smith's?

The second is that it involves a self-contradictory theory of value. If Smith's values *ought* to be subordinated to Brown's, then a direct self-contradiction is involved in asserting that at the same time Brown's values ought to be subordinated to Smith's.

Many a young married couple stumble into the absurdity of this. The young husband offers to take his wife out wherever she would like to go. But in her love she wants singlemindedly to make him happy, so she wants to go where he wants to go. The argument goes back and forth until a real deadlock develops and the evening is ruined. In a society of two or of billions, if everyone were to seek *only* to please someone else, no one could be pleased.

Yet we feel that something is missing here. We do need to subordinate ourselves, else life becomes selfish, or at least too calculating as regards self-interest over against other-interest. Yes, we do, indeed, need and are obligated to subject our personal interests, not to single individuals, but to the values of the group to which we belong.

This does not mean that the individual surrenders his *conscience* to the group, seeking the values which the rulers or the majority of the group favor. God forbid! It does mean that he considers what, in his judgment, would be to the best interests of the group, devotes himself to those interests, and subordinates personal gain to gain for the group.

The young couple may escape from their impasse if they begin choosing, not for the pleasure or other value of him or of her as an individual, but for the best strengthening and enriching of the little group they have formed by their marriage. The needs of the individuals will not then be ignored. The home needs members who are growing in their own value experience. But individual interests are now judged in the light of the couple—and probably later a family— in all its relationships.

This makes sense, for the whole is greater than any of its individual members, and the values of the whole group—whether family or other group—are greater than those of any individual in it. Moreover, as the Principle of Cooperation has established, the whole of a cooperating community is much greater than the sum of its noncooperating parts.

To what group should the individual subordinate his personal interests? There are some groups of which he is inevitably a member, including usually family, neighborhood, nation, and world. There are others which he may choose to join, including bridge club, political association, and church organization. The individual will have to decide the relative priorities of the different groups, in accordance with the various Principles, especially the Principle of Coherent Valuation and also the Principle of the Ideal of Community to which we must soon turn.

Social devotion must be carefully related to self-realization. The individual, as a valuer, has his own intrinsic worth, and not simply as a contributor to the group of which he is a member. Even while subordinating his own interests to the interests of the group, as he sees them, he must still see that the interest of the group in the full development of its members, including himself, is of essential importance.

Such balancing of individual and group interest is, of course, impossible unless such values are chosen for self and group as are compatible. The totalitarian demands of a fascist state, for example, are inimical to full development of its individual citizens. Likewise, the interests of an irresponsible playboy are incompatible with devotion to a family, a nation, or a church.

b. Christian Devotion for the Salvation of All.   The New Testament and the history of Christianity are full of exhortations to self-sacrifice and also present to us numerous examples of such sacrifice, from Jesus himself to Martin Luther King, Jr.

For whom are the sacrifices properly made? What group is to command final subordinating, serving devotion? Does one's family come first? One's particular church? One's nation?

For Christians, Jesus and the Gospels provide the supreme normative answer. The best known passage in the New Testament declares,

> For God so loved the world that he gave his only Son, that whoever believes in him should not perish but have eternal life. For God sent the Son into the world, not to condemn the world, but that the world might be saved through him.   [John 3:16–17. Cf. 12:32]

Similarly, Paul represents the life, death, and exaltation of Jesus as intended for the salvation of *all* people,

> that at the name of Jesus every knee should bow, in heaven and on earth and under the earth, and every tongue confess that Jesus Christ is Lord, to the glory of God the Father.   [Phil. 2:10–11]

Paul himself is true to this vision as he travels about the Mediterranean basin, earning his living with his tentmaking, but incessantly preaching and teaching, guiding in the formation of churches, warning, encouraging, and spending himself without stint. Finally, when he awaits execution or another of his remarkable deliverances from prison, he writes that even his imprisonment and sentence to death are for the good. These events spread his testimony in the praetorian guard and strengthen faith and courage in Rome and elsewhere. Since "what has happened to me has really served to advance the gospel," he writes, "I rejoice. Yes, and I shall rejoice" (Phil. 1:12, 18–19).

The Christian is to subordinate his own interests to those of family and nation. But all must be subjected to the cause of Christ in service to the whole world. Thus the Principle of Social Devotion is broadened in Christian teaching to include the whole world and to specify "the best interests" of the world in terms of faith and the fullness of life offered by God through Christ.

3. The Principle of the Ideal of Community

Every person ought to form and choose all of his ideals and values in loyalty to his ideal of what the whole community ought to become; and when possible to participate responsibly in groups to help them similarly form and choose all their ideals and values.

a. Exposition and Validation. This Principle leaves open for every individual the obligation and privilege of forming his own "ideal of what the whole community ought to become." It assumes that he does not have the right to attempt life as an isolated individual. Reasons have been stated under the last two Principles discussed.

The Principle of the Ideal of Community also excludes the supposition that we need only to form ideals of what individuals ought to be, try to influence the formation of such individuals and let good communities result as a matter of course. This supposition underlies some types of church life aimed only at the conversion of individuals. If we have a community of truly born-again individuals, with love in their hearts, can we not be confident of a good community? By no means! Such individuals would still need to give the most careful attention to best possible forms of economic, political, and social organizations, to ways of assuring good education for all, to provisions for the variously handicapped, to intercultural and international relations, to best techniques and quantities of taxation, and many other problems.

Even knowing clearly what constitutes a good individual gives no guarantee of knowing what constitutes a good community. When Plato considered a city-state to be simply an individual "writ large," he made one of the worst blunders of his whole remarkable career. The result was to present in *The Republic* the blueprint for an amazing mixture of idealism and an oppressive police state where only a small minority of people—if any—would have a chance of developing into the kind of persons he regarded as ideal.

In order to seek the maximum of coherent value for individuals, we must give much attention to the kind of community needed. We must also work responsibly in the various groups to which we have access in order to exert our influence for the forming of such community.

In the statement of this Principle the community spoken of is "the whole community." We live in a day in which decisions made ten thousand miles away may radically alter all the conditions of life within hours. "The whole community" to which we ought to give responsible attention, then, is the world community which includes all mankind. Formally, a person has responsibilities only for the largest community in which he is aware of living and being able to participate. Materially, all human beings ought to be made aware of responsibilities for the whole world community which in fact affects the interests of all individuals on earth.

b. Ideal Community and Reign of God.   That "the whole community" must, for the Christian, include all mankind and be subject to Christ has already become clear. But we have seen that the concept of the ideal individual cannot be simply transferred to the community. There must be carefully formed also the "ideal of what the whole community ought to become," and all of our other ideals, values, and choices must be made subject to that.

There cannot be any question what, in general terms, is the Christian ideal of the whole community, nor can there be any question of Jesus' command that all our other ideals, values, and choices must be subject to it. That ideal is the kingdom or reign of God over all people and in all things. Regarding material needs of food, drink, and clothing, Jesus exhorts his followers not to be anxious. It is not that you do not need them; indeed,

> your heavenly Father knows that you need them all. But seek first his kingdom and his righteousness, and all these things shall be yours as well.   [Matt. 6:32–33]

Marxians object that the notion of the kingdom of God is too vague to be a guide to action, as well as being unacceptable because of its reference to God. It is true that we need much more specific guidelines concerning the structures of government and social policies generally. The generality of the Christian ideal, however, marks its strength as well as its incompleteness. Particular programs and policies are related to historical periods and situations. A structure of government or an economic system which serves a people well in a nomadic period may be highly defective when most of the people have turned to permanent residence and agriculture. A predominantly urban, industrial society makes new demands.

On the other hand, the kingdom of God is not wholly without specification. From the Beatitudes and other passages we learn that it is characterized by faithful obedience to God's commands in Christ. In the kingdom, the people are characterized as merciful, pure in heart, courageous, self-controlled, and kind. The community is just and at peace. The whole is infused with loving-kindness. The further characterization of this ideal and its demands upon us in this present age will occupy much of our further study.

E. PRINCIPLES OF ETHICAL ONTOLOGY

1. The Principle of Quest for the Source of Ethical Obligation

Every person ought to seek to know the source and significance of the harmony and universality of these principles, that is, of the coherence of the moral order.

a. Exposition and Validation. The very possibility of such a system of Principles as we have been examining is further evidence supporting belief in the objective reality of moral obligation. How has such obligation come to be a part of reality? In the world of atoms, rocks, and stars there is much of necessity and considerable indeterminacy as well. But duty? Right? Obligation? What is the source and ground of these?

The question becomes even more urgent when we observe deep, underlying relationships between the acceptance of obligations and the knowledge of truth. Apart from acceptance of the obligation to be consistent and honest, science and fraudulent pseudoscience have equal claim to acceptance. Moreover, self-discipline, cooperation, loyalty, industry—all moral virtues—have cleared much of the way to the scientific knowledge which we possess. What, in the very root or ground of being—the being of mankind and the being of all else that is—accounts for this deep harmony among moral obligations and rational ethical principles and between these and the world of matter and physical force?

Every person ought to seek the source of this basic harmony and relevance of ethical principles. We have noted that we are under obligation to consider the situational context of our choices. Whatever situations come and go, we are all continually in this total situation of a morally relevant universe where a system of ethical principles can be discovered. We are obliged to see the basic nature of this total situation. In the long run which the Principle of Foresight requires us to consider, it makes a great difference what kind of world we inhabit. Is it a chance interplay of blind forces? Is there a purposive God who is our Creator, our Sustainer, and the Goal of our destiny? Is life a brief and fitful scene in an indifferent universe, and after it the darkness? Or is there an endless call to yet higher life? The answers to such questions need to be sought, not only to give the intrinsic intellectual value which all quest of truth generates, but also to guide our appraisal of various styles of hope, aspiration, and conduct which are open to us.

b. Biblical Affirmation of God as Source. The first Principle of Ethical Ontology recognizes a universal human obligation to raise a question and to seek the answer. It does not state nor even postulate an answer.

The Christian faith, however, is based upon an answer, namely, the conviction that the one almighty God who is creator and sustaining ground of all being is also the source of the ethical dimensions of existence. Because we are the creatures and subjects of God our Father, we can fulfill our lives and be fully human only in terms of the purpose with which he has made us. God is the source of the moral order, and he alone has empowered us and can renew us for its fulfillment. When we are alienated from him, we place ourselves in an unnatural and false position. We cannot then be true to our own deepest selves. Sin as condition is precisely this alienation from God, hence from true human nature in ourselves and in other human beings. Paul tells how men thus alienated from God became "filled with all manner of wickedness, evil, covetousness, malice" (Rom. 1:22–32).

Since this alienated life is evil, we are under obligation to turn from it. We can do this only by turning to God, the source of freedom and of goodness, as well as the source of the moral order.

2. The Principle of Ethical Adaptation to Ultimate Reality

Every person ought to form all his ideals and choices in relation to his conception of the ultimate reality which is the ground of ethical obligation.

a. Validation and Exposition. The same considerations which require that we seek to know the source of ethical obligation, as they have been stated in support of the last preceding Principle, require also that we make use of that knowledge by taking it into account as we make our ethical decisions.

Moreover, the reality which is basic to all obligation is therefore essential to all valuing and to all true values. Accordingly, whatever a person may find to value, he has reason to value supremely the ground of all values. Other values must then be sought in proper relation to this supreme value.[19]

At this point ethics stands at the doorways into metaphysics and religion. The undertaking to fulfill the Principle of Quest for the Source of Ethical Obligation by theoretical, rational speculation leads

19. Cf. H. Richard Niebuhr, *Radical Monotheism and Western Culture* (New York: Harper & Row, 1960).

one into metaphysics. The effort to relate oneself in living reverence and supreme loyalty to that source is religion.

We may compare Frederick Ferré's definition of religion as "one's way of valuing most comprehensively and intensively."[20] He says further, "Ideally . . . every other valuation, including the sum of all other valuations, will, under appropriate circumstances, be sacrificed to this one. The object of religious valuing, in other words, is 'sacred' " (*ibid.*, p. 66). Ferré does not hold that the "sacred" must be already real, much less ultimate reality. Most philosophy of religion, as well as common usage, understands religion as relating to an object of prior reality, an object regarded as source or ground of value, as well as itself supremely valued. On the other hand, Ferré would have the support of considerable usage by existentialists. Both he and the existentialists would *include* in their definitions, even though not themselves accepting, the kind of religion which we see approached by the Principles of Ethical Ontology.

b. Absolute Devotion to God Alone. Again in this second ontological Principle and the last in the system, reference is made to the source or ground of moral law, but we are not told what it is. In the Scriptures the reference is to the one only God.

We are not to form some ideals and choices in relation to God's commands, while being left at liberty to develop some aspects of our lives in independence from him. We are to worship God alone and serve him only (Deut. 6:13; Matt. 4:10). To do otherwise would be idolatry. It would also divide us against ourselves, violate the unity of the moral order, and renew our alienation.

The system of General Principles rationally discovered by examination of human moral experience moves at last, in the ontological Principles, to the quest for the source of the moral order and the obligation to subordinate all else to that source. However, this is only a rational *ordo cognoscendi;* the order in which human reason comes to know the Principles. The *ordo essendi*, the order of ethical and ontological reality, is precisely opposite. God is "from everlasting to everlasting." Man is a recent arrival among his creatures. "In the beginning God." All being—and, of course, this includes the moral order—begins with God and all is subject from first to last to his sovereign judgment.

While the last of the Principles speaks of the "concept" of the source of the moral order and our obligation to subject all our ideals and choices to that concept, the biblical teaching goes much further. Not only does it identify the source as God, but this teaching bids me be faithful to God, not merely to my concept of God. Of course

20. *Basic Modern Philosophy of Religion*, p. 69.

I am obligated to be true to my best understanding of God, but this is only my more formal obligation. My material and final obligation is to be faithful to God himself, as he truly is. God, and not my poor concept of God, is finally my judge. Hence, in the midst of all my efforts to be true to my best understanding of God, there must be the continuous quest both to understand better who he is, and also to know him more fully in personal relationship.

F.   DIALECTICAL TENSIONS AND RESPONSIBLE FREEDOM

We noted that the *ordo cognoscendi* and the *ordo essendi* of the General Principles are opposite. We should now note that the same is roughly true of the order in which the Principles have been rationally expounded and the order of the Christian's loyalties. Everything begins with the Ultimate Reality, God. Under his reign in our lives we are called to enter into all the other considerations required by the General Principles.

More specifically, in determining his own style of life and in deciding particular ethical questions, the Christian is called to begin with obedient faith in God as known through Jesus Christ. Such faith requires as comprehensive goal the reign of God over an inclusive community united by ties of love. The Christian's ideal of personhood is the spirit of Jesus Christ as predominantly represented in the New Testament. Christian living dynamically unites loyalty to this individual ideal with the inclusive loyalty to the whole ideal community of love under God's reign. All values and choices are to be related freely but faithfully to these complementary loyalties, with due attention to changing situations, actual possibilities, and responsible regard for consequences.

The responsible freedom of Christian life is thus found in the interplay of dialectical considerations, especially the following:

1. The eternal purposes of the righteous God and the changing needs of aspiring, sinful, needy, imperiled human beings.
2. Loyalty to the ideal community, the kingdom of God and to the actual communities such as family, church, nation, and world.
3. Devotion to the community and affirmation of the individual.
4. Loving service to the neighbor and realization of the highest values in the self.
5. The call to perfection and the need for achieving the best possible in actual situations.
6. The requirement of consistent, principled integrity and the need for creative adaptability to changing circumstances.
7. The cultivation of faith, hope, and love in a life of prayerful,

meditative, inward devotion to God and the outgoing, active life of service to the world.

The principles of God's purpose learned by rational examination of human experience and more concretely taught and illustrated in Scripture save us from antinomian anarchy. Without principles we should be left to the mercy of social pressures and the whims of desire in the moments of decision. But if principles could be structured into a rigid system, with corollary rules for every circumstance, the moral life would be reduced to computerized bondage. That might be comfortable, but it would lack the creative freedom of faith. The General Principles, as here outlined, do constitute a system, but it is an organic system, rather than a mechanical one. As a biological organism has its dialectics of anabolism and catabolism, afferent and efferent nervous activity, growing and aging, so the system of General Principles contains dialectical tensions. Since these tensions are ever present, the Christian lives and decides in freedom. The result is responsible freedom.

Such life is bound to produce anxieties and guilt. Most decisions to which we give much thought are of sufficient complexity and ambiguity so that we cannot be sure we are deciding in the best possible way. Dialectical freedom can be creative, but it can also make us insecure and guilt-ridden.

We can deal with the resultant accumulating of guilt by either of two basic approaches besides sinking into emotional sickness. A very common way is to develop a shell of callous indifference. That way leads to spiritual death for the individual and disaster for society.

Christian faith offers a better way which is at the heart of our faith itself. This is the dependence upon grace. We are not saved by works, but by God's freely given loving mercy. We receive the grace of God by faith. Faith commits us to the intention of utter obedience. This must be unfeigned and includes earnest effort both to learn and to do what is truly God's will in all issues we face. When such effort is made we are assured that it is accepted and blessed by God, even when we are mistaken.

When we fail to make the best efforts, we still have access to God's forgiveness by truly repenting and seeking renewal of his Spirit in us.

Here, then, is one more dialectic of the Christian life, and one which is basic to all else—the bipolar living by grace and by obedience. Such living requires an alternation of attention. The Christian turns regularly and frequently to God in worship and prayer, for forgiveness and renewal. Then with fresh spiritual sensitivity he turns again to study and perform his responsible tasks in the world.

In this book we are primarily concerned with the study and action. Yet all this is approached from the background of assurance that God is gracious and merciful. Such assurance, when genuine, gives rise to no easy indifference. Instead, it sends us to our task, gratefully thanking God for his gifts so freely bestowed and seeking eagerly to share all the best God has given with the world in its appalling need.

part II

APPLIED CHRISTIAN ETHICS

chapter eight

From Principles to Action

———————•⌒⌒•———————

A. Considerations Which Must Be Joined

As we move from laying philosophical and theological foundations to the making of decisions for action, we seldom find the task simple.

It is one thing to say that a judge should be just. It is another to know what verdict he should render in a complicated civil suit growing out of an automobile accident. It is one thing to say that we should all be kind and generous. It is a different matter to say what wages a businessman should pay his employees, in view of the prevailing wage scale, the rising cost of living, the sharply competitive market, and the knowledge that a miscalculation could bring not only financial disaster to himself and his family, but also the loss of employment for his workers.

As we move now from basic principles to particular issues which require decision, we need to look a little further into two of the dialectical tensions noted in the last chapter. These are: (1) the tension between our understanding of the eternal purposes of God and the changing needs of human beings; and (2) the tension between grace and obedience. The aspect of the first which we must now examine further is the bipolar relation of basic principles and situational facts. The form in which the second requires brief, but pointed additional notice is the dialectical combination of resultant human attitudes, namely, confidence and urgency.

1. Principles and Situational Facts

Traditional Roman Catholic moralists have taught that to tell a lie is always wrong. On the other hand, the situationist says we cannot tell whether speaking the truth or lying is better until we know the situation. Circumstances will determine what is right.

Yet most traditionalists will grant that the situation has much to do with defining what *is* lying or truth-telling and with the question *how* one ought to tell the truth. Many will concede that under some circumstances it is morally right to deceive a hearer or to cause him to deceive himself, while they will still insist that this must be done by means other than telling a lie—for example, by using an ambiguous form of words likely to be interpreted in such a way as to be misleading.[1]

The situationist, for his part, cannot draw from the circumstances any moral directive without referring to *some* principle of obligation. Thus Joseph Fletcher maintains that we ought always to do what love requires, though love requires different kinds of acts—lying or truth-telling, taking or saving life—in different situations.

Following our General Principles and the basic injunctions of Christian ethics, we must in every moral dilemma seek to be true to Christian principles, especially *koinonia* love, taking account of the situation in which we are to act. Both considerations must always be included. The moral principle or ideal provides the ethical perspective. The situation makes possible the relating of the principle to the proposed act in view of its predictable consequences. Only by considering both can we know the moral significance of the act.

Moreover, we usually face more than the two possibilities of performing or not performing a certain act. What the possible choices are can be discovered only in view of all obtainable relevant facts in the situation.

2. Confidence and Urgency

An important aspect of Christian faith is the confident trust in God. Church people readily recall the words of Jesus in the Farewell Discourses of the Fourth Gospel,

> Peace I leave with you; my peace I give to you; not as the world gives do I give to you. Let not your hearts be troubled, neither let them be afraid.   [John 14:27]

Many other passages will come to mind, with messages of trust, peace, and assurance.

In American churches of the twentieth century such teachings have been and still remain popular. Unlike Jesus' disciples and many early readers of John's Gospel who were being prepared to undergo martyrdom for their faith, many American churchgoers are affluent and comfortable people who have no intention of taking any heroic risks for the sake of faith or justice. With some feelings of guilt and

---

1. While not going into detail, Dietrich von Hildebrand is typical when he absolutely condemns lying, but says concerning "the deception which is connected with lying" that it "need not in every case be morally illegitimate." *Christian Ethics* (New York: David McKay Company, 1953), p. 148.

occasional uneasiness about the ominous state of the world, they look to the church for soothing insulation against care.

Such understanding and use of biblical reassurance is simply perversion. The peace of Christ approaching crucifixion has nothing to do with the peace of complacent hiding from the anguished needs of the world. It is not gained by escape from the fear of injury, death, or failure. Rather, the peace of Christ is given to him who for the sake of God's own righteousness and love accepts injury, death, and failure. This peace is on the other side of fear. Only he who passes *through* fear to faith can know it.

In the peace of Christ one works without the hurry of anxious panic and yet without the ease of complacency. Because human beings for whom Christ died still hunger for food and truth; because God's children still fight and kill; because men and women still die without reconciliation and without hope, no one who loves God can take his ease. But because the end is in the hands of God, we need not be fretfully anxious. Hence we "work without haste and without rest."[2]

B. PRIMARY PRINCIPLES AND SECONDARY PRECEPTS

As we move from principles to action there are way stations. Thomas Aquinas recognized in natural law a distinction between primary principles and secondary precepts. R. A. Armstrong has made a careful study of this distinction. He shows that Thomas makes two different approaches to secondary precepts. Only the second need concern us here.[3] Secondary precepts, he says, are derived from primary principles of natural law much as we derive corollaries from general principles of speculative knowledge.

Thomas apparently regarded as primary only such principles as he considered self-evident—e.g., that we should "do good and avoid evil." However, such statements are little if anything more than tautologies, so such a classification would reduce all our General Principles of Moral Decision and the law of love to secondary status.

We could redefine secondary precepts in such a way as to place them a little nearer the empirical data and further from the most abstract generalizations than our General Principles or the basic Christian teachings of love to God and neighbor. We could not avoid facing

2. From the prayer, "Grant to us such a vision of Thy power and glory that we may work without haste and without rest." For that prayer I am indebted to the late Edwin P. Booth, who adapted it from Henry Sylvester Nash.

3. In the first, he describes such precepts as forbidding acts which make a primary end more difficult, though not impossible, or which hinder or prevent attainment of a secondary end. See Armstrong, *Primary and Secondary Precepts in Thomistic Natural Law Teaching* (The Hague: Martinus Nijhoff, 1966), p. 64.

immediately, then, the question whether a proposed secondary precept would be valid under conditions nowhere existing on earth now, but conceivably present in the distant past or some unforeseen future. Such discussion might be interesting and possibly even useful speculation on rare occasions.

However, a more promising procedure would seem to be an immediate turning to examine the actual institutions and problems of the present day and, by reference to our basic principles, to seek guidelines for our decisions under existing conditions. This procedure will serve to give greater emphasis to empirical data and to safeguard Christian freedom in meeting the ever-changing conditions of modern life.

C. PRINCIPLES AND SITUATIONAL GUIDELINES

We observe with James Russell Lowell that "New occasions teach new duties." Solemn obligations of one time and place may differ considerably from those pertaining to other occasions.

On the other hand, many situations remain for considerable times, with little change to affect the validity of certain ethical decisions. There are also many situations which have numerous close parallels. The important relevance of the situation to moral decision need not, then, mean that each decision for action must be made as if the problem, in its ethical essentials, had never before been confronted.

An American citizen observes that his government's expenditures for the military are many times as high as those for the elimination of urban and rural slums. After studying the various perils to his country, he decides that while this situation continues, with domestic needs acute and foreign relations little altered, he will support efforts to change priorities. Now when new bills for military appropriations or for better housing, more job opportunities, or sounder income support for the poor are introduced, he does not have all his thinking about priorities to do over again.

Such a citizen might formulate a *situational guideline* in some such terms as this: relative to present high expenditures on military strength and low expenditures on correction of flagrant domestic ills, Christian love and my ideal of community oblige me to work for a change of national priorities. Therefore, I will seize all possible opportunities to support congressmen and specific measures to correct the domestic injustices and provide opportunity for deprived people, while likewise opposing the maintenance of present high military appropriations.

Such a situational guideline does not absolve the individual from the obligation to examine each specific candidate or measure. A candidate may appeal vocally for his vote on the very grounds the citizen approves; but the candidate's record may show that his predictable performance will be much different. An introduced bill may look, at first sight, like a measure to relieve poverty, but the fine print may show it to be actually an open invitation to a maximum of corruption and a minimum of aid to the poor. A bill purporting to cut military appropriations may actually have the effect of transferring items from one category to another and of starting new projects which have built-in assurances of growth into much greater proportions.

In short, situational guidelines do not eliminate the need for alert watchfulness, examination of new details, and sensitiveness to relevant change in the situation. They do enable one to begin preparation for specific decision from a base much more concrete and immediately relevant than a General Principle or basic Christian teaching.

If this multiplication of premises from which decisions are to be reached looks complex and artificial, try to describe the way in which morally responsible people make decisions all the while. Here is a legislator who is convinced that the greatest problem of the country is crime and that the main path to improvement is the way of stronger police power, fewer judicial safeguards for the interests of suspects, and judges willing to pronounce severe sentences. As long as crime continues to increase or remains at high level, he intends to act on the basis of these convictions. They are his situational guidelines concerning a rather wide range of decisions.

Situational guidelines are not new, then, but are actually in universal use among people who maintain some degree of consistency or stability in their behavior. It is contended here simply that such guidelines ought to be formulated with great care on the basis of our general principles (philosophical and Christian) and from study of the situation. As must be apparent, our situational guidelines are of utmost importance in actual day-to-day decisions. Too often they are adopted on the shallow basis of prejudices expressed by neighbors or other associates, of misinformation, or of some one or few emotionally charged experiences.

D. Initial Presumption

Philip Wogaman has suggested a further ethical consideration of which we need to become aware if we are to act responsibly. This is the *initial presumption* with which we approach decisions.[4]

Often the initial presumption is only a kind of temperamental in-

4. Wogaman has developed this concept in class lectures at Wesley Theological Seminary and has written about it in an article, "Christian Moral Judgment," in *Christian Action*, Vol. 2, No. 5 (Jan., 1970), pp. 3-23.

clination of which the person holding it is unaware. Sometimes it represents a complex of attitudes developed consciously or unconsciously through a series of experiences. It may or may not be directly related to an adopted situational guideline.

1. Activism and Inaction

Here is a young woman known as a "militant activist." When she hears that there is going to be a demonstration at the city hall, her immediate inclination is to join it. If the cause being espoused is at all congenial to her, while the time and place do not pose extreme difficulties, she will be there. She is similarly inclined to circulate petitions, attend legislative hearings, and wear buttons proclaiming political slogans. She has an initial presumption in favor of personal involvement and action, especially for unpopular causes. This does not mean that she will join every such movement which comes along. But she feels that in a world badly out of joint she ought to be involved in efforts to bring change. Hence she views calls and opportunities for such involvement with favorable initial presumption.

On the other hand, there is many a person with quite the opposite inclination. In a presidential election of the United States, more than one-third of the eligible voting population do not cast ballots. Since 1920 fewer than 47 per cent of people of voting age actually voted in any Congressional election not in a presidential election year.[5] It is obvious that the initial presumption of more than half the people is that they will not take the trouble to vote in a Congressional election unless a vote can be cast for president at the same time. A much greater majority see any call to more vigorous, time-consuming, and potentially embarrassing political action with initial negative presumption. Even more people would be difficult or impossible to recruit for the kinds of action for change which are viewed with initial favor by the young lady first described.

There are many reasons and causes for such initial presumption in favor of inaction. One is sheer inertia. It is easier and more pleasant to stay at home and watch television. Another is a fair degree of satisfaction with things as they are. Then again, so many issues are complex that many persons who are dissatisfied with present conditions are thoroughly confused about the kind of change they should seek. Moreover, in middle-class American society, demonstrations and even petitions are widely identified by people as subversive or fanatical movements of which they want no part. Politics, even in the major parties, tends to carry a tainted reputation with which respected people do not want to soil their hands. This is especially true of local ward

5. *The Statistical Abstract of the United States: 1968*, p. 369.

politics where political influence begins. Some people have, on some occasions, made vigorous efforts to support change, and the effort either failed or brought about change which proved disappointing. Yet others are in business or in professional careers which may be injured by entering controversial activities.

Considering all these reasons and influences which can support inaction, it is no cause for wonder that the initial presumption of most Americans relative to most calls for social action is negative! It generally requires either a case of clear self-interest or a crisis of major emotional impact to overcome this presumption and stir large numbers into action.

2. Other Initial Presumptions

Another kind of initial presumption can be seen in characteristic responses to an appeal for gifts of church members to support the mission of a church in a foreign land. Regardless of the specific cause to be supported—a school or hospital to be built, a seminary to be supported, or a missionary couple to be sponsored—anyone who knows the congregation well can predict with fair probability good responses from some parishioners and little or no response from others. Yet some of the "mission-minded" people may give less than many others in a campaign for air-conditioning in the home church.

It is evident that even though the goal of the current appeal may never have been presented before, the appeal meets different kinds of initial presumptions about priorities in some minds than in others.

In this instance, there is probably a considerable system of beliefs underlying each initial presumption. These beliefs may have to do with understanding of the Christian gospel itself, stereotyped images of "missionaries" and "missions," breadth of information and personal acquaintance, and many other factors.

There are a number of United States senators who have found different reasons for opposing each proposed civil rights bill to reach their committees or the Senate floor. More important than those stated reasons for opposing particular bills is the fact that these men have opposed every measure which would decrease discrimination against blacks. Their discourses on rights of property owners, on due process, on local autonomy of school districts, and even on states rights are relatively superficial as compared to their initial presumption that racial separation and discrimination are desirable.

Other initial presumptions may be observed in our responses to proposals for revision of the United Nations Charter, or for the establishment of wildlife refuges, to strict enforcement of traffic laws, or to the sexual behavior of the girl next door.

3. Need for Critical Examination

The discussion of initial presumptions is not for the purpose of assisting decision whether or not to have them. Everyone does exhibit them in responses to questions large or small decided every day. To a large extent initial presumptions constitute what we consider to be a person's character and also his image in the community.

Initial presumptions need discussion so that we may become conscious of them and so that we may examine critically the ones which largely control our behavior. If we make such critical examination we shall often find that the reasons we give ourselves and others for our decisions are drawn from superficial levels of our decision-making processes, while the major controlling factors are in the initial presumptions which we brought with us to the issues. This will be true no matter whether we are considering a special effort to welcome the new family in the neighborhood or a proposed reformation of the social welfare laws.

If we are to grow ethically as Christians, it is not enough that we examine our particular decisions in the light of reason and of Christ, although this must be done. It is necessary that we also bring deliberately to consciousness and into critical study the initial presumptions which mainly determine the way we live.

E. Motivation

However much we know about our duties and opportunities and about the will of God as shown in Christ, such knowledge is no guarantee that we shall live accordingly. There is an aphorism which runs, "Wisdom is knowing what to do; skill is knowing how to do it; virtue is doing it." The study of ethics should assist in the cultivation of wisdom and even, at the more general levels, of skill. Virtue requires the additional ingredient of motivation. Motivation is of primary concern to the parent, the pastor, and the personal counselor, as well as to the aspiring person himself, rather than to the study of ethics, whether Christian or other. Yet we cannot properly treat the movement from principles to action without giving brief attention to the motivation involved in the transition.

Paul writes,

> I do not understand my own actions. For I do not do what I want, but I do the very thing I hate. . . . I can will what is right, but I cannot do it.   [Rom. 7:15, 18]

Why this discrepancy between knowledge of the good and good

resolution, on the one hand, and actual performance, on the other? The strength of habit is often an important factor. The appeal of immediate pleasure is another. The social pressure of people near us, and above all, the dominance of self-concern override, in the event, many good decisions made in advance.

Both Thomas Aquinas and Aristotle would include initial presumptions brought to each situation from past experience under the general head of habits. In any event, the presumptions are important and often exercise at the crucial moment of action more power than newly formulated judgments.

Underlying both the dominance of self-concern and the inhibiting initial presumptions are the defensiveness, anxious insecurity, and emotional loneness which characterize our guilty alienation from God and true community. Freedom from these moral handicaps is to be gained as a gift of grace offered by God through Christ and the faithful community and appropriated by personal acceptance.

Positive motivation to do the good we know is gained in part by sheer determination. William James was faithful to experience when he declared that a human person does not, like a physical object, move always in the direction to which pressures push or pull. There is also this ever-new force of volition which can be exercised at the moment of decision, tipping the scales in one direction or the other.

However, there is much more to it than this. Underlying decisions and actions are practices of thought and the influences to which one has subjected oneself beforehand. Behind the quiet courage of Christ before Pilate were long nights of prayer, and many years of study, especially in the great prophets. Even the enemies of the gospel could see something of the forces which accounted for the effective strength of the apostles on trial. So we read,

> Now when they [members of the priestly council] saw the boldness of Peter and John, and perceived that they were uneducated, common men, they wondered; and they recognized that they had been with Jesus. [Acts 4:13]

Their association with Jesus had given them both an urgent message and the courage to deliver it in any company, however learned or threatening.

The Christian draws basic assumptions and also motivation from participation in the Church's remembrance of Jesus and its faith in him as God's action in history. In the corporate worship, preaching, study, and work this participation is actualized and renewed. By his reading, his associations, and his daily habits of thought and conversation, the individual prepares the inner springs of motivation from which action arises.

F. INDIVIDUAL AND COMMUNITY

The ethical subject of conduct is the individual. The character of organizations, communities, and institutions is shaped by the decisions of numerous individuals. It is often assumed, therefore, by Americans of pietistic tradition, that all the social problems of the world will be solved when enough people are converted to an earnest Christian faith. In our study of the General Principles of Community we saw that this idea is far wide of the mark. Indeed, a genuine Christian life must be formulated within the broad context of devotion to the reign of God over the total community of mankind.

Social groups, small and large, are also significant units of action. I am called upon to work for the development of a righteous nation in a peaceful and just world community. I cannot do so effectively unless I join with others in efforts to move toward these goals. Many individuals, each working alone, could not provide educational and economic opportunity for all people or stable international relations. Significant advance toward those goals can be made only by organized effort to develop structures of law, organization, and economic relations suited to the purpose. It is of the most vital importance that we see Christian love as providing formative purpose and motivation for skillfully designed institutions and corporate effort, not as substitute for them.

When this truth is recognized it can be seen also that effective expression of Christian purpose in modern society requires much use of technical knowledge.

G. CHRISTIAN ETHICS AND TECHNICAL KNOWLEDGE

1. The Need for Facts

A moral decision must be made in one situation and not everywhere in general. Consequently, if the decision is to be sound the relevant facts of the situation must be known as well as the situation permits. The relevant facts are often complex and capable of being known only by the help of precise and specialized study. Hence moral decision requires the use of knowledge made available by the physical sciences and the sciences of man.

It is folly to decide at what level to set the speed limits on a highway without consulting the statistics of accidents relative to speed on that or similar highways. Food and drug laws and regulations cannot be responsibly enacted without analysis of much information from the medical, chemical, and biological sciences. Moral decision on personal, national, or international policies concerning methods of birth limitation requires the taking account of expert analysis of numerous facts. The needed information concerns, first of all, population trends and effects of these trends on the quality of human life, and then the known physiological, genetic, psychological, and social effects of different contraceptive methods.

On none of these or many other ethical problems can any one person collect at first hand the information imperatively needed for moral decision. Even the highly competent specialist in one field must depend heavily on colleagues in the same field and much more on information made available by specialists in other fields related to the decision which must be made. Most of us are not expert in any of the scientific specialties involved at a given time and so must depend on authorities who are. Christians who are not educated sufficiently even to do the reading and reference work required to learn the facts from the sciences need to learn to rely on people who do make such careful study and who share their own Christian seriousness, rather than deciding on the basis of uninformed emotional harangues, political slogans, or traditional dogmas which have not been reexamined in the light of present-day problems and new information.

2. The Necessity for Principles of Valuation

On the other hand, moral decision cannot be made on the sole basis of factual information or of biological, chemical, psychological, sociological, or other scientific analysis. No amount of knowledge concerning present human and environmental realities and trends can provide in itself premises from which ethical conclusions may be drawn. Even if it be shown that a policy under consideration would bring an end to the human race on earth, it is not established that the policy is immoral unless one believes that the human race ought not to be destroyed.

Often, the difference of decision when the same facts are faced is due to different *priorities* of value in the ethical premises adopted. During the 1968–1969 national debate on antiballistic missile systems (the ABM), neither Senator Richard Russell nor Dr. George Wald, 1967 Nobel Prize winner in physiology and medicine, believed that human beings ought to be exterminated from the earth, nor that great numbers of them should be killed. Both contemplated the possibility that the ABM proposal might lead to the extinction or near-extinction of man. But in a public address at Massachusetts Institute of Technology, Professor Wald said,

> A few months ago, Sen. Richard Russell of Georgia ended a speech in the Senate with the words: "If we have to start over with Adam and Eve, I want them to be Americans; and I want them on this continent and not in Europe." That was a United States Senator holding a patriotic speech. Well, here is a Nobel Laureate who thinks those words are criminally insane.[6]

Senator Russell regarded the superior power and future ethnic dominance of Americans as supremely important, while the prospects of the human race generally seemed to him secondary. On the other hand, Laureate Wald regarded the future of human beings, including Americans, as worthy of first consideration, the relative position of different nationalities being minor by comparison.

It is impossible to state, apart from a concrete situation, how various kinds of value should be related in order of priority, from most important to least important. We can recognize that some values are "higher" and others "lower," but that must not be understood as implying that the higher values should always be chosen in preference to the lower.

Judging, in general, which values are higher, we may place intrinsic worth, such as an educated mind, above instrumental values like money, the more permanent, like goodness of character, above such transient values as the taste of a well-cooked meal. Values which are peculiarly human, such as wisdom, saintliness, and aesthetic enjoyment, have often been placed above physical health and sexual indulgence as such, which are present also in many lower animals. Again, values which can be shared without diminishing them in the experience of the original possessor would be widely regarded as higher than those which must be divided to be shared. Thus, I cannot share one hundred dollars with fifty other people without reducing my own possession. On the other hand, if I share a piece of knowledge with fifty others, I actually gain firmer possession of the whole of it in the process.

Following such tests as these, we can form a scale of values. Such a scale was constructed by W. G. Everett, who placed the various kinds of value, from lowest to highest, as follows:

---

6. *The Washington Post*, March 30, 1969, p. B3. Wald's complete speech, delivered extemporaneously on March 4, was also printed in the *Congressional Record* on March 17 and in an extraordinary technical violation of Senate rules, four subsequent additional times, by request of two Representatives and three Senators. In one printing the reference to Senator Russell's remarks was deleted. Cf. *The New Republic*, May 17, 1969, pp. 8–9.

I. Economic Values.
II. Bodily Values.
III. Values of Recreation.
IV. Associational Values.
V. Character Values.
VI. Aesthetic Values.
VII. Intellectual Values.
VIII. Religious Values.[7]

We may debate any particular scaling in detail. I would, for example, place character values above the aesthetic and intellectual. Other classifications of the types might also be urged, but Everett's scale will sufficiently serve our present purpose.

In general, the higher values are the ones which give depth and meaning to human life. Most people will applaud, even if they will not imitate, a man who gives up wealth, sacrifices his health and pleasure, and even lays down his life rather than deny what he believes is true, betray a friendship, or act contrary to God's will as he sees it. In this sense, the higher values do rightly take priority over the lower.

Notice, however, that the conflicts of values just mentioned are all among values in the experience of one individual. Even in individual experience there are times and seasons. Greater moral and religious value may usually be achieved by an individual who gives reasonable care to his body, and who seeks sufficient income to avoid being a burden to others, than to one who in young adulthood totally disregards economic needs and refuses to eat, while devoting all his time to serving others and praying.

When we turn to the values of people other than the deciding subject, it is much more obvious that a scale of higher and lower values is of little help to sound ethical choice. When a neighbor is hungry or cold or about to be evicted for lack of rent money, if I possess or have access to food, clothing, or money to relieve his distress, my highest choice is not to invite him to prayer or to the intellectual values of a book loan. Indeed, some of the worst evasions of Christian responsibility by churches consist in exclusive concern with other people's "spiritual" values, while the members take very good care of their own health and comfort.

The space shots sending men to the moon afford a good analogy of the relations between classes of values. The first stage of the rocket lifting the whole machine and its human cargo from earth may be

7. *Moral Values* (New York: Henry Holt, 1918), Chap. VII. Cf. the discussion of value scales, in Edgar S. Brightman, *Moral Values;* Wilbur M. Urban, *Fundamentals of Ethics* (New York: Henry Holt and Company, 1930); and Peter A. Bertocci and Richard M. Millard, *Personality and the Good.*

compared to the evolutionary process by which God has lifted life from the soil and water of earth to the level of human existence. The process of putting the front section and module into orbit around the earth may be compared to the process of securing and stabilizing the lower values of human life. Without the body and food and warmth there would be no more of human value. But this low orbit is not the justification for the journey of life. It is from the earth orbit that the module is sent on its journey to the moon. From the secure physical and economic base, God intends that man "take off" into the eternal life of truth, faith, hope, and love. It is that life in fulfillment of the higher values which constitutes the meaning and goal of the whole journey on which we have all been launched.[8]

We must not despise the launching base in the earthly environment around us. Great care must be taken to see that all human beings are provided with those earthly values which will give them a secure and stable orbit. While providing this stability and security of the lower but basic values, we must use great care not to exhaust all energies or do anything contradictory to the supreme human and divine values which constitute our real reason of being. To act dishonestly, disloyally, or selfishly in securing our own economic values, for example, is so to distort our lives as to clog and fetter all aspiration for the higher gifts.

Our task, then, is so to relate all together in individual and society that lower and higher value-achieving may be coordinated in a grand harmony. Only then can we report gratefully and joyously, like the space technicians, "All systems are go!" as we move toward the stars of our heaven-destined goal.

3. *Principles of Value and Factual Knowledge*

Sound procedure in reaching moral decisions requires, then, both the most adequate possible knowledge of the situation and also true ethical principles. The sciences are needed to provide understanding of possible alternative courses of action and their predictable consequences. Ethical principles define the good we should will.

Any one structured, step-by-step procedure in decision-making seems impossible to prescribe for all kinds of problems and situations, even when we assume a standpoint of Christian faith. A man's decision how much if any money to give in response to the latest financial appeal in his mail would not usually involve the same steps as would be taken by a committee of a large denomination in determining what stand to take on nationally uniform divorce laws.

8. For the analogy I am indebted to a sermon preached by Dr. Theodore R. Bowen at Foundry Methodist Church, Washington, D.C., on May 19, 1969, just an hour before the launching of Apollo 10.

Yet the basic ingredients of moral decision are the same, whatever the problem. They must include clear defining of the issue as presented in the situation, noting the values at stake, and weighing the alternative possibilities in the light of basic Christian principles and such rationally defined principles of decision-making as were presented in Chapter Seven, above. Usually the movement of thought goes back and forth many times between situational facts and ethical principles.

For the Christian it is also important that he frequently renew the liveliness of his faith by worship, prayer, and interaction with people of devoted faith. In the tasks of decision-making he will be equipped for sound action only if ethical principles have become for him living, personal commitments, expressed in prayer and in community with his fellows.

It is right, then, that we should begin our more concrete study of ethical problems with the Church. The Church provides an essential part of the distinctive situation from within which the Christian makes his moral decisions in every sphere.

chapter nine

The Church

---··◦—⟨∾⟩—◦··---

A. Why a Church?

Many people are asking whether there is any reason for the Church to be at all. We live in a secular age. The decisions affecting the future of the world appear, at least, to be mostly in the responsibility and power of government, the mass media, and the big economic organizations, especially business corporations and labor unions. In a way less visible publicly the family doubtless has its important functions. But where, in modern, secularized society, is the place for the Church? If Christian faith is important, then why not let that be passed along in the family and among friends? Why incorporate it in the special organizations we call churches?

In answer, we can point out the need for carefully organized Christian education and the importance of support for parental Christian nurture given by classes and other groups within the churches. We might also point to the pioneering work which churches have done in educating most of the black leadership in Africa—before governments and other agencies were interested in such work and at a time when it was often extremely dangerous and costly. We can speak also of many pioneering activities in the United States in medical care, education, welfare service to the aged and the poor, and in the fostering of useful legislation. Much more could be said concerning such publicly observable contributions of the Church to the larger society.

The principal answer, however, must be concerned with the integral relation between the Church and the Christian faith itself. The New Testament knows nothing of individual Christian faith apart from the covenant community. By its very nature Christian faith, when genuine, leads to a drawing together by *koinonia* love into a congregation.

The Church is in a continuous dialectical tension between its relationship to God and its existence in the world. In the view of faith Christians see the Church as it is represented in the Scriptures. Its present actuality in the world is described as other institutions and organizations are commonly described by sociologists.

B. THE BODY OF CHRIST

In the New Testament several descriptive terms are used of the Church, and "the body of Christ" is but one.

The very word translated "church" has its own meaning, already rich in historical tradition. *"Ekklēsia"* (cf. Latin: *ecclesia*) is a term used commonly for any assembly called together at a particular time in a Greek city. However, its use in the New Testament is colored by its appearance in the Septuagint as translation of the Hebrew *qâhâl*, used of Israel as a people assembled by God through his chosen leaders. As Israel was called together and brought out from Egypt through the wilderness to the Promised Land, so the Church is called together by the Holy Spirit, brought out from the world, and led through trials and persecutions to life eternal.

This heritage is made quite explicit when Christians are called "Israel" or "the Israel of God" (Gal. 6:16) and when references are made to "the new covenant" by which Christians are called to live.[1]

The Church is also characterized as "God's field" in which his chosen workmen are planting and watering while God gives the growth (1 Cor. 3:5–9). Again, it is "God's building," with Christ as the foundation on which his ministers build well or badly, and "God's temple," a structure made holy by the Spirit of God and so to be treated with care and reverence (1 Cor. 3:9, 16–17).

The Church is "a chosen race, a royal priesthood, a holy nation, God's own people" (1 Pet. 2:9). One can hardly miss here, once more, the analogy with the ancient doctrine that Israel was the chosen people of God. However this new "chosen race" is also "a royal priesthood," all the people of the Church being called to mediate the love and mercy of God to all the world and to "declare the wonderful deeds of him who called" them "out of darkness into his marvelous light" (1 Pet. 2:9).

Paul compares the relation of the Church to Christ with the relation of a wife to her husband (Eph. 5:22–23). As Alan Richardson points out, this comparison is used as if it were already "accepted teaching in the early Church."[2] In John the Church is related to Christ as branches to a vine (15:1–8).

1. As in Heb. 8:6–15 and Matt. 26:27.
2. *An Introduction to the Theology of the New Testament* (New York: Harper & Row, 1958), p. 257.

However, the most vivid figure of all is the metaphor by which the Church is called "the body of Christ" (Rom. 12:4–8; 1 Cor. 12:12–27). In both the passages which most elaborate this concept Paul stresses the intimate relationships of mutual support which Christians have for one another, and hence their deep unity. In the same passages he emphasizes also the different talents and functions of the various individuals, by which they serve other Christians and also non-Christians. Christ is "the head" of this body.[3] All are joined with him by faith and while sharing his life obey his bidding. As Christ lived a life of service to all, so he has enjoined his disciples to serve all (Mark 10:43–45). The Church, then, continues his life of service to others. How else could the Church be regarded as his body?

The body of Christ is not an organized institution to which individuals are attached or a kind of mystical entity floating somehow above the human beings who choose to join it or leave it. Paul is quite explicit in excluding any such quasi-separation or even differentiation of the Church from its members. "Now you are the body of Christ," he says, "and individually members of it." Yet the Church no more exists apart from its members than does the human body apart from the various organs which compose it.

We may marvel as we read Paul's description to the Corinthian Christians of their church where "If one member suffers, all suffer together; if one member is honored, all rejoice together" (1 Cor. 12:26)! If there were any doubt that in so describing the body of Christ he is speaking of the very Corinthians whom he is addressing, the doubt is dispelled in the verse immediately following, where he says, "Now you are the body of Christ."

However, any modern minister or layman inclined to envy the perfection of the Corinthian church will be disillusioned when he reads the entire letter in which these words occur. For there he will learn that these very Corinthian Christians are divided into quarrelsome factions;[4] that some of them rush to the table of the Lord's Supper to eat up the bread and drink the wine before others can share in it (11:20–22); and some are engaged in lawsuits against brother Christians in the pagan law courts (6:1–8).

What kind of double talk, then, is this? Are the Corinthian Christians the harmonious body of Christ, or are they the quarrelsome, litigatious, greedy lot elsewhere described? Paul's answer is that they are both. In their proper identity as people of faith they are the deeply communal body of Christ. Doubtless they have experienced that reality at times also.

---

3. Eph. 1:22, 4:15, 5:23; Col. 1:18.
4. 1:10–13; 3:3–4; 11:18–19.

In the purpose of God, as he calls them and creates the *koinonia* which is the Church, the Corinthians are the body of Christ at all times. In the experience of its human members the Church does not have a continuous *existence*, but *occurs* occasionally. It was so in Corinth; it is so wherever there is a local church today. The Church may occur in response to a particularly moving sermon by the pastor, calling the congregation to a courageous Christian stand against the dominant class bias and selfishness of the larger community. It may occur in a spontaneous movement to support a loved family in deep distress. When it occurs, the people know in their experience what it means to be the body of Christ.

C. HUMAN ASSOCIATION

As viewed by the candid and critical observer, the church is a type of free association, like a labor union or a political club. Its members join together to reinforce certain common beliefs, to form pleasant and useful friendships, and to promote their ideas and folkways in the community, especially among their own children.

Like other free associations the churches compete with each other for support, and in this competition they use similar devices. They try to present more attractive buildings, to offer equipment and service more appealing to prospective members, to claim economic and social advantages, and to cater to popular ideas and attitudes or at least avoid offending them. For all these devices they may give biblical, historical, or theological "reasons" which sound convincing to people who have not seriously studied and who find it more comfortable to be convinced in any case.

The objective social observer knows it is no accident that the un-educated poor whites, in their church, maintain that the Bible teaches segregation of the races with white people in superior position, while in a neighboring church of uneducated and poor blacks, it is quite clear that the Bible teaches the full brotherhood of all people. The difference is not due to divergent theories of hermeneutics. The biblical preaching and teaching reflect the social interests and attitudes of the two congregations. This is not to say that both views are equally true or false, but that as a very human association each church is affected throughout its life by the condition and prevailing social attitudes of its own members and their daily associates.

Within the church, too, the functioning of its organization closely resembles that of other associations. There are positions and committees of higher and lower prestige. There are tasks which are onerous and largely invisible and which are therefore difficult to fill. In the effort to "climb" the ladder to the places of prestige, laymen use their wealth and worldly position, their political skills, and their circles of friends within the church. The clergy similarly use their ability to raise money for general church causes and their success in increasing memberships and building attractive church structures, along with subtle or overt political effort—handshaking, cultivating the "right" people, and all.

So sympathetic a sociologist as David O. Moberg repeats the common criticism that the church is a conservative or even reactionary influence. It has opposed "the use of anaesthetics," critical study of "mental illness and the phenomena of demonism, witchcraft, and evil spirits," stirred hostility, even violent conflict and persecution among different religious groups, and supported corrupt and evil public officials on the ground that they were good family men.[5] As Moberg indicates further, the church, like other organizations, is easily subject to development of overgrown bureaucracies, overelaborated institutional structures, proud display of material wealth, and the idolizing of complacency, all radically contradicting Christian principles.

The contrast between Christian profession and institutional practice of the church is often striking. Many examples of such discrepancy are afforded by the nearly universal segregation or near-segregation of the races in local churches as contrasted with the pronouncements of all large American denominations as national or world bodies. As W. Seward Salisbury puts it,

> The present movement to do away with segregation (an ultimate ideal) has stemmed mainly from the churches. By the mid-1950's all major bodies in the North and the South had issued statements officially adopting the principle of desegregation. The churches have found, however, that it is one thing to verbalize the ideal on a national level and something quite different to implement it at the parish level.[6]

Such conditions emphasize the dual nature of the Church. As its informed members understand its origin and message, it is an instrument of God in which God himself is continuing his redemptive action in the world. Its members, though sinful human beings, are learning, aspiring, and growing in Christian life, individually and communally, embodying the Word of God and communicating that Word—even Christ—to the world. At the same time, because they are sinful men, themselves part of the world, they also draw back from their high calling, hypocritically contradict their own teaching, are blinded by

5. *The Church as a Social Institution* (Englewood Cliffs, N.J.: Prentice-Hall, Inc., 1962), pp. 179–81.

6. *Religion in American Culture: A Sociological Interpretation* (Homewood, Ill.: The Dorsey Press, 1964), p. 469.

selfish interests and the prejudices which surround them, and participate in the war, injustice, and sexual immorality of the wider community.

D. Ethical Responsibility

The Church is responsible to God. By reason of its origin, profession, and functions, its relation to God is essential to its very reason for being. This responsibility requires faith—the maintenance of its commitment to God and its reliance upon him. Its primary concern must be to please him. It must therefore seek above all else to be obedient to his purpose. If it is to be obedient, it must be continually involved in study, prayer, and action. Even with utmost effort to learn God's will it is sure to make mistakes, mislead its people, and become a stumbling block in the way of God's children. It must therefore be repentant, as it seeks to leave old, wrong ways behind and press forward in his service.

The Church has also responsibility for its members. This does not imply that the Church is an association of people who engage a pastor to provide them with "spiritual" service, even though many laymen so understand it. The responsibility to members is borne by all the members for each other, for all are to have "the same care for one another" (1 Cor. 12:25).

This internal mutual responsibility in the Church, however, provides only the base from which it performs its major task, its ministry to the world. God, to whom it is responsible, commands it to teach, heal, preach, and otherwise serve all kinds of human needs in the world. This ministry is discharged both by corporate bodies of the Church, such as local congregations, and by individual churchmen; both by direct ministration to individuals in need and by strengthening and influencing other social institutions, from the family to the United Nations.

E. The Church in Tension with Culture

When the church is truly the Church of Jesus Christ, it is not able to be comfortable in its worldly surroundings. Even the most casual view of the world shows clearly that no nation, city, or village is Christian. If a congregation fits smoothly into its surroundings, it has so gravely compromised its word and life that it partakes more of the world than of Christ.

H. Richard Niebuhr demonstrated convincingly that American

denominations divided and formed on lines of ethnic, class, and cultural differences in the community at large.[7] Will Herberg describes religion in the United States as an accepted "normal part of the American Way of Life." He continues, "Not to be—that is, not to identify oneself and be identified as—either a Protestant, a Catholic, or a Jew is somehow not to be an American." This does not imply that these three faiths are especially vital and intense in this country. Rather, America "has its underlying culture-religion—best understood as the religious aspect of the American Way of Life—of which the three conventional religions are somehow felt to be appropriate manifestations and expressions."[8] Robin M. Williams, Jr., writes,

> Although there is a prophetic and radically ethical strain in the basic religious tradition, the corporate actions of the major churches appear to have been mainly shaped by external forces rather than by the immanent development of religious value-orientations.[9]

We must now note some of the particular characteristics of contemporary American society especially inimical to professed Christian values.

1. Materialism

The dominant mood of present society in the United States and among many peoples is materialistic. Men and women are ranked in "upper" or "lower" classes according to economic wealth or income. To ask, "What is he worth?" is to be answered in dollars.

On the other hand, Jesus said, "Take heed, and beware of all covetousness; for a man's life does not consist in the abundance of his possessions" (Luke 12:15). We are warned that a man of wealth will find it hard to enter into heaven. A rich young man is told to sell all that he has and give to the poor. Material values are clearly subordinated to the values of personal character, faith, and loving-kindness.

It is painfully evident that many churches have accepted the world's measure of worth. They value wealthy members above all others; they compete for prestige by lavish expenditures of wealth on buildings and decorations. A recent commercial advertisement reads, "If you got it, flaunt it." Many churches demonstrate such conspicuous consumption.

7. *Social Sources of Denominationalism* (New York: Henry Holt and Company, 1929).

8. *Protestant-Catholic-Jew* (Garden City, N.Y.: Doubleday & Company, 1955), p. 274.

9. *American Society: A Sociological Interpretation* (New York: Alfred A. Knopf, 1952), p. 340. Cf. also Gibson Winter, *The Suburban Captivity of the Churches* (New York: Doubleday & Company, 1955); and Ralph E. Dodge, *The Pagan Church* (Philadelphia: J. B. Lippincott Company, 1968).

2. Pleasure and Comfort

The mass media and popular folkways support the quest for self-indulgent pleasure, with stress on comfort, ease, and security. The Gospel blesses those who are "persecuted for righteousness' sake" (Matt. 5:10), who give up all for the kingdom, and who willingly die, even as Christ has died. Yet at the first sign that a faithful application of Christian principles to a current issue would bring unpopularity and loss, many, perhaps most, church members discard the idea as "impractical." The church, like a bank or a manufacturing firm, must be "successful," and its people must live in comfortable "peace of mind."

3. Aggressive Competition

The world, particularly in America, teaches aggressive, egoistic competition. The Gospel teaches humility, and serving rather than being served. We must "not be haughty, but associate with the lowly; never be conceited" (Rom. 12:16). If we compete we are to "outdo one another in showing honor" (Rom. 12:10).

The teachings of the New Testament on egoism and competition are not always matched by the performances of the churches themselves, to say nothing of their members. Too characteristic was a business meeting of a local Methodist board. The pastor proposed a substantial advance in the resources which the church offered to youth. He based his appeal on felt needs of the youth and the need to teach them effectively Christian faith and life. After his appeal every speech by a board member expressed opposition on account of the considerable expense involved. Then the pastor made a new appeal, on the ground that a nearby, competing church had just adopted an even more ambitious and costly program. Quickly the mood changed and in that very meeting the board voted favorably without dissent. Among the businessmen who controlled the board, the language of service had been less persuasive than the language of competition.

The unseemly competition of denominations is often defended as a means of improving church ministrations to the community. However, it operates with this effect mostly in producing service to the more well-to-do and respected people, not in reaching and helping "the poor, the maimed, the lame, the blind," of whom the Lord spoke (Luke 14:13). Meanwhile, the competition of churches augments and further intensifies the aggressive, hostile, and egoistic motivations of the people.

4. Racism

a. In the World.   There are strong attitudes of ethnocentrism and racism throughout the world. The people of Europe and their descendants in other lands have an especially bad reputation for their assumptions of superiority and their efforts to dominate other peoples. The imposition of British, French, German, Dutch, Spanish, and Portuguese rule on large areas abroad, in the last four centuries, has left a heritage of hostility and racist countermeasures from which the world will suffer for a long time. Yet in honesty it must be pointed out that the Chinese needed no European example to launch their perpetual warfare of the eighth to fourth centuries B.C. No more did the tribes of Africa depend on Europe to learn the intertribal warfare, invasions, and conquests of which archaeology, oral tradition, and present deep-seated enmities bear testimony. The enslavement, slaughter, or exploitation of foreign people was practiced by ancient Egyptians, Babylonians, and the predecessors of the Incas and Aztecs long before they felt European influence. Ethnic pride and hostility or contempt toward people of strange appearance or culture is exceedingly widespread.

It was so throughout biblical times, and this makes the testimony against it in the New Testament the more impressive. More radical contempt or hatred of one race or people toward another can hardly be found than that of Greeks toward Scythians or Jews, Jews toward Romans, or Romans toward Libyans in the first century. The Old Testament provides much support for implacable hatred of Israelites toward other peoples and for strict segregation from them.

Some remnants of such attitudes occasionally appear in the writings of the New Testament. In some passages their place is taken by expressions of hostility toward "the Jews," even though these expressions seem especially strange when uttered by Jewish-Christian writers or concerning Jewish persecutions of other Jews who were followers of the Jew, Jesus of Nazareth.

But the major thrust of the New Testament is a powerful and complete repudiation of racist and segregationist ideas and practices.

b. Creation of All Men as Brothers.   The roots of authentic Christian attitudes concerning race are in the doctrine of creation as contained in both Old and New Testaments. It is not the character of some particular race or nation, but our common humanity which is represented to be in the image of God.[10] The light of God which shone radiantly in Christ is described as "the true light that enlightens every man."[11] All men share in the wretched heritage of sin, but all have sufficient awareness of right and wrong so that none can claim exemption through ignorance so long as he brings any charge against another.[12] All men are, by God's creation, brothers under the one Father and also under a common burden of sin.

10. Gen. 1:26–29, 31. Cf. Jas. 3:9 and Eph. 3:14–15.
11. John 1:9. Cf. 1:1–11.
12. Rom. 1 and 2, especially 2:1.

The earth and the whole world of natural resources we share also. These are the creation of God which we hold in stewardship for all. As we view the world today we can plainly see, in appallingly practical terms, that the deadly pollution of the atmosphere knows no national nor continental boundaries. All mankind is threatened by the reckless exploitation of the earth and by the proud hostility in which we use God-given resources to prepare destruction for our brothers. Mankind is inextricably bound together from creation to the end of history.

c. Mankind One in God's Redemptive Act. All men stand in need of forgiveness for their sin. None has ground for self-righteousness and boasting, for "all men, both Jews and Greeks, are under the power of sin, as it is written: 'None is righteous, no, not one' " (Rom. 3:9–10). No favored birth insulates anyone against the common need for humble repentance and a new life (Matt. 3:8–11).

God gave his Son in love for all who would believe—regardless of nation or race. The gift of Christ is in order that *"whoever* believes in him should not perish but have eternal life" (John 3:16). The disciples were slow to understand this, but the dawning of the truth of Christ's universality upon them is graphically epitomized in the story of Peter and Cornelius (Acts 10:1–48). The Apostle Paul frequently emphasizes the point, as when he writes,

> For there is no distinction between Jew and Greek; the same Lord is Lord of all and bestows his riches upon all who call upon him. For, "every one who calls upon the name of the Lord will be saved." [Rom. 10:12–13]

If we do not forgive and seek reconciliation with our brothers, we should not expect forgiveness by God.[13] The ground of this forgiveness and reconciliation has nothing to do with race or nation. It is the reconciling act of God himself. All Christians are exhorted to be "forgiving one another, as God in Christ forgave you" (Eph. 4:32).

While all are brothers in sin and all stand in need of forgiving one another, the strong and favored are under the greater obligation. "Every one to whom much is given, of him will much be required" (Luke 12:48). In race relations there is, consequently, a greater responsibility upon the group in power to take the initiative for justice and brotherhood.

d. Unity of All in the Church. When the Church was formed, people of all the known continents and races and of many nations were called into unity by the Holy Spirit. There is doubtless considerable mythological and symbolic coloring of the account in the second chap-

---

13. 1 John 4:16–21; Matt. 6:14–15; Luke 15:11–32.

ter of Acts. But it is no accident that the writer (presumably Luke) stresses heavily the intercontinental and international character of the Church from the very day of the Church's origin at Pentecost. Not only are Africa, Asia, and Europe all heavily represented in the nations listed, but the unity described is intimate and all-embracing.[14]

Paul declares explicitly and repeatedly that among Christians there can be no distinctions of race, nation, or class. Among the harsh contempts and hostilities of the peoples in the Near East of the first century, he writes, "Here there cannot be Greek and Jew, circumcised and uncircumcised, barbarian, Scythian, slave, free man, but Christ is all, and in all."[15] It would have been easy to exclude from the primitive Church all excepting the Hebrews from whom came its first leaders—such as Paul, the Twelve, and even Jesus himself. If others were to be admitted, a strong case could have been made for dividing into separate congregations along ethnic lines. But Paul would have none of this. For "in Christ Jesus," he declares,

> you who once were far off have been brought near in the blood of Christ. For he is our peace, who has made us both one, and has broken down the dividing wall of hostility.[16]

e. Interracial Unity in Mission. The mission of the Church is inclusive, not only in the universality of its object, but also in its interethnic base. The first account we have of the ancient Church commissioning members to a missionary task emphasizes this fact. When Paul and Barnabas were sent from Antioch, we are told, the Cypriot Barnabas and the Asiatic Jew Paul were "set apart" with the laying on of hands by Manaen, of Herod's court, Lucius of North African Cyrene, and "Symeon who was called Niger" (Acts 13:1-2). "*Niger*," the Latin word for black, would seem to imply that Symeon was very dark in color. In any event, the first missionary-sending party apparently consisted of at least one person and perhaps two from Africa, along with one from the Palestinian court of Herod.

The Church, itself interracial and bridging every worldly barrier of class and prejudice, was from the beginning sent to bring into its own body all peoples, according to the Gospel commission: "Go therefore and make disciples of all nations, baptizing them in the name of the Father and of the Son and of the Holy Spirit" (Matt. 28:19).

14. Note especially Acts 2:44-47.
15. Col. 3:11. Cf. Gal. 3:28.
16. Eph. 2:13-14. Of course I am aware of the reasons given for doubt that Paul himself wrote the Letter to the Ephesians. While I have not found the arguments compelling, the debate does not deeply affect our present concern. If Paul was not the author, the actual writer closely followed his ideas, and the point being made in this passage resembles and is completely congruent with passages in Paul's Letters to the Galatians, Colossians, Corinthians, and Romans.

Meanwhile, we are commanded to love every neighbor, regardless of differences and worldly hostilities. Jesus so taught indelibly by interpreting and universally expanding the ancient Levitical commandment through the Parable of the Good Samaritan.

Such life in the Church must cut across the common divisions and prejudices of the world, whether in the ancient Mediterranean basin or in the modern United States or South Africa. But the means of accomplishing this is provided along with the command.

> For the love of Christ controls us, because we are convinced that one has died for all. . . . From now on, therefore, we regard no one from a human point of view. . . . Therefore, if any one is in Christ, he is a new creation; the old has passed away, behold, the new has come.[17]

f. The Nature of Christian Love.   In our earlier defining of love in the full New Testament sense, we noted that it implies an active desire for a deep sharing of life's treasures and very being as gifts from God. Hence the central principle of Christian ethics directly challenges every level and kind of racial discrimination or segregation. Even the utmost benevolence or justice or insistence on "equal rights" is not enough to satisfy the demands of love. Love stands directly opposed to notions of "separate but equal" opportunity. Both in the churches and out in the world, love demands brotherhood and a fellowship of sharing.

g. The Shameful Hypocrisy of the Churches.   There is nothing else which shows so dramatically the massive faithlessness within the churches as the racial practices within them. In the United States, government, manufacture, commerce, organized labor, and education have all moved much further toward an inclusive society than have the churches.

In all fairness it must be said that the more impersonal the human relationships, the easier is racial desegregation in a culture where prejudice is strong. Hence impersonal economic relationships may bridge racial barriers even while the same people involved in these relationships would balk at the desegregation of social clubs which provide intimate personal acquaintance in depth. The institution most resistant of all to desegregation is the family, precisely because it includes the most intimate of all relationships. Indeed, resistance to integration of membership and ministry in the churches is augmented by fear that the sharing of worship, Christian education, and social activities in the church will lead to interracial marriages.

Yet the New Testament will not permit us to escape on any such grounds. We are called to a new life in which the old is crucified with

17. 2 Cor. 5:14-17. Cf. vv. 18-20.

Christ and the new arises. In this new life, the old worldly divisions simply cease to exist. True Christians

> have put off the old nature with its practices and have put on the new nature. . . . Here there cannot be Greek and Jew, . . . barbarian, Scythian, slave, free man, but Christ is all, and in all.

F. Pastoral and Prophetic Functions

The churches generally recognize that they have both a pastoral and a prophetic responsibility. On the one hand, they are bound to care for the members of their congregations in the various crises of life and in the nurture of their understanding and faith. Closely related to this function of caring for individual members is the work of keeping the congregation united in one body. On the other hand, the churches have an obligation to direct the attention and action of their members and of other people to the great discrepancy between Christian ideals and the present lives of individuals, churches, and society.

1. Conflict of These Pastoral and Prophetic Tasks

These two types of function tend to be in conflict one with the other. When the preacher pronounces God's condemnation of racism or calls for policies of aid to the poor, or for changes in national priorities from major expenditures on military preparation and minor expenditures on housing and training for the unemployed, many people are offended. It then becomes harder for them to accept from him supporting visitation in illness and sorrow or counsel in the personal problems of family life.

2. Toward Resolution of the Conflict

The problem is irresoluble if one conceives the pastoral task as one of maintaining a comfortable "peace of mind" in individuals and pleasant social compatibility in the congregation. These goals are, however, far from authentic, if one judges authenticity by rootage in the New Testament. The peace of which the Gospel of John speaks is not the soft peace of conformity with the world. It is the peace of the Christ who has challenged earthly powers, is about to be crucified by them, who gives peace even while promising tribulation, and who says he has "overcome the world" (John 14:27; 16:33). The oneness of the Church of which the Gospel and Paul speak is not the unity of superficial agreeability but of faithfulness to the crucified Christ and of love which holds together despite many differences.

Pastoral responsibility is not concerned with maintaining comfortable self-satisfaction. Quite the contrary! The pastor is to help his people to grow, and spiritual growth is incompatible with proud self-satisfaction. The peace and comfort which the Church in its pastoral functions is called upon to convey are of a kind which no one can experience without repentance, sacrifice, and risk.

On the other hand, the prophetic function is not to be identified with those angry denunciations by which a preacher may express his own pride, personal insecurity, or repressed hostility. To be truly Christian, a prophetic utterance must arise from love for the victims of injustice or other evil and desire to bring all who are involved into a community of forgiveness, grace, and mutual assistance.

So understood, these functions are not in real conflict, but are mutually supporting. Sometimes, indeed, the race prejudice, violence, and other evil of a person can be excised only by a caring personal ministry. In such instances, the friendly counsel of a kind pastor may bring not only Christ's healing to the offending individual, but also, at the same time, relief to the victims of his vicious conduct.

In practice, it is often difficult to select the best tactics. Whether to denounce and condemn or to befriend and counsel in a mood of personal acceptance may be so hard to decide that at best the answer is uncertain. In general, it is likely to be better to be kindly and affirmative, though candid, with the individual, even while publicly condemning in terms worthy of an Amos, Isaiah, or Jesus the hypocrisy, cruelty, injustice, and folly of society or of people belonging to certain types or classes. For example, in this day the Church must condemn flatly the devices by which neighborhoods and apartment houses exclude people by race. At the same time, the Church seeks to minister to the individuals engaged in such practices in a positive way which will remove their fears and hostilities, expand their perspectives, and eliminate their prejudiced activities.

G.   Ordained and Lay Ministries

Pastoral, prophetic, educational, and administrative functions of the churches all belong in various degrees and forms to both ordained and lay people. All alike are called to Christian ministry in the world. The spiritual and ethical reformation of the world is a task for laymen as well as clergy.

Clarence C. Goen writes directly to the point. He illustrates by brief references to "authentically Christian ministries" of politicians, businessmen, teachers, housewives, and others. He continues,

As theologically mature, dedicated and informed members of Christ's Church, they could literally redeem the world. . . .

Whose vocation is it, then, to call forth the lay apostolate, enlarge its vision, clarify its faith, sensitize its conscience, focus mission, and equip it for its work in the world? The answer of the New Testament is that God has given to his Church "pastors and teachers to equip the saints for the work of ministry" (Eph. 4:11-13).[18]

Christian ethics, then, is a subject in which every ordained minister is called upon to instruct laymen in order that they may perform their ministry in the world according to Christian norms of worldly conduct.

H. Gathered and Scattered Church

The Church gathers together for worship, instruction, renewal, and planning. Then it scatters for its work of ministry to the world. In both phases of its existence it is the Church. At the scheduled hour of worship on Sunday, the Church, if its members are faithful, is mainly in the place of worship. There will be other hours of united study and planning, all together or in groups, in the church building or elsewhere. But during most of the week, the Church is not in any one place, but in many offices, factories, classrooms, homes, fields, courtrooms—wherever its members are doing their worldly work in the spirit of Christ and according to God's will.

If the members of a local congregation are not the Church in this sense during the week, it is highly doubtful that they are the Church when they are gathered on Sunday in the building which they call their church. True worship must send the worshipers to mission in the world as surely as the work of mission sends them back to further meditation, instruction, repentance, and new resolve.

I. Situational Guidelines on the Church

Guidelines on the wide range of contemporary ethical problems are not being formulated at this point in the book. That would be premature. However, it is not too early to lay down several, having to do with the Church's own life style for the present period of history. The center of focus in this attempt is the Church in the United States.

18. "The Place of the Ordained Minister in the Servant Church" (Washington, D.C.: *Wesley Theological Seminary Bulletin*, Summer, 1969), p. 5.

1. Emphasize the Distinction Between the True Church and the World

Many articles and books, in recent years, have deplored the easy identification of Christianity with American patriotism and "the American way," in a bland culture religion. Goen discerningly laments,

> As a conglomerate of one-class congregations mistaking social compatibility for Christian *koinonia*, we are hard put to identify ourselves in this broken world as a Christian community living under divine judgment and grace.[19]

One evidence of the bland melting of the churches into culture is the prominence of the national flag in places of worship, a kind of display rarely matched in other countries. A more basic evidence is the wide resentment among church people when ministers or organizations of the churches criticize any national policy, particularly in international affairs or military preparedness. Another is that in a country where 60 per cent or more members of the population profess church affiliation, all the occupations which are mainly concerned with direct service to persons as persons are in seriously short supply excepting only a recent upturn in recruits for teaching. If 60 per cent of our people accepted the precept that the highest standard of greatness is serving people, would we be experiencing serious shortages of trained ministers, nurses, social workers, and family physicians?

While this condition exists, the churches should emphasize strongly that the moral demands and order of loyalties taught in the Scriptures and sacraments are in striking contrast to the prevailing standards of American life. A church which is only a bland echo of the world might as well die outwardly as it has died inwardly. If it covers the materialism, pride, and selfishness of the nation with a cloak of sanctity, it is worse than useless, for it then makes reform even more difficult.

2. Increase Instruction

If laymen are to fulfill their ministry to the world, they must be much more adequately equipped for the task than they are at present. Large numbers of laymen, as well as ordained ministers, are aware of this. Frequently, requests are made that theological seminaries offer extensive programs for laymen, both at the institutions of instruction and out in the churches. It is hard to see how such programs can be manned without seriously weakening the preparation of clergy and

19. "The 'Methodist Age' in American Church History," *Religion in Life*, Vol. 34, 1965, p. 569.

the scholarly work of faculties to blaze new trails of thought for the church. Occasional conducting of lectures, discussions, and workshops by professors can be handled, but this activity barely touches the massive problem. Two other approaches seem more promising.

Some seminary-trained men, with further advanced preparation, may enter the specialized vocation of lay instruction. Engaged by conferences, associations, or presbyteries, they will continuously plan and direct lay institutes in localities easy to reach from a number of churches. After a time they will develop local clergy and laymen to assist in instruction.

More important is seminary preparation of ordained clergy to perform this task in their local parishes. Much highly important work can be done in the regular Sunday hour of worship. Preaching is widely judged solely on the scale of its "inspirational" quality. Results achieved by such preaching are largely dissipated before Monday morning. More lasting effects are gained by the implanting of new knowledge, insights, and perspectives. Often it will be found that such instructive preaching stirs the feelings and will, as well as providing the ideational basis for renewed support for Christian life in other days. Such teaching from the pulpit can lead into individual and group study under the pastor's guidance.

3. Develop Small Groups

Not all laymen in our present bland churches will care to bestir their minds to this extent. Many want to hear only what they already know or believe. But in this day as in other times the renewal of the Church to perform its rightful task in this world must come from a "saving remnant," a "little church within the church" ("*ecclesiola in ecclesia*"). A considerable number of churches large and small are in process of radical growth in ministry to the world through the skillful development of groups meeting for study, prayer, and mutually reinforced action.

Some of the potentially most important small groups are already organized in most churches as committees or commissions formed to direct financial planning and effort, evangelism and extension of membership, Christian education, or inclusive planning of policy. The trained pastor may, through the judicious stimulation and leadership of such groups, make the whole administrative task an educational and spiritually nurturing one as well.

4. Devote Special Effort to Seeking and Serving Black People

In recent years many churches with long traditions of white exclusiveness have decided to open their membership rolls and activities

to all people regardless of race. They have advertised their new decision and have been surprised that no black people have responded.
What is now lacking?

It must be recognized that many black people are deeply imbued
with a subculture different from that of the white majority and will
continue to prefer separate membership and worship. Their free choice
must be respected. In a few places different services have been arranged at various hours, in the different traditions, within a single
church, hoping that such an arrangement would lead to a gradual
blending of cultural contributions to mutual advantage.

On the other hand, many blacks have had a long and deep association
with whites in education, business, labor unions, politics, and other
secular activities. Many such people would prefer to be in a fully integrated church now. But they want to be sure that it *is* fully integrated, that in it their families would not be insulted, patronized, admitted only to selected activities, or exploited as false tokens of an
inclusive church. They need repeated personal invitation and the cultivation of genuine personal friendships by some people of the church
—all standard procedures in cultivating especially desired white members.

At the same time the Church must reach out in broad, costly, and
practical service to the long exploited and deprived black community.
Churches have participated shamefully in the racial injustice of America. Local churches, denominations, and church institutions must now
discriminate in favor of black people to compensate morally and to
help them into full participation in the community.

5. Use Clear and Literal Communication

The churches suffer badly from archaic and inflated rhetoric. Many
thousands of ordained ministers weekly lead their congregations in
solemnly affirming many things they themselves do not believe—from
the virgin birth of Jesus to "the resurrection of the body" of every
true believer. The seminary-trained minister may understand that he
is using historical language to affirm a historical continuity of tradition. He may mean to affirm a symbolic significance of the words he
speaks, not their literal meaning. But few laymen are even aware of
these understandings, to say nothing of having accepted them. They
often suppose either that the minister must be a fool for believing
these propositions as literally understood, or else a hypocrite for saying he does when in fact he does not.

Is it any wonder, then, that many congregations can hear and speak
and sing about the brotherhood of all mankind and the unity of the
whole Church without the slightest impact on their attitudes toward
members of other races or classes?

Care must be taken, in trimming our language, not to reduce all that is spoken to the terms fully intelligible to our less well-informed parishioners. Worshipers' concepts and imaginations need to be stretched. Language must be frequently used which points beyond our understanding. But the Apostles' Creed and some other passages in our liturgies were not intended as poetry or open indicators of mystery. They were intended as sharp, literal statements of orthodox beliefs precisely excluding views now held by millions who use them.

We need to learn more plainly to say "Yes" and "No," as the Lord taught, and to mean what we say. Such plain honesty is itself required by our ethical norms (especially Principles of Consistency and Personal Conscience) and is also needed to restore proper force to our various Christian ethical convictions.

6. Stress the Concrete and Specific

The Church has a special responsibility to cultivate loyalty to ideal norms of conduct (according to the Principles of Ideal Control, Ideal of Personhood, and Ideal of Community), especially the ideal norms taught by Jesus and New Testament writers, and above all, inclusive *koinonia* love. To focus discussion on specific actions, especially in the complex sphere of social issues, is to risk dispute over technical issues of predictable consequences. In such discussion of economic or sociological theory of cause and effect the ethical question what ends ought to be sought easily becomes lost.

For example, a minister wants to teach the Christian requirement of justice and love toward all men regardless of race. He is aware that most blacks and Puerto Ricans of his city live in a ghetto where the schools are notoriously poor. He gives concrete form to his concern for racial justice and brotherly love by urging that many children of the ghetto and others of the predominantly white suburbs be exchanged between the schools by bus, with a simultaneous effort to upgrade the quality of the ghetto schools.

Immediately the issue of justice and love becomes complicated by arguments over the desirability of having young children attend school in their home neighborhoods, the need for local involvement in school decisions, the peril of handicapping some children by forcing them into inferior education, and the subjecting of suburban children to dangers of disease or personal attack which they are poorly prepared to resist.

On the other hand, to preach the general norms without effort for concrete implementation leads to idle abstraction, vague self-delusion, and hypocrisy. If such ideals as justice and love are to have any ethical meaning, they must have meaning for particular action in particular circumstances.

Church instruction must move back and forth between the persuasive clarifying of sound principles and effective calls to specific action. But at present there is such wide formal acceptance of Christian principles in theory and such gross violation of them in practice that the churches need to move far over into emphasis on specific applications. This requires careful study of means as well as ends, hence enlisting technically trained economists, educators, sociologists, political scientists, and others. Even with the exercise of utmost care some mistakes will be made. Attempting to correct evils, good people will sometimes produce new evils. Careful preparatory study can reduce such mistaken effort to a minimum, but it will still sometimes occur. In such instances Christian people depend on justification by faith and learn from their experience. Without such effort they neither learn nor accomplish anything for the realizing of justice or love.

7. *The Church as Social Welfare Agent*

It is important that the churches learn, especially in the inner city, to perform many acts of social service which they have been inclined to leave to specialized agencies, often of government. Various organizations within the local church, the local church as a whole, and larger church bodies all need to go on from verbal instruction of their people to the actual doing of some work to meet the material and other "secular" needs of neglected people in ways to complement more specialized agencies.

While most churches have not been accustomed to doing much work of this kind in the inner city, it has often been taken for granted in the country and the small town. There it has seemed natural and right for a congregation or an organization within it to find work for a family man to do to support his family, to contribute furniture and clothing for a family who have lost their personal property in a fire, or to put in the crops or paint a barn for a farmer laid up from an accident.

The inner city poses more formidable problems, however. The impersonal relations, the alienation of groups, the unemployability of many persons, the long-term character of many needs—all these and more make the needs of people in the inner city particularly hard to reach and meet. They also make the appeal more urgent.

Some churches are working increasingly to give aid both beyond and within their congregations. One church, for example, while not operating an employment service, does provide directions for securing employment service. It also operates a day nursery for working mothers—with government assistance. It offers classes in cooking, child care, and budget management for wives and mothers. At certain hours vol-

unteer lawyers give legal aid. It operates a "clothes closet," collecting
clothing from the relatively more affluent people and distributing it
free of charge to people referred by schools and welfare agencies. It
operates an extensive program of social and athletic activities for the
neighborhood youth, who are desperately short of recreational resources. Some churches are serving as agencies to direct government-
financed integrated housing projects.

Such activities must be carefully planned, and the people engaged
in them must be ready for endless disappointments and frustrations.
However, the very demands which such work makes upon the virtues
of patience and love make it particularly valuable for Christian growth.
It provides also means for improving government services and render-
ing invaluable aid to people in all stages of anxiety and despair.

Even the young people in a church—sometimes especially the young
people—may render highly significant service in the inner city by tu-
toring younger children, assisting in recreational leadership, staging
cleaning and painting parties, and the like. The learning by doing such
things may exceed even the very considerable direct assistance given
to people in need.

The one emphatic note of caution which must be sounded is the
warning that any suggestion of pride or paternalism is likely to be
ruinous to both the participants and the recipients. Hence there is
necessity for careful preparation of spirit and understanding before
and during the work.

8. Other Situational Guidelines

In the remaining chapters, related to many kinds of contemporary
problems, many other situational guidelines will emerge, guidelines
which should be taken seriously both by churches as groups and by
individual Christians.

J. INITIAL PRESUMPTIONS

Another way of stating the situational guideline regarding emphasis
on the concrete and specific is to say that in approaching every issue
today the initial presumption of churchmen should be to lean toward
the more specific rather than the more general, toward action rather
than toward verbal statement of general principle alone.

Another appropriate initial presumption of churchmen today should
be in favor of interchurch cooperation rather than individual church
effort in social action. There are many situations in which a church
must move alone or not at all. But the first inclination should be to
seek cooperative effort. The social forces corrupting political life,

continuing injustice, exploiting natural resources against the general interests of humanity, and accelerating the arms race—for a few examples—are so strong, even in most local communities, that combined efforts are needed to study how best to overcome them and then to put plans into successful operation. Moreover, the whole theme of unity and that of reconciliation imply the movement of churches into ever closer fellowship, and specific proposals for such movement should be viewed with favorable initial presumption, even while they require careful particular examination.

chapter ten

Marriage and the Family

————•—•⟨∞⟩—•—————

A. Variety of Forms

It has often been assumed that the institution of marriage arose out of earlier human promiscuity. This, however, is questionable. No human society observed by anthropologists or reported in history has accepted general promiscuity. Moreover, while many lower animals are promiscuous, others maintain well-defined polygamous patterns and a few are strictly monogamous.

However, there is a wide range of socially approved patterns of sexual behavior and family structures in known societies, as well as much individual deviation from approved ways. Some peoples accept considerable sexual experimentation before the first pregnancy—though Margaret Mead's early reports on the Samoans have been challenged.[1] Many approve polygyny[2] for men who can afford to secure and keep more than one wife and her children. A few have practiced polyandry.[3] Some have small groups within which two or more men share two or more wives and the children are reared together. Some societies provide for easy dissolution of marriage.

Many peoples maintain large family groups in which child-rearing is widely shared in clan and village. Thus, in many tribes of Africa a child recognizes a number of women, who may be related in complex ways, as "mother," and all share responsibility for the child's care. The number and types of relationships of "brothers" and "sisters" in many African villages is puzzling to all outsiders who have not studied the local tribal customs in great detail. These complex larger families

1. See her *Coming of Age in Samoa* (New York: William Morrow & Company, 1930). Cf. John D. Copp, *The Samoan Dance of Life; an Anthropological Narrative* (Boston: Beacon Press, 1950). Cf. also Bronislaw Malinowski, *The Sexual Life of Savages in North-western Melanesia*, 3rd ed. (London: Routledge and Kegan Paul, 1932).
2. The form of polygamy in which one man has more than one wife.
3. Polygamous marriage of one woman to more than one man.

have obviously great survival value where life is precarious and children therefore often lose their natural parents, and where an infant not breast fed cannot be fed at all.

Regarding functions and relative authority of the members, also, marriage and the family have shown wide variations. Rule by wife and mother (matriarchy) has prevailed in very few societies. Dominance of husband and father has been most common, though in widely differing degrees. The responsibilities of family members in work depends largely on the economy of the society. Where the food supply and materials for clothing depend on fishing and hunting, the duties of men tend to be restricted to these activities and their equipment, often supplemented by fighting hostile tribes. In such societies the men are arduously and dangerously employed at times, but may have also long periods of idleness, while the women and children do the daily work of collecting wood, carrying water, making and cleaning clothes, caring for the hut, preparing food and caring for the infant and infirm members of the household. By contrast, in many households of our industrial society, when the children are grown the man may spend most of his days at work or commuting, while with mechanical aids the wife spends the larger portion of her time at leisure or in voluntary activities of community service or pleasure. To an increasing degree children have little to do in the family economy and are expected to spend their time in their own education or amusement. These patterns may be transitional and unstable.[4]

B. Natural Law Ethics of Sex and Marriage

1. Practices Excluded by General Principles

The General Principles of Moral Decision formulated and defended in Chapter Seven clearly imply the unethical character of some common practices in sexual and family relations.

a. Exploiting Others. When a man or a woman uses a sexual partner for the satisfaction of sexual desire, for pride, or for other individual purpose, without genuine respect for the partner's present and future interests and well being, this is a flagrant violation of the Principle of Altruism, to say nothing of Christian love. Such violation is also, as

4. For an old but classical and still informative account of the variety of human customs regarding marriage, see Edward Westermarck, *The History of Human Marriage* (London: Macmillan and Company, 1903). A shorter, but recent and authoritative account is *The Family in Various Cultures*, Second Edition, by Stuart A. Queen, Robert W. Habenstein, and John B. Adams (Chicago: J. B. Lippincott, 1961). Cf. also Margaret Mead, *Male and Female: A Study of the Sexes in a Changing World* (New York: William Morrow & Company, 1949).

Kant clearly saw, a violation of the Categorical Imperative, or what I have reformulated as the Principle of Personal Conscience. For plainly, no one wants to be similarly exploited or to have a person for whom he truly cares—perhaps a wife or a daughter—so exploited.

Because the sexual relation is so intimate and normally communicates so immediate a personal caring for another, such sexual exploitation of another is especially destructive of the offender's personal integrity and damaging to the victim's self-confidence and social trust.

Other relations in the family are also subject to serious abuse, however. Parents frequently try to use their children to satisfy their own frustrated ambitions. Youth try to use their parents to finance or justify their own selfish behavior, without regard to the parents' economic and personal needs. One sibling often uses another for his own advantage.

The obligations of altruism are particularly clear and important in relations within the family, even when sex is not involved. For here the individual is met face to face, is especially well known, and shares much in a common heritage. If he cannot give and receive personal respect and concern in the family, then where may he be expected to do so?

b. The Double Standard.   Ages-old is the double standard by which a woman is held accountable for her illicit sexual acts, while a man goes free of any severe penalty or even of censure. This is but a special case of exploiting another. For the woman in such cases, whether ancient Tamar or the girl next door, is treated as a means to the man's pleasure, and not herself as a person of worth, whether he be Ammon the Hebrew crown prince or the careless local boy following his latest passion.[5]

c. Parasitical Roles in the Family.   When one or more members of the family needlessly live in idleness or unproductive pleasure while others work, the workers are being used as means, not respected as persons. The parasitical ones are also failing in the self-development and fulfillment required by the General Principle of Self-Realization.

2.   *Values to be Served*

The Principles of Valuation require that we consider the values which can and should be furthered by the institution of marriage.

a. Propagation and Nurture of Children.   Sexual relations and reproduction would, of course, be possible without the institution of marriage. Yet some writers believe that general promiscuity would have lowered fecundity and brought an end to the tribe practicing it.[6]

5. For the story of Ammon and Tamar, see 2 Sam. 13:1–37.
6. E.g., see Westermarck, *The History of Human Marriage*, p. 115.

In any event, marriage customs of wide variety secure feeding, care, and training of young children, services essential to the survival and well-being of the race.

b. Love.   Human beings need more than mere physical gratification to fulfill the highest possibilities and find the deepest satisfactions of sexual life. Sexual desire may be goaded by pride, contempt, jealousy, or even hate. However, when it expresses personal admiration, concern, tenderness, and loyalty, in a total life relationship, it becomes not only a secure bond to guarantee care for children, but also the means of nurturing love at some of its highest levels.

Erich Fromm writes that the animals, with their instinctive adaptation to their environment, securely belong to their world. But with man's emergence into reason and freedom of choice, "he has transcended nature—although he never leaves it—and yet once torn away from nature, he cannot return to it."[7] As Fromm recognizes, this separation and loss is dramatically symbolized in the Genesis story of the Fall. Once he has become self-conscious in his freedom, man cannot return to the automatic security of an anxiety-free innocence. If primitive man tried, he found that the way back was blocked by "a flaming sword which turned every way, to guard the way to the tree of life" (Gen. 3:24). As Fromm says,

> When man is born, the human race as well as the individual, he is thrown out of a situation which was definite, as definite as the instincts, into a situation which is indefinite, uncertain and open.   [*Op. cit.*, pp. 7–8]

A man, aware of his insecurity, alone between birth and death, "would become insane," says Fromm,

> could he not liberate himself from this prison and reach out, unite himself in some form or other with men, with the world outside.   [*Ibid.*, p. 8]

The deepest, most secure, and most satisfying form of such uniting is mature and loyal love. This union between human persons may still not be enough and it may not be able to stand alone, without support of a union with the divine. But it can be confidently affirmed that, whatever more is required, the human being must love if he is to be fully human. His loving need not be a sexual loving; for some of the most mature and complete persons of history and of the present have found and expressed love in other forms. But for countless millions

7. *The Art of Loving* (New York: Harper & Row, 1956), p. 7.

of persons marriage has provided the form and structure for learning the most secure and complete overcoming of aloneness by a loving relationship which they have experienced. From their marital school of learning many have gone on to love their children and others.

c. Protecting and Stabilizing Community. Among the Mashona there is a wise saying that "the place where the rafters [of the circular hut] meet is under the roof." This may seem so obvious as to be foolish. But what is meant by this typically concrete and symbolic African saying is that the members of a household meet and love and quarrel most intimately within the family circle, out of view, and so not disturbing the wider community. This is an important function of the family, which is based upon marriage.

In the relationships of daily life, many irritations accumulate and threaten to break out in an angry outburst which would disrupt the peace of a whole neighborhood, or office or other public place. Recently I observed a screaming verbal explosion of a woman in the face of a hapless gateman before hundreds of shocked observers, at Grand Central Station in New York, and I marveled at the relative rarity of such scenes. It was not insignificant that her husband was the person who succeeded in quieting her and taking her to her train.

Ordinarily the drawing off of accumulated hostilities by husband or wife occurs in the privacy of the home. This serves to insulate the outside world from innumerable upset tempers, and to prevent great numbers of people from performing rash acts which would disrupt employment or, in the eyes of the law, "disturb the peace."

Not only anger, but discouragement, self-pity, and other undesirable attitudes are commonly expressed and assuaged at home, and at the least this protects the wider society from their more intense and disturbing outpourings. While they can be extremely unpleasant in the home, there are few people there to receive the shocks and, because of the small numbers, far less frequent episodes than there would be if all the people in a large office or industry were to inflict upon the others their fresh wrath or the full weight of their disappointments.

This is, of course, no excuse for thoughtless imposition upon others in the home. Indeed, a further function of domestic life is the learning of self-controlled and smooth social relations by both children and parents, in the intimate security of the family circle.

d. Other Service to the Community. The home is not an adequate final object of loyal commitment. The General Principle of the Ideal of Community refers lesser loyalties to the "ideal of what the whole community ought to become." The Gospel commands that we "seek first the Kingdom of God." "The whole community" is the most inclusive community which the individual can conceive and serve. For no normal adults and for few children of the world would that community be the family. The family itself is obliged to serve the wider community. It can and very frequently does train its own members for service in the larger world and provides moral, religious, or economic support for such service. It is tragic that many young people who commit themselves to lives of service to especially needy persons, in their home country or abroad, find that their parents bitterly charge that they are "disloyal" to the family because they are going far away or because they will not be earning enough to maintain family pride or security.

The family which turns in on itself as the most inclusive and final goal fails in its highest function. The internal loyalties are likely to become progressively more unattractive and more strained. Families, like individuals, find themselves by losing themselves for a larger good.

3. Social Superiority of Monogamy

The only serious rivals of monogamous marriage in the modern world are the polygynous forms of polygamy, easy divorce, and formal monogamy coupled with surreptitious premarital and extramarital sexual intercourse. All of these social arrangements undermine to some extent the security of personal relationships which we have seen to play a vitally important role in supporting the various values served by marriage and the family. This is least true of polygyny at its best, but that brings other evils.

Wherever this form of polygamy exists the double standard, with all its injustice, is entrenched in the legal social system itself. There are other evils, too. As several Old Testament narratives illustrate, a plurality of wives brings jealousy and intrigue into the most personal relationships of life. Occasionally a favorite wife may attain a status of wide influence and respect in some polygamous societies, but in general every culture which tolerates polygyny debases women to a status only a little above such property as livestock. We can readily understand why in Muslim countries where women have begun to assert themselves, one of their foremost demands has been and is the abolition of all polygamy.

Polygyny has been regarded as desirable among people who have been mainly concerned with women's labor or with the satisfying of male sexual desires—both implying the subordination of women. Westermarck, who writes without commitment to Christian or other religious authority, rightly concludes,

> When the feelings of women are held in due respect, monogamy will necessarily be the only recognized form of marriage. . . . The refined feeling of love, depending chiefly upon mutual sympathy and

upon appreciation of mental qualities, is scarcely compatible with polygynous habits.[8]

Easy divorce, if it is only available for men, subordinates women as do the double standard and polygyny. If it is equally available to men and women, then this is not the case. There are, however, other attendant evils.

In this section I am not discussing the question of best legal policy regarding divorce as a recourse to terminate occasional marriages intended as permanent monogamous unions but found later to be intolerable to one or both partners, a question to be examined later. We are now concerned with a policy of deliberately accepting easy divorce and remarriage as a normal, socially approved way of life.

An example is to be found in some American social circles, especially of the entertainment world. Legal arrangements may be complicated, but money can take care of those. It is not uncommon to read of movie stars who have married and divorced up to four or five times, and occasionally oftener. It is significant, however, that life in those social circles is highly charged with alcoholism, drug abuse, and suicide. Few ironies of American life equal the fact that the very people who are most widely looked upon by youth as the darlings of good fortune and the models for romantic love are in extraordinary proportion self-confessed failures in love and marriage. For they do acknowledge, again and again, as they go back to the divorce court that their quest for that magic happiness of love which they so often portray on the screen has failed. They hope that in the new marriage they will reach the elusive goal.

In this world of ignorance and sin it is to be expected that some marriages will fail. But every time a marriage breaks up, the separation not only brings many a wrench of pain to one or both partners, and injures the children if there are any; it also weakens in various degrees the secure confidence of many a married couple acquainted with the parting pair. When such separations are made an accepted and common custom in any society, the intimate confidence of innumerable husbands and wives in the security of their married love is immeasurably weakened and something of the anticipatory glow of many a marrying couple is diminished.

The fact is that the people of no society can, in marriage customs, have their cake and eat it too. They cannot have both the deep and solemn joy of utter loving devotion and the confident security of lasting love and also the implied reservation that marriage is an experiment, perhaps to be followed by another and another, if this one fails

8. *The History of Human Marriage*, p. 509.

to measure up to expectations. Such fearful reservations are, in fact, self-fulfilling and doom from the start the highest possibilities of love.

Similar are the defects of that other deviant from monogamous marriage, the indulging of premarital and extramarital sexual episodes, while retaining the formal and public structure of monogamous marriage. These episodes detract both from the completeness and integrity of the individual's commitment to the married partner and from the confidence which each partner feels in the other. We have seen how important such commitment and confidence are to the highest values in marriage.

The individual may grant that the custom of faithful monogamous marriage is good. He only wishes to make an exception of his own case sometimes or on one special occasion. At this point the Principle of Personal Conscience is emphatically violated, for the individual is acting contrary to his own approved norm of conduct.

4. Mutual Respect in Differing Roles

In many tribal societies the roles of different family members are clearly and rigidly structured. Husband, wife—or various wives from oldest to youngest—and the different children all have their own positions of responsibility or dependence relative to the family economy and relative to the deference or obedience due other members of the household.

In modern society of the Western nations, and increasingly throughout the world, such customary rigidity is being replaced by almost infinite variety. Not only do the roles vary from city to farm, from the wealthy to the poor, and from families of working wives to those of full-time homemakers; they differ widely also within each of these and other categories.

Between husband and wife, for example, the placing and degree of dominance vary extremely, from the still common dominance by the husband through rough equality to strong dominance by the wife. Studies of happiness in marriage show very happy and also deeply unhappy marriages of all these types. In American society some men like to hold the initiative, both sexually and in processes of decision about financial matters, place of residence, schooling of the children, and the like. Some women like to have it so. On the other hand, some women prefer to have it appear so while they actually dominate. Yet others are unhappy with any but a roughly egalitarian relationship, with roles of dominance changing according to the matter involved and the relative interests of the two partners at a given time. Obviously, there will be strains and probably some permanent sense of lack in marriages involving the dominating type of husband with any but the more willingly dependent and passive wife. On the other hand, there are similar differences among men. A man may be very happy with a decisive and dominant wife if he prefers a more dependent and passive role.[9]

There is clearly no right or wrong, good or evil set of roles at which all couples should aim. There is, however, a need for careful matching and an ethical obligation to respect the partner in any marriage as a person with special individual needs. Such respect is basic to satisfactory mutual adjustment both before and in marriage. When such respect exists, with a high sense of responsibility and strong personal attachment, even two strongly aggressive and dominant persons do frequently adjust in roughly egalitarian ways which become highly satisfying and enriching to both.

C. The Christian Ideal

Thus far we have related the actualities of marriage and family life to the General Principles of Moral Decision, which were validated without reference to Christian assumptions. Now we must see what light explicitly Christian teaching and history have to throw on the ethics of marriage and the family.

1. A Sadly Mixed Tradition

The history of thought concerning sex and marriage among Christian theologians is strewn with wreckage. Many writings from Augustine to Thomas Aquinas and on to some utterances of Pope Paul VI reflect more influence from pagan sources—and not the best—than from Christ and the dominant teaching of the New Testament.

There have been several causes of these subchristian views.

a. Low Conception of Natural Law. First, there is the disastrous basing of much Church teaching on the natural law of man's animal nature. As pointed out in Chapter Six, this conception of natural law was derived from the Roman jurist Ulpian, through Justinian's *Corpus Iuris Civilis*. Because of this baneful influence, much Church teaching has interpreted sex as good only for propagation of the race and otherwise evil, "carnal" in an invidious sense, or a regrettably necessary concession to concupiscence. The positive values of the whole relation between husband and wife have, in such interpretation, failed to come into view at all.

b. A Minor Strain in Paul's Teaching. It is false exegesis which finds in Paul's opposition of "flesh" to spirit a denigrating of the physi-

9. Cf. Ernest W. Burgess and Leonard S. Cottrell, Jr., *Predicting Success or Failure in Marriage* (New York: Prentice-Hall, 1939), especially Chap. XI.

cal body and its desires as compared with the mental or spiritual aspects of humanity. Paul includes among the sins of the flesh such things as "idolatry, . . . enmity, . . . dissension," and "party spirit," which are certainly no more bodily than such "fruit of the Spirit" as "love, joy, peace," and the like (Gal. 5:20, 22). The "flesh" is nearly always, in Paul's writing, simply unregenerate or natural humanity, as contrasted with the Spirit of God working in and through man. Unfortunately, however, Paul does, on occasion, write about sex in a deprecating mood. The worst instance is in 1 Cor. 7:8–9:

> To the unmarried and the widows I say that it is well for them to remain single as I do. But if they cannot exercise self-control, they should marry. For it is better to marry than to be aflame with passion.

Such admonitions as this are connected—indeed this one is explicitly related by Paul—to his expectation that the age will soon end. It is better not to have the complications of wife or husband and family while approaching the distress of the final world crisis (1 Cor. 7:25–31). Even so, he explicitly states that to marry "is no sin," even though "he who refrains from marriage will do better" (1 Cor. 7:36, 38). On the other hand, Paul speaks emphatically of the sacredness of the body. Sexual immorality is evil, not because the body is base, but because the "body is a temple of the Holy Spirit" and is therefore not to be defiled by irresponsible union (1 Cor. 6:15–20). Unfortunately, other conditions of the early Christian centuries led to more emphasis on negative than on positive New Testament teachings concerning sex.

c. Prevailing Sexual Practices.   In the Graeco-Roman environment of early Christianity, the dominant image of sex was of sensuality, polygamy and concubinage, and various perversions. In such a setting it was doubtless difficult to think of sexual relations as good or holy.

d. Personal Experience of Theologians.   Much of the traditional attitude of Christian writers toward sex is traceable to Augustine. Throughout his writings one can observe a tension between the moral revulsion which he feels for sexual expression and his duty to represent faithfully the biblical teaching that God ordained and sanctified the institution of marriage. It is easy to understand his spontaneous revulsion when one remembers that Augustine's experiences of sex had been experiences of using women, not of love for them, of moral defeat, not of ennobling fidelity. In his own life sex had meant temptation and fall. He had escaped from its degrading clutches only by embracing vows of celibacy. Other Church Fathers had similar memories which helped harden the tradition of viewing marriage as at best a state of life for people who could not rise to the higher calling of celibacy. The experience of all celibate priests, who must always view sexual desire as temptation to sin, further confirms the tradition.

e. Hellenistic Dualism. Influential also has been the dualistic thought of ancient culture in which the material world was widely regarded as a debasing or imprisoning force which kept the spirit of man from rising to its rightful destiny. Such dualism took many forms, but was especially prominent in the Neoplatonism of Plotinus, some forms of Gnosticism, and the Manicheanism to which Augustine adhered for a time before his conversion. As Catholic theology united with Hellenistic philosophy to form both the Platonic and Aristotelian syntheses, such dualism, even when not openly avowed, tended to affect value judgments. Reason, mystical visions, and ascetic self-denial were then highly prized, while bodily appetites and especially sex were regarded as foes of true Christian life.

f. Virgin Birth and Celibacy of Jesus. The fact that Jesus was single until death and, even more, the doctrine of the Virgin Birth, contributed further to the idealization of the celibate life. Wherever the cultus of Mary is emphasized, much is made of her virginity, with a common assumption that virginity is superior to the state of a faithful wife.

2. Basic Norms

If one seeks the norms of Christian marriage from the perspective of central and distinctive gospel principles, the denigrating of marriage is seen as a sub-Christian aberration, despite its recurrent prominence in the writings of celibate priests. We must now seek to formulate normative Christian principles.

a. Marriage Optional. When his disciples concluded that if divorce was forbidden it was "not expedient to marry," Jesus replied, "Not all men can receive this precept, but only those to whom it is given," and continued with his saying about eunuchs by birth, by mutilation, and by their own choice "for the sake of the kingdom of heaven" (Matt. 19:10–12).

Karl Barth properly writes,

> There is no necessity of nature nor general divine law in virtue of which every man is permitted or commanded to take a wife, or every woman a husband. If this is permitted and commanded, it is a special distinction, a special divine calling, a gift and grace.[10]

In short, the all too common assumption that there is something strange or abnormal about a man or woman going through life unmarried is

10. *On Marriage*, ed. by Franklin Sherman (Philadelphia: Fortress Press, 1968), p. 1. From Barth's *Church Dogmatics*.

false. Marriage would more often be entered responsibly and wisely if there were not such a social pressure to marry. Unfortunately, the churches often increase this pressure by the unrestrained sentimentality with which they observe such occasions as Mother's Day, with rarely a word to recognize the beauty and completeness of lives achieved by many unmarried adults.

While Roman Catholics traditionally elevate celibacy to a superior status, Protestants often indulge in equally regrettable one-sided glorification of marriage and childbearing. This is especially inexcusable in a day when a population explosion threatens all human life worthy of the name.

b. Sacramental Monogamy. Derrick S. Bailey points out the high significance of Paul's teaching in 1 Cor. 6:16–17, including the correct translation in the margin ("one flesh"):

Do you not know that he who joins himself to a prostitute becomes one body with her? For, as it is written, "The two shall become one flesh." But he who is united to the Lord becomes one spirit with him.

Says Bailey of this passage:

St. Paul contrasts two kinds of union. There is, first, that of the believer with Christ, expressed in the metaphor of the body and its members—a spiritual, metaphysical union analogically exemplified in the true *henosis* of husband and wife: "he that is joined unto the Lord is one spirit." Second, there is union with a harlot—a parody of the true *henosis* and so of the marriage between the heavenly Bridegroom and his Bride. . . .

His use of "body" (*soma*) instead of "flesh" (*sarx*) shows how well St. Paul understood the significance of sexual union. . . . Intercourse therefore is much more than a mere physical act . . . ; it involves and affects the whole man and the whole woman in the very centre and depth of their being. . . .[11]

A traditional form of Christian marriage ritual speaks of

holy matrimony; which is an honorable estate, instituted of God, and signifying unto us the mystical union which exists between Christ and his Church. . . .[12]

To many modern ears this has an archaic and unrealistic sound. To relate the marriage of a man and a woman to the union of Christ and

11. *The Mystery of Love and Marriage* (New York: Harper & Row, 1952), pp. 51–52.
12. *The Book of Worship for Church and Home* (Nashville: Methodist Publishing House, 1965), p. 28.

his Church appears to be a remote analogy at best. Actually the relation is much more than analogy.

Josiah Royce wrote of "loyalty to loyalty" as the foundation of all other loyalties.[13] A man's loyalty to his friend, to causes which he espouses, to every ideal he holds, and to his wife, alike root in a basic commitment to loyalty as such. But this loyalty is not an abstract ideal; it is embodied in the community in which I participate. My faithfulness to loyalty is my acceptance of membership in the whole community of men, my responsibility to that community, and my commitment to further the loyalty of my fellows. For the Christian this community is the Church in its union with Christ.

There has been much discussion of the relation between love and fidelity in marriage.[14] The precise psychological relation undoubtedly varies in different instances. In some the intensity of love teaches and confirms a fidelity hitherto not strongly developed. In others strong fidelity holds firm the ties of a marriage in which love is initially weak and vacillating until love deepens. In yet others strong love and the deep fidelity of emotionally mature persons blend together in even union. But always where a sound and happy marriage is to hold fast, "for better, for worse, for richer, for poorer, in sickness and in health"[15] until death, love must be deeply blended with fidelity. Emotion is notoriously variable and in no relationship continues constantly at high pitch. Fidelity must carry love through some times of stress.

The resources and riches of loyalty to Christ and his Church in the world are brought to the Christian marriage relation. Since intercourse, as Bailey has said, "involves and affects the whole man and the whole woman in the very centre and depth of their being," it is sacramentally expressive of the whole Christian commitment. That is, it is so if it is in truth the consummation of a Christian marriage. To be such a consummation it must be an unreserved, total giving of the two persons to each other. But when there is such giving, faithful monogamy is implied.

The affective dialectic of monogamy is similar to that of monotheism. Ancient Israel did not come to exclusive belief in one God through rational speculation, but through a kind of implicit rationale of feeling and will. Believing that many gods existed, Moses and the prophets nevertheless proclaimed that one alone should be worshiped by Israel. Other peoples might serve other gods; but Israel was to

13. *Philosophy of Loyalty* (New York: The Macmillan Company, 1930), pp. 118–21.
14. E.g., by Emil Brunner, in *The Divine Imperative* (Philadelphia: Westminster Press, 1947), pp. 357–58:
15. *The Book of Worship for Church and Home*, p. 29.

worship and serve Yahweh only. As this loyalty intensified other gods came to be regarded as inferior, unworthy to be called gods, and finally as sheer fabrications.

So the lover (man or woman) who is in earnest sees one woman or one man who stands out from others as the chosen one. The sexual kind of interest in others falls away until there is only one with whom the compact of marriage is entered. To be sure, the husband does not deny that other women besides his wife exist (!) but affirms that there is only one woman *for him*. The polygamist and the philanderer are only dilettantes who know little of love, in the full humanistic sense, let alone the Christian sense.

c. Responsible Care for Children. In relations between parents and children, as between husband and wife, there are many patterns of roles. It would be stupid to expect Christian parents in Tokyo to train their children in the same way as those in rural African Botswana. Different patterns are acceptable on a Nebraska farm than in Manhattan. Even within a single city, various subcultures make their own varied demands. These variations are to be respected within limits. The limits are imposed by the universal needs of children and the requirements of orderly society. Within these limits moral decisions must be made in relation to the specific situation, physiological, economic, psychological, and cultural.

Such General Principles as Altruism and the Ideal of Community apply to relations of parents to children, of children one to another and to the parents, and of all to the family as a whole and to the larger community. Of course, such obligations rest upon the members only to the extent of their capacities and so normally weigh most heavily upon the parents and not at all upon young infants.

Fully in accord with the General Principles and also with the most basic Christian norms are these famous apostolic admonitions:

> Children, obey your parents in the Lord, for this is right. "Honor your father and mother" (this is the first commandment with a promise), "that it may be well with you and that you may live long on the earth." Fathers, do not provoke your children to anger, but bring them up in the discipline and instruction of the Lord. [Eph. 6:1–3]

Children need to learn early obedience to their parents for their own protection from physical danger and from acts which would limit and undermine their future. Obedience to parents is not an end in itself, however. It should be a steppingstone to moral autonomy and obedience to God in responsible service to the larger community.

If obedience is to be taught in a way to accord with this purpose and with a minimum of provoking to anger or resentment, thoughtful care is required. Discipline is necessary, but it must always be gentle and with loving purpose. Parents must avoid the attrition of good relations by overattention to trivial immaturities. When a child's desires must be frustrated by negative commands, parents need to give special care to cultivating positive supporting relationships. There is a kind of book-balancing of credits and debits needed in these relationships. When a parent becomes chiefly a nuisance from the child's point of view, disciplines of love become impossible and estrangement develops. It is especially important that the Principle of Altruism be observed, for children's habits are not to be managed predominantly for the convenience of their parents. No amount of monetary support and gifts can compensate for personal neglect nor for a habit of getting the children "out of the way" for the parents' pleasure.

An especially delicate art is the correctly timed and phased withdrawal of authority to let the growing son or daughter learn responsible self-management and decision-making. For better or worse, at some time in adolescence there remains little or no authority of parent as parent. The parents' hopes then rest upon the judgment of the youth. Their own influence now will be limited solely to the strength of the youth's love for them and respect for their ideas.

As the children grow in understanding and self-rule, their own obligations increase rapidly. They, too, are then bound by the Principle of Altruism, and they have their own responsibility for developing that community of mutual concern and sharing, and of service to the larger world, which is the Christian family.

D. SOME CURRENT PROBLEMS

1. *Premarital Conduct*

As parents and others have sought to guard the chastity of young people before marriage, they have generally laid heavy stress on the risks of illegitimate children and of venereal disease. There is a widespread belief that, thanks to new devices and medical developments, sexual intercourse can now be indulged with very little danger of conception or disease. Consequently, many conclude that the reasons for premarital chastity are now outmoded and the opposition to intercourse before marriage is only an archaic prejudice without sound contemporary reason.

We have seen that there are essential reasons for premarital chastity quite apart from conception or disease. But in actuality even the secondary arguments remain stronger than is commonly believed. The *rate* of illegitimate births *per 1,000* unmarried (never married, widowed, and divorced) women in the United States, so far from declining, rose from 7.1 in 1940 to 24.1 in 1968, a 239 per cent increase in the rate per 100,000, with the increase continuing to the last year included.[16]

As far as disease is concerned, it is true that deaths from syphilis and its sequelae have been sharply reduced, from 5.0 per 100,000 in 1950 to 1.2 per 100,000 in 1967. Between 1950 and 1968 the total number of syphilis cases among civilians has not declined so much as the death rate from this cause, but only about 56 per cent. On the other hand, the incidence of gonorrhea increased from 236,197 to 464,543 between 1955 and 1968, among civilians, or four and one-half times as fast as the civilian population (*ibid.*, pp. 58, 78, and 5).

The essential ground of the ethical obligation to premarital chastity is, however, in the nature of marriage itself. It should be noted that in discussing the ethics of faithful monogamy, up to the present subtopic, I have not so much as mentioned either disease or conception. Both are important, and responsible parenthood is especially so, but neither concerns the essential nature of the sexual relation between man and woman.

2. *Divorce*

The essential permanency of true marriage has been discussed. But despite all warnings and the regrettably inadequate instruction usually given by church and family, many couples do marry who do not, in some instances cannot, form such true unions as our General Principles require, while far more are unable to form genuine Christian marriages. Civil law which seeks to enforce the Christian teaching concerning marriage is counterproductive. When all marriages in a state are subjected to such laws, the result is a scandalous number of illicit unions and illegitimate births, as in many nominally Roman Catholic countries, or of unfaithfulness, dishonest collusion and evasion, as in the United States where state laws permit divorce on no grounds or only on extremely limited grounds.[17] For best results civil laws must be written with a view to realities in the total society and with the purpose of providing greatest actual stability under the circumstances. Making divorce too easy encourages casual and irresponsible marriage. Making it too difficult leads to a breakdown of the legal structure intended to protect marriage and so actually undermines the institution of marriage.

What, then, of the ethics of personal divorce by a Christian? Clear

---

16. *Statistical Abstract of the United States: 1970*, p. 50.
17. Cf. W. F. Ogburn and M. F. Nimkoff, *Technology and the Changing Family* (Boston: Houghton Mifflin Co., 1955), pp. 239-40.

New Testament teachings, as well as the basic meaning of Christian marriage, strongly oppose divorce. Hence the initial presumption in any instance is that the Christian ought not to seek divorce. Marriage should be permanent, and every Christian has the obligation to strengthen and not weaken customary expectations that marriage vows will hold fast until death. Hence all possible devices which humility, patience, and a forgiving spirit can employ should be used. Where needed and possible these should include the aid of a trained marriage counselor.

Yet there are cases in which, through whatever fault of ignorance, deceit, unguarded haste, later change of personality, or other cause, a marriage has failed to become a genuine union of two persons or, having once succeeded, has subsequently broken down. The couple may have tried to continue the relations of man and wife, but without love. Despite earnest effort by one, or even both, love and hope may now be dead. If there are children, they may be injured as deeply by the loveless relationship and its effects on attitudes toward themselves as they would be by the parents' permanent separation.

Despite the contrary initial presumption, the legal dissolution of divorce may be the least destructive way to deal with the existing tragic realities. The New Testament teaching against divorce, emphatic as it is, is not law but gospel. When Jesus said, "What therefore God has joined together, let no man put asunder,"[18] he was not laying down law regarding couples whom God evidently has *not* joined together. The "hardness of heart" which, Jesus said, had been the occasion for easy divorce law—for men—in ancient Israel is still present today, and it is necessary to take account of it.

When the question is raised whether a certain divorced person should be remarried as a Christian, to someone other than the original spouse, the problem is not to determine who secured the divorce at law. The problem is to determine as well as possible the probability that this person and the proposed new partner are prepared in every way to form a genuine Christian marriage. This is the same question which needs to be faced by *every* couple proposing to marry and every clergyman requested to bless *any* marriage. However, in the case of one or two divorced persons there is an emphatic initial presumption against the marriage, in view of the previous failure. The burden of proof now requires substantial evidence that this new marriage will succeed despite the previous record of failure.[19]

18. Matt. 19:6. Cf. vv. 3–12 and Mark 10:1–12.
19. Cf. the discussion of this subject, with different method but similar conclusions as to practice, by Karl Barth, in *op. cit.*, pp. 29–41. Cf. also Otto A. Piper, *The Christian Interpretation of Sex* (New York: Charles Scribner's Sons, 1947), especially pp. 204–5.

3. Responsible Parenthood

There is no biblical teaching that sexual intercourse should not be inhibited from leading to conception. When Jesus and Paul speak about the ethics of marriage and divorce, they discuss the nature of the marital relation itself, not its connection with reproduction. The two Old Testament passages commonly used by opponents of birth control are actually irrelevant. The story of Onan concerns a dishonest violation of the ancient Levirate law which required the brother of a deceased man to beget a child by the widow (Gen. 38:7-10). The other passage used, the command "Be fruitful and multiply" (Gen. 1:28), is placed in the context of a world with only two human inhabitants—not over three billions, heading for six or seven billions in thirty years!

If, as I have maintained, and as most Christian theologians agree, sexual intercourse has primary meaning in the love of husband and wife, then in our present world it should be freed from the peril of producing unwanted children. In principle this has been conceded even by the Roman Catholic Church, which now contends only against "artificial" means of contraception. As pointed out earlier, that position is based on no religious grounds, but on a concept of natural law giving top priority to man's animal nature. That concept, derived from the pagan lawyer Ulpian, is indefensible. So is the gnat-straining effort to distinguish between the dependence on "the rhythm method" of birth control and the "artificial" methods. The restricting of intercourse to a few days per month which physiological examinations, wide experimentation, and mathematical computations have designated as "safe" is about as artificial a method as anyone ever proposed —besides being ineffective.

The present "population explosion" and the heavy burdens of large families among the poor are the result of artificial interference with sickness and death. Unless we similarly inhibit births, we shall soon face the alternatives of mass extermination by war or mass starvation and plague. Meanwhile, in America most couples do practice family planning according to means, desire, and sense of social responsibility. Unfortunately, a combination of ignorance, unavailability of help, and outmoded religious prejudice still keeps many of the people least able to rear and educate useful citizens from participating in planned limitation of their own parenthood.

Common humanity, as well as Christian love, requires that clinical aid be provided for the poor who wish to escape the ever-increasing burden of unwanted children, along with couples of larger means. This is also important to meet the now urgent threat of unbearable *total* population pressure. Of this threat more will be said in Chapter Eleven.

Aid in family planning for the poor provides another example of the interaction among different ills and problem areas of our society. A minority, but still a disproportionately large minority of poor people in America belong to ethnic minorities of the population. The offering of assistance in family planning to these minorities, especially black people, predictably raises the charge of "genocide." Elimination of racism is essential to effective social cooperation to relieve mothers of excessive childbearing burdens.

The providing of contraceptive information and means such as "the pill" to unmarried women raises more serious questions. Clearly, Christian personal ethics forbids the individual from practicing premarital intercourse. If all our citizens were living by this standard, the question of public policy would not be raised. Actually, large numbers are not living by such standards. The number of illegitimate births continues to rise, with all the accompanying tragedies. Under these conditions it is better to provide means of birth control to young women who request such means, and to accompany such provision with instruction about the social and personal cost of premarital sex even without conception. The tragedy of unchastity is evil enough—and has evidently been chosen already when the single girl asks for contraceptive aid. There is no need to add the further tragedy of unwanted and homeless children.

4. *Abortion*

Induced or surgical abortion is much more serious than contraception, and the initial presumption must be against its being employed. However, there are many cases in which it is the ethically preferred alternative. When a woman has been raped or when the condition of a pregnant woman is such that her life is gravely imperiled by continuance, or when there is sound medical reason to expect that the conceived child will be abnormal, abortion should certainly be an available choice. The prohibition of it in such cases can hardly be interpreted as an expression of Christian love. Should the law prohibit abortion at all? Should the law rather provide a generous structure within which medical and ethical questions can be decided by the pregnant woman and her physician?

The contention that abortion is sinful under any and all conditions is generally based on the view that the human embryo is a human being and that therefore to deprive it of life is murder. The traditional Roman Catholic view is that from the very moment of conception, that is the joining of a sperm with an ovum, the fertilized egg is a human being and hence inviolate.

Obviously, such a one-celled embryo does not have the defining characteristics of a human person—whether bodily form, intelligence, or other. But a baby born at full-term does not exhibit the signs of intelligent personality; yet obligations of Christian love are universally regarded as including the loving care of a baby, however young. He is so visibly and imminently on the way to becoming a person that he is regarded as possessing the right to life as surely as an older child or adult.

We must ask, then, at what stage the embryo or fetus comes to possess such inviolable right to life. One traditional view is that the critical point is the assuming of recognizably human form—after about three months.[20] Another tradition is that when the expectant mother first feels the quickening, that is the normative sign of a human being. In medical practice the decisive condition is often held to be the time when the fetus becomes able to live outside the womb, breathing air and taking food by mouth, rather than being supported through the umbilical cord within the womb.

In an age of population explosion there appears to be no compelling reason why civil law should require a woman to bear a child resulting from rape or incest, or almost certainly doomed to be deformed, or even unwanted, just because she has become pregnant. Love for the woman and for other children, and concern for the community which must often accept the burden of supporting such children, would militate against such legal compulsion. Moreover, when abortion is prohibited, great numbers of illegal abortions are performed by unqualified people in unsanitary conditions. In short, the foreseeable consequences of legally prohibiting abortion in the present world are not such as to be acceptable to a person with loving concern for all who are affected. The embryo or fetus itself is in all probability not yet capable of experiencing either value or disvalue. On balance it would appear better that in a world where there are limited resources for additional people, place should be reserved for normal and wanted children rather than for those who if born will live in misery and inflict misery also on their mothers and others.

As for the time after which abortion should not be permitted by law, rather generous freedom of decision might well be left to the prospective mother and physician, while yet placing a safe distance between abortion and infanticide. Perhaps six months of pregnancy might be set by law as the latest limit beyond which any method of abortion designed deliberately to terminate the life within the womb must not

---

20. Tertullian seemed to express this view in the second century when he wrote, "The embryo therefore becomes a human being in the womb from the moment that its form is completed." *A Treatise on the Soul*, Chap. 37. However, Tertullian did not hold this view consistently.

go. Of course, the little creature may be removed from the womb by Caesarean section or induced labor at any later time, as well, for sound medical reasons, but in such instances normal effort should be made to preserve the life, as in any case of premature birth.[21]

5. *Responsibilities of the Church for the Family*

The present responsibilities of the church would emphasize especially early instruction regarding the sacramental meaning of love and marriage. Churches need also to establish standards for due notice and premarital consultation by their clergy before marriages by church rites. Special classes for young married people are helpful both in solidifying marriage and in preparing for wise parenthood. Much is being attempted in support of parental instruction of children. Much more is needed.

When strains appear in marriage, a church counseling center can be a great boon, if manned by ministers well-trained for the task. Seminaries are increasingly preparing ministers for pastoral counseling, including marital counseling, and this trend is to be encouraged.

In the legislative field, too, the church has responsibilities for the support of wise and uniform legal structures supportive of stable marriage and responsible families—along lines already set forth.

In all its approaches the church should emphasize the positive sacred meaning of marriage and family relations. The approach of Christian love and grace is always the authentic one. There must be negative prohibitions, but it must be stressed heavily that they are for protection of the sacred good of sex, marriage, and family life. At the same time, the celibate life must be carefully respected as a valid option for both men and women.

21. For a closely argued view with radically different conclusions, see Paul Ramsey, "The Morality of Abortion," in Edward Shils and others, *Life or Death Ethics and Options* (Seattle: University of Washington Press, 1968), pp. 60–93. Cf. also the articles on abortion by Charles H. Boyer, K. Danner Clauser, John Moore, and John Pamperin, in *The Christian Century*, May 20, 1970 (Vol. LXXXVII, No. 20, pp. 624–31).

chapter eleven

Our Natural Environment

A. URGENCY OF THE PROBLEM

In November, 1961, a special task force of nationally known scientists met at Greenbank, West Virginia, to determine the probabilities that communication could be established with an extraterrestrial civilization somewhere in the universe. A part of the task was to ascertain the life expectancy of any civilized species which might come into existence. This question brought their attention back to earth. Now that human beings have developed to a technological stage capable of interstellar radio communication, how much longer is the human race likely to endure? The answer might tell us something about similar creatures possibly existing elsewhere in our galaxy.

Working under the auspices of the Space Science Board of the National Academy of Science, they examined present trends, various growing threats to human existence, and the likelihood of reversing fatal trends before final disaster. Some participants thought that probably *in less than two hundred years* the human species would be extinct.[1] If we estimate that the human race has been in existence for about one million years, this would mean that our species had finished about 99.8 per cent of its life expectancy. A more generous consensus was that all might depend on the surmounting of the international and environmental crisis looming immediately before us. Hence the future of the human race or any other comparable species of intelligent, technologically communicative beings might be "less than a thousand years." On the other hand, if such beings could "surmount the crisis," their species might then "continue development almost indefinitely, perhaps for periods of the order of hundreds of millions of years."[2]

1. Report by David Adamson, head of the Space Physics Group, Aero-Physics Division, Langley Research Center of NASA, in illustrated lecture to the Virginia Methodist Pastors Assembly, Blackstone, Va., Oct. 3, 1967.
2. J. P. T. Peerman, in a report on the Greenback consultation kindly supplied to me by David Adamson, and entitled "Extraterrestrial Intelligent Life and In-

If we survive two hundred years or more, it will probably be because we shall have gained a new political and cultural maturity so that we shall be working together for the future of us all. In that case the human race might endure for as long as the conditions of the solar system remain of such character as to make it possible.

This would, however, require radical change of human priorities, with nationalism, the conflict of political systems, the independent right of couples to beget children as they please, and the constant drive for a larger gross national product all being subordinated to the conservation of conditions of life for all. A radical turning must come within ten to twenty years if catastrophe is to be avoided. The time may be shorter. In view of the way we are using our powers, it seems probable that, sinful egoist that he is, man made a fatal mistake when he developed scientific technology. A human future on earth will be possible only if technology can be put into uses radically different from those which are now dominant.

In such reversal, the United States would have to lead the way. This is true because the highly industrialized United States is continuously destroying more necessary resources of life per capita than any other nation, is threatening vastly greater additional destruction than any other, and at the same time has the greatest capacity for reversing the fatal trends.

B. The Basic Threats

1. War and Preparation for War

What are the forces which are feared as our probable early destroyers? The most immediate threat is, of course, war. With the newly developed means of nuclear bombs and various forms of biological warfare, we now possess the power to kill hundreds of millions in a matter of minutes, but also, at the same time, so to pollute the human environment as to doom the remaining human life to early extinction.

Moreover, the United States is currently polluting and upsetting the ecology of Indochina by deliberate military policy. The drainage of the soil into the sea, the export of foodstuffs, and the migration of wildlife all prevent such reckless destruction from being isolated with certainty from the rest of the world. A first hopeful step was taken when President Nixon ordered the military services to limit developing and stockpiling bacteria and viruses for the spreading of plague

terstellar Communication: an Informal Discussion." More alarming views and much useful information will be found in Garrett De Bell, ed., *The Environmental Handbook* (New York: Ballantine Books, 1970).

among a possible enemy and to begin disposing of some of these supplies. We continue, however, to increase our other means of mass destruction. We still remain both the greatest present military destroyer and the greatest potential military threat to the whole human race, including ourselves.

2. Pollution of Air

The average American puts 1,500 pounds of air pollutants into the atmosphere per year, making a total for the American people of 142 million tons. Much of this material is known to be toxic.[3] The worst offender is the automobile with its highly inefficient internal combustion engine spewing lead and unburned hydrocarbon in its wake. Additional serious offenders are jet airplanes, burning dumps, oil refineries, utility plants, and other industrial burners of oil or coal. Apart from one deadly smog in London, and the serious intermittent problems of Los Angeles and New York City, the public has not generally noticed cause for alarm. However, the polluted atmosphere outdoors is known to be an important cause of pulmonary disease, including lung cancer, although less deadly generally than tobacco smoke pollution indoors, especially, though not solely, in the lungs of the smoker. It is the accelerating concentration of automobiles and hence rapid increase of air pollution which is the main cause for alarm. If we wait for obvious and widespread injury to result, before heroic measures of relief, it will then be already too late to avoid huge human cost and perhaps some irreversible ecological effects.[4]

3. Pollution of Water

Water is being polluted most seriously by sewage disposal, industrial waste, runoff from erosion of soil exposed by the bulldozer, DDT and other nonbiodegradable compounds, radioactive waste, and thermal change due to industrial use of water for cooling purposes, with resultant ecological havoc.

4. Upsetting of Ecological Balance

Rachel Carson's book *Silent Spring* alerted many Americans to the problems which could result from speedy use of promising chemicals

3. Symposium of nationally gathered authorities at Airlie House, as reported in *The Washington Post*, Nov. 26, 1968.

4. "Ecology" is the biological science of the interrelation between different forms of life and their environments. The word means also a system of such relationships. Human ecology is the system of relationships in man's natural environment upon which his life depends.

for destruction of unwanted pests. When DDT first appeared it seemed too good to be true. Sprayed over barn walls or over trees and lawns it effectively eliminated flies and mosquitoes for a long period, for it kept its deadly properties indefinitely. However, it was only long after its heavy use that it was discovered that it had also sterilized great numbers of birds involved in food chains which included insects, worms, frogs, lizards, and fish. As the American bald eagle was threatened with extinction and the numbers of many insect-eating birds were sharply reduced the rapidly reproducing, short-generation insects developed new varieties resistant to DDT—and now their natural enemies were few or missing.

Many species of animals have become extinct because of our reckless upsetting of ecological balance. We manage without them even though the loss is real, and we can survive loss of the bald eagle if the very small present reproductive rate proves insufficient to sustain his kind. But the next time it may be mankind which will be nearly or altogether wiped out by some such unforeseen effect of our hasty massive use of new intervention in the delicate web of life.

5. Exhaustion of Oxygen

The earth is well supplied with free oxygen. We should quickly exhaust the supply, however, were it not recycled by plant life which uses the carbon dioxide which we and other animals exhale and gives off oxygen. Now we are seriously threatening this recycling process and hence our oxygen supply. We have done this by reducing forest acreage—a process now ended at least for the present[5]—and by replacing fields and orchards with houses, paved highways, and parking lots. Another, slower change may in the end be even more disastrous. The pollution of streams is in turn polluting the large lakes and the ocean. The biggest helpful factor by far in the oxygen cycle is the vast quantity of minute life in the ocean known collectively as plankton. Some areas of ocean water have been observed to be significantly changed and the plankton sharply reduced. It is too early to know how seriously forces we have already set in motion will inevitably alter the ocean's indispensable recycling of our atmosphere.

6. Overpopulation

One basic root cause of our increasing environmental problems is the exploding population. When the Pilgrim Fathers landed at Plym-

5. Hans H. Landsberg, *The U.S. Resources Outlook: Quantity and Quality* (Washington, D.C.: Resources for the Future, 1968).

outh in 1620 there were about one-half of one billion people on earth. In 1965 the United Nations Statistical Office estimated the world's population as about seven times as high, or three and one-half billions. Not only does the population rapidly grow; the rate of growth also grows. Thirty-five years later the population is expected to be doubled to seven billions. In 345 years from 1620 to 1965 the population increased to more than three billions. In the *next* 345 years, at the present rate, there will be an increase to over 3,000 billions or 1,000 times the 1965 population.

The earth cannot remotely approach the support of any such population as that. The only question is what will be the means of holding it down or cutting it back. As population becomes more congested there is a marked tendency to increased irritability and aggression. Hence the prospect may be for increased violent conflict. If so it might not only reduce, but altogether eliminate the population, bringing human history to an end. The food supply per person has already gone down every year since 1962 and starvation on a vast scale may develop soon. Meanwhile, the bigger the population the more the pollution and exhaustion of irreplaceable resources.[6]

7. *Affluence*

It may seem strange to speak of affluence as a problem. However, it is precisely because of American affluence that much of our unequaled pollution and exhaustion of resources is taking place. Affluence brings air-polluting automobiles, enormous waste in garbage and trash which pollute both air and water, the rapid use of irreplaceable oil, coal, and metals and, added to breathing by ourselves, the great consumption of oxygen by our machines and furnaces. It is because of affluence, then, as well as the enormous waste and destructiveness of our military machine, that we are despoiling the natural environment far more per capita than any other people on earth.

8. *Reckless Disregard*

Each of the problems and perils we have noted is serious. Even worse is the wanton relentlessness of man's exploitation of nature as a whole. Whatever purposes the world may have apart from human use, it is, of course, absolutely essential to the continuance of human history. Hence all the biblical admonitions to love our neighbors and our children reinforce the heavy obligations we bear for the care and conservation of the natural resources on which mankind depends. How

6. For a factually informed and shockingly pessimistic view of the future, see Paul R. Ehrlich, *The Population Bomb* (New York: Sierra Club-Ballantine, 1968).

concerned are we? The Canon of Westminster, Edward F. Carpenter, writes of

> man's relentless assault, in a global context, upon the universe around him—that is on God's creation—an attack on the air which he pollutes; the natural waterways which he befouls; the soil which he poisons; the forests which he hews down, heedless of the long-term effects of this wanton destruction. This attack is piecemeal and uncoordinated. Scant regard is paid to any balance of nature and consequently little sense of responsibility for what one generation owes to another.[7]

C. Biblical Views of the Natural Environment

1. Subject to Man's Dominion

Our Christian tradition has been especially destructive in its ecological fruits because of some bad hermeneutics.

The fateful verse is Genesis 1:28—"Be fruitful and multiply, and fill the earth and subdue it; and have dominion over the fish of the sea and over the birds of the air and over every living thing that moves upon the earth."

We people of the biblical tradition have obeyed this injunction in its worst sense. In fact, so deep in our whole Western tradition have we implanted the notion that to conquer and exploit nature for our own benefit is positively virtuous that we have a special responsibility for undergirding a new attitude toward nature with a sounder theology.

"Subdue" and "have dominion"—these are the commands we have been so eager to obey. The Hebrew *kâbash* and *râdâh* are even worse than the English, for both carry the notion of tramping down or conquering like an enemy. We have treated the lower animals and the earth itself accordingly. Now we have even started to do the same with the moon.

But the Bible has very much more to say about the world of nature that we have overlooked only because of our sinful egoism. This egoism has called to its support such abuse of Scripture as would have fooled no one had it not pleased men's selfish impulses.

The single emphasis on subduing and dominion results from bad hermeneutics in two respects.

First, it results from dwelling on one verse of Scripture seen in

7 "In Context," *The Modern Churchman*, Vol. XII, No. 1 (Oct., 1968), p. 111. Cf. R. C. Mortimer, *The Elements of Moral Theology* (New York: Harper & Brothers, c. 1947), p. 11. Mortimer was prophetic in his time. However, Carpenter goes well beyond him when he shows concern for nonhuman creatures as well as human beings. See *op. cit.*, pp. 104–17.

isolation from all the rest that is said on the subject in the Bible and even in Genesis. Subduing and having dominion need not always have so ruthless an implication. In this instance they can hardly be so intended, since the same writer has just represented God as five times pronouncing that the natural order was good before he created man. Before we can see the main weight of biblical teaching, we must look at the rest of the testimony.

A second hermeneutical requirement is that we seek the new thrust of divine truth for our time among dated expressions of ancient prejudice or perspectives relevant to situations long past. In the human biblical reports of God's disclosures there is much which represents prescientific thought about the world, or bias belonging to the social institutions of ancient cultures. Biblical scholars of many schools commonly and rightly find ways of ignoring, dismissing, demythologizing, or figuratively interpreting such materials before declaring God's word to the present age.

The command to subdue and have dominion is ascribed to God at the very beginning of human life on earth. It is one thing to attack and acquire mastery over forests and plains infested with poisonous snakes, deadly diseases, and ravenous lions; it is quite another to maintain a similar attitude of determined conquest in the world of today. Now men have so completely dominated the earth and its nonhuman inhabitants that the principal threat to their existence is the human race itself. Human beings are now by far the most dangerous and destructive animals on earth.

For God's word through Scripture to us today, we must turn to other themes much more prominently represented and widely distributed in both Testaments.

2. To be Tended with Care

According to the older creation story, God put man in the garden which he had created "to till it and keep it" (Gen. 2:15). The Hebrew word to "till" here is *âbad*, to work, or serve, as well as to cultivate. Even more significant is the word translated "keep." This is *shâmar* and it means to guard, preserve, or protect—precisely what conservationists are now asking us to do with the garden earth in which we have been placed.

3. Good in Itself

Even in the priestly narrative, with its talk of subduing and having dominion, there is material for a very different view of nature. For in the story of creation in Genesis Chapter One, as we noted, God is reported as five times pronouncing things of nature good before he created man.[8]

Albert Schweitzer's widely known "reverence for life" has good biblical ground here and elsewhere. But we can go further. We need to learn, like Jonathan Edwards, to have "reverence for *being*"—the being of sun and moon, of rocks and fields and oceans, as well as for living things. Even before any man saw the splendors of King's Canyon or Mount Rainier they were already of value because God made and loved them.

4. Object of Wonder and Respect

It has been customary for many theologians to scoff at all such talk of nature as "nature worship" and to insist that only in Jesus Christ have we evidence of God. But in the Bible itself are many passages which show a wonder and respect approaching reverence for the things around us. I mention only a few.

"The heavens declare the glory of God" and the rest of Psalm 19:1–7 come at once to mind. Rich in implication for our case is the opening of Psalm 24: "The earth is the Lord's and the fullness thereof, the world and those who dwell therein; for he has founded it upon the seas, and established it upon the rivers." In a mountain thunderstorm we may well ponder that indeed "the God of glory thunders" (Ps. 29:3), and the rest of Psalm 29 is equally fitting and eloquent.

Even when mentions of nature are only figurative expressions concerning spiritual realities, the attitudes expressed often show a deep respect for the nonhuman world around us, as in the great Psalm of God "our refuge and strength," with its reference to the mountains which "shake in the heart of the sea" and the "streams" which "make glad the city of God" (Ps. 46:1, 2, 4).

Again, as Walther Eichrodt writes fittingly,

> Ps. 104 is outstanding for the way in which its picture of the world is completely filled with the idea of the unity, the coherence, the harmonious order of the cosmos. Even when account is taken of the stimulus which the singer received from Egyptian poetry, the force with which the Yahwist faith permeates his material, and shapes it to his own sense, is unmistakable, and compels one to conclude that here Israelite feeling for the natural order found the expression best suited to the absolute claims of belief in Yahweh.[9]

Gerhard von Rad points out that the Old Testament hymns do not

---

8. Vv. 10, 12, 18, 21, 25.
9. *Theology of the Old Testament*, Vol. II, tr. J. A. Baker (London: SCM Press, 1967), p. 113. Cf. pp. 152–53.

stop with praising God's wonderful creation and preservation of the world.

> Since it was so wonderfully created by Jahweh and is so wonderfully preserved, it has a splendour of its own, from which praise and witness issue: in other words the world is not only an object which calls forth praise, but is at the same time also the subject which utters it. "All thy works praise (confess) thee," "the heavens praise (confess) thy wonders" (Pss. CXLV.10, LXXXXIX.6 [5]). The later hymns point quite assiduously to those spheres which are remote from the community and which lie altogether outside the cult—the ends of the earth, the sea, the islands, the wilderness, the dwellers in the desert of Arabia; what do these know of Jahweh and his people? And yet from all of them issues praise (Is. XLII.10–12).[10]

We must not leave the Old Testament without mentioning Job 37–41, with its unparalleled outpouring of praise to the majestic, the overpowering, the terrible, the mysterious, and the gentle wonders of nature in which God is at work.

In the Sermon on the Mount Jesus is represented as referring two separate times to the natural order, each time with deep appreciation and reverence for the Father's work there. God "makes his sun rise on the evil and on the good, and sends rain on [Gk. *brechō:* rains on or moistens] the just and on the unjust" (Matt. 5:45). Again, when he speaks of God's care for "the birds of the air" and "lilies of the field" (Matt. 6:26, 28–30), although his point is concerning God's care for his people, he speaks of God as directly caring for birds and flowers, as also in his reference to the fall of a sparrow (Matt. 10:29).

5. *Sharing in the Dread Result of Man's Sin*

On occasion man's natural environment is pictured as participating in the terrible judgment on man's sin and so sharing his death or agony. An early example is the depicting of a desolate area near the Dead Sea as the blasted ruin of the condemned cities Sodom and Gomorrah and even a salt pillar as the transfixed body of Lot's wife (Gen. 19:24–28). The story of the Great Flood represents all creatures of the earth as sharing the fate of wicked men, save only a tiny remnant, with Noah in the Ark. When doom is being pronounced upon the sinful people the prophets often speak of a time of terrible drought, or a plague of locusts, or disastrous floods, so that nature is both the scourge of God and also co-sufferer with man in the day of judgment.[11]

10. *Old Testament Theology*, Vol. I, tr. D. M. G. Stalker (Edinburgh: Oliver and Boyd, 1962), pp. 361–62.
11. Cf. Eichrodt, *op. cit.*, pp. 152–54.

Perhaps most eloquent and pointed of all is a very brief passage from the Apostle Paul, which carries us on also to a theme of hope. To read it one would think Paul knew how terribly man in his selfish sin was already exploiting and denuding the earth and would yet do so more disastrously before being divinely restored to righteousness and releasing nature with him for a glorious future. For Paul says that "the whole creation has been groaning in travail together until now" (Rom. 8:22). But thank God! there is more, both in the passage and in a possible future for us and the earth.

6.   Place in Eschatological Hope

The whole passage from Paul reads:

> For the creation waits with eager longing for the revealing of the sons of God; for the creation was subjected to futility, not of its own will but by the will of him who subjected it in hope; because the creation itself will be set free from its bondage to decay and obtain the glorious liberty of the children of God. We know that the whole creation has been groaning in travail together until now; and not only the creation, but we ourselves, who have the first fruits of the Spirit, groan inwardly as we wait for adoption as sons, the redemption of our bodies. For in this hope we were saved.   [Rom. 8:19–24a]

I am not meaning to suggest that Paul was a conservationist nor that he had twentieth-century understanding of the delicate web of life which joins man with the world around him. Neither would I suggest that his eschatological hope was intended by him to support conservation as a policy. Yet I do affirm that he and various other biblical writers sense, as indeed many men much less scientific than he feel deeply, the bonds which hold mankind and the natural environment together in a common earthly destiny. He therefore declares spontaneously by a prophetic or poetic vision that the creation which cradles man both suffers with him and will share the glory of the new day when our highest hopes are fulfilled.

There are foretastes of such vision in the Old Testament when we are told of the animals sent into the Ark with Noah, and when the prophets describe the days of God's mercy on his repentant people as days when deserts will turn to gardens; likewise when they describe the future peace among men as a day when lions and lambs and little children can walk or lie down together without fear or harm.

Traditionally, Christian hope is intimately related to the Incarnation. That, too, is a biblical theme deeply related to ecology.

7. *The Web of Life and the Incarnation*

The Incarnation did not begin with the conception in the womb of Mary. Paul's doctrine of the preexistent Christ offers one approach to this truth. The Logos doctrine of the Fourth Gospel offers another. The Synoptic Gospels and Pauline Letters also teach that the Incarnation began in a preparatory sense, here on earth, long before the conception of Jesus. The calling of Israel out of Egypt and the work of the prophets prepared the way until in the fullness of time, the *kairos*, God's purpose of Incarnation and Redemption was fully revealed in Jesus of Nazareth. Indeed, there is repeated suggestion that the beginning was much earlier, as when the genealogy of Jesus is traced back to Adam and when the Prologue of John's Gospel represents the *Logos* which has been made flesh in Jesus as having participated also in the creation of "all things" from "the beginning."

Our present understanding of "the web of life" enables us to see this preparation in a new light.[12] Many hundred millions of years ago the surface of the earth was composed of lifeless rock. In the fullness of geological time, as rain and carbon dioxide formed corrosive acids, the surface of the rock was pitted and partially disintegrated. Life invaded the land in the form of lichens, then mosses and fine-rooted grassy plants. As these plants lived and died they laid down the soil base which could support larger plants. Plant life, by its use of carbon dioxide, freed oxygen. Thus was the way prepared for animal life which, in turn, combined oxygen with carbon to form the carbon dioxide so vital to the plants. Among the animals, again in the fullness of time, came human beings.

Today man lives within a vast web of life so complex and delicate as to intrigue and baffle the greatest biological scientists and to require also the most penetrating and creative poetic vision properly to describe. When a single species in this great network of interdependent life is too greatly diminished, it sometimes turns a whole region back into lifeless desert. Of all creatures in this intricate complex, man is by a wide margin the most destructive but also at times the most helpful. Whether destroying or assisting, man is embodied in the network so that he is an integral part of it all. He is utterly dependent upon it, interacts with it, and continuously contributes to it, for good or ill. As

12. For a highly readable introduction to this concept see John H. Storer, *The Web of Life* (New York: New American Library, Signet Book, 1953, 1956). Cf. the more recent attractive and able theological statement of a similar "inclusionist" point of view, Frederick Elder, *Crisis in Eden* (Nashville: Abingdon Press, 1970). Cf. also the scientific-theological symposium, *Christians and the Good Earth*, edited by Alfred Steffelrud, published by The Faith-Man-Nature Group and sold by the Bookstore of Wesley Theological Seminary in Washington, D.C.

the ecologist sees me, a man, I am a kind of mobile cell in a vast organism which includes all animals, plants and microorganisms, but also rocks, soil, seas, and the sun which is so essential to all terrestrial life.

When the divine Word was made flesh, then, God became incarnate not only in human flesh, but in the world's flesh. Jesus Christ, in his earthly life, was of the same flesh with men and women, yes, but also with deer and fish, with trees and plankton, with seas and mountains. I mean not only that his body was of the same chemical elements to be found in these things, but that the substance of his body was literally drawn from them. His very breath participated in the oxygen carbon-dioxide cycle by which all plants and animals enable each other to live. By being a part of the web of life Jesus Christ has sanctified not only humanity but the whole fabric of life in which human life exists.

8.   *An Ecological Insight into Holy Communion*

Christianity is an incarnational faith and therefore also, in a unique sense, a sacramental faith. Particularly in Holy Communion we cele-brate God's redemptive sanctifying of our common life through Christ and his sacrifice.

In the light of our new ecological awareness, how fitting it is that we should eat and drink the products of grain and fruit in this celebration! In Jesus' earthly life grain and fruit provided the very flesh of his body and blood of his veins, even as they become also our flesh and blood. In the Sacrament we who are members of his mystical body signify this by eating bread and drinking wine as his body and blood. We thus acknowledge anew our dependent and responsible membership in the body of the earth which God has brought to life, by which he sustains us, and which he has sanctified in Jesus Christ. What he has thus sanctified we are called to respect, preserve and nurture.

Jesus took bread and wine in his hands and said, "This is my body; this is my blood." We must now learn that these words actually im-plied also of *all soil and life, all streams and oceans, "This is my body; this is my blood."* For so they are—his and ours.

D.   SITUATIONAL GUIDELINES OF CONSERVATION

Considering our time in history, with rapidly increasing congestion of population, the state of our technology, and the warnings of some experiences and of our ecological experts, we have a number of criti-cally urgent obligations in the field of conservation. In this field the Principle of Foresight is of decisive importance in seeing what love of God and man requires.

1. Disarmament and Peace

We must turn back the frightful waste and destruction of war and preparation for war. The worst influences man is loosing or threatening to loose on his environment are related to war or are greatly augmented by war and the arms race. The use of oil and natural gas, the pollution of atmosphere and water by hastily expanded industry and by the actual use of military equipment in war or testing and practice for war—all these have very rapidly increased in the late sixties, indeed 19 per cent in three years, at a level 40 per cent higher than the total expenditure on education.[13] A more profligate waste of natural resources would be hard to devise. If the most deadly nuclear bombs and weapons of biological warfare are ever used on a large scale, the human race may be extinguished, partly by direct destruction and even more by the wrecking of the human environment through radioactive pollution and fundamental changes of ecology.

The problem of war will be discussed further in the last chapter.

2. Population Limitation

The earth is not unlimited. An overbalanced burden of support placed upon its resources will bring disaster, despite all efforts of conservation. The present outlook is ominous. At the present rate the world population would be 35 billions, or ten times the present number in less than one hundred years. The earth could not support so many. There will not be any such population. The question is what will limit it.

It may be nuclear war, which could kill hundreds of millions at once and leave such effects as to annihilate the human race altogether. It may be that the population will become so great that it will be limited by starvation, malnutrition, and resultant disease of massive proportions. It may be that the struggle for the means of existence will reduce masses of people to a savage struggle for life. Certainly none of these possibilities can be regarded as ethically acceptable. How can they be prevented?

The alternative to such disasters is a combination of mass communication to change attitudes and making means of contraception available to all, especially the vast throngs of the miserable poor. Such efforts are being made on a large scale in India, with voluntary male sterilization.[14] Yet the vast work needed to stop the disastrous population growth in that land is still mostly ahead. In Japan the congested

13. *The Washington Post,* Jan. 24, 1969, p. A6.
14. The millions so far sterilized are not changed in sexual feeling or potency, but need no longer fear the begetting of children who cannot be properly supported.

population has now become nearly stabilized. There is a positive relation between prior improvement in living standard and a declining birth rate.

The indication is, then, that there must be a great increase of technical aid by the industrial and prosperous powers to the impoverished and overcrowded countries, along with encouragement and assistance to them in their efforts to limit population. This, again, requires a basic change of priorities, as does the successful meeting of *any* major threat to humanity in the present world.

Even now rapid population growth produces distressing results in many places. Anyone who has seen the misery and starvation on the streets of Calcutta or even East Cairo is not likely to accept a future in which such conditions would be spread over much of the world.

Most underdeveloped countries have Gross National Products growing more rapidly than that of the United States. Growth rates of 5 per cent or more are common. But when the population grows by 3.5 per cent (Philippines, 1967) or 3 per cent (Brazil, 1967), the net gain in standard of living is very slow, indeed. Crash programs of school expansion in countless villages of Latin America and Africa have left more children without any opportunity for school than before, because population—especially youthful population—has expanded even more rapidly than schools.[15]

3. Measures Against Pollution

Running water has remarkable powers of restoration under sun and air. But when cities and towns all along our streams dump their sewage and industrial waste into the rivers by the millions of tons, the burden is too great. Cities downstream must go to great lengths to purify water for their own consumption, but most of the filth is sent back. It fills the stream beds and some of it destroys the life in the water. Meanwhile, our American factories, automobiles, jet planes, dump fires, and the like, go on putting 142 million tons of pollutants per year into the air we breathe, at the same time threatening the oxygen supply for a more distant future.

In the face of this problem, it is not enough to accept the pleas of municipalities, automobile manufacturers, and industries that drastic reduction of pollution is too expensive. Means are now known and are

15. For a graphic and factual description of such frustrating problems in a leaflet priced for mass distribution, see "Collision Course: Population Explosion vs. World Development," by Jessma Blockwick, reprinted from *The Church School* and sold by Department of Population Problems, Board of Christian Social Concerns, The United Methodist Church. For recent church pronouncements, see "Statements of Churches Concerning Problems of Population Growth," a compilation by the same Department issued in June, 1969.

spottily used. The responsible person should approach every question which involves pollution with an initial presumption in favor of drastic measures to prevent or decrease it.

4. Conservation of Mineral Resources

Reserves of oil are very great, of coal and iron enormous, but with dropping quality and rising cost of extraction. Many other metals in high demand are in short supply. Plastics are replacing metals in many uses and such substitution is a major help in this way, but they are nondegradable and so difficult of disposal. Changes like the introduction of plastics, the manufacture of aluminum, the development of new alloys by the hundreds, and more efficient methods of extraction have prevented many dismal predictions about mineral exhaustion from coming true.

However, our resources are not limitless and many, when used once, are gone forever. Considering the expanding world population and the long future of possible human habitation of this planet, we have no right to waste minerals in war or in sheer reckless disregard for the future.

5. Soil Conservation

All our food and that of most other living land creatures comes from the soil. Fortunately, maintaining productivity of the soil generally pays good dividends to land owners. It is therefore receiving more attention than most kinds of conservation. However, it occasionally happens that short-term exploitation and subsequent abandoning of land is profitable. Obviously, any such policy when deliberate is grossly immoral. Productive land must be protected by law, properly enforced, against ruin by strip mining, or denuding, so that great numbers of future generations may eat and live.

6. Guarding Against Ecological Upset

When new products or organisms are considered for introduction to solve certain problems in our biological environment, it is important that careful consideration be given to side effects and long-term effects. Ecological balance is a sensitive matter, despite its flexibility, and reckless alteration of it could be disastrous.

We need greatly strengthened food and drug laws, with devoted and able enforcement. Our technological ingenuity, together with the desire of manufacturers to be the first to market dramatic new products, must be checked by careful study designed not to make money but to protect present and future generations of men. There have been some narrow escapes and small-scale tragedies, such as the use of sugar substitutes which in large quantities sterilize the user, and some tablets which, when taken by pregnant women, predictably produced pitifully deformed babies. Such experiences should be warning enough of the urgent need for responsible action.

The Christian principle of love requires our ecological care for love of present and future human beings. If the interpretation of Scripture, of God's creative purpose, and of the Incarnation, in the earlier part of this chapter is correct, our love of God and neighbor implies also a more far-reaching concern.

Because we love God, and live in gratitude to him, we respect and care for the web of life in the midst of which he has placed us. We cultivate and guard the beautiful, grand, curious, and fascinating world around us, not only for the sake of other human beings, but for gratitude to God the Creator. We participate responsibly in the larger community of life in which the Word of God was made flesh in Christ.

Indiscriminate sentimentality will not do here. There are forms of life which are so destructive of other life as to require our unremitting attack. In fact, much of our war against pollution is of this kind. We must battle against rats in city tenements and alleys, and against the microscopic life which invades human beings as typhus, cholera, staphylococcus, and meningitis. We have responsibilities not merely to guard what is here, but to cultivate and nurture the good. An important part of cultivation is discriminate selection and weeding.

Yet it is still true that

> man has no effective way of living beyond or outside the kingdom of life. So whatever diminishes that kingdom diminishes him, both as a form of life and as a form of spirit.[16]

Our task as human husbandmen of the environment requires vigorous, thoughtful, discriminating hard work, not an attempt to let the world of nature go its own way. We are in it, we inevitably make a great difference in it, and we are responsible for seeing to it that we preserve and even improve it in every possible way—especially where we have polluted and degraded it. But we must approach the task with sensitive care.

The story of Babel is a parable with two suggestive teachings for us. When we set out to build our cities, our pleasures, and our technology in ever-mounting pride, we are preparing for a fall which could be of catastrophic proportions. There is much we do not know. Before we introduce new insecticides or new drugs or make radical

16. Julian Hartt, in a lecture to The Faith-Man-Nature Group, at Airlie House, Va., Nov. 28, 1969.

changes in the conditions of the earth, we need to pause long for thought and preliminary small-scale experimentation.[17] The tower of Babel which was intended to reach up to heaven may also symbolize for us man's effort to provide for his comfort with ever more artificiality and growing indifference to the natural environment.

As we form our ideal of community for the future and work toward its realization, it is imperative that we include in it that larger community of life and being in which the human species is inextricably joined. Otherwise human history will foreseeably end by man's own folly. On the other hand, by grateful, responsible concern for that larger community we may so relate ourselves to the work of God himself as to participate in the realization of the Christian hope for both earth and heaven.

7. *Preservation of Wilderness*

Serious conservationists distinguish carefully the two technical concepts included in the broad notion of conservation. One is *preservation* and the other *conservation* in a narrowed sense.

Conservation is the careful, responsible management of resources so that they may be used with high effectiveness for an indefinite period of time, or at least as long as possible. Good management of soil, so that after years of farming its fertility is undiminished or increased, is the commonest example. Forests selectively cut and protected against fire so that fresh crops of valuable lumber can be harvested indefinitely is another. Conservation includes, likewise, farseeing management of water supplies, efficient extraction and use of petroleum and natural gas, and programs of flood control. Obviously, conservation is of vital importance.

But preservation, too, is of high significance. By this term is meant the protection of some areas and resources from all uses excepting limited recreational enjoyment and educational study.

With our large and growing populations, most land areas which can be productive of foods or materials important to human life should doubtless be carefully used with the best conservationist practices in effect. However, we need also to have many areas, some of them large, preserved as nearly as conditions will permit, in a state of wilderness. Such areas will vary from the wild, scarcely explored regions of the Alaskan mountains to wooded parks in our great cities. All alike serve as areas where sky, trees, birds, and animals may be observed, loved, studied, and respected for their own sake. If conservation is needed

17. Those people are wise who are urging, for example, that we not be hasty about constructing a sea-level canal between the Atlantic and Pacific oceans, in view of drastic changes in ecosystems which could result, with currently unforeseeable results.

for man's body, preservation, at all levels of wilderness, is needed for his soul and for the sake of the natural order itself.

At the least, a wooded park provides a partial escape from the hard, mechanizing, dehumanizing forces of the city, and from the pressure of too many people. At most, it offers a vision of the earth without man, a place where a human being can take fresh bearings in the nature from which he came, and on which he still depends, so seeing himself in renewed perspective. In such a place, too, one may learn to appreciate the meaning of the ancient poet who wrote, "And God saw everything that he had made, and behold, it was very good."[18]

18. Gen. 1:31. Four classics of ecology and conservation are the following, in order of first publication: Aldo Leopold, *Sand County Almanac* (New York: Oxford University Press, 1949; enlarged ed. 1967); Loren Eiseley, *Immense Journey* (New York: Vintage [Random House], 1957); Rachel Carson, *Silent Spring* (Greenwich, Conn.: Fawcett Crest Books, 1964); and René Dubos, *So Human an Animal* (New York: Charles Scribner's Sons, 1968).

chapter twelve

The Economic Order

A. An Order of Means

The world of money, wages, profits, and taxes is a world of instrumental values. Persons, beauty, love, and truth have value in themselves. Money has value only for what it will buy—from groceries to the personal satisfaction of achievement. How little value it has in itself is quickly discovered when a currency collapses, so that it will not be accepted in exchange for anything else. Houses, television sets, and automobiles are desired and enjoyed in themselves and so have some intrinsic worth, but are mainly valuable as means to ends of a more personal and immediately satisfying nature—such as love, entertainment, comfort, rest, personal growth, and friendship.

All these values and many more may be found in the market place, for human beings are there, with all their interpersonal network of interests, fears, loves, and hopes. When we speak of the economic order, we are speaking of human beings as they are related in the production, distribution, and consumption of goods and services.

B. Common Errors

In thinking about the economic order there are a number of common myths which oversimplify and so misrepresent the realities. Many bad policies result from these misconceptions.

1. Economic Reductionism

Many men believe, or act like men who believe, that the all-determining force of history is the striving for material gain. There are radically different forms of this myth in the present world, under Marxian and capitalistic names.

a. Marxian Economic Determinism. According to Marxian communism, "the ideal is nothing else than the material world reflected by the human minds, and translated into forms of thought."[1] Religion, art, government, and all the works of human thought are then regarded as mere appearances on the surface of the basic struggle for material advantage among men. Through the ages of slavery, feudalism, and capitalism history has been a class struggle, in changing forms, between exploiters and exploited. The violence of oppression and of war will end only when the workers rise up and overthrow the capitalistic government and economic system, to replace them with the "dictatorship of the proletariat." This transitional form of government is to place all the means of production such as farms, mines, and factories under the ownership and control of the working people themselves. Oppression being ended, crime will cease, there will be no cause for going to war, the state with its police and prisons will "wither away," and all will be well in the "last stage of socialism."

Something has gone wrong with the Marxian prophecy. Within the Communist lands crime has not ceased, the state is more omnipresent and more sternly enforcing law and order than before, and the pressure for aggressive expansion continues.

The evils of human relations are evidently not to be eliminated simply by a change of government and of economic systems. In the Soviet Union remarkable economic and educational advances have been made since 1919. Yet even the economic system is not working without coercive pressures, considerable use of political prisoners for the most burdensome labor, exploitation of the satellite states, and the restoration of limited opportunities for private profit. There is a deep spiritual unrest. Even after fifty years of materialistic propaganda many Soviet citizens know that man was made to live *Not by Bread Alone*.[2]

b. Capitalistic. On the other hand, capitalism has been preserved in the United States and elsewhere only by such large modifications as to make our economic system today a "mixed economy" and no longer simply a capitalistic one. Defenders of pure private enterprise contend that if everyone tries to get ahead financially, all the needs of deserving people will be served, with the exception of a few handicapped unfortunates who will have to depend on relatives, private charity, or "the poor house." In a land of open competition, it is argued, if some need is not being met, someone will see the chance to make money by serving that need and so the gap will be filled. Prices and wages will seek their proper levels by the "law of supply and demand," and economic justice will be automatic.

It has not worked according to that ideal. The wide areas of severe

---

1. Karl Marx, *Capital,* tr. and ed. by Frederick Engels (Chicago: Charles H. Kerr and Co., 1919), p. 25.
2. Title of a searching novel by Vladimir Dudintsev, tr. by Edith Bone (New York: E. P. Dutton & Company, 1957).

poverty, the recurrent depressions, and the great needs not met by private enterprise—such as high risk ventures, adequate housing for people of low income, and retraining for workers displaced by industrial change—have brought ever more governmental action in the economic field. Moreover, the higher development of industrialization, with ever higher costs of capitalization for expensive machinery, has developed strong trends toward monopoly, stifling and threatening to kill competition. In all countries, whether under the rule of "conservative" or "liberal" parties, governments have intervened to limit monopolistic trends, to protect labor, to provide neglected services, to support the aged, to attack unemployment, and in other ways to correct and supplement private enterprise.

It has too often escaped notice that many defenders of capitalism make a materialistic assumption of a kind usually charged against communists. This is the assumption that man is primarily motivated by materialistic aims so that no other purpose can adequately motivate production. This one-sided image of "economic man" will not stand critical empirical or theological examination.

2. Individualistic Pietism

A favorite myth among economically comfortable church people is that when enough individuals have been converted the economic problems will be solved quickly. Hence the church has the solution by attending to its evangelistic business and not "meddling" in political or economic affairs. The teachers of this doctrine generally denounce as "statism" or "socialism" all government intervention to restrain the powerful or assist the poor.

Such individualism is both bad theology and false economics. The Christian is not called to be a lone operator, but to be a member of the serving community which is the body of Christ. Whether in worship, judgment, or work he is called to be united with others in mutual sharing.

In the economic field a person with the most humane motives often helps produce vicious results. A well-intentioned man votes for a pious-talking senator who helps defeat safety legislation to protect coal miners from "black lung." A kind old lady who lives on her modest income from the stock in her deceased husband's estate casts the deciding votes to engage a new superintendent who promises to increase production and lower costs. She is not worried about his hostility to labor unions and their demands because she has heard that union leaders are trouble-makers anyway. Little does she suspect that because of her, faithful older workers will lose their jobs with no one to defend them.

Love as basic purpose is indispensable to ethically sound economic policy. But sound knowledge and planning are also indispensable.

Moreover, sound policy in a complex economy like our own is difficult or impossible for the individual alone. For example, a merchant in a highly competitive business in which others are taking advantage of legal loopholes to sell shoddy or even dangerous goods or to pay wretched wages may face the dilemma of being forced out of business and leaving his employees altogether unemployed or violating his conscience in his own business methods. Most major injustice and other evil in our economic order requires concerted attack with carefully planned, well-informed, and systematic effort.[3]

C. Love and Distributive Justice

Love and justice are often regarded as quite separate principles in severe tension. When love is seen as the profoundly communal reality it is in the New Testament, the positive connection is clear. If love is an earnest and active desire to share God's gifts in a community of experience, then justice is the structuring of relationships to bring about or encourage such sharing in community. Justice is the expression of love in a situation of conflicting interests.

Justice in the economic sphere requires at least that none shall be in painful poverty while others are in abundance of luxury. Whether community would actually be best promoted by economic equality may be argued, with consideration of differing needs, differing functions, and the need for material incentives (among others) to production. But such dismal and wretched poverty as besets millions of Americans, alongside such colossal wealth as is held by a few, is a flagrant denial of justice. It is also a judgment upon lack of love—not only of the rich who will not share, but also of all citizens who tolerate the system which produces, perpetuates, and is even exacerbating the bitter discrepancy.

1. Economics in the Christian Ideal of Community

No one system of economic relations would be ideal for human beings in every condition or situation. A system serving well a society living by hunting and fishing would be grossly inadequate for a tribe

3. Cf. Reinhold Niebuhr, *An Interpretation of Christian Ethics* (New York: Harper & Brothers, 1935), pp. 181–82. Niebuhr is wrong, however, in identifying "liberal theology" with simplistic moralism oblivious to need for changed social structures, even though some liberals and many nonliberals have fallen into this delusion. The names of Walter Rauschenbusch, Francis J. McConnell, and Walter G. Muelder should be enough to lay to rest the myth of any inherent connection between liberal theology and simplistic individualism. Many others could be cited.

of farmers. As much of the world's population moves from predominantly agricultural to industrial and on to increasingly automated industrial economics, the forms of economic organization must be radically changed. Land, water, disposal of waste, transportation, media of exchange, property of many kinds, the roles of the young and the aged, the relations between education and production—all take on new meanings with these changes. We do not know what demands the future will place upon the economic order, although we must foresee and plan as well as we can. To plan a single system of economic organization and call it "the Christian" system would, therefore, be the height of folly.

We can say in more general terms, however, what are the norms by which any economic order should be judged by Christians. Having in mind the requirements of *koinonia* love, principles of responsible Christian freedom demand of an economic order that it provide in high degree the means for the following:

1. Useful and creative work by all during the potentially productive years.
2. Adequate food, clothing, shelter, and medical care from birth through old age to death.
3. Security against disaster whether of natural or human causation.
4. Safeguards for conservation of natural resources and protection of the natural environment.
5. Education of all according to ability and desire.
6. Time and resources for rest and recreation for all.
7. Freedom to pursue spiritual values of wide variety.
8. Control of economic means by persons for personal values—both individual and communal—with opportunity for all to participate meaningfully in the processes which determine economic goals.[4]

When we consider the sheer productivity of the economic order in the United States, it is obvious that it falls shockingly far short of maximum attainment relative to such norms as these. Indeed, it seems to great numbers of Americans at all economic levels that their lives are devoted to serving an impersonal monster, the economy, whereas the economic order, when operating in proper relationships, provides means for full personal life.

Let us now examine one of the most serious of our present economic problems, the pitiful poverty which exists in the midst of unprecedented American affluence.

4. For some of the ideas here I am indebted to Walter G. Muelder, *Religion and Economic Responsibility* (New York: Charles Scribner's Sons, 1953), especially pp. 161–65.

2. *Poverty and Wealth in the United States*

On the one hand, 20 to 30 per cent of Americans live on a level of real poverty. Roger L. Shinn, using the Health, Education and Welfare (HEW) figure of $3,000 per year per household as defining the poverty level, writes,

> With this yardstick we find that 1 family out of 5 in this country lives in severe poverty. This lowest fifth (more than 9 million families) get less than $3,000 a year. More than half of them receive less than $2,000 a year.[5]

The Commerce Department, in 1966, defined the poverty level for a city family of four as $3,335 per year, or for a woman of 65 living alone in the city as $1,560 per year. The level in other situations was defined accordingly, on a sliding scale. In 1966, according to the report, 41 per cent of all Negro individuals, or 34.9 per cent of Negro families, were living below the poverty level, compared with 12 per cent of all white individuals or 9.9 per cent of white families. Progress had been made in decreasing the numbers of the poor in both races since a similar study in 1959. Yet the gap between the races continued to be scandalous and the number of poor in the midst of rapidly growing and unprecedented affluence was appalling.[6]

In 1968 the money income of the tenth of people in the contiguous United States having the least income was unavailable. The income of the second tenth began at a low figure of $1,930 per family unit. This was $430 more than in 1960, little more than the increase in cost of living, while it was actually a lower real income than in 1965. The lowest fifth received only a total of one-twenty-fifth of the money income of all families, the lowest tenth about 1 per cent of the total.[7]

These are the people who live in rat-infested tenements, often unheated even in winter as far north as our national capital, or in makeshift rural shacks without running water and with seriously deficient diet. Lack of protein food is dooming many of the children to a life of low energy and dull achievement, no matter what they may have to eat later. Most have no dental care and rare medical attention.

At the other end of the scale, the highest tenth had, in 1968, 30 per cent of the total income, up from 28 in 1965 and 27 in 1960 (*ibid.*). The rich are getting richer and the poorest are not gaining. The gap is not being narrowed, but is widening.

5. *Tangled World* (New York: Charles Scribner's Sons, 1965), p. 43. Cf. Gabriel Kilko, *Wealth and Power in America* (New York: Frederick A. Praeger, 1962).
6. Associated Press dispatch in *Washington Post*, May 5, 1968.
7. *Statistical Abstract of the United States: 1970*, p. 323.

Not only income, but also ownership is important. When sickness or unemployment or advancing age comes or when a family considers some new move, the amount of economic security and freedom enjoyed depends on the money in the bank or other kinds of wealth held. Differences in wealth are much greater than discrepancies of income. At the end of 1962, 9.8 per cent of all American households owned nothing. On the other hand, 200,000 households owned over one-half million dollars of wealth each.[8] About thirty-five individuals, in 1957, owned over seventy-five million dollars each, which they had themselves assembled, and about forty-two are said to have inherited wealth of more than seventy-five million.[9] The wealthiest seven were believed to own over 400 million dollars each.

But do not the wealthy earn their money by their great contributions to society? Many among the moderately wealthy undoubtedly contributed much in invention, creatively imaginative meeting of needs, or contributing to pleasure through entertainment. Many of the older wealthy families have contributed greatly out of their wealth to education, art, religion, social service, and economic development, although their gains were often made at tragic human cost to other people. In this group one must think of the Rockefellers, Carnegies, Fords, Mellons, and others. However, a look at the road traveled by the newly rich is especially disillusioning.

Of the thirty-five newly rich presented by *Fortune*, only nine are known to be college graduates, while sixteen are known not to be. Their money-making has been more conspicuously characterized by speculation, manipulation of markets, and special favors from politicians than by service, whether by work or benevolent giving.[10]

The great concentration of wealth in the hands of a few Americans, especially of people with as little public spirit as most of the new super-rich seem to have, is dangerous as well as unjust. By owning well-placed, controlling blocs of stock in the great corporations they exercise economic power far out of proportion to their huge wealth. The top 500,000 owners of wealth have effective control of nearly all corporate economic power in the country (*ibid.*, p. 295). These are one-fourth of 1 per cent of the people, but they are the millionaires and most of their wealth is in corporate stocks which multiply their power many times over.

This vast economic power, in turn, exerts preponderant political

8. Both figures are from a study for the Board of Governors of the Federal Reserve System entitled *Survey of Financial Characteristics of Consumers*, p. 151, and are quoted by Ferdinand Lundberg, in *The Rich and the Super-Rich* (New York: Bantam Books, 1968), p. 15.

9. Cited from *Fortune* by Lundberg, *op. cit.*, pp. 159–62. There is a slight overlapping of the two lists.

10. Lundberg, *op. cit.*, pp. 35–61.

power. Through the control of television and radio stations or programs, newspapers and magazines, through carefully placed political contributions and outright corruption, they stoke up the international arms race, protect the tax privileges and economic subsidies of the very rich, and heavily influence the nomination and election of legislators and officials of government.

The maldistribution of wealth and income also perpetuates the gross racial injustice in America. By providing great advantages to those who begin life with a nest egg and parents who can support a good education, as well as by outright discrimination in jobs and housing, our society keeps down the Negro people. "Nonwhite families suffer a poverty risk three times as great as white families do, but 7 out of 10 poor families are white."[11] A disproportionate number of those poor whites are in the South where for a century politicians have invested more energy in keeping Negroes down and protecting special privileges for their wealthy sponsors than in development of the economic well-being of state or region as a whole.

3. *What Love Requires*

When Jesus spoke of the Judgment, the only requirement he described was providing for the needy—the hungry, unclothed, friendless, and imprisoned. What we do or fail to do to them, he said, we do or fail to do to him (Matt. 25:31–46). In many other ways the New Testament stresses the obligation to relieve and care for the poor. In a country like the United States where so many have so much, the presence of people suffering in poverty lays an especially heavy burden on the Christian conscience.

In protest it is often asked, "Is not voluntary private charity the Christian way?" There is great need for personal assistance to other people in want, especially in emergencies of illness, accident, bereavement, or sudden material loss. There will never be a substitute for such person-to-person caring.

However, millions of people are today unemployed or underemployed because of farm mechanization, automation, malnutrition, chronic illness, and massive shifts of emphasis to new industries for which displaced workers lack skills. The massive task of reeducation, job training, housing, and provision for the health of all these millions is scarcely touched by private philanthropy. Unless people of goodwill join together to do this work in a cooperative way through the agencies of government which we voluntarily establish for this purpose, we are choosing not to feed, clothe, house, or aid the Christ who is identified with "the least of these."

11. *Social Security Bulletin* (Jan., 1965), p. 5.

It is often complained that through government we are being required to support "give-away programs." Actually, the very Congressmen and lobbyists who voice this complaint most loudly are also urging big give-away programs, not for the poor but for the rich—in the form of subsidies, oil depletion allowances, and large sums to wealthy landowners for not growing crops on their land. Many owners, including an ultraconservative senator, receive more than $100,000 for not raising cotton or wheat on their land. A fitting question is, who are the Americans who should receive government aid, the wealthiest or the poorest?

The need, however, is not generally for gifts, whether private or public. It is for such changes in the structure of our economic order as to permit all to participate in ways suited to their potentials, in the active years, and to retire in dignity when those years are done.

What form should the change take? To move toward suitable answers, some basic economic and ethical requirements must be further examined.

D. NEED FOR INDIVIDUAL INCENTIVE AND RESPONSIBILITY

Just distribution of wealth or of consumer goods means little if there is little to be distributed. To secure the well-being of growing population there must be growing production. If the individuals in a society find little incentive to work, there will be little work and little production.

This was a problem faced by Plymouth Colony in its very early years of shared labor and land. In a sermon of December, 1761, Robart Cushman complained that

> men blow the bellows hard, when they have an iron of their own a heating, work hard whilst their own house is in building, dig hard whilst their own garden is in planting, but is it so as the profit must go wholly or partly to others; their hands wax feeble, their hearts wax faint, they grow churlish, and give cross answers.[12]

Although Cushman himself was condemning this sinful selfishness and urging generous communal spirit, Governor William Bradford decided that "seeing all men have this corruption in them, God in his wisdom saw another course fiter for them" (*ibid.*, p. 303). In 1623 some of the land was divided into family plots, though only for present use, not

---

12. William Bradford, *History of Plymouth Plantation 1620–1647* (Boston: Houghton Mifflin Co., 1912), Vol. I, p. 299n.

inheritance, and Bradford reports an immediate sharp rise in productive work.

There are many kinds of incentives. The carrot-and-stick method alone has its own practical drawbacks, especially in mass production. When large numbers of employees are held between constant hope of individual raise of wages and fear of demotion or firing, tension and unrest are rapidly built up to a point of explosion. Under such conditions steady production can be maintained only under coercive methods which are closer to police-state tyranny than to democratic freedom. In a reasonably free society, sheer material individual incentives have to be supplemented by a sense of common purpose, recognition of personal worth, and confidence in a fair measure of security.

Some kinds of work are constantly done best under incentives other than individual material gain. A very large bloc of productive work is done in the home by housewives and mothers. They could not be motivated to render half their present service if they lived between a constant fear of being "fired"—separated from husband and children— and a hope of some increment in personal allowance. In various other kinds of work, too, experience has shown advantages in security of tenure and income. This is especially true where creative imagination, original thinking, or sensitive personal understanding are needed, as in teaching, nursing, and scholarly research.

So far as human beings are reduced to the image of "economic man," they are dehumanized. When a man regards himself and his work as a mere means to material ends, he is made into a dull, clock-watching slave. The common expectation that men will work only for ever more monetary gain is a self-fulfilling prophecy. But we should be badly mistaken if we concluded that the desire for individual material gain was the one universal human motive sustaining productive work. It is undoubtedly one motive and has some importance in support of work by great numbers of persons, perhaps most, but it is not the only motive impelling most people to work. Nearly everyone does some work as a neighborly service, or in order to have an attractive lawn and garden, or to support a fund drive for church or charity, or to develop a union, fraternal organization, or club.[13]

Suppose it be granted that at present, in a free society, given our general selfish materialism, a large place must be left for individual incentive of material gain. If we are concerned with the whole humanity of persons, as we must be as Christians or even as reasonable hu-

---

13. See the further study reported by Adam Curle, in "Incentives to Work: An Anthropological Appraisal," in *Human Relations* (Vol. II, No. 1, 1949), pp. 41–48; cf. also Walter G. Muelder, *Religion and Economic Responsibility*, pp. 48–62, 82– 89.

manists, then we must desire to see other motives developed as much as possible. Even where the desire for material gain is foremost, it should be positive and not the fear of starvation or utter deprivation of the worker or his family.

To be encouraged are such arrangements as will develop group incentives, opportunity for maximum self-expression according to ability, interest in the relation of the particular job to a whole enterprise, and recognition of the worker as a person of varied responsibilities and interests.[14]

E. GUARANTEED ANNUAL INCOME

The people of the United States have been sufficiently influenced by humane concerns characteristic of Judeo-Christian moral teaching so that the vast majority want to prevent anyone in this country from dying by starvation or lack of medical attention. The federal government, states, cities, counties, and towns have accordingly developed a great variety of "welfare" programs. Beginning with the old "poor house" or "poor farm," these efforts to save the poor have moved to aid for widows and orphaned children, unemployment insurance, Social Security, free lunches for children, food stamps, Medicare, and Medicaid. The result of this gradual and undercoordinated development is a crazyquilt pattern with much overlapping in some categories and total neglect or gross underattention to other categories of needy people.

In recent years a number of people representing radically different points of view have proposed that much of this pattern be replaced by a single program which would put a floor of minimum income under all people in the United States. My own first substantial introduction to it was at a meeting under the sponsorship of the United States Chamber of Commerce, in November, 1966. Guaranteed Annual Income was demanded by the 1968 Poor People's Campaign of the Southern Christian Leadership Conference. Forms of the proposal are urged by economists as different as Robert Theobald, radical English economist, and Milton Friedman, economic adviser to Barry Goldwater in the 1964 presidential campaign. Several such proposals are and will continue to be under consideration by Congress.[15]

14. Cf. Muelder, *op. cit.*, pp. 116–29.
15. For some useful writing concerning such proposals, see Philip Wogaman, *Guaranteed Annual Income: The Moral Issues* (Nashville: Abingdon Press, 1968); Milton Friedman, *Capitalism and Freedom* (Chicago: University of Chicago Press, 1962); Robert Theobald, ed., *The Guaranteed Income: Next Step in Socioeconomic Evolution?* (Garden City, N.Y.: Doubleday & Company, 1966).

One of the most intriguing and popular proposals would handle minimal support for the poor by "negative income tax." All household units would file income returns. All above certain levels would pay income taxes based on such returns just as they do now. Others, within a narrow margin of incomes, would file returns but pay no tax, even as now. But all within a third group, whose returns showed income below a prescribed minimal or "floor" figure, would receive from the federal government a "negative income tax" sufficient to bring their income above the level of unacceptable poverty. The better proposals specify a graduated scale of support, so that a person who earns anything will gain somewhat by so doing, although if the earning is of a considerable amount he will receive less from the government than if he were completely dependent on the public support. Of course when his earnings increase beyond a specified point all public support ends. This is in sharp contrast to present welfare aid and Social Security which are on an all-or-nothing basis and are cut off altogether if the recipient earns more than an insignificant amount.

Many of our present programs are destructive of both morale and morals. For example, many unskilled male workers or mothers with limited time to spare from their children would like to take small jobs by which they could start earning a little. Through such jobs they might learn to do more and meanwhile sustain positive interest in self-support. But they are effectively prevented by laws which cut off public assistance if they start earning. If the husband and father in a home is unable to get work, the only way he can get public support for his family, in many jurisdictions, is to desert his family and stay away. The better proposals for Guaranteed Annual Income are free from any such cruel, immoral indignities and, through sliding scales of support, like income tax in reverse, provide incentives for self-support to the limits of people's ability.

Guaranteed Annual Income confronts an ethical objection which is often urged against other programs to aid the poor, but an objection which seems particularly relevant to it. Is it right to tax the earnings of hard-working people in order to pay money to everyone who earns little or nothing? Some of the poor are lazy or sexually immoral. Some have criminal records. Do they deserve help?

Much apparent laziness is due to malnutrition or illness. The heaviest burdens of poverty fall upon the aged and infirm, the children, and the handicapped. Many of the most miserable poor are honest, industrious, upright people, yet are humiliated and despised rather than helped in their misfortune. Are we to start judging who are morally worthy of living or where on the economic scale they deserve to be placed? Many of the lazy and socially destructive people are wealthy! None of the richest have earned their wealth by their work. Most of them inherited large sums with which to begin their escalation into the stratosphere of riches. Did they deserve to be born into wealth? Are we to try judging people's rightful place on the economic scale by personal moral deserts only as regards the poor?

For true Christians these questions are beside the point. We know that we have reaped where we did not sow, and all of us are heirs to much—both good and ill—for which we did not pay. "While we were yet sinners," God loved us (Rom. 5:8). All that we prize we have had by the free gift of grace, not by our deserving. As Christians we ask not what our neighbor deserves, but what we can do to help him and if possible to encourage him to become more deserving. The command is not to lecture the neighbor about his deserts nor to judge and scorn him. The command is "Love your neighbor as yourself" (Matt. 22:39).

F. INTERNATIONAL AID

Great as is the gap between the superrich and the poor in the United States, there is an even wider chasm between the rich in this country and the vast multitudes of poor in other lands. Indeed, despite all the poor people here, the general economic level of life in the United States seems fabulous by comparison with most of the world. There are more telephones in the United States alone than among the fifteen times as many people in the rest of the world. Many other items are similarly distributed. Roger L. Shinn writes,

> While the United States puzzles over its agriculture surpluses, many people within the country worry about expanding waistlines. But elsewhere 10,000 people a day die of starvation or malnutrition, and more than half the world lives in continuous hunger.[16]

This kind of gross inequality cannot long endure.

The British economist Barbara Ward speaks of four important revolutions which are simultaneously under way throughout the world.[17] First is the revolutionary demand for less inequality—of nations and of individuals. Second is the revolutionary idea of material progress. Third, biological revolution has vastly increased the rate of population growth. Fourth, the application of science and of capital is changing the economic order with revolutionary speed and deeply affecting everything in our culture.

All of these revolutions, she says, started in the nations around the

16. *Tangled World*, p. 126.
17. *The Rich Nations and the Poor Nations* (New York: W. W. Norton & Company, 1962).

North Atlantic Ocean. Most of the other nations lack the capital resources to provide the education and the machinery for full launch
into this new technological, industrial age. Americans were able to
gain the necessary capital by a combination of thrift and ambition
with unparalleled resources in virgin territory. The British first and
then the other peoples of Western Europe used their colonies. Once
a point is reached in the capitalization of industry, increasing quantities
of profit are used for further capitalization. The problem is to reach
that "takeoff point."

The Soviet Union has gained its capital by exploiting its satellites,
by opening large new resources, especially in Asia, and by compelling
its people to pay in labor much more than the amount required for
consumer goods. China is using the latter method under the severely
difficult conditions of an overpopulated and desperately impoverished
people. These methods require police-state rule, for no people will
voluntarily live on the border of starvation in order that their labor
may go into the construction of large-scale industry for the future.
China is now beginning to reward its people for their suffering by a
slow rise in the standard of living.

The example of China is impressive in many nations of Africa, Asia,
and South America, where there is despair of capitalizing industrialization by the voluntary savings of free people or by large-scale low-
interest investment from the industrial democracies of the West.
Capitalization by American and European interests which take most
of the profits back to the already advanced countries is little or no help.
It is naturally viewed as simply a perpetuation of colonial exploitation
by the rich nations.

If the undercapitalized nations are to come up to the "takeoff point"
in industrialization without giving up the various degrees of freedom
which they have, they must be capitalized principally by large-scale
aid or low-interest loans from the Western governments. The lion's
share must come from the one which is wealthiest by a wide margin,
that is the United States.

Barbara Ward points out that the four revolutions will not necessarily lead to more freedom.

> They can yield us freedom or its opposite. . . . Have we measured
> the margin of choice given us by our new capital resources, our new
> technology, our new ability to create the means of wealth? . . . And
> given our ability to assist in the process of modernization, have we
> really grasped its relevance to the grand question of our time: whether
> the developing world society will be closed or open, slave or free?
> [*Ibid.*, p. 156]

Americans commonly assume that the United States is more generous with foreign aid than any other country. That is far from the truth. To be sure, the number of dollars from the United States is the greatest. However, generosity must be measured in proportion to means, as Jesus clearly taught by his account of the widow's mite. In 1968 the United Nations Conference on Trade and Development asked the wealthier nations to commit 1 per cent of their Gross National Product to aid, loans, and private investment in the underdeveloped nations. Only two nations had reached that proportion in 1967, namely, France and the Netherlands. The United States ranked tenth, even including its $357 million to Vietnam and the 95 per cent of its aid which it required to be spent in the United States.[18] The United States can provide 66 per cent of its federal budget for the military, to pay for past and future wars, while less than 2 per cent goes to nonmilitary international relations, including the U.N. and foreign economic aid. Can anyone believe that such a budget is defensible in terms of Christian ethics?

We preach to other nations about the advantages of freedom over Communism. But the advantages of Western democracy are not apparent to most people who can never go to school, who are fighting a weekly uncertain battle with starvation, and who see us who talk so much passing them by with little or no help. "But God is not mocked," writes Barbara Ward. She continues, speaking to the whole North Atlantic community words which are especially relevant to America:

> We reap what we sow and if freedom for us is not more than the right to pursue our own self-interest—personal or national—then we can make no claim to the greatest vision of our society: "the glorious liberty of the sons of God." Without vision we, like other peoples, will perish. [*Op. cit.*, p. 159]

G. Some Situational Guidelines for the Economic Order

The economic realities in our present situation, a few of which have been reviewed, now require a number of situational guidelines to be adopted by any American genuinely concerned with putting Christian faith into action.

As we prepare for decisions in the economic sphere we may be tempted to think we are now in a realm apart from faith and ethics. That would be a grave mistake. A faith which does not penetrate in

18. Report in *New York Times*, July 10, 1968, summarized by John M. Swomley, Jr., in "Food and Famine—a World Problem," *Current Issues* (undated).

an effective way deep into our decisions on the economic order is phony. It is still true that "where your treasure is, there will your heart be also" (Luke 12:34). Where your treasure is to be will be decided as much by corporate and political decisions as by individual choices—in the long run more.

Love calls us to form an ideal of the kind of economic community that would best provide for the persons and total world community which the spirit of Christ leads us to envisage. Then with all possible technical aid we must support policies best calculated to lead toward realization of these ideals.

1. Critically Examine the Present Order

Most Americans have long made the initial presumption that their country was basically sound and right, in both her domestic and her foreign policies. They have supposed that their economic order was sound. Were we not the most prosperous people of all history? Were we not generously extending aid to all kinds of unfortunate people at home and abroad?

Now if we have eyes to see, we find that something has gone radically wrong. Relative to norms of Christian community, our present economic order is badly out of joint. We are engaged in continual indecisive war or preparation for war, with ever fewer allies and friends abroad. At home poverty is more conspicuous, even if not more prevalent, than ever, while the children of our affluence despise the material price tags and the mechanical numbers affixed to them. Our wealth intended to sustain our humanity seems somehow to be dehumanizing us and threatening our complete downfall in a mess of crime, pollution, moral confusion, incorrigible injustice, and war. This is a time calling for critical examination of facts, fresh appraisal of ethical norms and of proposed changes, and action to dethrone from power leaders whose response to the present challenge is only flag-waving and slogans.[19]

2. Join with Others in Study and Action

The individual alone is unequal even to the task of thinking through to sound conclusions many current complex ethical problems about economics. This is a task for cooperative effort of people with different skills and approaches. How much more is the task of changing our

19. The inadequacy of slogans for political guidance was well illustrated in the 1968 presidential campaign. George Wallace stressed "law and order" and promised to make Washington safe if he was elected. Ralph McGill wrote, "Yet in the last year Mr. Wallace was governor, Birmingham's murder rate was 12.2 . . . per 100,000 persons while Washington's was 7.7" *Atlanta Constitution*, Sept. 23, 1968.

national economic course a work for united and not for lone effort! The habits and assumptions of individualistic pieties will not measure up to the present hour.

3. *Change Economic Priorities from Death-Dealing to Life-Healing*

We shift attention now from questions about the guidelines for individuals in the present situation to the identifying of guidelines to public policy which the individual should support.

We must change from our national preoccupation with military preparation and war to a similar emphasis on reconciliation, protection, and healing of human life throughout the nation and the world. The placing of highest priority on military containment of the great Communist powers has wasted our resources, brutalized and exploited our youth, inflated our currency, and paralyzed efforts to relieve poverty. This policy is threatening the very life and culture we have meant to protect.

4. *Close the Racial Gap*

Even though more than half the poor are white, they constitute, as we have seen, but 12 per cent of the white population, while 41 per cent of American blacks are poor. The difference in opportunity confronted by a black and a white child is intolerable. The poverty of anyone in present-day America is needless and belies our pretensions. But the net of discriminations which still entangles and frustrates great numbers of our black youth is both a scandal and a fearful waste of human resources. The National Advisory Commission on Civil Disorder analyzing the basic causes of the 1967 disorders, reports,

> Of these, the most fundamental is the racial attitude and behavior of white Americans toward black Americans. Race prejudice has shaped our history decisively in the past; it now threatens to do so again. White racism is essentially responsible for the explosive mixture which has been accumulating in our cities since the end of World War II.[20]

Such statements in the *Report* have caused many charges of unfair oversimplification. But to be fair we must observe that the Commission goes into a vast amount of factual detail in showing the truth of this conclusion. Particularly, the *Report* shows how racial attitudes have produced pervasive discrimination in every aspect of education and economic life, the black migration to northern cities, the exodus of

20. *Report of the National Advisory Commission on Civil Disorders*, p. 91.

white populations from those cities, and the resultant frustrated and destructive ghettos.

The efforts of many private businesses, of schools and colleges, and of countless individuals to break these patterns and extend to blacks new opportunity to participate in American affluence are praiseworthy. But no amount of such efforts can fully overcome the massive inertia of the present racial patterns and handicaps. We must also move together by use of our one inclusive cooperative agency, the government. By our own tax money we must will to catch up with decent housing, good schools, risk capital, subsidized job training, and medical care. We can if we will. A nation which put Western Europe on her economic feet by the Marshall Plan, and could spend thirty billion dollars a year on a fruitless intervention in the Vietnamese civil war, can finance the rejuvenation of both rural slums and decaying cities if we will.

5. Seek the Right "Mix" of Private Enterprise and Public Service

Slogans of "free enterprise," "socialism," and the like neither describe the realities of our present economic order nor point the way to solving our urgent problems. We live in a mixed economy as do the people of all political democracies.

Our problem is to find the right combination for our own time and place. As we confront each economic problem we need to face it with firm purpose to serve all our people and also the world in the most ample way possible. Then with careful marshaling of facts and considerable experimental pragmatism we must work out the best solutions we can find in an imperfect world.

As we make such efforts, the defenders of special privilege among the wealthy and powerful will try to divert us as they do now and always have done. Here the Christian has a vitally important function of holding attention on the needs of human beings as persons, whatever their color, age, class, parentage, or nation. Love can do no less.

6. Enact Broad Tax Reforms

Again and again, when Congress has been in process of legislating taxes, there have been angry calls for tax reform. The graduated income tax was supposed to place the heavier burdens on those best able to bear them, but actually provides a number of wide loopholes for the rich. As a result some of the wealthiest Americans including some with incomes above one million dollars per year pay no income tax at all and it is said that few of the millionaires pay a much larger percentage of their incomes than do the upper middle class professional people.[21]

Tax loopholes constitute only one example of many ways in which our laws favor wealth and property over persons. New and effective efforts must be made to correct these inequities and place justly the burden of supporting the great and expensive tasks which we must as a whole people perform.

7. Enact Guaranteed Annual Income

The precise form and method, the minimal figure to be established, and the name to be chosen are matters to be determined. But by whatever name and in whatever exact form, a nation of such resources as ours must in the name of common human rights, to say nothing of love and grace, guarantee the basic minimum of life with dignity to every person in this land.

8. Extend Educational Opportunity

Too many promising young Americans are denied opportunity for good schooling. Others, having demonstrated superior potential in public schools, are still unable to meet the costs of college or technical education. Educational opportunity should be determined by student potential, not by the means of parents. We cannot afford to have a youth grow up in America without education of whatever extent and kind is best suited to his aptitudes and interests. Our technically complex economy requires trained people to operate it. By the same token, to live usefully in such an economy requires the best preparation which can be provided. Such training will pay for itself in the country as a whole. At the same time, if the awesome power we have produced is to be wisely used, the ablest possible youth must be provided with the broadest and deepest possible education so that they may see issues of world life and death in broadest perspective.

9. Provide Greatly Increased Foreign Aid

In 1969 the United States maintained three thousand "minor military installations" and four hundred "major bases" abroad, requiring "a million servicemen to staff them in addition to 250,000 foreign employees." The maintenance of these bases cost four to five billion dollars per year.[22] Most of this money and very much more would be

21. Some of the devices used for legal escape from taxes are described by Ferdinand Lundberg in *The Rich and Super-Rich*, pp. 388–464, and by Kenneth Lamott, in *The Moneymakers* (Boston: Little, Brown & Co., 1969), pp. 270–92.
22. *The Washington Post*, July 13, 1969.

better spent in helping the nations to reach the economic "takeoff point" for their own industrialization, sound self-support and defense. More must be said on this in the chapter on International Order. But such is the interrelation of domestic and foreign affairs that the American economic order could not be honestly treated without a brief view of our responsibilities abroad also.

All these guidelines together cannot solve even one precise problem of economic choice. They do, however, set basic directions, and propose a framework within which particular decisions must be made in the light of the best up-to-date information obtainable.

chapter thirteen

Some Problems
of Technological Advance

―――――――――――・∽・―――――――――――

Most ethical problems in the world today are affected by our developing technology.[1] All could be discussed under other titles. However, it is useful to focus attention especially on some types of issues which are new in kind or in such extreme degree as to require examination of technology as such and the directions in which it is taking us.

The application of science has brought so many things we like that it may seem ungrateful to question whether more of such application would be good or whether at some point we should cry, "Enough!" A technology which has lengthened our life expectancy, relieved housewives of many tedious chores, provided even heat in winter and cooling in summer, enabled us to talk directly with distant friends, and taken the first men to moon landings, seems to many of our older people too good to be true. Why question it? Why not enjoy it, be thankful for it, and extend it in every direction possible?

We have already cautioned that technology offers means by which we may destroy ourselves in war or poison ourselves with polluted air and water. But for response to pollution do we not immediately look for technological answers? We may grant that war is a special case, for in war destruction is deliberate and technology now makes it possible to destroy with vastly greater effectiveness. It may still be thought that so long as technology is directed to useful production and the service of life it can only be good. In actuality, however, even when used for such good purposes the application of new scientific technique creates some grave problems which drive us to consider the most basic principles and meanings of human existence.

1. Technology means here applied science, especially of the more recent discoveries and methods of physical science, to practical problems.

A. AUTOMATION AND LEISURE

Although the term "automation" is sometimes used broadly to include all power machinery or even all useful tools, it is used in a much
more limited sense in this discussion.[2] Here we mean by automation
the use of

> an apparatus, process or system [controlled] by mechanical or elec-
> tronic devices that take the place of human organs of observation,
> effort, and decision.[3]

The simplest familiar example is the door which opens as you approach. A more complicated example is the sending of men to the
moon in a space vehicle operated much of the time by automatic devices and even when under manual control operated according to formulas signaled to the men on board from the computers.

In 1964 the Congress, by Public Law 88-444, authorized appointment
of a fourteen-member National Commission on Technology, Automation, and Economic Progess. The instructions to the Commission
were broad and were intended to seek knowledge about the directions
in which technology was taking our economy and our people. There
was particular concern lest the rate of unemployment, growing at the
time, might portend much worse unemployment to come, especially
among poorly educated people.

The concern with unemployment was considerably allayed when
the proportion of the unemployed began turning down, even as the
Commission was being organized, and dropped 20 per cent within one
year. The Commission concluded that the greatly increased productivity per man-hour achieved by automation would not need to cause
unemployment and was not causing it in 1965. But there was a catch
to it. The increased productivity per man-hour would not cause unemployment *if* the Gross National Product increased fast enough to
use the growing number of available man-hours in a growing population, despite the higher productivity, adjusted for shorter work weeks.[4]
Automation and other forms of technology are said by the Commission
to be increasing the productivity of labor about 2.8 per cent per year.
The labor force is increasing about 1.9 per cent. Making necessary ad-

2. For an example of the broadest usage, though stressing the narrower meaning also, see Donald A. Laird and Eleanor C. Laird, *How to Get Along with
Automation* (New York: McGraw-Hill Book Company, 1964), especially pp. 4–6.
3. *Webster's Seventh New Collegiate Dictionary*, slightly amended.
4. See the report by the Commission: Howard R. Bowen and Garth L. Mangum,
eds., *Automation and Economic Progress* (Englewood Cliffs, N.J.: Prentice-Hall,
Inc., 1966), pp. 10–21.

justments these figures mean that the Gross National Product must increase 4 per cent annually to prevent increasing unemployment.

Some classes of workers have suffered seriously from mechanization and automation. This is especially true of coal miners and even more of agricultural workers. In agriculture,

> a 5.7 per cent annual rate of productivity increase accompanied by only a 1.4 per cent increase in farm output has reduced the number of farm owners and farm workers from 8.2 million in 1947 to 4.8 million in 1964, or 42.3 per cent. . . . Too many, suffering from deficient rural education, lacking skills in demand in urban areas, unaccustomed to urban ways, and often burdened by racial discrimination, exchanged rural poverty for an urban ghetto.   [*Ibid.*, p. 16]

These facts of selective displacement of workers emphasize the need for special, large-scale assistance to the particular groups affected so that they will be retrained, relocated when necessary, and brought into full participation in the advantages of a technologically developed economy.

Yet there remains the necessity of that 4 per cent annual increase in the GNP. The Commission failed to acknowledge that in 1965, about which such satisfaction was expressed, the United States was just in the process of escalating its material and human involvement in the Vietnam War. In that year and every year from 1965 to 1969, much of our advance in GNP went overseas or was expended in unproductive armament. What if we had to expand our GNP 4 per cent per year without resort to such colossal waste?

The Commission does attack this problem by pointing to such "unmet human and community needs" as "improvements in health care, transportation, control of air and water pollution, and housing" (*ibid.*, p. 56). It is also anticipated that there will be a far greater increase in services than in material production. In many types of person-to-person service, automation is of minimal importance and cannot displace the human being.

Even when all these possibilities are taken into account, mechanization escalated into automation will increasingly provide us with basic and vitally important choices. The Commission points to several broad options.

First, we may take all the gain in productivity in added income. By 1985 we could then have an annual real income per individual of $5,802. Second, we could lower the hours of work to twenty hours weekly, or cut the work year to twenty-seven weeks or set retirement at thirty-eight. Third, we could invest much effort into humanizing the work and its environment to make labor more creative and satisfying.

There is the possible use of labor under government direction to satisfy unmet personal and community needs. Finally, we could "use a portion of our continuing gains to help the less fortunate in other parts of the world" (*ibid.*, p. 40).

I venture the prophecy that we shall continue to choose, in a rather haphazard way, to do a combination of these things. Every one of us will be taking his own part in making the decisions. We do, in fact, make such decisions every time we choose the use we make of our leisure time or of our rising incomes.

There is nothing which can show more clearly our actual convictions, our real faith. When I am confronted by new hours of leisure, I am deprived of my excuse that I do not have time to do the good works which have been presented to my conscience. This is true of the housewife with labor-saving devices in the home, the professional or businessman who moves to and from work more rapidly and with less toil, or the skilled worker of office or factory with shortened hours. What do we now do with the time?

Many a man of the self-employed or of the management class simply devotes the additional time to more of the same work. Whether this is good or bad depends on his personal needs, the nature of his work, and the true inner purpose of his added labor.

It will be no less than tragic if, as a people, we decide—in all our individual and communal ways of choosing—that we want mainly to escalate our feverish growth in production and consumption of material things. "Man shall not live by bread alone." A GNP perpetually increasing by 4 per cent and consumed by a national appetite for more things made insatiable by all the devices of advertising would bury us in gadgets and waste. The utter ruin of our environment lies not far down that road. It would not bring us the abundant life we seek. Jesus has warned us, "Take heed, and beware of all covetousness; for a man's life does not consist in the abundance of his possessions" (Luke 12:15). That is true even when the possessions are as attractive as technical wizardry in production and marketing can make them.[5]

The community which can provide deepest, widest, and most lasting satisfactions to its members is a community of the highest shared values. Increasing realization of such community will not be gained by a growing GNP. If growth in the community for which love

5. For interesting and useful discussions of automation, technological unemployment, and leisure, see Robert Theobald, *Guaranteed Income;* Walter A. Weisskopf, Raghavan N. Iyer, and others, *Looking Forward: the Abundant Society* (Santa Barbara: Center for the Study of Democratic Institutions, 1966); and Charles Markham, ed., *Jobs, Men, and Machines: Problems of Automation* (New York: Frederick A. Praeger, 1964). See also Vance Packard, *The Waste Makers* (New York: Pocket Books, Inc., 1960, etc.).

yearns is to be gained it must be by deliberate choice of plans carefully made for that purpose.

B. THE AUTOMOBILE

Few inventions of a mechanizing age have affected human life in the United States so much as the automobile. It is so familiar that it is often thought of as having come before the age of technology. The easy way of taking it for granted is a part of our trouble.

The automobile has intensified the problems we have with some old evils and brought to us some new ones. It has intensified the problems of teenage premarital sex and illegitimacy. It has made commission of crime and escape from crime easier and so added new difficulties to the task of law enforcement. The automobile is itself a major temptation to theft—both of whole cars and also of parts and accessories.[6]

1. *Destructiveness*

Ethicists have had too little to say about the killing and maiming of people by automobile drivers.

The fourth most common cause of death in the United States is accident. This is by a wide margin the principal cause of death of young people. Of every 100 accidental deaths in 1967 nearly 47 were of people killed by automobiles. When an airplane crashes, killing as many as one hundred people, we are horrified; but on the average over one thousand people are killed every week in traffic accidents, or a total of 56,400 in 1969.[7]

2. *Situational Guidelines*

The automobile is far too useful to be outlawed. Yet there are both needed public policies and personal responsibilities clearly indicated by the facts. In public policy, responsible public opinion should support realistic speed laws and their enforcement. Improvement of highways and the regulation of traffic can make significant impact on traffic deaths. The enforcement of laws against driving after drinking alcoholic beverages is important.

Love requires the protection of life. The Principle of Foresight guides us to use the growing body of technical knowledge about causes of accidents and means of safety for the achieving of such protection.

6. In 1968, 298,782 automobiles were known by police to have been stolen in the United States. *Statistical Abstract of the United States: 1070*, p. 146.

7. Based on figures in *Statistical Abstract*. 1970, pp. 57, 59 and 552.

As population becomes denser and highways more congested with automobiles, it is plain that far too heavy reliance is being put on private motor cars for personal transportation. No city has tried harder to clear the way for automobiles to carry its commuting population into and across town than Los Angeles. Yet, with over six-tenths of the inner city area taken over by parking lots, streets, and expressways and the high speed roadways radiating in profusion, every morning and night the lines of cars sit bumper to bumper in massive traffic slowdowns or complete paralysis. It is not easy to transfer now a large proportion of urban transportation to high speed electric railways, but the city planners know it must be done. Indeed, this must be done also in the long "megalopolis" corridors, and in many other locally congested areas. The federally subsidized experiments in new high-speed comfortable rail service along the densely populated eastern corridor is a promising step toward relief from the dangerous and strangling congestion of the highways and also from the new and similar problems of the airways. United States Secretary of Transportation John A. Volpe rightly calls for a balanced system in which public ground transportation such as railways and subways will carry a much larger proportion of the passenger traffic than now.[8] Unfortunately, the enormous material interests involved in highway construction and the automobile industries have thus far effectively smothered large-scale efforts to move in this direction. Our legislative bodies continue to appropriate billions of dollars for highways, thus subsidizing automobile transportation on a huge scale; while efforts to secure funds for mass transportation are crushed or reduced to minor proportions by charges of "socialism," "statism," and the like.

Meanwhile, all of us have clear moral obligations. Because the motor vehicle is a latecomer in man's long history, we do not *feel* the same force of conscience about our conduct at the wheel as we feel in other relationships. People ordinarily considerate of their associates often become inconsiderate and dangerous at the wheel. The church has a share of responsibility for cultivating a national conscience in the restrained and safe operation of motor vehicles.

We must correct the tragic fact that as streets are widened and superhighways built through our cities, the worst sufferers are usually the poor. Living in crowded tenements of the inner cities, most are able to secure the bare living they get only by being close to their urban work. When the buildings are torn down to make way for speeding automobiles, these slum dwellers are thrust out, often with little or no provision for new dwelling places within reach of their jobs.

8. Address to the American Society of Civil Engineers, meeting in Washington, D.C., July 21, 1969.

C. Mechanizing of Human Relations

1. Bigness and Depersonalization

The sheer size of the world's exploding population tends to increase a sense of insignificance in the typical individual. What is one among so many? Moreover, people are rapidly moving into big cities, finding work in big corporations or big government agencies, joining big unions, forming big associations, attending big schools and universities. When an organization is small, its affairs are usually managed in face-to-face personal relations, where coordination of effort and mutual confidence depend on personal acquaintance and trust. If it grows larger the time soon comes when rules must be adopted and governance by personal acquaintance and informal cooperation gives way to governance by regulations. This is necessary to protect the rights and interests of all concerned, especially the subordinate members, but it reduces the sense of personal significance.

2. People as Numbers

Management by rules, dealing with large numbers of people, is made more efficient by technology. The worker punches his card in the time clock so the hour of his arrival and departure will be known exactly. Then neither he nor the firm will be short-changed if the rules themselves are fair. Absolute identity is simply and surely established by an identification number on a card. Payrolls are made up by computers which have been programmed according to all the rules. The computerized records hold without forgetting all the times of late arrival at work, the sick leaves, length of service, and often the numerically measurable achievements of each worker. All is mechanically efficient and icily cold.

Customers, too, find themselves to be numbers on cards, and woe be to the buyer who discovers that something has gone wrong with his account! He is likely to find himself able to correspond, it seems, only with a machine, answering his complaints by form letters which repeat the error or give explanations which do not fit at all his precise situation.

Even patients in a hospital often find themselves reduced to numerical terms precisely when they are feeling most sensitive and needful of some genuinely personal attention. A boy admitted in emergency with a painfully broken and mangled finger lies on a stretcher in the hall awaiting his turn for an hour, then hears a cold voice on the intercom over his head saying, "X-ray, X-ray, the finger in the hall is number 15,726." With a wry grin the boy says, "That's me!" So it is

—a suffering human being reduced to the number assigned to a finger for an X-ray film.

Some complaints running through many disorders and through many more orderly but anguished protests on university campuses have to do with this matter. Every college student is wanting to be someone. He is striving to find out precisely what he is and will be. Then he finds himself subject to the indignities of an identification card with its all-important number. Without the card he cannot register for a course, take a book from the library, enter the swimming pool, nor eat in the dining hall. But anyone else who carries his card may be able to do all these things. His card seems more important than he, for the rights and privileges belong to the card, not to himself.

The problem is not really with numbers and machines as such; it is with social relations—whether of student and teacher, buyer and seller, or employer and employee—relations which are attentive only to the conceptual abstractions capable of being computerized. In such relations the unique individual, the living, desiring, concerned, choosing person is lost to view.

3. *Situational Guidelines*

a. Limitation and Distribution of Population.   As was emphasized in another connection, we face the urgent necessity of bringing to a halt the exploding increase of world population. This must be mentioned again here because the sheer congestion of people in limited space creates serious social problems, quite apart from problems of the economic order and ecology.

When a number of people are thrown together in close relationship from which there is no escape, there are problems even if the persons were good friends at the beginning. Experiments with the apes and monkeys most like human beings show that even when there is plenty of food and when sex rivalries are not involved, the presence of too many individuals in limited space sharply raises the level of hostilities. It is probable that a similar tendency is present among human beings.[9]

Various compensatory devices commonly come into play to reduce the feelings of pressure and the trend to hostility. The modern custom of vacation trips is helpful for those who can take them and who choose wisely. The increasingly complicated structure of law helps control the symptoms and alleviates some occasions for hostile expression. The religious teaching of love may be viewed from one perspective as a compensation, as Konrad Lorenz does interpret it. Indeed, Lorenz looks to this as man's supreme hope for the long run (*ibid.*, pp. 289–

9. See Konrad Lorenz, *On Aggression* (New York: Bantam Books, 1966, 1967).

90). One important compensation, however, increases the depersonalization which we have been considering. This is our strong trend in all crowded cities everywhere to avoid personal relations with most people near us. Most people in crowded cities are not personally acquainted with the majority of their closest neighbors. Many know none at all. Such anonymity is especially prevalent in modern high-rise apartment houses. It is often convenient but it is also dehumanizing.

In addition to policies for the limiting of population growth, we need to distribute the people we have in ways which encourage small neighborhood groups. Millions are doing this for themselves by moving to far-out suburbs—whether of Calcutta, Buenos Aires, or New York—though this movement is leaving the congestion in the inner city undiminished. Much can be done by imaginative planners and architects even within large apartment houses. Providing the necessary housing construction and transportation will require much labor, but as we face an excess of productiveness, the labor cost is only a matter for sound application to the right tasks to make our world more livable.

b. Providing Beauty and Convenience. When we live in square, uniform boxes, ride on overcongested, malodorous streets or noisy and ugly trains and subways, and work in offices and factories obviously designed only for efficient accomplishment of impersonal functions, we are being treated as nonpersons. The more of our time we spend in such environment, the more we lose our true humanity. On the other hand, when we live in homes planned both for efficient use and for beauty, and walk through clean streets to our transportation, we feel refreshed and liberated. It is ironical that it is the Soviet Union which has produced a subway system, in Moscow, famous for its spacious and artistically decorated stations. Why not elsewhere? Many a factory and office building is now being built for gracious and attractive living as well as for getting the job done. It is often reported that the job itself gets done better by the whole persons then working than by the human robots who work in the imprisonment of ugly walls and machines. Good enough! But even more important is the fact that since people are living a large part of their lives at work—even with the reduced hours—they are being enabled to live more fully.

c. Using Small Groups. Individuals who find themselves depersonalized by the mechanization and massive numbers of the present world can rediscover and develop true personhood in well-planned and skillfully led small groups. Such groups are increasingly used in American schools. In the history of Christianity they have been effective means for the deepening of faith and the organizing for action—from Jesus' twelve apostles to John Wesley's class meetings and to many contemporary efforts at church renewal.

Churches should increase the use of small groups. In some situations most of the need is met by regular committees, teaching staffs, church school classes, and similar groups in the community. However, as churches become larger, relations within them often become as anonymous and impersonal as in factory or apartment house. Here deliberate effort must be made to offer small-group membership to all, and in relation to a wide range of functions and interests.

d. Resistance and Planned Compensation. Some large colleges and business firms have deliberately resisted the often recommended installation of computerized records of student work or customer accounts. A few have even discarded such systems after adopting them, because the decision makers have decided that the mechanized procedures exacted too great a toll of human personal relations.

Whenever it is decided to use the technical, mechanized systems, every effort should be made to introduce simultaneously compensatory arrangements for the strengthening of fully personal relations.

e. Accent on Personal Loving-kindness. In the present situation, we ought to respect the desire of many persons for anonymity and for impersonal functional relations with us. However, we should also be continually alert for opportunities to introduce personal relations of respect and consideration, even in normally casual business transactions and chance meetings. Sometimes such relations will lead to further associations and may finally offer occasion for much more significant expressions of neighborly love. Certainly there was never a time when loving and being loved were both so critically needed by so many as now. This need is at the heart of Christian duty and privilege.

D. Medical Technology

New drugs, new machines, and new surgical procedures for the treatment of disease are confronting physicians, nurses, patients, and families of patients with a whole complex of critically important and difficult ethical problems, two of them, drug dependence and high costs, being aggravations of old problems. The others involve more of novelty.

1. Drug Dependence

The use of alcohol and some other depressants is of ancient origin. Some stimulating drugs and hallucinogens have also been employed for many centuries among various peoples. The more acute social problems of addiction and exploitation, however, have developed since the commercial spreading of opium smoking through China in the eighteenth century, the building of modern distilleries, and the technical production of the concentrated morphine derivative heroin and other new drugs.

a. Recent Increase. In the twentieth century drug abuse and dependence have greatly increased in the United States. There are believed to be several causes. The tensions induced by extremely rapid change and high mobility drive many persons to look for comfort or escape. Some of the same factors have created general moral confusion so that a larger proportion of our people may feel morally free to try alcohol and drugs than formerly. Technical changes in medical practice are other highly important causes.

During the American Civil War morphine was much used to deaden the pain of wounded or sick soldiers. Some of the men thus treated became addicts. Hence morphine addiction became known for a period as "army disease."[10] Ever since the introduction of general anaesthesia into hospital surgery, in 1846, there has been a growing use of pain-killing drugs and procedures in medical and surgical practice. The benefits of such use are beyond all estimation. Indeed, most of modern surgery would be impossible without it. The problem arises with the many abuses.

In hospitals and under the care of physicians at home, millions of people are instructed to use prescribed or publicly available medicines for the relief of headaches and other pains, for the relief of tension, and for the inducing of sleep. Thereafter many find it easy to turn to such drugs for relief from every kind of discomfort, physical or psychological. Alcoholic drink may serve a similar purpose. There are vast numbers of persons in our society who are not "addicts," in the traditional sense, and who do not use "habit-forming" drugs, but who are nevertheless in the habit of depending upon alcohol for relaxation or to stimulate moods of gaiety, and on aspirin for relief of headaches and the inducing of sleep. The same people may look to strong coffee, concentrated caffeine pills, or tobacco for aid to vigorous wakefulness in the morning or when work or pleasure calls for special alertness. Moving always from depressants to stimulants, they may become difficult to know for what they themselves intrinsically are. Using such means in daily routine, they find them quite inadequate in more serious need. A personal crisis may send the moderate drinker into alcoholism or lead the daily user of aspirin to amphetamines and barbiturates, then on to obtain opiate "sleeping pills" from the doctor. He may move finally to the escalating cycle of demand which constitutes true addiction.

Meanwhile, many university students have turned special attention

10. Elliot D. Luby, in *Drug Addiction and Habituation*, ed. by Delbert D. Konnor (Detroit: Wayne State University College of Pharmacy, 1968), p. 1.

to certain drugs by which they seek new psychic adventures. They may try marihuana—which is probably fairly analogous to alcohol in the seriousness of its effects, though less addictive physically than alcohol. Someone introduces a hallucinogen like LSD, which is genuinely dangerous. The escalating addiction, however, is likely to begin when heroin enters the picture. Even then only certain ones of the experimenters will be "hooked."

b. The People Who Become Addicts. Tommie L. Duncan writes that most real drug addicts are persons characterized by more than usual emotional distress. "The addiction-prone neurotic person is looking for something to relieve his anxiety." But

Two other conditions are required for a person to become addicted. First, he must be introduced to drugs. Second, he must have a personal attitude that permits him to use a socially disapproved method of relieving distress.[11]

The experimenters who fall into addiction "are usually young people from the heavily populated, low economic, minority-centered areas of our larger cities" (*ibid.*, p. 33). Yet there is a serious problem among the affluent also.

Drug dependence is disastrous in direct effects on the helpless addicts themselves—their feeling of hopelessness in the advanced stages, their misery when craving new dosage, and their loss of the freedom which is the essence of full personhood. But a massive additional social evil flows from drug dependence in the form of crime. We do not know the proportion of serious crimes committed by drug addicts but we know it is large. The insatiably escalating demand of the addict for his expensive drug drives him to obtain ever-increasing amounts of money. Usually he has quite limited means, and as his habit increases he is unable to work steadily even if he has done so in the past. He resorts to crimes of larceny, robbery, or burglary, or else to selling drugs for a supplier—an activity which is also a crime. If we include in the list the crimes committed under the influence of alcohol, then the criminal consequences of drug dependence are massive.

c. Policy Concerning Addictive Drugs. The causes of drug dependence are evidently complex and various approaches must also be made to dealing with the problem. Certainly there must be continued vigorous effort to cut off the supplies of illicit addictive drugs. Medical doctors have an obligation to be conservative in their prescription of

11. *Understanding and Helping the Narcotic Addict* (Englewood Cliffs, N.J.: Prentice-Hall, 1965), p. 27.

drugs which may lead to dependence and to urge patients to tolerate much discomfort without artificial aid. Such policy would be contrary to very widespread practice now.

Some conditions which prevail in much present American life clearly play a major role in the great curse of drug abuse. These conditions include family disorganization, unemployment, bad housing, and generally depressing conditions of urban slums, moral confusion throughout society, severance of ties with religious sources of consolation and moral convictions, and the sensate materialism so heavily promoted in popular television. All social evils are interrelated and this interrelation is well exemplified in the causation of the illicit drug traffic.

As far as beverage alcohol is concerned, we must raise the question why we should tolerate the expenditure of many millions of dollars per year in the effort to gain more users of a drug of such potent addictiveness. In 1945 a Special Commission appointed by the state legislature of Massachusetts, in a 381-page report said that in 1943 known alcoholic-related costs to the state for penal, rehabilitative, and other expenses had totaled at least $46,474,953.74 (over three and one-half times the tax revenue from alcoholic beverages).[12] Costs to individuals, business, and private agencies were not included. In 1957 the National Safety Council estimated that a "drinking driver was involved in about 30 per cent of all fatal accidents in 1956."[13] Morris E. Chafetz and Harold W. Demone, Jr., describe alcoholism as "third only to heart disease and cancer in incidence."[14] Whatever may be the pleasure which many receive from it without falling into alcoholism or being in fatal accidents, it scarcely seems to be in the public interest to urge its claims upon all the population by the myriad devices of advertising today.

In dealing with the generally illegal addictive drugs, the best informed and experienced authorities recommend a combination of education, rigorous, well-enforced laws against dope-peddling, and rehabilitation of addicts without the stigma of criminal records.[15] Education and rehabilitation are important also for reduction of alcoholism.

The church has special responsibilities for pastoral care of alcoholics and drug dependents. Through some involvement in such care its min-

---

12. Roger Burgess, *Drinking Problems* (Washington, D.C.: TEM Press, n.d.).

13. *Ibid.*, citing "Accident Facts 1957 Edition" (National Safety Council, 1957), p. 51.

14. *Alcoholism and Society* (New York: Oxford University Press, 1962), Preface.

15. See, e.g., H. J. Anslinger and William F. Tompkins, *The Traffic in Narcotics* (New York: Funk & Wagnalls Co., 1953), pp. 294–303. Cf. Alfred R. Lindesmith, *The Addict and the Law* (Bloomington: Indiana University Press, 1965). Lindesmith is extremely critical of Anslinger and advocates main reliance on rehabilitation.

isters and laymen can become even more useful in giving preventive care to persons near the borderline of addiction.[16]

In dealing with the whole range of problems having to do with drug dependence, special emphasis must be laid on the positive task of making life wholesome and meaningful for all our people, the very task of love to which God calls us. This is a work for businessmen, government, city planners, engineers, labor union leaders, and homemakers. God's call is to all people. None is exempt. In this task the churches have a central role.

2. *Medical Costs*

John H. Knowles, director of the Massachusetts General Hospital, says,

> Any practical, reasonable man would agree that the costs of medical care are prohibitive today for 99 per cent of the American people. There must be an insurance mechanism to protect people against this kind of economic ruin.[17]

For people who can pay for it medical care in the United States is very good indeed. But for the population as a whole it is far from the best among the nations, and probably the prohibitively high costs are among the causes for our shortcomings. "The US lags behind 14 other nations in infant mortality and behind 17 in life expectancy (for US males, 66–8 years)" ("TRB," *ibid.*).

Some of the rising costs of medicine, hospitalization, and physicians' fees are due to the introduction of many new procedures, machines, and drugs which are expensive. If our physicians had relied on the knowledge and procedures available thirty years ago, many of us would have died long ago. We have little ground for personal complaint if we have had to pay more money than our parents for medical service which they could not have at any price.

How expensive some of the new procedures are, we are told in a recent editorial of the *Journal of the American Medical Association.* We are informed that the cost of hemodialysis (use of an artificial "kidney") and renal (kidney) transplantation now totals about an average of $15,000 to $16,000 per patient for the first year and $10,000 to $12,000 "during the ensuing years of survival."

16. A good treatment of these functions, especially pastoral care of the drug dependent, is Tommie L. Duncan, *op. cit.*

17. Quoted in "TRB from Washington," in *The New Republic*, July 12, 1969, p. 8.

This is an extreme example. But the total of many less expensive technically advanced but more commonly used items is much greater. The combination of higher medical fees, expensive technical advances, higher wages and salaries for hospital employees, and general inflation have raised the annual cost of our national health care system from $26.4 billion in 1960 to $60.3 billion by 1969, of which increase two-thirds is "due to higher costs alone, not to improved or expanded care," says a *New Republic* editorial, adding, "Medical costs are rising today at a rate twice that of over-all prices."[18]

If our whole population is to have the advantages of both preventive medicine and medical treatment, it is evident that there will need to be an extension of federal health insurance to cover all. If this is done it will have been over the determined, skillful, and heavily financed political opposition of the American Medical Association.

Curiously enough, when Theodore Roosevelt's Progressive Party advocated national compulsory health insurance in 1912, the AMA was favorably inclined and a committee of the AMA named in 1917 reported in support of such a plan as preferable to voluntary health insurance which could not reach the neediest people.[19] Since that time the AMA has become a staunchly conservative body, opposing not only government-supported health insurance but also such things as federal unemployment insurance as tending toward "socialism" or "communism." With a political budget of millions, it maintains one of the most powerful lobbies in America outside the incomparable military establishment. In the 1970 meeting there were loud rumblings of revolt and signs of hope for change in the AMA position. All who are concerned with the health of the whole nation and not only the privileges of the more affluent—both patients and physicians—should support such change. The national health plan which love and foresight require will come sooner and operate more effectively with the hearty cooperation of the medical profession than without it.

The limited facilities for training medical doctors—limited partly by AMA policy opposing federal sponsorship of new medical schools—have left us with a serious shortage of doctors. The scarcity tempts many to charge exorbitantly. The resulting loss of public confidence in the medical profession is becoming serious. Fortunately, many physicians maintain faithfully the finest tradition of devoted, unselfish medical service, with self-restraint in fee schedules, and are resisting the benighted politics of the AMA. Their spirit is the hope for the future.

18. July 12, 1969 (Vol 204, No. 10), p. 11. The totals stated above are from *Statistical Abstract*, 1970 p. 62, and show an even greater increase and a higher total for 1969 than stated by the *New Republic*.
19. TRB, *New Republic*, July 12, 1968, p. 8.

3. Genetic Issues

For many thousands of years, only physically fit human beings survived to reproduce. Thanks to great medical advances, millions who would have died in youth, even fifty years ago, now live to have children. As a result, in many instances the inheritance of inferior traits is transmitted. Similarly, throughout most of man's long life on earth people of inferior intelligence or initiative usually fell victim to the severe hazards of primitive life and so did not live to reproduce. Now such persons are protected and supported, either in institutions or at home, and more do have children. Some of the defects (by no means all) are hereditary, and so the proportion of defective people in the world increases.

Leroy G. Augenstein writes that there are three possible choices for our society to make in the face of this trend. We may continue as now but know the predictable dreaded consequences. We can make the change of withholding medical care from some defectives or practice compulsory sterilization or abortions to prevent their propagating their undesirable strains. Finally, despite "all the hazards involved, we can embark upon the road of genetic manipulation."[20] Augenstein favors this third choice.

Genetic management of a kind has been possible as long as selective animal breeding has been understood. In fact, it has been practiced in a way for many centuries. When families have selected mates for young people of marriageable age, usually they have arranged marriages between families of similar class. Whatever the motivation, a result has been at least partially to avoid the serious deterioration of good genetic stock by intermarriage with inferior strains. The modern trend around the world is toward individual choice by the young people themselves, as in the United States. These choices are often based on superficial kinds of attraction and may join families of superior ability and health with others inferior both mentally and physically. The result may be to upgrade an inferior strain, but it may be the opposite.

Some eugenicists are advocating use of artificial insemination by selected donors. It is "estimated that 10,000 artificially inseminated conceptions occur in the United States every year, and the number is rising."[21] Presumably, when a couple decide to have a baby by AID (artificial insemination by a donor) the choice of a donor, though made by their physician and kept anonymous, is made with effort to select a representative of a healthy and intelligent family. This sug-

20. *Come, Let Us Play God* (New York: Harper & Row, 1969), p. 32.
21. Gordon Rattray Taylor, *The Biological Time Bomb* (Cleveland: World Publishing Company, 1969), p. 159.

gests one way to develop a large-scale eugenics program. People would marry whom they pleased, but let conception be by artificial insemination, donors being selected on objective eugenic grounds by genealogical research committees.

Other suggestions have come from enthusiasts about the new discoveries of the hereditary code carried in the chromosomes by the molecules of deoxyribose nucleic acid, commonly known as DNA. However, the human DNA is said to contain a billion nucleotides, and our knowledge of combinations producing desirable and undesirable traits is very limited and crude. Chemical and radiological alteration of the genetic code may have uses in producing better grain and in altering insects, but to tinker with human genes would be to run enormous risks of producing monstrosities. It would be, indeed, to "play God" in the worst sinful sense. Human life is too sacred for such recklessness.[22]

What about AID? A couple whose desire for children has been long disappointed may learn through a fertility clinic that the obstacle is the sterility of the husband. Most such couples who are still especially eager for children adopt a carefully selected homeless child. But some now choose AID. Several problems should be thoughtfully faced if this alternative is to be ethically chosen. Are both husband and wife sure that the knowledge that the child borne by the wife is by conception from the semen of another man will not divide their own feelings toward each other or toward the child? Are they sure they can trust the physician to keep absolutely to himself the knowledge of their identity and the donor's? Can they trust his selection of the donor? Is the semen collected in an ethical manner? Can they be sure the donation is not impairing the character of the donor or his relationship with his wife? In view of the needs for fit parents to adopt homeless children, the complex psychological and ethical questions which need satisfactory answers in any individual case, and the present population explosion, I should conclude that the initial presumption would be against resort to AID. But this presumption need not be in all cases identical with the final decision after sensitive and thoughtful exploration.

As a general eugenic program AID offers much more serious obstacles. Cattle breeders know exactly what traits they wish to develop. Artificial insemination of hundreds of cows from a single bull carrying these traits to superlative degree is a useful expedient. But the human

22. A good treatment of the scientific facts and some problems, in nontechnical language, is in Gordon Rattray Taylor, *op. cit.*, pp. 158–85. A thoughtful scientist's discussion is P. B. Medowar, "Genetic Options: An Examination of Current Fallacies," in Edward Shils and others, *Life or Death: Ethics and Options*, pp. 94–113.

traits we most need are genetically complex in the extreme. Who will decide precisely what combinations of traits are to be propagated? Do we want a maximum of computerlike genuises? Or do we need people more sensitive to nuances of feeling in other people? Do we want artists or scientists, mystics or administrators? If all, then in what proportion? Knowing that all such complex traits require a combination of heredity and environment, do we know how to produce the proper heredity for a given environment? Moreover, we must ask whether millions of couples able, so far as they know, to raise children of their own will consent to a program substituting AID with the donor selected by others for natural conception in their own marital love. If life and love are to be respected as Christian ethics and even a genuine humanism require, *such* a program of positive eugenics must be rejected as unethical.

There are, however, two kinds of eugenic policies which can and ought to be adopted.

First, parents, churches, and schools should teach older children and youth the great eugenic responsibilities of love and marriage. Most young people want to have families of which they can be proud. It is difficult, often impossible, to dissuade a young man or woman from a contemplated marriage when love has become strong and intimate commitments have been made. It is quite another matter to assist earlier, by thoughtful instruction, in developing the youth's image of the kind of person he or she would be able to love and marry and the kind of family which would be seen as desirable grandparents and other blood relatives of his or her children.

Second, a program of "negative eugenics" is practicable, socially desirable, and ethical. There are traits of feeble-mindedness which are hereditary (although much subnormal mentality is not) and which are certainly undesirable. I have personally met in an institution a woman and twelve children, all her sons and daughters, and all, like herself, helplessly dependent in their low mentality.

In the face of such tragic propagation of pitiful defectives, society has the right and the obligation to say, "Enough!" Some states have laws which require sterilization of people institutionalized and found by special boards to be bearers of defective hereditary strains. Some also provide for voluntary submission of people to sterilization when they themselves believe that for some reason they ought not to bear children although they do wish to live normal married lives. Limited in scope as such provisions are, and must be, they are nevertheless useful and proper measures for defending a proper respect for the human person.

Compulsory sterilization is widely viewed with deep suspicion, not only because of intense personal feelings about sex, but also because of abuses practiced under Hitler and possible under any prejudiced government. Certainly it must be closely limited by law to extreme types, with decisions of individual cases in the hands of boards well insulated from political influence. There is, of course, no preventing the practice of genocide by a sufficiently evil and powerful government. But for such purposes laws providing sterilization are not necessary. A military draft and the arbitrary structures of military discipline will serve as well, with or without deliberate and wholesale murder in death camps.

As far as the invasion of private sex life is concerned, it must be understood that sterilization such as we are discussing does not affect sexual expression between two people, but only prevents conception. Many defectives now kept in special homes, with the sexes separated, could be permitted to marry within or outside such institutions if they

There are two especially serious and difficult ethical questions concerning the transplanting of human organs from one body into another. When there is a limited supply of machines or other equipment required so that some people must be selected to have a chance for life while others must be left to die, how is selection to be made? The same question arises relative to scarce life-sustaining machines not concerned with transplants. The other question concerns the circumstances under which it is ethically right to take a single vitally necessary organ, such as the heart, from one human body and place it in another.

a. Who Shall be Selected to Live?   According to the editor of the *Journal of the American Medical Association* there is now equipment to provide for about 1,000 of 7,000 patients per year well suited to have their lives saved by use of hemodialysis and a kidney transplant. It would cost nearly one billion dollars for the first six years to provide were first sterilized.

4. Transplants

facilities and personnel for the rest.[23] The surgical team in a hospital equipped for this procedure has applications from seven patients who have been referred for it and have proven to be suitable subjects. There is an available donor for each. Which one will be chosen, in the knowledge that the rest will die of uremia?

We may support the plea that more resources and personnel be prepared so that surgeons will not have to make such choices. But the surgeons must decide today who will be chosen and who must be left to die.

Both professional training of the physician and the background of a Judeo-Christian culture make the very question distasteful. Every person is of worth beyond calculation. God cares for the least, as well

23. Vol. 204, No. 10 (June 3, 1968), pp. 923-24.

as for the greatest. Granted. Nevertheless, now the choice must be made.

I see no way of avoiding a calculus in which account is taken of many factors. First must come the medical considerations. Which one has the best chance of survival with the transplant—assuming that all have been found unable to survive without it? Which has the most suitable donor? Assuming that the issue has not yet been settled, some nonmedical considerations must now be faced. Whose life—under the somewhat impaired health predictable—will be most valuable to other people? Here must be faced the questions of dependents—economic or personal—and of broader social usefulness. Who might be expected to have the most years of useful life ahead if seen through this present crisis successfully? None of these questions can be answered with certainty. However, I believe the Principle of Foresight indicates that an otherwise healthy person in the twenties should have priority over a similar person in the seventies. Many other comparisons would be equally clear. When such objective grounds are not clear, the decision should be made by lot or by order of application. The surgeon or team of surgeons, with any other consultant they choose to invite, must do the best possible to decide aright, with humble dependence upon God for purification of motives, guidance of thought, and forgiveness of mistakes which may yet be made.

b. When Are Heart Transplants Justified?   The Board of Medicine of the American National Academy of Sciences issued a public statement proposing guidelines on the undertaking of heart transplants. Pointing out some troublesome features inherent in this particular type of transplant, the Report continued, "Thus the procedure cannot as yet be regarded as an accepted form of therapy, even an heroic one."[24] Hence it is believed that the doing of a heart transplant can be justified only under highly restricted conditions. It must not only be judged to offer the only hope for the recipient, but there must be resources present for gaining maximum scientific value for the future of medical service. Exacting requirements should be made of the institution where the operation is to be performed.

In the report to which reference has been made there is a proposed requirement that a donor be selected only with unanimous written agreement by a "group of expert, mature physicians—none of whom is directly engaged in the transplantation effort." This opinion must be based on "evidence of crucial and irreversible bodily damage and imminent death" (*ibid.*).

Does this mean that the heart may be taken from such a person before he has actually died? Apparently so. It is specified that death must

24. *British Medical Journal*, 23 Mar. 1968, p. 762.

be "imminent," but not that it must have occurred. This would appear to imply a plain case of medical killing, even though the purpose is not to kill this patient but to save another. The medical profession generally would reject the rightness of this provision. So I think would most moralists.

Much more authoritative in American practice is the Report of the American Medical Association Judicial Council to the AMA, approved by vote of the House of Delegates in June, 1968. It is too long to reproduce here. It specifies rigorous requirements regarding the physicians, the medical institution, and the selection of both recipient and donor. Regarding the latter, it states,

> When a vital, single organ is to be transplanted, the death of the donor shall have been determined by at least one physician other than the recipient's physician. Death shall be determined by the clinical judgment of the physician. In making this determination, the ethical physician will use all available, currently accepted scientific tests.[25]

The Report specifies that before death the donor must be provided with all the care which would be given to any other patient in his condition, and lays down other conditions to protect his rights and those of his relatives.

But when is a human being actually dead? This was formerly a matter of holding a cold dry mirror to the lips, the feeling of the pulse, or the attempt to produce a reflex in the eye of the patient. But now it is not so simple. In these days both breathing and heart action may stop and yet the patient may be restored to life and recover.

Some neurologists have advocated using electroencephalography to determine when activity of the cerebral cortex comes to an end. However, at the twenty-first annual meeting of the American Academy of Neurology in Washington, this procedure was a subject of some controversy.[26] We can readily see the wisdom of the AMA Report insisting that several criteria of death be employed and not one alone.

There remain some additional important considerations.

Any change in the body as radical as the transplanting from another of an important organ may produce psychiatric complications, usually from change in self-image or side effects of drugs used to prevent rejection. Transplantation of the heart brings other potential trouble-making factors into play. In literature and common usage the heart is symbol for emotion, for the depth of personal identity, for moral conviction, or, as in ancient biblical literature, for the intellect. To have

25. The Report may be secured by request sent to the AMA Judicial Council, 535 N. Dearborn St., Chicago, Ill., 60610.
26. *The Washington Post*, May 18, 1969, p. A28.

a new heart, then, may lead the patient to expect a new life, new loves, and new abilities. The knowledge that one's new heart is that of a dead person may lead to depressing thoughts. The fact that the heart is an organ of such obvious and constant activity, of which a heart patient is likely to be frequently and keenly aware, adds to the danger of unhealthy emotional effects.

That the danger of such effects is serious is well attested by Donald T. Lunde, experienced psychiatric consultant to a cardiac transplant team at Stanford University.[27] Dr. Lunde tells of psychoses induced by transplants and also of undesirable effects upon members of a donor's family who felt that their own loved one had not completely died so long as his heart was beating in the chest of another. As a result they followed the recipient's fortunes with abnormal anxiety and suffered a new trauma of grief when he finally died.

Such complications give further reason for conservative policy regarding cardiac transplantation. They indicate also the need for taking pains to instruct the recipient and his family and also the family of the donor to allay the effects of traditional mythology about the heart. When it is understood that the heart is the central blood pump of the body and not a physiological center of either emotional or mental life, most of the psychiatric complications of heart transplants should be prevented.

The extraordinary demands on medical resources made by heart transplantations constitute a further inhibiting consideration. The number of people in critical need who are unable to receive hospital care or medical service even in our national capital has become an open scandal. It is probably worse in many rural areas and other less publicized places. The total investment made for the possible extension of one life for a relatively brief period by a cardiac transplant might have brought many years of good health to many persons needing only ordinary preventive or curative medical service.

Probably it is right that a very few of the teams in the nation now doing heart transplants should continue quietly and with great care, for the sake of future breakthroughs to more satisfactory and less costly procedures. But until we establish a far better ratio of health equipment and personnel to population and distribute these resources far better, we cannot afford to expend so extravagantly very much of the inadequate resources available.

Organ transplantation is closely related to questions about the prolonging of dying. To these questions we must now turn.

27. See his "Psychiatric Complications of Heart Transplants," *The American Journal of Psychiatry*, Vol. 126: No. 3 (Sept., 1969), pp. 369–73.

5. Prolonging Dying

a. "Not Allowed to Die." A letter to the *British Medical Journal* tells of a venerable and able physician who was incurably ill and suffered cardiac failure. By heroic measures he was resuscitated and lived on in great pain, with further deterioration of his hopeless condition. He gave explicit instructions, orally and in writing, that if he were to undergo another cardiac failure he was to be allowed to die with no further effort to resuscitate him. Yet when there was another such episode the attending physician again took heroic measures and was again "successful."[28] Has a patient no right at all to say when or whether he wishes to undergo a procedure at the hands of his physician? It often seems that no such right is recognized.

Every experienced pastor and innumerable other people have observed extreme measures used by physicians in hospitals to extend the half life of people reduced to a level of existence worse than death. Thoughtful provisions made for surviving dependents are often used up in the heaping of indignities and pain upon him only for the unwanted prolonging of his dying.

Physicians must not suppose that I am writing with pretensions of moral superiority or that I do not appreciate the awesome, complicated, and harrowing responsibilities which they must frequently face in relation to these issues. On the contrary, I am deeply impressed with the conscientious and thoughtful responsibility which the doctors generally display, and with the excessively heavy moral burdens they must frequently bear. I write of these matters, rather, because I believe they should not carry these burdens alone. Other points of view besides the doctors' should be considered. Patients have a stake in these matters, as well as physicians. So also do nurses and the many persons who need medical care but who are not brought to the doctors' attention at all. It is the business of the moralist to consider such questions in the broadest possible perspective.

b. Maintaining Half Life. It is possible now to maintain some biological processes for months, sometimes for years, after all recognizable human personhood is gone. Artificial lungs, hemodialysis, transfusions, drainage through tubes in stomach and bladder, and other artificial devices can often keep blood flowing and lungs inhaling and exhaling for a long time after life has ceased to have positive meaning or value for the victim.

I am not here speaking of euthanasia, the deliberate taking of a person's life at his request or the request of next of kin when he is incapacitated for decision. This I oppose. Life is too sacred and the con-

28. "Not Allowed to Die," *British Medical Journal*, 17 Feb., 1968, p. 442.

fidence of every patient in the medical profession too sensitive and important to permit medical doctors serving at times as agents of death, however benevolent their motivation. The live ethical questions are at different points.[29]

c. The Right of a Patient to Decide.   One is the question whether a patient who engages the services of a physician and enters a hospital under his care loses thereafter the right to say whether he chooses to receive or not to receive specified further treatments which the doctor proposes. No sound ethical principle would support a doctor or hospital in assuming such loss of basic right. Primary responsibility for care of my body is my own.

If I have become mentally incapable of judging responsibly, my next of kin and the doctor may decide what is best for my interests. In the case of a treatment which offers some hope of curing my ailment or even, without cure, restoring me to such meaningful life as I could rationally choose to have, they ought to employ that treatment. If the treatment promises, at most, to prolong some of my vital processes without hope of my returning to meaningful, conscious life, or to restore consciousness but only for a period of great pain and continued deterioration until early death, then they are obligated to decide the issue on the basis of concern for my own best interests.

d. Bodily Life Not the Highest Good.   The American Medical Association referred some questions about treatment of terminally ill patients to Brian Whitlow, Dean of Christ Church Cathedral, Victoria, British Columbia, and to Fred Rosner, M.D., Division of Hematology, Maimonides Hospital, Brooklyn, New York. Dean Whitlow, in his thoughtful response, writes,

> The notion in much contemporary thought, that life as such (the vital or biological principle) is the highest good, is an error. It is far removed from the Christian view that there are many things more important than mere existence.[30]

I suppose that most people would agree that there are causes worth the cost of dying. We do honor martyrs of the state, of science, and of faith. There is in principle, then, a wide agreement that there are more important values than the continued biological existence of a human body.

It must be noted that in martyrdom the price is paid for the sake of

---

29. For thoughtful support of euthanasia and also useful discussion of other issues pertaining to medical attitudes toward death, see the publications of The Euthanasia Educational Fund, Inc., 250 West 57th St., New York, N.Y., 10019.

30. *Journal of the American Medical Association*, Oct. 23, 1967 (Vol. 202, No. 4), pp. 226–28.

values (such as freedom, truth, sanctity) to be experienced by other persons. There is nothing of value apart from actual or potential experience of a person—human, divine, or other if there be other. But a radical distinction must be made between the biological existence of a human body or its organs and the life of a person. A kidney, stomach, or heart kept biologically alive in a nutritive solution is obviously not a person. Neither is a larger part of the human body nor a whole body in which various biological processes are occurring to be equated with a living person. Such a body may exist without any sign that it embodies a person capable of desiring, suffering, appreciating, loving, or enjoying, that is capable of setting a value or disvalue on anything at all.

Again, a body may be so far deteriorated in vital functions that it is irreversibly moving to death. It now becomes possible for the physician to intervene and retard the process. Meanwhile, when the patient is conscious he may be plainly living a nightmarish existence, with anguished pain, with the sacrifice of personal dignity to helpless dependence on mechanical equipment and on other persons for care of his ordinary bodily functions, and with sustained processes of thought and communication impossible. The sheer maintenance of life in such a body is not necessarily a service of love to the patient or to his family.

e. Initial Presumption the Duty to Extend Life. Whenever a physician or anyone else faces a question what to do about an injured or ill individual, the initial presumption must be to sustain the life and to do all that is possible to restore it to health. The burden of proof is on the patient or doctor, next of kin or friend, who is making the decision, to show cause why such life-sustaining efforts should *not* be made. But there are many circumstances in which the necessary countermanding evidence is at hand.

When the patient himself is making or participating in the decision, his primary concerns must be for faithful stewardship of his earthly life and for love of others whom his life affects. He has not the right to despise and destroy the life which God has given. Even if life has become a burden to him, if he is still capable of receiving and communicating love and faith in relations with others who love him, he is morally bound to choose continued life. He may, however, decide, while he can rationally choose and clearly communicate his decision, that under certain predictably probable conditions the efforts to prolong his bodily life are to be discontinued. If he senses that death is near and he believes it is God's will that he now enter it, he may ask that no one interfere. If his choice has been rationally made, it should be respected. Indeed, if the ailment is believed by the doctor to be incurable, the physician has no right to force on the patient, under such circumstances, treatment which the patient has chosen to reject.

f. Ordinary and Extraordinary Treatment. Whitlow and many other churchmen have maintained a distinction between ordinary treatment and extraordinary or heroic treatment, the former being always obligatory, the latter optional under rare circumstances. Extraordinary treatment is understood to be "very costly, or very painful, or very difficult, or very dangerous." Certainly the difference must be taken into account.[31] The pain or danger attending a proposed treatment will be of concern to the patient and must be weighed in the balance against the possible hours or months of extended life the treatment might bring. So will the cost if financial means are not unlimited and survivors will genuinely need the money. Since these matters would be of concern to the patient, they must be also to others who may be compelled to decide in view of his incapacity to do so. Of course in the latter case, both the physician and the family must take heed to keep their own motives pure.

While the distinction is relevant and may be decisive in some cases, it is not conclusive in itself and in principle. Stewardship of life and love for others affected must be primary concerns. In relation to them empirical facts of the individual case must be decisive.

g. Restoring the Living, but "Only Caring for the Dying." As Paul Ramsey insists, we must never cease "caring for the dying"; but we are not always called upon to interfere with the process of dying. Indeed, love may dictate that we are not to interfere.[32] Similarly, Whitlow emphasizes that "essential medical or nursing care must always be given." On the other hand,

> If the Christian physician concludes that death, not recovery, is God's will for the patient, he will believe himself morally justified in ceasing to obstruct the process of dying and in beginning instead to cooperate with it.[33]

Without the theological language, Rosner adopts a similar position in his own report to the AMA. He says,

> Most people would probably agree that withholding of treatment or discontinuation of instrumentation and machinery in an incurably ill

31. For citations of some Jewish and Roman Catholic authorities who make this distinction decisive, see Robert B. Reeves, "Recognizing the Death of the Individual," in *The Right to Die with Dignity* (New York: The Euthanasia Educational Fund, 1969), p. 11.

32. Lecture on "Only Caring for the Dying," at Wesley Theological Seminary, May 14, 1969.

33. Report in the *Journal of the American Medical Association*, Oct. 23, 1967, pp. 226–28.

patient would be permitted if one were certain that in doing so, he is shortening the act of dying and not interrupting life.   [*Ibid.*]

The distinction made by Rosner, Whitlow, and Ramsey between shortening life and interfering with dying is helpful. But it seems to me not decisive. Every human being alive is inexorably set on the course of death. Most of us do not know what will finally deliver the fatal blow, but we are all on the way to it and no medical science can prevent it. All that medicine can do about the death of anyone is to delay it and perhaps ease the dying when it comes. But in most instances such inexorable coming on of death provides no reason for refusing treatment to slow the process and delay death.

It will be protested that there is a great difference in time here. Very well, then. How little time must there be of life in prospect before death, in order to permit the discontinuance of treatment to extend it? And by how much time must the treatment offer hope of extending it to make it ethically mandatory?

h. The Decisive Consideration.   A little thought will quickly show that time is not the decisive factor, though it is highly relevant when taken with other considerations. The decisive question must be: What quality of life is there hope of extending?

But can the doctor be sure that while extending bodily processes for a little time he or someone else may not find a further way of renewing meaningful and valued life once again? When there is reasonable doubt, certainly the initial presumption must hold. Treatment must be given. Reasonable doubt, however, does not include the theoretical possibility unsupported by facts, that an absolutely unexpected miracle might occur. No rational ethical decision can be based on such a consideration. We have to judge as reasonably as we can, on the basis of available evidence.

When a physician, patient, or relative must decide such a question, Christian faith offers an invaluable resource for meeting consequent anxieties of guilt. God who has offered us his love in Jesus Christ extends to us justification by grace through faith. Faith requires our humble, prayerful effort to be wholly obedient to his will. But we are not thereafter guilty before God if our best efforts fail.

i. True Obligation to the Dying Person.   To decide not to use treatment of an incurably ill person only for the hope of extending a life that is either meaningless or negative in meaning to him and his loved ones must not lead to his abandonment. The obligation to love and care for the dying is as deep and is even more urgent than such concerns for others, because the patient's need is more poignant and the time to show concern for him is short. To love and care for the patient who is dying is the one all-inclusive obligation to him.

A right which is too little observed in these materialistic, body-oriented days is the right to be respected and so to die with all the dignity and all the communication of love which the condition of the patient will permit. Here again it must be insisted that the life of the body is not all-important. Because physicians, by the nature of their work, tend to make it so, the hospital room of a dying man is often more like a biology laboratory than the chamber of a child of God. Wife or husband and family may even be sent out so that they will not be in the way of all the apparatus.

The physician tends to be preoccupied with postponing death and to regard the death of a patient as defeat for himself. A distinguished physician writes,

> The personal threat that death presents for the physician can best be illustrated by the enormous activity that goes on in hospitals in prolongation of life and which acts as a mechanical barrier to the patient himself. We are all familiar with the apparatus that in American hospitals stands between the patient and the physician, and also between the patient and the family.[34]

Certainly when the incurably ill patient is in intense pain and wants sleep-inducing relief, relief should be administered. But while he is conscious, it is far more important that such a patient be in fellowship with his loved ones than that technical means be employed in hope of postponing a little further the processes now pushing him irreversibly away from even partial recovery. Love is for the loving, aspiring person, not for a mere body.

j. The Right to the Truth.   The initial presumption should always favor the doctor's telling the truth to his patient—directly or through a chosen mediary. Indeed, if one had to choose one way or the other, it would be better for all physicians always to tell patients the truth, with care and concern, yes, but the truth, rather than to have the predominant evasion and withholding of truth which now prevail.

Thomas P. Hackett says, "One hundred years ago every physician told his patient the truth. Nowadays about 30–40% do." He adds, "Dr. Herman Feifel has shown that while 69–90% of doctors do not tell their patients the truth, 78–89% of these patients desire to know the truth."[35] Hackett reports a current trend toward more truth-telling by physicians, a trend which he emphatically supports.

34. Charles H. Goodrich, M.D., "Educating the Medical Profession about Death," in *The Right to Die with Dignity*.
35. "Current Approaches to the Care and Understanding of the Dying Patient: Overview of a Conference." *Archives of the Foundation of Thanatology* (New York: Foundation of Thanatology, Vol. 1. No. 3 Oct. 1, 1969), p. 110. Cf. Frederic P. Herter, M.D., "The Right to Die in Dignity." *Ibid.*, pp. 93–97.

There are, it is true, irrational or seriously neurotic patients who might speedily become much worse or even die of heart failure if told the truth. But such cases should be regarded as the exception. Most people have remarkable capacity to meet a crisis of life and death when they know the facts about their situation.

For the serious Christian the knowledge that death is near provides opportunity for some of the most effective testimonies of faith. When once it is granted that the life of the body is not the ultimate good, then it should be apparent that the soul—the living, aware person who relates in love or anger, hope or despair to other persons and to God—has claim to the truth which usually supersedes any real or presumed danger the truth might offer to the doomed body.

The withholding of truth keeps from the patient what is due to him as a person, and so prevents his making decisions and performing acts in full view of reality. It also isolates him psychologically from people around him at the very time when he needs them most. In the misguided effort to shield him, doctor and family and friends spread around him a curtain of evasion. Again and again, first as son of a father who slowly died at fifty-one, and later as a pastor and friend of many dying persons, I have been told by the fatally ill that they felt this isolation and the need for someone who would talk with them openly. In many instances, probably most, a person fully conscious when coming near death knows it or at least deeply suspects it. Other people try to hide the truth from him. He thinks they do not want to face it and so he joins in the evasion. Thus they play games with each other instead of meeting in the full light of truth and seeking each other's love and God's grace together in conquest of death.

k. The Test of Faith.   The way in which doctor, patient, and loved ones deal with dying expresses as clearly as any decision we ever make our understanding of life and our ultimate faith. If the life of the body is ultimate, if as people often say, "the main thing is to keep your health," then death is simply defeat. One can understand why a person who believes that might sacrifice truth, dignity, fellowship with family and friends, and funds long saved for a loved one's support, to fend off the enemy until the last possible minute. Yet even then it would seem more worthy of a man or woman to accept that final defeat for what it is believed to be than to evade it or pretend that life was still going on as long as some machinery could keep blood flowing and cells alive in a miserable remnant of the body.

But if one is a Christian or anyone who believes that bodily life is not ultimate and that death has not the last word, then radical revision is needed in our common present attitudes toward death and many current decisions about care for the dying.

chapter fourteen

The State

———•◦⟨∞⟩◦•———

A. Its Use of Power

In modern life the state is extremely important and continues to increase in its relations to various human interests. This trend seems to advance inevitably in the complex and widely interrelated character of modern life. An irony of the present day is that the very people who most angrily declaim against "statism" also call most loudly for "law and order" and for increased governmental powers to enforce law.

The question of the proper province of government and the relation of its basic responsibilities to its use of power is an ethical question about which a number of views have been held.

1. Machiavelli's View of Amoral Power

In his *Discourse on Livy* and private correspondence, as well as in his more dramatic and well-known work *The Prince*, Niccolo Machiavelli set forth a plausible and influential philosophy of government. The supreme good of the state, according to this view, is the maintenance of order in society. To secure this end, the ruler must have power to punish lawbreakers, to repulse invasion, and to prevent dissident factions from disrupting the order. The use of power must be so aggressive and ruthless that potential rebels will be deterred.

Machiavelli thought that in quiet times a broad sharing of power with the people would be good, and the more the better. But order must take precedence over freedom and all other goods. Unfortunately, the conditions present in his own time were far from peaceful and the luxuries of freedom and mercy could not be permitted. If the ruling prince is soft and restrained, violent challenges are likely to arise and plunge the country into civil war. It is better that the prince should use every available device, not hesitating to deceive, spy, and even murder members of his own family, in order to strengthen and extend his own monopoly of coercive power. It is better that a few should thus die than that the whole country should be plunged into a bloody civil war.

Christian standards of conduct are good for personal relationships. But woe be to the state ruled by a prince who tries to apply Christian standards to affairs of state. In the end the people of such a state are likely to pay with their blood and treasure for the misguided mercy which allows crime to flourish, revolutions to be incited, and ambitious invaders to violate her territory.

2. Tolstoi's Pacifist Anarchism

It is a long jump in time and spirit from Machiavelli to Lev N. Tolstoi. Yet there is a broad base of agreement between the two men. Tolstoi agrees that the existence of the state depends on raw power. This may appear in the form of armies or of police, but they are ethically the same. Both have the function of enforcing the sovereign law of the state and to maintain that law must use as much and as ruthless force as the seriousness of the challenge requires.

Tolstoi and Machiavelli agree also that there is a radical conflict between the precepts of Christianity and the necessary use of force by the state. But whereas Machiavelli concludes that it is so much the worse for Christianity, Tolstoi advocates rather the giving up of the state. He holds that when people were troubled by the crimes of their neighbors against them they should have turned the other cheek and spoken gentle words of love as Christ commanded. Instead, they joined with other neighbors in hiring thugs (police, soldiers, and hangmen) to do for them the dirty work of beating offenders against them into submission. This appeared to work rather well in the neighborhood, aggressive violations of neighbors and property being put down or kept under control. But alas! Whereas Christ's method of nonresistant love removes the sinful hostility which is the cause of the trouble, the method of organized group violence only suppresses some of the sin while extending belief in violence. So neighborhoods have found themselves in violent conflict with other neighborhoods. Then it seemed that what was needed was a superpolice force. Thus the units of violent force went from clans to tribes to city-states to confederations of city-states and to the great modern states. Now when these states go to war with each other the violence is worse than ever. The solution is not to proceed with the formation of international leagues or superstates. Rather we should dissolve the whole apparatus of the state and return to the direct relations of neighbor with neighbor, there to turn away wrath with gentleness and overcome evil with love.[1]

3. Brunner's View of the State as Necessary Evil

Emil Brunner, too, contrasts the state's use of "the sword" with Christian *agape*. But he acknowledges that the world is not Christian and does not live by *agape*. The Christian, going from the Church out into the world, enters an alien territory where sin and force rule. Yet he should acknowledge that the state, sword and all, is God's appointed instrument preserving men and even protecting the Church in the midst of a sinful world. The state is thus seen as a kind of necessary evil which for our sinful condition is relatively good.[2] One is not to expect nor attempt the forming of governmental law by reference to *agape*.

4. Inadequacy of These Views

All the theories of the state we have mentioned thus far include a view of the relation between the state and power which is far simpler than the reality. All consequently underestimate grossly the degree to which grace and the kingdom of political law interpenetrate and the larger degree to which it is possible to introduce grace and *agape* into the state.

No state can depend wholly on physical coercion to enforce its laws and maintain its rule. A number of people, and in a great modern state a very large number of people, must be willing to join in enforcing the laws. In 1968, there were in the United States, 408,286 state and local policemen, or more than one to every five hundred people. In addition, we must consider the more than three million men under arms and the additional millions of reserves and National Guardsmen.[3] Obviously no single ruler nor minute coterie compels all these millions by force to don military or police uniforms. There are various kinds of coercion, it is true, and several are used to obtain quotas for the armed services. But if most people did not, on the whole, believe in the usefulness and essential validity of the government it could not be made to stand by force. Even under a dictatorship,

1. While these themes run through various writings, the best introduction to Tolstoi's basic philosophy of anarchistic pacifism is *The Kingdom of God is Within You*.

2. *The Christian Doctrine of the Church, Faith, and the Consummation*. Dogmatics: Vol. III (Philadelphia: The Westminster Press, 1962), pp. 310–13. Cf. *Justice and the Social Order* (New York: Harper & Row, 1945) and *The Divine Imperative* (New York: The Macmillan Company, 1942), Chaps. 36–37.

3. *Statistical Abstract*, 1970, pp. 150, 255.

great numbers of people must serve willingly and most people must obey most of the laws voluntarily if order is to be maintained. An army of one country may occupy another and cow its people into submission, but such government by a foreign occupying force is not a state.

5. MacIver's Account of the State

To understand the nature of modern states, we could hardly do better than to observe Robert M. MacIver's account. As he describes it, the state is not the society, "not even the *form* of society." It is one of the associations within society, though the most inclusive and in some respects the all-inclusive one. "Its achievement is a system of order and control. The state in a word regulates the outstanding external relationships of men and society."[4] The life of the society is not created by the state and is never wholly controlled by it (*The Modern State*, pp. 5, 7). To some extent, at least, the state is itself formed by traditions, customs, ideas, and the style of its people which were present before it came into being. In one sense only, the state is all-inclusive.

> By its very nature the state must include under its control all persons who live within its territorial bounds, whether they are properly members of the state or not.   [*Ibid.*, pp. 7–8]

Because the state must possess the supreme human power in its territory in order to be the state, its very nature is often taken to be power. Augustine knew better when he said that states without justice were only "gangs of robbers" (*The City of God*). MacIver puts it well when he says, "Coercive power is a criterion of the state, but not its essence" (*op. cit.*, p. 223). Laws are obeyed and order kept more by training, conviction, and public opinion than by coercive force. The more of such voluntary and intangible social order there is, the less coercion there needs to be and the more free is the society.

When there are gross inequities of opportunity and participation in the goods of the society, more coercion is needed to maintain order. If its rulers are wise they will seek, not simply to defend a static order, but to change the laws with changing conditions in constant effort to meet the needs and reasonable expectations of all its people. Only through such movement can a state keep inwardly strong in a changing society.

4. *The Modern State* (London: Oxford University Press, 1926), p. 5. Cf. his later book, *The Web of Government* (New York: The Macmillan Company, 1947), pp. 87–94.

6. The Modern State and Christian Love

a. The State's Need of Coercive Power.   If all citizens were angelic in Christian love, many functions of the state would still be needed. Traffic would still need to be directed according to uniform regulations. Orderly public transportation, education, water supplies, sewage disposal, maintenance of streets, parks, the limited available wavebands for radio and television, these and many other functions would still require control by a public agency or agencies of some kind. Even if character and motives were perfect, there would still be a wide disagreement about the wisest way of managing many of these things. Somewhere even a society of saints would of necessity place responsibility and commensurate authority to decide which of the various rival schemes would be adopted. Then, presumably, all the saints would obey the regulations for the good of all.

In the real world, Tolstoi's program would lead quickly to disaster. If all the people who want peace and reconciliation were to renounce police power, this would not be the end of the coercive state. Even if there were no invasion from without, some gang of self-seeking men would begin threatening and robbing their neighbors. Soon the gang would have been set up as the ultimate coercive power of the area—perhaps after a bloody warfare between rival gangs. The last state in that society would be much worse than the one which the idealistic anarchists had persuaded to die. Actually there is no danger of this happening because states do not voluntarily yield to anarchy.

Does this mean that Christ's precepts are impractical? If one takes them to be laws, yes. But they were not so intended, as we saw earlier. If we understand the words about loving enemies and turning cheeks to be rather symbols of a life style, then they have much to teach us, not only about one-to-one relations between individuals, but also about the state.

b. Love's Requirements of the State.   Love requires the state to enforce laws for the protection of the weak against strong predators, to enable industry and commerce to operate with confidence, to prevent general disorder from disrupting the peaceful pursuit of family life, religious observance, and processes of democratic political decision, and in general to make possible a broad sharing of opportunity and value in the society. The enforcement of law requires the use of such coercive force as proves necessary to maintain order. A government by laws can neither gain nor long retain actual authority without securing and being prepared to use as much coercive force as necessary to put down any forces which violate its laws or challenge its rule within its sphere of authority.

At the same time, love requires the most strenuous efforts to minimize the coercive force required. There must be a constant search for alternatives to hurtful use of force. Such alternatives to be sought are adequate information to all segments of the community, two-way communication so that officials will be aware of grievances and tensions, and provision for adequate education, employment and active recreation for all, especially for energetic and adventuresome youth. When force must be used, the injury of people by it is to be kept at the lowest possible level. Thus, verbal command is preferred to physical seizure, grasping to clubbing, tear gas to shooting. Similarly, when feasible the securing of court appearance by summons alone is better than seizure; bail or bond is better than holding in jail. When record of conviction alone is enough, mere filing without sentence is good. When a stronger hold on the offender is needed, a suspended sentence may be used. When further direct punishment is required, fine is better than imprisonment. When more personal punishment is needed, imprisonment is not to be used unless probation with or without supervision is believed to be ineffective for protecting the public order. Of course when there must be imprisonment it must be as short and benign as possible to accomplish the purpose.

In the whole matter of law enforcement the Christian must live with an uneasy conscience. Too little force gives too much rein to violence and in the end injures everyone. Too much does undue injury to the convicted persons, spreads resentment and strain in society, reduces respect for human life and freedom, and tends to increase public trust in violence. The calculus of the right measure is a difficult art, at best uncertain.

It must be emphasized that love seeks always to get at the source of individual or social trouble and to serve the human needs discovered. Considering the task of maintaining order, then, we are led to see in larger perspective the total work of the state, which includes many other tasks. Even if it sought only to maintain order, the state could not do that for long without doing much more.

B. Dual Functions of the State

1. Messner's Natural Law Theory

Johannes Messner, applying traditional natural law concepts to the modern conditions, defines the state as a community constituted by a people inhabiting a definite area and endowed with supreme authority for the all-round establishment of its common good.[5]

The state's fundamental function "of establishing and safeguarding the legal order is the prerequisite for all other characteristic activity of the state" (*ibid.*, p. 544). But it has much more to do.

> The end of the state is not confined to the preservation of law and order; in addition, it consists in making possible the fulfillment of all the existential ends of its citizens.

This broad second function Messner calls "the welfare function" (*ibid.*). It must be observed, however, that this is much more inclusive than what Americans commonly call welfare in political context.

2. The Limited Authority of the State

Messner's basic theory of the state seems generally sound. We must make two reservations about his initial definition, however. First, Mac-Iver is right in insisting that the state is not the community, but is an association within it, since the community includes many other associations which are not parts of the state. Second, the state is not "endowed with supreme authority," but only with the most inclusive human authority in the area of its jurisdiction. For earnest Christians, Jews, and many other religious people, God alone has supreme authority. Moreover, in some restricted matters, great numbers of citizens would regard other human authorities as taking precedence over the state. Indeed, it is because of this fact that when it is wisely led the state seeks to avoid invading too deeply the provinces commonly assigned to such other authorities as the church and the family.[6]

Roman Catholic thinking in the present more progressive mode would concur with these reservations, and like traditional Protestant thought is especially concerned to defend the integrity and freedom of individual conscience. Thus Charles E. Curran writes,

> Modern political thought also emphasizes the freedom and respon-

5. *Social Ethics: Natural Law in the Western World*, tr. by J. J. Doherty, rev. ed. (St. Louis: B. Herder Book Co., 1965), p. 542.

6. For an excellent Protestant view of the state, its responsibilities and proper limits, see Philip Wogaman, *Protestant Faith and Religious Liberty* (Nashville: Abingdon Press, 1967), especially "V. The Responsible State in Protestant Perspective," pp. 148–80.

sibility of the individual person. People are citizens and no longer subjects whose lives are completely governed by those in authority.[7]

There is a complex relation between the broadly inclusive functions of the modern state and the freedom of the individual. On the one hand, the broad services of the state enable it to remove sources of tension and demoralization in society, thus decreasing the need for coercive restriction of freedom. On the other hand, as the activities of government become more various and inclusive, less room is left for the operation of other associations. The totalitarian Nazi and Fascist states provided horrible examples of such encroachment upon the liberties of church, labor union, and other free associations. Similar examples are present in the various Communist states, although with more of partially compensating services to the people.

The problem for citizens of the modern state is to use the state for the largest possible securing of human rights in a broad spectrum and to avoid so fattening its coercive powers, in the process, that individual liberty and the freedom of other associations are stifled. To look more closely at this problem we must examine the nature and scope of human rights.

C. Human Rights

The idea of human rights or "the rights of man" has come down to us from the Stoics through the long tradition of natural law. Through the work of John Locke a statement of such rights appeared in the famous Bill of Rights enacted by the English Parliament in 1689. Another statement of them appeared in the Virginia Bill of Rights of June, 1776. Then, in July of that year, appeared the momentous words of the American Declaration of Independence:

> We hold these Truths to be self-evident, that all Men are created equal, that they are endowed by their Creator with certain unalienable Rights, that among these are Life, Liberty, and the Pursuit of Happiness.

This notion of inherent human rights has become so powerful that most political constitutions drafted in the present century make reference to them. It might surprise some Americans and also some Russians to learn that the Constitution of the Soviet Union, in Article 125, states:

7. *Christian Morality Today*, p. 30. Of course we are frequently reminded that we are subjects as well as citizens, for we are subject to the laws enacted by the government in which we participate as citizens.

The citizens of the U.S.S.R. are guaranteed by law (a) freedom of speech; (b) freedom of the press; (c) freedom of assembly, including the holding of mass meetings; (d) freedom of street processions and demonstrations.[8]

Under the chairmanship of Eleanor Roosevelt, the United Nations Commission on Human Rights recommended, and the United Nations Assembly adopted in 1948, the "Universal Declaration of Human Rights."[9] While the Preface speaks of "equal and inalienable rights of all members of the human family," the first paragraph of the Declaration proper describes it as "a common standard of achievement for all peoples and all nations" and speaks of the aim that all individuals and organizations "shall strive by teaching and education to promote respect for these rights and freedoms," and to achieve their full realization in all "Member States."

The Declaration was intended, then, to be both a statement of inherent natural law rights and a commitment to promote the striving for their realization as a goal. The Declaration was not an enactment into positive law—even such positive law as the United Nations could legislate. Unfortunately, from the beginning there was much ambiguity, yes, even hypocrisy, in the attitudes of many national representatives toward it. The Western Powers were eager to include their traditional statements of civil liberties which embarrassed the Communists. The latter were eager to include the universal "right to work," and other economic guarantees which have seemed more important to Communists than the freedoms which, though stated in the U.S.S.R. Constitution, are more at home in the West. When the Covenants which were supposed to provide legislative support for the Declaration were taken up, there was consequently much foot-dragging all round. The United States, no less than the Soviet Union, refused to support even the enacting Covenant on political rights (or civil liberties), to say nothing of a second Covenant on economic and social rights. The United States has never signed either Covenant. In 1969 fifty-two Soviet citizens courageously appealed to the U.N. to note widespread violation of the Declaration in the U.S.S.R. The U.N. could only show the appeal to the Soviet government and notify the petitioners of its powerlessness to act.

For all that, the whole Declaration states rather accurately the demands of people around the world so far as they have moved into the modern industrial era. The declared economic and social rights to

8. Text quoted from the useful book by Maurice Cranston, *What Are Human Rights?* (New York: Basic Books, 1962), p. 6.

9. A convenient place to read the text, together with a critical history and commentary, is the book by Maurice Cranston, to which reference was made above.

work, paid holidays, health care, security in case of disability, old age, or the like, and free education, no less than the rights to free speech, assembly, worship, and petition, make rapidly mounting appeal to the conscience, as well as the desire of mankind. Nearly every government in the world is subject to increasing internal pressure to honor them.

D. Civil Disobedience

1. Its Seriousness

We have observed that even the much imprisoned Apostle Paul had high regard for civil law and urged Christians to be law-abiding citizens under the rule of imperial Rome, pagan and oppressive though it was.

There is more reason for respecting the law in the United States. Most American adults have had opportunity, whether used or not, to participate in the process of making laws and choosing the men to enforce them. We are not living under a foreign power imposed upon us from without. Moreover, there are few of us, indeed, even in the most abused minority groups, who do not depend upon and profit by some services of government.

The alternative to law-abiding order must also be considered. If this order were to be broken down generally, business and transportation would be quickly disrupted. In the cities where most of our people live, food would soon become unavailable. In a common scramble for life's necessities, the strong and ruthless would plunder and destroy, while the weak and helpless would be trampled under foot. Widespread civil disturbance would be far more destructive than in former years, because elaborate industrialization and dense population have established such a delicate fabric of complex interdependence. To take part in breaking down respect for law is an exceedingly serious act.

Actually, if disobedience to law becomes so massive as to threaten a complete breakdown of the social order, there will certainly be a powerful reaction, with suspension of civil liberties and massive use of armed police and troops to control the outbreak. Every act of disobedience to law is in danger of serving as part of a provocation to establishment of a fascist police state.

Why, then, would intelligent and idealistic people who wish to uphold civil liberties and personal rights ever advocate the deliberate violation of law? Most lawbreaking is, of course, indefensible private action for selfish purpose, an expression of impatience, anger, lust, or greed. Some of it is deliberately organized by an underworld of crime for profit. The civil disorders in a number of American cities during recent years have much more complex causes. Both crime and civil disorders are to be examined later. At present we are concerned with the different, often opposite, acts of rationally deliberate, conscientious disobedience to law.

2. Reasons for Civil Disobedience

It is plain that in Paul's experience the authorities did not punish only what Paul regarded as evil, nor did he meekly do only what the lawful authorities permitted. There was already good precedent. Peter and John had stirred riotous responses to their public speeches, so the Sanhedrin had arrested them and commanded them to stop. When they were arrested again and rebuked for their disobedience, "Peter and the apostles answered, 'We must obey God rather than men.' "[10] Even before that Jesus himself had performed an act of flagrant illegality. When he drove the merchants out of the temple and "overturned the tables of the money changers" there, he was directly challenging the economic, religious, and political establishment of Judea (Mark 11:15–17). Obviously such action as his would be contrary to law in any country. In the early centuries of the Church, Christians were frequently violating the laws of Rome, usually in secret, but sometimes in public defiance.

American Christians have conscientiously violated laws for three different reasons in varying circumstances.

a. Testing and Overthrowing Invalid Laws. In the United States many laws have been passed by municipalities and states in violation of the federal Constitution or of state constitutions. Although invalid, these laws have been enforced for generations, especially against blacks who, without votes or money, were powerless to resist them. On many occasions since the 1950's such laws have been deliberately violated by people of prominence, after arranging for ample witnesses, and sometimes after making advance arrangements also for legal counsel. The violators of these spurious laws have been arrested and convicted. Then they have appealed, sometimes all the way to the U.S. Supreme Court, which has then invalidated the laws. Ordinarily, there is no way to test a law believed to be unconstitutional excepting by such violation and appeal.

In such cases it may be argued that there has not been any real law-breaking because the statute or ordinance violated was not a true law at all. In a proper sense this is true. However, the statutes were called laws, had been long enforced as laws, and their violation was usually denounced angrily by respected people in the community as "law-

10. Acts 5:29. Cf. 4:18–19.

breaking," "criminal behavior," and the like. Moreover, although men and women who engage in such violations are advised by good legal counsel that the obnoxious law is unconstitutional, the courts may finally decide otherwise. In such an instance, not only may the violator be required finally to serve a sentence, but, contrary to his intention, he will find that he has broken a genuine law. Yet without such risks, innumerable injustices are perpetuated and the lawlessness of legislators and enforcement officers goes uncorrected.

b. In Forced Dilemmas of Conscience. "We must obey God rather than men." When an earnest Christian must make a choice, he should follow the example of Peter and his companions. If the state commands what the citizen is convinced God forbids, and the citizen obeys the state, he has made the state his God. "One nation under God," to quote the American Pledge of Allegiance, is not for him, since he has placed the nation above God.

The principle that under some circumstances a citizen is obligated to disobey law, even in the armed services, has been given increasingly impressive acknowledgment, even in political circles of late. After World War II the United States actively supported a movement in the United Nations to bring to trial various German Nazis for acts of crime "under international law." The International Law Commission established for the purpose formulated seven Principles to govern the Nuremberg Tribunal in the trials. They are all worth recalling, but I quote only Principle IV, one of the Principles especially relevant to the obligation of an individual to violate the commands of his own Government:

> The fact that a person acted pursuant to order of his Government or a superior does not relieve him from responsibility under international law, provided a moral choice was in fact possible to him.[11]

Under this provision many men were, in fact, judged guilty and hanged or sentenced to terms of imprisonment.

The Law of Land Warfare, U.S. Department of the Army Field Manual No. 27-10, similarly acknowledges the personal responsibility of individuals for their conduct, even in the armed forces and in combat. Thus, it declares,

> Any person, whether a member of the armed forces or a civilian, who commits an act which constitutes a crime under international law is responsible therefor and liable to punishment.[12]

11. As formulated by the International Law Commission, June–July 1950. Text taken from *In the Name of America* (New York: Clergy and Laymen Concerned About Vietnam, 1968), p. 43.
12. Section II, Article 498. Text from *In the Name of America*, p. 53.

In a subsequent article (501) it is made clear that when subordinate soldiers commit war crimes, the responsibility may rest with their commanders as well as "with the actual perpetrators." But nowhere is the individual freed from responsibility for his own conduct.

Now what of the young man who is ordered by his Selective Service Board to report for induction into the armed services, but who is convinced that to do so is to make himself liable to participation in war crimes—whether in the legal sense or in the religious and moral sense? It may be replied that provision has been made for conscientious objectors and he should take advantage of these provisions. He may try. However, many such young men have found that their conscientious scruples did not satisfy either their draft boards or the appeal boards.

This is especially common for the many young men who are so-called "selective objectors." They are not absolute pacifists. If their country were actually attacked, they would be willing to defend it. But they see the American armed forces of today serving very different functions in distant places around the world. Many of the regimes which they see the armed forces directly or indirectly supporting, from Franco's government in Spain to the Thieu-Ky government in Saigon, they regard as oppressive, inhumane, and unworthy of American military defense. From the news they know that if they once enter the armed services, they will be subject to strict military law and despite the Army Manual's warnings of individual responsibility for war crimes, they will be very severely punished for refusing to perform any act commanded, even if it is clearly a war crime as defined by international law and the Manual. Under such circumstances they are forced to decide now between unconditional subordination to a military rule they regard as evil in its main contemporary action and, on the other hand, saying, "I must obey God rather than men."

This is the most common case of conscientious disobedience in forced dilemmas in the United States, but there are others. In Communist countries many Christians have been forced to choose between worshiping God and obeying the state. In China and especially in North Korea, the choice of worship has led frequently, perhaps usually, to death. Such acts of disobedience are regarded by Americans generally as heroic and admirable. But the principle is precisely the same when our own government forces a choice between Christian obedience and acts which seem to a citizen to be acts of infidelity to God and to humanity.

c. Means of Revolutionary Change. The United States gained independence through revolution against the English Crown. Leading up to the actual war were acts of deliberate refusal to pay taxes, to obey British officials, and to acknowledge the authority of laws made in London. The Boston Tea Party was a particularly well-known act of civil disobedience with the intent of bringing about revolutionary change. There was still hope that by this dramatic act Parliament would be persuaded to correct the American grievances. When such efforts failed, direct and violent force began to be used.

When Mohandas K. Gandhi led his massive campaign of civil disobedience in India, he was escalating his demands for justice from petitions and lawsuits to dramatic and dangerous, though intentionally nonviolent action. As he and his followers made salt by evaporation at the seashore, in defiance of the law, it was not because of a forced dilemma nor to have a law declared invalid. It was to compel the British government to face the embarrassment of Indian jails filled with people for the "crime" of making salt. By a long series of such embarrassments Gandhi finally persuaded the British to grant India independence.

Even in a democracy the majority may impose on a minority conditions which are intolerable. Despite petitions and campaigns of political persuasion, lawsuits and appeals, the injustices may remain uncorrected. What then should the aggrieved minority do? Or suppose it is a disenfranchised majority, like the Africans of South Africa or Rhodesia. Is there any sound Christian principle which limits gravely mistreated bodies of citizens, whether minorities or majorities, to methods of protest legally permitted by their oppressors?

Certainly anyone in such circumstances who considers massive civil disobedience must think of the grave danger that this will deteriorate into violence and massive bloodshed. He must weigh the question whether so much of violence is being done to human beings under present law as to merit the risk of greater violence in revolutionary action.

In present-day America, the social system is itself doing great violence to many of the black and the poor, a violence in which churchmen who abhor violence unwittingly participate.[13] Condemning children to live in rat-infested tenements, to be permanently handicapped physically and mentally by low-protein diet, to have self-respect crushed by racist attitudes, or to be bullied and sometimes killed by sadistic and prejudiced police—this is violence and it is intolerable to Christian conscience. Such violence justifies radical protest and drastic means of change. However, it is still necessary to calculate the best means for redressing the wrong with a minimum of damage to people —especially the people now suffering most.

Important in this calculus must be the question whether all peaceful

13. Cf. J. Edward Carothers, *The Churches and Cruelty Systems* (New York: Friendship Press, 1970).

and legal channels of redress have been exhausted. A resort to deliberate violence is bound to set back so badly every legitimate purpose of the protesters as to be clearly unjustified unless it is a last resort and the way can be seen through it to a quick end with less damage to people than is being done by the present evil condition. The use of massive, legal demonstrations has helped greatly to move this country along toward justice. Some small-scale civil disobedience deliberately designed to focus attention and stir action may be useful in some places and times in this country, but there are more promising channels open and used only to a fraction of their potential.

In short, harm to human beings should be kept to a minimum. Where great violence is now done to people by present conditions, action must be taken to correct it. That course of action should be taken which promises to do least harm and bring most good. Initial presumption is strongly against violent revolution anywhere. Initial presumption opposes also civil disobedience which is not forced or aimed at the invalidity of laws by court tests. But there have been and doubtless will be again conditions where any one of these options may involve a smaller total of injury to people than letting the status quo continue or using any alternative method for attempted redress.

E. PENAL JUSTICE

The Christian Gospel is concerned, at its very heart, with the treatment of the wrongdoer. God's justice and his forgiving love, man's humble repentance, his grateful receiving of God's grace, and his generous, forgiving, sharing love for his neighbors—these are the great Christian themes. It is especially strange, therefore, that most books on Christian ethics have little or nothing to say about the meaning of doing justice to the person labeled as wrongdoer by human courts of law. Moreover, this is an important and timely subject for consideration.

1. The Present Crisis in Penal Justice

The enlarging scope of civil law, increasing crime rates, growing complexity of legal procedures, and other factors have brought a serious crisis in penal justice. More serious than most conditions receiving more publicity is a deep confusion regarding the question what is true justice to the convicted violator of criminal law. Both in the general public and in the legal profession there is much difference of opinion and no little confusion regarding the purpose of penal justice. The question, What is a just sentence? will elicit a variety of answers, often inconsistently held.

The question is vitally important to all the work of the state. A private charity can solicit all the people for gifts to aid the handicapped; but only the government can tax the people, thus *compelling* them to contribute to this cause. The National Safety Council can urge all drivers and pedestrians not to venture on the streets under the influence of alcoholic liquor; but only the state can *command* such cautions. The unique power of the state to do the many things we ask of it depends upon its ability to invoke penalties against those who disobey its commands.

But how do we, including the sentencing judge, determine *what* penalties are appropriate? What is justice to the lawbreaker? Because of the widespread confusion on this subject, the processes of criminal justice do not have the public support which they need to be effective. Many people do not wish to cooperate with the police because they think that even if there is a conviction, the judge will not be severe enough to make the effort worthwhile. Others refrain from cooperating because they do not wish to have part in a process which may result in merciless, vindictive injury to some poor unfortunate person. Yet others think of the whole procedure of prosecution and punishment as confused and irrational. Such lack of public confidence reflects confusion and conflicts of aim in the judicial process itself. If we are to have a stable and orderly society, one of the necessities is a stabilized understanding of penal justice, both in the judicial system and among other citizens whose intelligent cooperation is indispensable.

2. Simple Current Theories of Penal Justice

a. Legal Positivism. Among lawyers, justice is frequently defined as the prescription of positive law; that is, whatever the law requires is what is meant by justice. If the legislator then wishes to know what penalty would justly be prescribed for a criminal offense being newly defined by a statute now being drafted, he is told by the legal positivist that it would be the penalty which previously enacted statutes, the precedents of court decisions, and the present trends of customary practice would lead an intelligent lawyer to expect.

Advantages of continuity in society commend this view, but it comes near to idolizing the status quo or at least the present trends in a society. When neither the past nor the present trends are adequate, we need to look deeper than the positivists would recommend.

Moreover, there are so many diverse trends to which appeal could be made that different jurists who alike subscribe to this theory actually appeal covertly to some ideals of their own to decide the issue. Morris R. Cohen, a searching critic of legal positivism, points out that those who oppose "all natural law or normative jurisprudence" may be found "implicitly assuming some ideal of what the law should be, often some idealization of the status quo."[14] Besides the inadequacy of such a method for meeting new problems or for making advance, Cohen observes that the failure to state explicitly the ideals implied leaves them without critical examination.

Benjamin N. Cardozo protests the tendency of legal positivism to foster in society "distrust and contempt of law as something to which morality and justice are not merely alien, but hostile."[15] He welcomes the renewal of interest in natural law as a basis for positive law despite the too rigid terms in which natural law is commonly stated. For the legal profession does need to renew the search for norms of true justice and right by which to evaluate critically the structure and proposed changes of positive law.

b. Retribution. In popular discussion of legal cases, in appeals to juries by prosecuting attorneys, and in conventional Roman Catholic writing on the subject, the *Lex Talionis* is still the dominant notion of justice.[16] Justice is giving the criminal "his due." It is making the punishment fit the crime in a quantitative sense. This view is symbolized by the bas relief on many courthouses depicting a blindfolded goddess (no respecter of persons) holding a pair of scales. In one pan the criminal has put his offense. Now the court must place in the other an equivalent punishment so that the scales will balance.

Emil Brunner contends that the Gospel requires, not the abolition of the *Lex Talionis*, but a refinement of it to take account of the intention as well as the outward act of the wrongdoer. "By its very nature," he says, "justice is proportion, like for like." Hence

> one thing is clear; reform or improvement can never be the determining principle of punishment. The sole and exclusive principle of punishment is and remains atonement, that is, the restoration of order by symbolic restitution.[17]

Perhaps it is not strange, then, that Brunner even regards capital punishment—in which the principle of retribution cannot be adulterated with notions of rehabilitation—as especially "the expression of God's holy wrath" (*ibid.*, p. 223).

I fear that in speaking thus, as often in his ethical writing, Brunner was reading the New Testament through a very thick lens of aristo-

14. In Joseph W. Bingham *et. al.*, *My Philosophy of Law* (Boston: Boston Law Book Co., 1941), p. 35. Bingham defends a form of legal positivism in the same volume.

15. *The Nature of the Judicial Process* (New Haven: Yale University Press, 1928), p. 134.

16. Cf. Messner, *op. cit.*, pp. 645–46.

17. *Justice and the Social Order* (New York: Harper & Row, 1945), p. 224.

cratic Swiss legalism. If he had had pastoral experience inside a prison, and studied the case records of the living persons whom he was so well satisfied to see getting their due, he must surely have been compelled to revise such opinions. We can agree with his stressing that every sane person is responsible for his acts and yet find many levels of accountability for the same intended kind of act and many degrees of shared responsibility among other elements in the community. A little Christian humility would then make the identification of human executions with "God's holy wrath" stick in one's throat.

Indeed, we are now near the heart of a very serious objection to the retributive theory of penal justice. By what right of sublime wisdom can any man presume to judge the moral desert of another? I am not here questioning the propriety and necessity of having human judges. But is the true moral responsibility and desert what a human court properly tries to determine? What man knows the powers of discernment or the measure of volitional freedom in another? How can one know precisely what scars have been left by wrongs done to another in early life? Often a close study of a criminal's life shows that, serious as his crimes may be, he has been even "more sinned against than sinning." Is it not a serious offense of presumptuous and sinful pride for a human being to judge the gravity of moral culpability in the intention of another person when he committed a criminal act?

Even if we could somehow leap over this hurdle, so as to know precisely how guilty in the moral sense another is, there remains an insuperable problem. What kind of quasi-mathematical operation is this by which we equate three months of imprisonment to the degree of a man's evil intention in snatching a purse? How much pain or deprivation does it take to equal the evil lust of a rapist or the greed of a cheater at the customs station?

Yet there is some limited validity in the retributive theory.

First, it suggests proportional limits on sentences imposed for other purposes. Without professing to judge moral intentions or the degree of responsibility, we do need to see that to impose twenty years in prison for stealing two dollars from an unmanned newspaper dispenser, while assessing a five-dollar fine for a mugging robbery, is not just. There should be some rationality in the relative penalties for types of criminal acts according to the gravity of injury done or the threat posed to persons and property.

Second, relative to crimes for profit, penalties should be severe enough to make the action emphatically unprofitable. There are many instances of law crying out for correction because of the very fact that stealing a little by a dramatic act like burglary in an unoccupied house calls for a heavy penalty, while stealing from a city treasury millions of dollars by corrupt practices may be punishable only by a fine which amounts to a small fraction of the ill-gained profit. Penalties need to be so proportioned to crimes as to make crime unprofitable.

Third, the punishment of crime is a means of expression by which the state says emphatically, "This is a kind of conduct which our society regards as intolerable." The more abhorrent the crime the more emphatic the expression and so the heavier the punishment. Penal justice thus expresses the outraged disapproval of the society and so has a moral educational value which is not equivalent to fear.[18]

c. Deterrence. Often when there have been many unsolved cases of a certain type of crime in a community, for example arson, and then at last a culprit is caught and convicted, the judge passes an especially severe sentence. He may acknowledge the severity, but says that he and the whole community are so disturbed about this kind of crime that he is now "making an example" of this man. In other words, he is punishing him severely enough so that it is hoped other persons tempted to commit arson may be deterred. Even though they know that they have a good chance of escaping, the penalties, if they are caught, are likely to be so severe that they will not take the risk.

The theory of deterrence, then, is the theory that a convicted law-breaker is punished in order that others may not be disposed to follow his example.

One objection to this history is that it makes the punishment of one person the means of influencing other persons. This implies using a person as mere means and not respecting his dignity as an end also. It appears to be, therefore, a deliberate violation of the General Principle of Altruism, to say nothing of Christian love.

Closely akin to this objection is another. According to this theory, the more prevalent a crime becomes in a community, the more severe the punishment would need to be. Likewise, the smaller the proportion of culprits caught, the more heavily they must be punished. Yet these are the very instances in which moral culpability might be lessened by customary acceptance. Here also the disparity between treatment of the one person caught and his many fellow criminals would be most extreme. In these instances one's sense of the partial truth in retributive theory stands opposed to the consistent application of the theory of deterrence.

On the other hand, deterrence has its positive social value. I should not care to drive on highways where no one feared punishment if he violated the code of safety. Similarly, when heavy fines are assessed against violators of laws governing labor relations or codes of safety in coal mines, this is not to put more money into the treasury. It is in-

18. Cf. the carefully reasoned and impressive study of A. C. Ewing, *The Morality of Punishment* (London: Routledge and Kegan Paul, 1929).

tended to deter such violations and it does have a deterrent effect. Along with other considerations deterrence has validity as a partial means of maintaining an orderly community in which personal rights are safeguarded. To that extent it has the support of the General Principles of Community and is required by Christian love.

d. Disablement. When a crazed man has been assaulting and killing young women in a community, a pall of fear falls upon the population. Then, at last, he is caught, convicted, and imprisoned. There is a general sigh of relief, not because some theoretical balance between immorality and symbolic restitution has been achieved, or fear struck into the hearts of potential criminals, but because this dangerous man is "out of the way" behind prison walls.

Other means of disablement are the forced surgical unsexing of a rapist, the removal from public office of a man who has abused the public trust, and the execution of a murderer. All these punishments, whatever else their merit or evil, are means of making the offender temporarily or permanently unable to repeat his crime. He may have the same inclinations as before, probably excepting the rapist, but he is unable to enact them. He may not be in the least improved in moral character, but he no longer endangers the life or property of others as before.

Disablement seems to be an inescapable obligation of the law in many instances. It is not a kindness even to the culprit to allow him to go unrestrained, accumulating new occasions for guilt. Certainly love for other persons requires that they be protected by putting the individual who endangers them or their property into such a place or condition as will effectively stop his depredations.

The trouble with disablement is that if it is by imprisonment as in most instances it must be, then when the sentence is finished and the prisoner goes free, he will—so far as disablement goes—be as dangerous as he was before. If we imprison only to disable, then all the people in prisons would either be kept for life or freed with due apologies. Actually, many people are made more dangerous by imprisonment because behind the walls they feed on their bitterness, they live in demoralizing idleness, and they are in especially bad company. Many prisons are described truly as "schools of crime."

e. Rehabilitation. Whatever may be the penal theory of the prosecutor and judge who send a lawbreaker to prison, unless the warden or superintendent is a callous brute, he will try to reeducate the prisoner so that when released he can live a useful life. Often the resources provided for this purpose are slender, for it is hard to obtain public money for giving aid to convicted criminals. Many people set their interest in "protecting the public from criminals" over against "softheaded" efforts to rehabilitate them. Yet actually most prisoners are released sooner or later. In fact, among the relatively serious convictions which are the general rule among prisoners in federal institutions, the average first sentence is three years, while the term actually served is nineteen months.[19] Obviously, the greatest aid the prison could give in protecting society would be by reforming the prisoner so he would commit no more crimes. This becomes especially clear when we observe that among the prisoners committed to federal institutions in 1966, 60 per cent had records of previous commitments. In municipal and state prisons the percentage of repeaters is often much higher.

Most states have official policies of seeking to reform juvenile delinquents, but serious efforts to rehabilitate adults are very spotty. Many are difficult to change, and it is much harder to get appropriations for personnel and equipment to treat adults. The professional staffs of many institutions, faced with crowded space, minimal equipment, staff personnel of inadequate number and quality, are badly frustrated in their hard task. Often it seems that about all they can hope to do is to help guide a few of the most promising cases and simply keep the others under lock and discipline until time for release.

3. Pound's Theory of Interests

Roscoe Pound, prolific author on jurisprudence and long the Dean of Harvard University School of Law, thought all simple and absolute theories of penal justice to be impractical of application or evil in effect. Various personal and social interests bear upon every question of justice which must be resolved at the bench or in legislative halls. Different individuals and groups have conflicting special interests of their own. For example, a burglar usually wishes to be set free as soon as possible, while householders in the neighborhood of his exploits will probably want him to be out of circulation for a long time for their protection. At the same time, there are different philosophies of law and of ethical behavior in the community, and the interests arising from these are also frequently in conflict.

The legislation of law and the processes of judicial decision, Pound contended, should be flexibly responsive to these varied interests. Justice, according to this view, represents a point of reasonable balance among them. It is neither a hard adherence to absolute standards believed to be timeless and unchanging nor a mere following of statutory law and judicial precedent. Maintenance of stability is an important interest, so expectations based on the past are basic; but society constantly changes and the law must be responsive to changed conditions. Pound also believed that the law should be especially responsive to

19. *Statistical Abstract of the United States: 1970,* p. 160.

religion, both because it represents so much of accumulated wisdom and because it expresses many of the deeper and more lasting interests of society.[20]

4. *Justice as Love in Situations of Conflict*

It is an intolerable presumption for any human judge to pretend that he is pronouncing a moral judgment on a convicted criminal, assigning to him the sentence that is in accord with his moral culpability before God. But a judge does act as God's minister when he makes his decision with loving concern for all involved—the criminal, people who have been injured by him, others who fear further depredations by him and persons like him, parents fearful lest their youth will think the offense committed was a small matter, the youth themselves who might be thus misled, and the whole body of citizens concerned with the maintenance of a stable but free and humane society.

Christian love also seeks the wholeness, unity, and openness of the community so that all may share God's gifts in gratitude. It takes up all the proper concerns of Pound's theory of interests and also renews and lifts to a new level the higher purposes of primitive justice. At the same time, penal justice properly informed by Christian love must be concerned to recognize and defend as far as possible the dignity and freedom of each individual, even the flagrant wrongdoer, the Prodigal Son of the Father. The goal is always the forgiving reacceptance into the community, though not with the submergence of the individual which is common in primitive societies and in totalitarian states.

In Christian love we can never be content simply to put a criminal behind bars. Often we must, regrettably, resort to imprisonment. But we do so with heavy heart, recognizing that, warped in character and threatening injury as he may be, he is still in society, though in a segregated part of it where he may still be injurious to fellow human beings. We must acknowledge, too, that his evil represents the evil of a society which can lay no claim to righteousness, but is prone to idealize, even idolize, tough aggressiveness and the lucky gamble, which gives many of its highest rewards to the most brazenly selfish and ruthless competitors, and indoctrinates millions of its selected youth in the glories of cruel violence to be committed on command.

20. Pound's view is firmly grasped only after reading many of his books and articles dealing with different emphases of his complex thought. Among his more important books are: *Laws and Morals* (Chapel Hill: University of North Carolina Press, 1924); *Criminal Justice in America* (Cambridge, Mass.: Harvard University Press, 1945), and *An Introduction to the Philosophy of Law* (New Haven: Yale University Press, 1922). Of special relevance to our subject are also his articles "A Theory of Social Interests," in *Proceedings of the American Sociological Society*, 1921, pp. 16–45 and "Law and Religion," in a Rice Institute Pamphlet of April, 1940, pp. 109–72.

The primary emphasis of Christian love relative to crime must be on its prevention by the redeeming of society and of all individuals in it.

With the convicted criminal our first concern must be with his rehabilitation and restoration to useful citizenship.[21] Whereas much penal justice is preoccupied with the past, penal justice worthy of Christian support looks chiefly to the future, with love informed by all the facts, and the social sciences can tell us of probable consequences to be expected from alternative courses of action.

Christian love cannot tolerate capital punishment. Large-scale experiments of states and nations in eliminating it indicates that there are no more homicides where executions are never practiced than where they are employed. By execution, a government and its agents declare their absolute and final rejection of the wrongdoer as a worthless thing. Even in life imprisonment there can be attempt to rehabilitate the prisoner, seek his redemption before God, and win him to a life of constructive usefulness among his fellow prisoners. By an execution a government teaches emphatically that human life is not always to be respected and that under some circumstances not involving imminent danger to anyone a coldblooded murder is justified.

At the same time, love for all in the community requires that with sparing regard for educational retribution, the purposes of deterrence and disablement be given ample place within the total consideration of interests which must be reconciled in penal justice.

True Christian love, then, when directed to all who are or will be affected, undergirds and guides a radically reformed penal justice under law. Such love limits justice in its typically impersonal character by requiring due heed to each person intimately affected, and by insisting on going beyond penal justice to prevention and to the assisting of the ex-convict as he returns "outside."[22]

5. Situational Guidelines on Criminal Justice

As already implied, Christians are called today to insist upon heavier than usual emphasis on preventing crime by eliminating its social causes;

21. An exception, of course, is the person convicted of no evil, but rather of opposing the evil of society imbedded in the law. The selective conscientious objector is a good example. The judge might well apply to him a sentence which will at once give him opportunity to witness to the depth of his convictions and enable him to use his sensitive conscience in ministering to others.

22. Among published books of my acquaintance, the most sustained and genuine effort to apply Christian norms to penal justice is Norman L. Robinson, *Christian Justice* (New York: Doran, 1922). Robinson recognizes inadequately the motifs other than rehabilitation and prevention, but his book is a rarity in taking love seriously for the defining and guiding of penal justice. I recommend also Dean Hosken, "Prolegomena to a Christian Philosophy of Penal Justice" (Boston University Ph.D. Dissertation, 1957).

to stress programs of rehabilitation; and to eliminate capital punishment.

Other specific objectives of penal reform which commend themselves to realistic Christian action include the providing of better trained and better paid police, probation officers, and prison staff personnel; and systematic provision for employment and reintegration of ex-convicts into the larger community. Some churches are developing programs in which strong and understanding laymen regularly visit convicts in their last months in prison and then sponsor them in their first years outside. Such work is difficult and at times discouraging, but also highly rewarding. Few tasks so directly bear witness to the spirit and teaching of Christ.

chapter fifteen

International Order
and World Peace

————————••⟨∞⟩••————————

Despite the errors of his idealistic anarchism, Tolstoi described accurately the general trend of political efforts to protect human beings from violence at the hands of their fellows. The movement has been toward the establishment of ever larger, more inclusive governments, to prevent or control violence between smaller units.

Just as the minimizing of violence within any small state is closely related to welfare functions in the broad sense, so it is when states form federations, regional associations, or such a body as the United Nations. Our economic, scientific, and cultural interdependence, and our relations of communication and travel, constitute a worldwide network. Even so vast a modern state as the United States of America or the Union of Soviet Socialist Republics is far too limited geographically to include a complete, self-sufficient community at present standards of living. Hence we have regional associations, like the Organization of American States and the wider international body, the United Nations, with all its many agencies. We have also the Permanent Court of International Justice and the most inclusive agency of all, the World Postal Union which includes even continental China.

It is the United Nations which principally represents the evolution of larger political units to restrain violence among its members. As presently constituted the U.N. does not have a permanent police force and it depends upon unanimity of the permanent members of its Security Council to take coercive action. It is therefore usually able to bring physically coercive forces to bear upon an offending member only when the great powers, especially the United States and the Soviet Union, are in agreement. It has consequently been of limited effectiveness in relation to quarrels between these great powers, but has had considerable effect in halting mounting belligerency between small powers. Even in regard to the smaller powers rival regional interests of the great powers can stifle U.N. effectiveness, as in the Middle East. There the common interests of the great powers in avoiding war long maintained a U.N. presence and dampened many a crescendo of fighting. At the same time, the rival interests in oil and strategic position prevented the kind of decisive united effort which could end the dangerous threat to world peace. Even the limited effectiveness of the U.N. observers was eventually undermined and destroyed.

There continue the intense distrust, the arms race, and the constant threat of war between the two largest Communist powers, on the one hand, and the United States and its anti-Communist allies, on the other. This "Cold War" constantly threatens to escalate each smaller war or episode of fighting between or within smaller nations into a cataclysmic war which would be far beyond comparison with anything ever experienced in human history. The same danger accompanies every episode of American or Soviet militancy which threatens to upset the uneasy balance.

War is still a reality of international life, while order is partial, fragile, and uncertain.

A. Evils and Perils of War

1. Destruction of Life

The perils to human life are considerable even in the most peaceful and favorable surroundings. As human beings evolved by God's creative power, they became more open and sensitive to their environment than are most creatures. This openness makes possible man's intelligent adaptation to his environment. A price paid for this superior adaptability is, however, his great vulnerability. He can be easily killed by bacteria, by many common chemical substances, by a hard fall, by drowning, by failure of water or food supply, by excessive heat or cold, and by many other accidents besides the old age which will end his life if nothing else does. It is the most ironical tragedy that fragile human beings, who depend on intelligence for survival, should set out deliberately to kill each other. The irony is heightened by the fact that the more man's knowledge has advanced, the more feverishly he has cultivated his ability to kill his fellows. In no other field of endeavor has technical ability increased more rapidly than in the power to kill.

The United States has not felt the deadliness of modern war, even in its preatomic version, since the Civil War, when about one-half million uniformed men died, or about one out of six in the contending forces. In World War II there were four times as many men in uniform, but fewer American deaths. It was the Soviet Union which suffered the massive losses. With the armed forces reaching a peak strength of 12.5 million, slightly more than the American peak, 7.5 million were killed in battle. The German forces lost 3.5 million, China 2.2 million, and Japan 1.2 million. These figures are for battle deaths alone, and of course do not include the even larger number of civilians who died in the bombings, fires, and epidemics, and from starvation.

A future war between major powers would, however, be in a completely different order of deadliness. The single uranium bomb dropped on Hiroshima on August 6, 1945, killed more than 70,000 people, and even a full generation later men and women are living with continuing radioactive injuries, while babies stillborn or defective are further pathetic fruit of that horrible moment.

A 20-megaton hydrogen bomb of the present stockpiles, however, is one thousand times as powerful as the Hiroshima uranium bomb. As early as 1961 General John B. Medaris had stated that the American arsenal contained nuclear bomb power totaling more than the equivalent of 20,000 pounds of TNT for every human being on earth.

> Between 1961 and 1969 the intercontinental nuclear delivery force of the U.S. was enlarged from 1,100 deliverable warheads to 4,200 deliverable warheads. . . . Apart from these, there are tens of thousands of other nuclear warheads mounted not only in short range devices, but in thousands of aircraft that are deployable from ground bases and from aircraft carriers as well, and therefore also capable of intercontinental reach.[1]

Robert S. McNamara reported that, assuming substantial Soviet growth and development, even in 1972 only 100 one-megaton warheads would destroy 59 per cent of all Soviet industry and kill 37 million Soviet citizens, while 400 such warheads would kill 74 million and destroy 76 per cent of Soviet industry.[2] McNamara also presented a table showing that even if the United States developed a 40-billion-dollar antimissile defense system and in the mid-1970s went all-out in a strategic nuclear attack on the Soviet Union, the Soviets could kill 90 million Americans in response. The estimates of deaths concern only people immediately killed and do not include the millions who woud die in ensuing fires and from injuries by radioactivity.

The deaths would by no means be confined to Americans and Russians exposed to shock, blast, and fire. The radioactive fallout would be distributed around the globe. No one knows how many people

1. Seymour Melman, in *New University Thought*, Spring, 1969 (Vol. 7, No. 1), p. 16.

2. Table reproduced in the same issue of *New University Thought*, p. 12, from *U.S. Armament and Disarmament Problems. Hearings before the Subcommittee on Disarmament of Senate Foreign Relations*, Feb. 3 to Mar. 3, 1967, 90th Congress. First Session, p. 58.

would be killed by it. Genetic damage from such vast quantities of nuclear fission would certainly be great, through succeeding generations of people if the race managed to survive. We cannot even imagine the conditions following such a nuclear exchange, with maimed, sick, and shocked people in many places trying to bury the larger number of dangerously contaminated corpses, while fighting for limited supplies of uncontaminated water and food. It is doubtful whether anything resembling civilized human society could survive such a catastrophe.

2. *Denial of Love*

In church schools and services of worship throughout the world pastors and teachers are declaring the supreme glory and responsibility of Christian love. Yet for years, in daily news accounts, Americans have been told how many of "the enemy" their young men have been able to kill and our "defense experts" have told how much more killing we could do if the military officers were given permission to fight in their own way without restriction. Meanwhile, the "games" theorists of the Pentagon continue to compute the numbers of Americans, Russians, and Chinese who might be killed without destroying all the future for their nations.

In short, the words of instruction in church speak of love, while national policy is frequently viewing people, both Americans and others, as expendable numbers, at best, while more than a billion in other lands are lumped together and despised as "the enemy," present or potential. In this atmosphere, even loyal Christian leaders in Cuba and Eastern Europe, who continue their brave witness under atheistic Communist governments, are viewed with cold suspicion or open hostility by many American church people.

If planning ways of inflicting the ultimate horrors of nuclear war upon the world for any purpose whatever be in accord with love, then there is nothing which would be a denial of love. Surely no sane person can believe that we can share God's gifts in gratitude and mercy, while engaging in such calculation of mass, indiscriminate murder and maiming of men, women, the aged, children, infants, and future generations. While we consent to such planning our words about love fall lifeless to the ground. We are training a generation in hard lovelessness and violence, or in schizophrenic effort to love and despise life at once.

War on the terms of a nuclear age is simply the antithesis of love and even of a decent, rational humanism. Considering all the means of destruction which technology is devising, it is also the road to suicide of the human race.

B. Peace by Balance of Terror

The indictment of nuclear war as unchristian and suicidal would be granted by many who still believe in the present American policy of *preparation* for nuclear, bacteriological, and chemical warfare.

1. *Its Actuality*

The argument plausibly maintains that war between the great powers is being prevented by the threat that an attacker would be immediately subjected to such devastation as the world has never seen and as no nation could endure. It is pointed out that both the United States and the Soviet Union have repeatedly backed off under provocations which would have precipitated war in any period before the nuclear age.

Thus, at the blockade of Berlin, the United States replied by an airlift of supplies, not by an armed assault on the barrier, and the Soviet Union did not shoot down the airplanes. In the Cuban missile crisis it was the United States which announced the ultimatum of blockade, but left an opening and it was the Soviet Union which saved the day by withdrawing the missiles. In Vietnam the United States bombed and shelled the North Vietnamese friends of the Soviet Union, and it was the latter which refrained from entering into direct confrontation with the Americans.

On each occasion when war might easily have begun, either the one nation or the other has backed away. This has happened because war between the two major nuclear powers would within an hour or two destroy in both countries a thousand times more than either could hope to gain or protect by it.

The strange new fact about nuclear defense is that it is only a psychological defense—a means of deterrent influence upon the minds of men contemplating attack. Of course psychologically deterrent defenses have often been used before. The new fact is that the force of the nuclear deterrent cannot be used as a physical defense at all. If it is ever used it will defend nothing. It will destroy what the user might have wished to defend.

Yet it remains a probable fact that open warfare has been as limited as it has been since 1946 because of this balance of terror. This is not saying very much. During this period, it is true, the Soviet Union has not been involved in any war other than the tragic brief invasion of Hungary and the contemptible but comparatively bloodless invasion of Czechoslovakia. The United States, however, has engaged in a long, bloody conflict in Korea, and a costlier war in Vietnam. Whether without the nuclear bombs the two great powers would have gone to war with each other since 1946 no one can be sure. We only know with certainty that both have possessed the nuclear deterrent and the war has not, in fact, occurred.

The leaders of the two governments are fearful that some miscalculation, accident, or the mad aggression of an individual or group controlling some of the bombs might trigger the cataclysm. Both sides have developed various means to reduce this danger, including the "hot line" directly connecting the offices of the chief executives. These efforts indicate that the fear of nuclear war does, indeed, have a strong cautionary effect.

2. Its Perils

On the other hand, the balance of terror holds incalculably great perils. Herman Kahn, an influential consultant on nuclear defense, writes,

> The major danger of the arms race lies precisely in the fact that the arms may be used; thermonuclear war may be unthinkable, but it is not impossible.[3]

Kahn categorizes the ways in which the "unthinkable" war may actually occur under the following headings:

1. *Unpremeditated war* (human mechanical error, false alarm, self-fulfilling prophecy, unauthorized behavior).
2. *Miscalculation* (game of "Chicken," rationality of irrationality strategies, escalation, over-confidence).
3. *Calculation* (. . . preventive war, preemptive war; world domination; solution to a desperate crisis).
4. *Catalytic war* (ambitious third nation; desperate third nation).
[*Ibid.*, pp. 18–19]

Kahn does not claim a reliable method for computing the odds against the dread thermonuclear war occurring within a given period of time. However, there have already been errors which have sent loaded nuclear bombers from our shores toward the Soviet Union. The errors have been discovered before the planes reached Soviet territory and the pilots have turned back. But what if Soviet radar operators had picked up the American bombers on their screens and sent their own bombers off toward this country? The crews of the hostile

---

3. "The Arms Race and Some of Its Hazards," in *Toward a Theory of War Prevention* (The Strategy of World Order, Vol. I), ed. by Richard A. Falk and Saul H. Mendlovitz (New York: World Law Fund, 1966), p. 18.

airplanes might have observed each other, confirmed that a hostile attack was under way, and so set off the wild destruction.[4] From all such possibilities some very rough computation can be made, although the likelihood is that because of many unknown possibilities the result would be an underestimate of the peril. I find blood-chilling the further comment of Kahn himself on the probability of a world-wide nuclear catastrophe:

> While it would be hard to convince me that it is as high as, say, 1 in 10 a year, if it were this high, the situation would be entirely unsatisfactory. Even if it were 1 in 100 a year, it would still be unsatisfactory, because the current state of affairs could not be allowed to continue indefinitely. One must eventually introduce a change in the situation, or expect to get into a war anyway.   [*Ibid.*, p. 21]

Kahn says the odds will become worse with the further proliferation and dispersal of weapons and increase in the number and diversity of governments possessing them.

These weapons "offer us nothing but a balance of terror, and a balance of terror is still terror."[5] Moreover, this balance of terror, if continued, will lead inevitably, sooner or later, to such catastrophe as the world has never known. The very military power which we have called into being to defend us, and which we sustain at a cost of eighty to one hundred billion dollars per year, will destroy our civilization and possibly, in the end, all human life.

3. Ethical Critique of the Nuclear Deterrent

It may be granted that the existence of the nuclear deterrent has probably occasioned restraint in policies of both the United States and the Soviet Union in some critical situations. At the same time the presence and threat of nuclear power have heightened the tension, so that small incidents have raised disproportionate fears throughout the world. Moreover, there are grave ethical objections to the maintenance of the threat, regardless of its actual use.

a. Deterrence Requires the Decision to Use. The existence of nuclear bombing power would not deter if the rival government did not believe that it would actually be used in response to attack. It is conceivable, though doubtful, that a despotic police state could maintain such credibility even if (improbably) the rulers had decided not ac-

---

4. Arkady S. Sobolev spoke of this danger in precise terms in the Security Council debate of April 21, 1958. The text of his remarks is given by Kahn. *Ibid.*, p. 20.

5. George Wald, address at Massachusetts Institute of Technology, March 4, 1969.

tually to loose nuclear retaliation and so incite further attack on itself even if subjected to a first strike. Credibility certainly could not be maintained by a democratic government under such conditions. Processes of decision making are too widely shared and the practices of an open society are too vulnerable to leaks and espionage. If the government of the United States is to keep the Soviet Union believing that an attack on the United States or on certain of its allies would lead to nuclear reprisal, the President and the Strategic Air Command must be steadfastly determined to carry out such reprisal if the occasion should arise.

Moral philosophers are agreed that the moral significance of an act is in the decision to perform it. Jesus presses this view to its very limit in his teaching that adultery is in the lustful intent and murder in the murderous anger. Whether the condition leads to the fulfillment of the intent is not the morally critical question. Hence the maintenance of a credible American nuclear deterrent must carry the full moral burden of making an actual nuclear attack.

b. To Use It Would be the Ultimate Sin. Actually to launch a nuclear attack would be the gravest sin which can be envisioned by the imagination. To choose a first strike would be even more gravely immoral than to retaliate against such an attack. Yet even a retaliatory second strike could not be matched by an act of any other kind.

Some will argue that such an attack would be justified to prevent a Communist victory over Western Europe or the United States itself. But "victory" and "defeat" would lose all rational meaning when the nations involved would have one-fourth to one-half of their populations instantly killed, a similar number maimed, the industrial plant and much of the agriculture destroyed, and future generations, if any, genetically damaged.

Probably not all people would be doomed to death by a major nuclear exchange, although no one knows for sure. But the task of the survivors, burying the dead, caring for the injured, and keeping alive, would be so massive and the conditions of existence so horribly altered that the differences of present economic systems and forms of government would be virtually meaningless.

Even if the United States had suffered a first strike from the Soviet Union, what would be the purpose of a counterstrike? It would take revenge, yes, and probably incite an additional strike against this country. But what good would it accomplish? How much would the American survivors of the first strike care for anything beyond their grief, their struggle to continue life, and such solace as they might find in their various faiths and philosophies of life and death?

Would the retaliation be designed to prevent a Soviet "takeover" of American territory? It is doubtful that the Soviet Union would care to take over a country with its industrial plant in ruin, its food and water contaminated for years to come, and millions of its people maimed and demoralized. If it did wish to move in to begin restoration of a viable economic life, that would be more help than harm to the shattered remnant left here. The identity and ideology of the government over the ruins would be of secondary concern under such desperate circumstances.[6]

I do not write thus because I am indifferent to America or democracy or Communism. I love my country and have worked for years to maintain and extend the democracy which is partially achieved here. I have seen Communism at first hand and I do not like it. But when one speaks of nuclear war, one is talking about disaster so catastrophic that there is nothing in history with which to compare it. When I have been with Christian people under Stalinist rule, I have seen that government is not everything even when it tries to be. The differences between Communist government and the American government are not of the same order as the value of hundreds of millions of American people and other human beings.

To choose death and ruin on this massive scale is to make the most sinful choice which has ever been within the power of men. It implies the idolatry of erecting a form of government into the supreme absolute and a contempt for human life which is the nadir of immorality.[7]

c. Its Maintenance is Corrupting Our National Purpose.   While our nuclear deterrent exists, we must train our highly selected young men in the Strategic Air Command to understand it, to know how to use it, and to will its use on order. At the same time the rest of the armed forces and the general public must be continually conditioned to accept and support it.

In order to maintain this policy, a kind of paranoid fear of other nations must be constantly incited, and political ideologies absolutized. At the same time human life must be cheapened in value, while hardness and violence are made acceptable. This corruption of values is not carried out only by direction of a small coterie of leaders in government. The moral poison of it has moved through the whole culture since Hiroshima. We are so addicted to this poison that we demand it and feed on it in the news, in fiction, and above all on television. So long as we can keep up a devil-may-care acceptance of callous violence, what we are doing to our youth in uniform and planning to do to whole populations on the day of nuclear holocaust does not hurt us so much.

6. Cf. Herman Kahn, *On Thermonuclear War* (Princeton: Princeton University Press, 1960).

7. Cf. Paul Ramsey, "The Infeasibility of Thermonuclear War," in *War and the Christian Conscience* (Durham: Duke University Press, 1961), pp. 244–72.

When American troops became deeply involved in the Vietnamese civil war, they were soon daily committing by command acts which the United States and other nations had, in 1960, joined in labeling international crimes.[8] But we were well hardened and the public shock was minor. So long as the opposing force could be labeled "Communist," everything was so relativized that even the minimal standards of civilized warfare seemed irrelevant.

What wonder that crimes of violence increase in our cities! Why should anyone be surprised that some youth, sensitized by the remnants of a humane culture, should think our whole establishment mad and try to find a way simply to escape or reject it?

The beginnings of a revolt in Congress against control by the military-industrial complex is an encouraging straw in the wind. If the revolt develops sufficiently, we shall be changing our national priorities. We shall place the feeding of the hungry, the education of the ignorant, and the housing of the homeless above the purchase of ever larger overkill. If such restoration of sane standards goes far, the whole policy of deterrence by nuclear terror will be reexamined and replaced.

d. Continuance of the Deterrent Will Bring Its Use. We have already noted that the deterrent can be effective only if our President and the SAC are willing to use it. But we must also recall that the continuance of the present policy will certainly bring the actual nuclear holocaust. Kahn was not convinced that there was a one-in-ten chance per year of its occurrence, but conceded that even if it were only one in one hundred the awful catastrophe would, sooner or later, occur. Whether by accident, miscalculation, the "catalytic" action of a third nation, or otherwise, the nuclear means of defense intended to prevent war will actually bring it to pass and in the most terrible form.

A responsible examination of consequences in relation to the General Principles of rational ethics or the norms of Christian faith will condemn the policy of nuclear deterrence as unacceptable.

Where, then, shall we turn? What will be the basic premises from which we should develop national policy relative to war and peace? In the face of the awful recent developments of modern warfare, Christian pacifism makes a fresh appeal to many thoughtful people.

C. CHRISTIAN PACIFISM

There are many kinds and degrees of pacifist rejection of war and violence. Few contemporary pacifists would join Tolstoi in rejecting all use of police and hence espousing the abolition of government. The

8. Hundreds of documented examples are given in the book, *In the Name of America.*

term "pacifism" generally means today the complete rejection of war and preparation for war. Even so, there are two radically different meanings of such rejection which must be distinguished.

First is *individual pacifism*, that is, the belief of a person that he ought never, under any circumstances, to enter or voluntarily support the armed services of any nation, or to fight in any war. This is the position of the conscientious objector legally recognized as such by the American Selective Service Act.

Second is *political pacifism* or pacifism as principle of national policy. This is the belief that a nation ought never to wage war, ought not to prepare for war, and hence should have no military forces nor equipment.

1. Critique of Individual Pacifism

A person who subscribes to individual pacifism may not necessarily work for the total disarmament of his own nation. He may recognize that most citizens are not pacifists of either type, so that pacifist strategies could not be operated. He may acknowledge that a man who accepts the presidency of the United States is morally as well as legally obligated to support and command the military defense of this imperfect nation in an imperfect world. But the individual pacifist himself has convictions which make it impossible for him to support such an effort without violation of conscience.

The Christian individual pacifist believes that Christ's commands in the Sermon on the Mount and the larger spirit of love which Christ taught and exemplified require that he stand ready to suffer and die at the hands of personal or national enemies, if necessary, but forbid him to participate in the organized killing which is war.

In a nation where few people hold such convictions, the individual pacifist may yet enter political activity in support of one military and foreign policy rather than another. This may lead to the charge of inconsistency or hypocrisy, since he will not support the implementation of the policies for which he expresses relative preference. But he may honestly believe that in political decisions he should always support policies less likely to lead to actual war than others, while in fidelity to his own Christian calling he is bound to refuse any personal participation in the military forces. Some individual pacifists accept noncombatant roles as medics, ambulance drivers, or chaplains; others refuse even these as auxiliary to the combat troops.

Such a position is worthy of respect in a nation where it is unpopular and generally suspected as an expression of cowardice or treason. It appears to be a simple, direct application of basic Christian teachings. By comparison with the common attitudes ignoring moral precepts to perform every act of villainy commanded in the name of patriotism, it brings a breath of ethical fresh air. As a personal protest and counterweight in a violence-prone society which spends the greater part of its national budget on killing or preparing to kill, it is a highly useful posture.

Yet, while being thankful for such counterweights, we must still question whether the position is the right expression of Christian responsibility in every situation. To refuse personal recruitment and support to any and all military preparation or action on principle cannot be ethically defended unless I believe that all persons ought so to refuse. But such belief commits me to the political pacifism of total unilateral disarmament. Without such belief, my own refusal means that I am willing for others to do what I believe to be morally wrong for myself. This looks very much like an individual escape from the dirty work which I prefer to see others do for me. In fact, if I refuse, someone else will need to carry my burden, both of danger and of whatever guilt I think is attached to individual military service or moral support of it. The General Principles of Personal Conscience, Altruism, and Ideal of Personhood forbid such a stance, while in explicitly Christian ethics the Golden Rule and the prohibition of spiritual pride likewise exclude it.

However, if a person accepts also political pacifism, as many, perhaps most, individual pacifists do, then no such charge can be made against him.

2. *Critique of Political Pacifism*

In the preceding chapter Tolstoian anarchism was rejected as both impractical and literally impossible. A government exists in this sinful world only so long as it is able and willing to put down, by force if necessary, any contrary power which challenges it within its geographical and social sphere of authority.

Many political pacifists distinguish between police power and military power, accepting the former as ethically legitimate. Police power, they say, operates under law, while military power operates lawlessly. Police seek only to bring the criminal to court where he is judged by the law; military power is partisan, seeking to crush the opposing force, killing, burning, and destroying all that supports it with little or no regard to personal deserts or justice. This distinction seems impossible to maintain in practice. Tolstoi is right in finding no distinction in principle. When members of a police contingent go out to arrest a defiant lawless gang, they must use as much force as is needed to overcome the hostile group. If the gang should have the support of a whole neighborhood or city, it may be necessary to call for the larger power of a military unit. Whether the gang be large or small, whether it rises out of the citizenry or comes over the border from a foreign country, the principle is the same. A police force is not necessarily more law-abiding and restrained than National Guard or Army. Indeed, in the handling of some urban disorders in 1965–1970, the opposite was true.

It may be suggested that what is needed is the supplementation of present police by mobile, more heavily armed organizations strong enough to maintain and defend the government, but still known as police. There might be values in such changes of organization and nomenclature, but it would not in substance conform to the political pacifist's rejection of all military force.

The uses of both police and military forces need strict limitation. The effort to eliminate either must, however, be regarded as misguided.

D.   JUST WAR THEORY

If a person generally opposing war grants that there is ever a justified forceful revolt against a despotic government, or, on the other hand, a justified forceful repression of a revolt, then he has adopted a just war theory. So he has also if he believes that a nation would ever have a moral right to defend itself by force against a hostile invasion or do battle in any other situation.

Just war theory has taken a number of forms, from some bare beginnings in the writings of Plato and development by Augustine, through elaboration by Thomas Aquinas, and legalistic codification by Hugo Grotius to the thought of contemporary Roman Catholics and such a Protestant as Paul Ramsey. All these views have in common the understanding that war is a great evil and that the burden of proof is on those persons who would justify the waging of war at any given time. Plato wrote in *The Laws* that the "highest good . . . is neither war nor civil strife—which things we should pray to be saved from— but peace. . . ."[9]

When we come to the Roman Catholic tradition as currently stated, we find a similar beginning and then the hard conditions which must be met if a war is to be regarded as just. Typical is Messner's formulation.

Because it is bound up with fearful evils, war is never justified as a means of policy but only for defense. Accordingly, *the conditions of a just war are:* (1) it must be waged for the defense of vital goods of a

9. *The Laws*, Book I, 628 D-E. The text is from The Loeb Classical Library translation by R. G. Bury (New York: G. P. Putnam's Sons, 1926).

state community, such goods being violated or directly and gravely threatened by attack from another state; (2) no superior authority can be called upon to restore the violated right; (3) war must not jeopardize still higher goods than those which are to be defended; (4) the intention of the defender does not go beyond the defense and restoration of the violated right; (5) the means of defense employed must not be unlawful in themselves; (6) the means employed must be proportionate to the purpose of defense, that is, they must not cause more evil than is necessitated by this purpose. If one of these conditions is lacking, a war cannot be just.[10]

The fifth condition obviously requires the statement of laws regarding acceptable means of warfare. Such laws have also been stated by Messner (p. 512), indeed at such length that here I must summarize. The "most important" of the principles governing justified means of warfare, he says, are as follows: (1) declaration of war before actual hostilities; (2) lives of noncombatants to be kept inviolable; (3) citizens in territory occupied to be free from deportation and forced labor; (4) state property in occupied territory to be possessed, but private property to be taken only for the kinds of emergency use which the troops of the citizens' own state would count sufficient reason for their own possession; (5) prisoners of war to be given the same medical care and food as the troops of the occupying force, and not to be subjected to forced labor; and (6) treacherous deceit and falsehood excluded.

Messner recognizes that a number of these principles are customarily violated in the twentieth century, but maintains that this fact does not modify their obligatory nature, excepting in repelling an aggressor who uses them, when no other means of repulsion exists. [Pp. 512-13.] Unfortunately, the exception opens a door wide enough to discount the effective meaning of the principles concerned.

The most prominent recent Protestant writer on just war theory is Paul Ramsey. In his prolific writing on the subject he has devoted most of his attention to the acts and means of war and relatively little to the other conditions of a just war. Indeed, most of his emphasis in his books and many articles defending or appealing to just war theory falls on a single principle that noncombatants must not be willfully attacked. His point is that a Christian may only approve the attacking of combatancy, not of men, even of men who are soldiers in enemy forces when they "by surrender or capture, have had the combatancy taken out of them."[11]

10. Johannes Messner, *Social Ethics*, p. 665.
11. *The Just War: Force and Political Responsibility* (New York: Charles Scribner's Sons, 1968), p. 533.

Other proponents of just war theory have not all agreed with Ramsey's applications of it. Some of the differences doubtless arise from varying assessments of the facts regarding nuclear force and regarding the Vietnam War, the two subjects to which he has most frequently applied his just war theory. But in the midst of the arguments differences of principle also appear. One is of critical importance.

Philip Wogaman, in a brief but telling critique of Ramsey's defense of American policy in Vietnam, writes,

> We must finally remind ourselves again that a justified war is always an exception to the moral norm. It is a lesser evil, which ought to be avoided if at all possible and which must, as an evil, bear the burden of proof before the Christian conscience. There is little evidence in the writings of Professor Ramsey on Vietnam that he is placing the heavy burden of proof upon the national administration and before the conscience of the nation.[12]

To this objection Ramsey replies that he has not overlooked the "burden of proof," but that he has properly placed it on political authority, while individual dissidents from the "magistrate" must bear the burden of proof once the nation has gone to war.[13] This reply fails to take seriously Wogaman's precise placing of the burden of proof on "the national administration and before the conscience of the nation." From the beginning both Wogaman and I opposed the American military intervention as unjust. Increasing political commitment to it did not change its unjust nature while the vast escalation made it progressively worse. In a country where citizens share in political authority, they cannot escape continuing responsibility. But more basically, there is a real difference in the way the two men interpret the burden of proof.

A major principle of just war theory as interpreted by both these Protestant moralists is the principle of proportionality. The surgeon does not cut off the patient's head to cure his headache. Likewise, in political decision the principle of proportionality would forbid a nation's seriously risking its very existence for the sole purpose of "correcting" a border to include a small strip of sparsely inhabited desert— or, on the other hand, destroying another nation for this relatively small gain.

But in interpreting this principle, Ramsey justifies the American intervention in Vietnam on the ground that "The principle of propor-

12. "The Vietnam War and Paul Ramsey's Conscience," in *Dialog* (Vol. 6, Autumn, 1967), p. 298.
13. *The Just War*, p. 275, n. 15.

tion, or prudence, can be violated by acts of omission as well as commission."[14] Hence we Americans must judge whether more evil would result from our *not* intervening in Vietnam than from our intervening. Why do Americans have the responsibility to make this assessment in Vietnam, Wogaman wants to know, and why does not Ramsey urge also our intervention in, "say, Paraguay, Angola, . . . South Africa, Spain, Haiti, Saudi Arabia," or elsewhere where tyranny exists?

Indeed, if we face the same burden of proof for *omitting* to go to war as for going to war, then the whole principle of burden of proof is nullified. Ramsey's broad interpretation of the responsibility of omission makes it deceptively easy for him to defend American intervention where he pleases to defend it, because he has undermined the principle that war must bear a heavy burden of proof and also the principle that decision to wage war must be made by legitimate and responsible authority. The latter requires more critical limitation of American responsibility than Ramsey has presented. Does the United States possess legitimate responsibility to determine what party or group of generals shall rule Vietnam—or country X in any other part of the world?

Such questions cannot be properly faced in the present world without considering the problem of international order and international organization.

E. INTERNATIONAL ORDER

The nations of the world are so deeply interdependent that any one of them can be plunged into economic trouble or grave physical loss at any time by decisions taken in distant parts of the world. It has been apparent for many years that peace and orderly progress everywhere in the world required world political organization responsible to the peoples of the world. As Woodrow Wilson tirelessly proclaimed while campaigning for the League of Nations, to choose unqualified national sovereignty as opposed to international government is to choose international anarchy, and to choose that is to decide for war. The United States Senate made the choice of absolute national sovereignty when it doomed the League of Nations. Twenty years later the hollowness of that sovereignty was exposed by a decision in Tokyo to bomb Pearl Harbor.

1. The Grave Obstacles to World Law

It is one thing to see the urgent need for a world order of law; it is quite another even to design theoretically such an order as would look

14. Quoted by Wogaman, *op. cit.*, p. 295.

plausible on paper. The difficulties of developing it in actuality are formidable indeed.

a. Conflicting National Interests.   At present, economic power is nearly all under national control. In 1963 Hubert Humphrey pointed out that the annual all-inclusive cost of the U.N. to the United States was "one-fourth the cost of the Enterprise carrier."[15] The low economic strength of the United Nations reflects the low priority assigned to its importance by the nations, including the United States.

Not only most, but all military power is under national control, although very minute proportions of it are occasionally loaned to the U.N. for temporary peacekeeping operations, as in the Middle East and the Congo. The U.N. military operation in Korea has had more of the character of a military expedition by national allies with U.N. sponsorship than of a U.N. action in the full sense. All the military units remain under national authority and pay, although temporarily under allied command.

Obviously, while the United Nations possesses so little economic strength—even that subject to annual national decisions—and no military strength of its own, its authority depends purely on the voluntary agreement of its members to accept it. From the beginning it was recognized that the U.N. could act coercively to stop aggression or threats to peace only when the great powers were in agreement on the matter in hand. Hence the well-known veto power held by the permanent members of the Security Council, which was insisted upon by the United States as well as the Soviet Union. As had also been anticipated, the U.N. cannot enforce any kind of action it may take against either of the great powers.

In actuality, however, even much smaller nations often defy the actions of the U.N., whether in the General Assembly or Security Council. South Africa, Israel, and the Arab states have given repeated demonstrations of such defiance. Israel and her neighbors can defy the U.N. because the Soviet Union and the United States have rival economic, political, and military interests in the Middle East, and are never able to unite in support of decisive action. South Africa has economic resources so valued by the United Kingdom and the United States that while they have plainly disliked the South African illegal annexation of Southwest Africa, they have never consented to any sanctions for enforcement of the U.N.'s will there.

To secure the peace it is essential to place real power in an international organization. But powerful nations are not inclined to yield

15. *The United Nations* (The Strategy of World Order, Vol. III), ed. by Richard A. Falk and Saul H. Mendlovitz (New York: World Law Fund, 1966), p. 742.

their power to defend their own interests to an organization which might act contrary to them on some occasions.

b. The Problem of Need for Basic Change. The one changeless fact about men and nations is that they are continually changing. National boundaries, federations of states, and politico-economic arrangements acceptable at one time may become flagrantly unsatisfactory at a later time. Disproportionate congestion of population occurs in some countries producing heavy pressures on boundaries, especially if immigration restrictions or discriminating laws prevent movement of people across boundaries. There exist now many small countries which are not economically viable without strong external support. Other countries, especially in Africa, are former colonies the boundaries of which bear little relation to demographic or economic realities, and which hold in high tension disparate and hostile ethnic groups. All these facts and more indicate the need for radical changes in the near and distant future. The more extreme instabilities of the Middle East, the divided Germany, mainland China and Taiwan, and the countries of Indochina, all illustrate the urgency of pressures for basic change.

How is an international government to provide for such change? Within such a federation of states as the United States of America, it is possible for the federal government to bring about mostly peaceful changes in the relations of the states and the varied elements in population (ethnic, urban, and rural, rich and poor) only by becoming the overwhelmingly predominant government. There is bound to be far more resistance to development of a world supergovernment with adequate power to maintain peace and accomplish changes as needed.

2. The Necessity of Strong World Organization

At the end of both World Wars the leaders of the victorious nations saw clearly that the escalating destructiveness of modern war was making international lawlessness intolerable. Yet since World War II the stockpiles of nuclear bombs and delivery systems have increased the destructive power in national hands by literally thousands of times.

After each of the World Wars an international organization was formed to preserve peace and to serve many other useful purposes. The League of Nations, even in its design, was too limited in membership and power to accomplish its purpose, and such hope as it held was blighted by the United States Senate. The plan of the United Nations profited by the earlier experience and has accomplished much, especially in the work of development which lessens many causes of war, but also in concerted diplomatic efforts and, in some instances, interposing of limited power. Yet it remains too weak for its task.

The main inadequacies of the U.N. are as follows: (1) the failure of the United States and other strong nations to commit to it their major investments in international development and diplomacy; (2) the enormous escalation of the arms race, especially in nuclear, chemical, and bacteriological weapons which even so strong a usual champion of American policy as Paul Ramsey sees to be irrationally and immorally maintained even for deterrence (*ibid.*, pp. 307–21), with consequent poisoning of the atmosphere for diplomatic progress; (3) the exclusion from membership of several nations, including China, alone comprising nearly one-fourth of mankind; (4) unstable and inadequate means of financing; (5) the unwillingness of many nations to limit their national sovereignty sufficiently to make its peace-keeping functions effective; and (6) the keeping of all military power under national control.

The need for limiting national sovereignty is the crux of the problem, and closely related is the arms race in weapons of terror. Unlimited national sovereignty and the maintenance of all these weapons will destroy modern civilization and frightfully cripple mankind if they continue unchecked. This truth has been declared by each recent president of the United States and by many other statesmen, including spokesmen for the Soviet Union.

The one government which has not only refrained from acknowledging it, but has repeatedly denied it is China. That government has been so ostracized and surrounded by hostile bases on all sides that it has predictably become irrationally paranoid in international attitudes. If, as it gains technical power, it is not seriously to threaten world peace, steps must be taken to ameliorate these attitudes. Two of America's best friends, Canada and Japan, are eager to help us in the reversal of American policy which such a course would necessitate.

The nearly unanimous agreement of informed statesmen that we must have nuclear disarmament and stronger international law gives some ground for hope. How, then, may the United States now move toward the actualizing of this hope and the making of world peace more secure?

F. Initial Presumption Peaceful

More than ever before, the initial presumption today must be against war. It must also be against the providing of arms to others. This latter point is underscored by such a recent event as Pakistan's use of American-supplied arms to attack India. Another warning example is Portugal's use of some American arms for brutal suppression in Angola and similar use of other arms which could be sent to Africa because arms from the United States were being supplied for defense in Portugal itself. Yet another occurred in 1969 when American arms were used by both Honduras and El Salvador against each other.

The initial presumption must also be against every proposal to produce more arms and likewise in favor of every proposal for arms reduction.

These initial presumptions do not constitute a subscription to the pacifist position. I have argued earlier that it is necessary to be prepared for use of some military force in case of necessity. Precisely how much the United States should have for its legitimate responsibilities no one can say now. But a nation with 400 major and 1,000 minor military installations abroad, an annual military budget in the neighborhood of 70,000 million dollars, with an arsenal of nuclear weapons for an overkill several times over of all targets which even the most jingoistic militarist could think worth destroying, and with millions annually devoted to development of radiological, bacteriological, and chemical (RBC) means of warfare, has far, far too much for its own good and for world security. Hence the initial presumption for disarmament relative to every proposal.

In some instances a proposal for a particular kind of new weaponry may be capable of justification. But under the circumstances it must bear a heavy burden of proof.

Finally, where warfare is now in progress, a friendly ear must be turned to any proposal for reducing or ending that warfare. The proposal may prove to be unpromising and subject to unacceptably serious objections. But the need to end hostilities and establish peace is critically urgent, both to stop the bloodshed and tragedy at the scene of war, and also to establish a more favorable climate for disarmament, rapprochement of the great powers, and the development of more effective world organization.

G. GUIDELINES OF AMERICAN FOREIGN POLICY

Christians in every country have obligations to do whatever they can for world peace and international order. The guidelines here are directed to the foreign policy of the United States because this book is written by an American, and also because the United States has the heaviest responsibilities and brightest opportunities to move the world toward the goals for which every person of goodwill and certainly every Christian must long. From these guidelines citizens of other countries can readily formulate similar ones for their own efforts.

1. End Such Interventions as That in Vietnam

During World War II the people of Vietnam, under Ho Chi Minh's leadership and with American support, successfully fought the Japanese invaders and won their freedom. After the war the French sought

to reimpose their colonial rule. The United States, fearful of Ho Chi
Minh's Communist ideology, supported France. Before France accepted defeat at Dienbienphu, in 1954, the United States was providing
most of the financial cost of the French military effort. On July 21,
1954, the United States pledged to respect the Geneva Agreement and
to "refrain from the threat or the use of force to disturb" the terms
of that accord.

Nevertheless, the United States supported the return from this country of Ngo Dinh Diem as premier and military dictator in Saigon.
Diem and succeeding military governments in Saigon had the support
of a considerable minority in South Vietnam but were kept in power
only by increasing application of American power, economic, diplomatic, and military.

Preoccupied as most Americans were with the single peril of Communism, it is not strange that many favored the closely limited military intervention which was begun by President John F. Kennedy. As
the character of the rule by Diem and his successors became more
widely known, and as the main burden of the war was taken over by
the United States under decisions of President Lyndon B. Johnson,
Americans in ever larger numbers became disturbed and then openly
opposed the intervention. By 1968 neither major presidential candidate
was willing to defend unequivocally the American presence in Vietnam. The prevailing assumption was that either the whole intervention
or the methods employed had been a mistake, but now we had the hard
task of finding the best way out.

Between 1961 and 1970 more than 50,000 Americans died in the In-
dochinese conflict, more than 40,000 of them in combat. Far more were
permanently handicapped by physical or mental injury. Over two hundred billion dollars had been spent in this adventure and the country
had been more deeply divided than ever before in this century.

Yet the Saigon government had still made none of the substantial
reforms demanded by the United States, was still unpopular, and continued to be dependent on American financial and military support for
its continuance. If American forces were ever to be withdrawn, North
Vietnam would still be at hand and nearby would be the power of the
Soviet Union and of China. In short, it was plainly not within the
power of the United States to guarantee that Communist forces could
not impose their form of government on South Vietnam. Fortunately,
even with the American invasion of Cambodia, China and the Soviet
Union had not thrown military forces into the fray. American military
pressures had, however, compelled both Vietnamese and Cambodians
to call in much Chinese aid and so, ironically, American policy had
caused a sharp increase in Chinese influence in Indochina where it had
been historically unwelcome.

Some will ask, then, how we are to deal with the extension of Communism by insurgency? If proper answers are to be found, we must begin by recognizing that this cannot be accomplished by military alliances—much less by active military interventions—in partnership with repressive regimes. Examples of such regimes would include that of Francisco Franco in Spain, the Portuguese rule in Angola and Mozambique, several aristocratic dictatorships of Latin America, and the successive governments in Saigon. The struggle with Communism is primarily a contest for the minds of men. Democracy cannot gain credibility by befriending corrupt and exploitative governments while the Communists, whatever their ultimate objectives, support landless peasants and oppressed workers.

The best defense against Communist insurgency is a combination of just and adequate meeting of human need along with a stable international order. Of the former we have spoken in Chapter Twelve, and somewhat more will be said below. There will be further discussion of the international order.

2. Stop Developing New Nuclear Weapons and RBC

Both the United States and the Soviet Union are in process of developing ever new weapons of mass destruction. Some theorists believe that the development of small nuclear weapons, of the kiloton and sub-kiloton classes, would be desirable. I must align myself with those who emphatically disagree. If a small nuclear bomb is ever used in war, the gate will be opened to rapid escalation of nuclear destruction.[16] No clear line can be drawn between the multimegaton giants and the small "tactical" nuclear bombs, even the sub-kiloton ones—which have their power measured in fractions of a thousand tons of TNT, so are themselves awesome weapons. No, we must start firmly on the road away from nuclear bombs, not go further in their development. This rule should hold with special firmness against efforts to multiply destruction—as by MIRV (multiple, independently targeted reentry vehicles).

The use of radiological, bacteriological, or chemical weapons would, by its very nature, indiscriminately destroy or imperil many noncombatants. Radiological weapons have the especially obnoxious quality of damaging the genetic chain and unpredictably injuring future generations. There is also much of unpredictability about bacteriological warfare, and what barbarism is this that prepares purposely to breed and spread disease among men! The chemistry of our environment is

16. Cf. Herman Kahn's view as quoted by Ramsey, *War and the Christian Conscience*, p. 292.

already so seriously polluted that its deliberate poisonous pollution is repulsive in the extreme.

3. End the Draft

Selective Service has taken an ominous grip on American life. Formerly the United States was a proud refuge for young men and their families threatened with unwanted and morally obnoxious military service in Europe. Many of our finest citizens are descendants of immigrants escaping from what we then called the slavery of conscription. Now it is our young men and their families who are the victims.

It is good that our laws permit conscientious objectors against all military service to perform "alternative service." But many of our most intelligent and conscientious youth who would be willing to serve in defense of their country under other circumstances cannot do so now without flagrant violation of conscience. They cannot in conscience participate in a military force based upon the strategy of nuclear terror. Neither can they accept the likelihood of being sent to fight in distant civil wars where "counterinsurgency" is the name for defending aristocratic military tyranny against Communist revolts appealing to desperate peasant victims of exploitation.

Even young men whose consciences are not violated are made to give years of military service, often mostly in idleness, and at subeconomic wages, while other people grow rich on the selling of military supplies. A smaller, professional army of men who choose such work would be more just and probably more efficient. We do not draft our ordinary police. Why should we draft the extraordinary police we call the military? We should have no need to do so if we reduced the inflated demands of our presumptuous foreign policy to legitimate levels.

4. Seek Broadest Possible International Agreement on Disarmament

There is not much likelihood of any major advance in arms limitation, let alone arms reduction, so long as the United States continues to wage war by its own decision, or threatens such war in remote areas of the world. But with the ending of such intervention and voluntary unilateral termination of development in nuclear and RBC weaponry, we should be in a strong position to press for progressive multilateral disarmament. Weapons of mass destruction should have first attention and then major offensive weapons of other kinds.

Many writers dismiss all suggestions of both unilateral and multilateral disarmament as utopian or unrealistic. But in the present time it is unrealistic in the extreme to think that the present level of national armaments can be continued without catastrophe which would dwarf all other disasters to which national foreign and defense policy could lead us. The nations *must* be persuaded. We must make urgent, immediate appeal to all to join in this risk for peace, expressing willingness to adopt generous formulas for doing so. However, it may be that all such persuasion will fall on deaf ears in the one nation which is a present arms rival, the Soviet Union. We must then move from the persuasion of words to the persuasion of further action.

5. Begin Public Disposal of Nuclear Weapons

The United States, by most accounts other than those emanating from the American military-industrial complex or from jingoists, has the most powerful military armament now in being. It certainly has economic ability to carry such a burden far more easily than any other nation—even though here it is at social cost we cannot afford. Hence the United States is in a uniquely favorable position to say *in action* that nuclear disarmament is urgently important to world security.

Would this be a utopian hope and too seriously imperil the security of the United States? It would represent the truth that the existence of nuclear weapons poses an intolerable peril to the security of this and all other nations, a peril greater than any other.

I agree with Paul Ramsey that the deterrent effect of our thermonuclear arsenal is greatly overrated because under no circumstances could it be rationally used and other nations must be more and more clearly aware of this fact. With explicit approval Ramsey quotes Franziskus Stratmann as affirming that

> "atomic armament no longer consists of 'weapons' in the proper sense of the word," and that "if the opponent should nevertheless start a war, in my opinion uncontrollable atomic weapons may even then not be used in defense, because this means is bad in itself" and also because "the damage, including the moral damage, will be greater if atomic weapons are stock-piled and employed by *both* sides" than by one only.[17]

Ramsey eloquently adds,

> I had rather be a pagan suckled in a creed outworn, terrified at the sight of hands made impure by any shedding of blood, than a skilled artisan of technical reason devising plans to carry out such a deed.
> [P. 170]

Note that Ramsey says "devising plans," a phrase which clearly includes the preparation in time of peace and not only the actual push-

17. *War and the Christian Conscience,* pp. 168–69, n. 47.

ing of the button. This is made more explicit and elaborated with emphasis at the end of the book.

It must be observed that I am not advocating pacifism. I agree with Ramsey that we must maintain military force for deterrent effect and, if necessary, actual use in justified war. However, I disagree with his acceptance of assumption by the United States of such global military responsibilities as are represented by present American policy. Accepting such responsibilities constitutes such irrational and immoral presumption by the United States as to force it into immoral means. This ethical error of Ramsey requires him to defend such vast military arming of the United States as to have driven him now to modify his strong repudiation of nuclear armament—at least above the kiloton level—which I have quoted.

If we are to lead the world into elimination of the balance of terror and the turning of priorities from arming for destruction to building for life, we must renounce the role of world policeman. The irrational assumption of that impossible role not only drives us into ever more immoral and irrational armament but makes us understandably feared and hated more and more widely, even in the populations we fancy ourselves to be protecting.

This is no advocacy of isolationism. Christian love requires a high degree of costly involvement but in support of life, not in destruction nor threatened destruction of life.

At every step we should make every effort to take the other nations with us in the reduction and elimination of nuclear arms. Yet if effort to get international agreement on this is not successful, we cannot keep waiting for another effort at such agreement, but must ourselves act decisively by publicly *renouncing* these weapons of mass destruction and destroying our own, preferably under international observation. As Ramsey says, in precisely this context,

> This will involve the decision, somewhere along the line, that a situation in which one people is destroyed is to be chosen over a situation in which two peoples are destroyed in retaliatory and counter-retaliatory warfare in any of its forms.[18]

Actually, however, such unilateral nuclear and RBC disarmament would not be a prescription for self-destruction. By this action we should greatly reduce the incentive for any nation to make a massive attack upon our population. We should be safer without our nuclear

18. *War and the Christian Conscience*, p. 323. This argument is not refuted or retracted by anything he has said in *The Just War*, even though, as I see it, some implications of it for a policy of deterrence are illogically denied in the latter work.

and RBC arms than with them, even though we might still need courage to withstand nuclear blackmail and to defend ourselves by limited counterforce means.

6. Call for Drastic General Disarmament

If the world is to be rescued from the constant fear and distorted priorities under which it now lives, the quantity of *all* armament must be reduced, along with the elimination of the nuclear balance of terror. With the persuasiveness of prior actions taken we should embark upon a program of proposals for general disarmament to much lower levels.

While risks for peace would be required in this effort also, it would require moving step by step, taking account of agreements and actions of other nations. For in such broader disarmament we should be dealing with weapons which nations could use—and not merely threaten to use—for nefarious political purpose and with weapons which in some conceivable circumstances we should be justified in using against hostile forces.

7. Commit Large Funds to Economic Development Through the United Nations

The United States, relieved of the excessive part of its present enormous burden of preparation for irrational warfare and presumptuous pretensions of world policing, should devote many billions per year to its long-postponed domestic needs and similar amounts to international development. The latter should be channeled principally through agencies of the United Nations. Such channeling would have the great advantage of avoiding the appearance and often the reality of fostering economic imperialism, with all the evil and resentment which that creates. It would also have the inestimably great advantage of strengthening the United Nations.

8. Seek Complete Rapprochement with China

Probably no other country has so much of national interest in common with the United States as Canada. Yet our good neighbor to the north has long followed a policy concerning mainland China based on a philosophy nearly opposite to our own. The United States has sought to ostracize and isolate the Peking government in order to weaken it, in the hope that it might fall and that it would at least be less well able to carry out aggressive schemes abroad. Canada, on the other hand, seeks to cultivate trade with China and in general to develop increased interchange of people and ideas, in the hope of overcoming the fears and hostilities of China and of preparing for her entry into a full peaceful participation in the community of nations.

Whatever might have been a defensible rationale for the American policy at one time, it has long ceased to be constructively relevant to the realities. The attempt to isolate China does not succeed in doing so, although it has pressed China to become as nearly self-sufficient as possible. The Communist government in Peking is not about to disappear because of our unfriendly policy. While it exists—and that will probably be for a very long time—its aggressive or pacific tendencies and its rational or irrational attitudes will continue to be strongly influenced by its relations with other countries. While bearing enormous domestic burdens of poverty and ignorance, it is in process of becoming a powerful nation. The all-important issue for the next decade is not whether China can be retarded somewhat in development but the question how it will choose to use its power as that increases.

We cannot expect that our first small efforts at reconciliation will receive much encouragement. Yet even small efforts of goodwill may somewhat soften the hostility that arises from resentment and fear. We must press forward steadily and persistently.

Our effort should include a forthright reversal of policy in the U.N. to join in inviting China to accept membership in the U.N., though this must not be at the price of expelling Taiwan or any other member. We should also directly offer full diplomatic recognition. This will cause the Nationalist Government in Taipei to fume in anger and possibly even break diplomatic relations with us. That would, however, be a hollow gesture since the government in Taipei owes its continued existence to our economic and military support. We cannot afford to continue an unproductive and long outmoded policy for fear of offending an aged dictator (or his son) and his absurd pretensions of power to recapture the mainland.

9. Vigorously Seek the Radical Broadening and Strengthening of the United Nations

The highest priority of our national policy ought to be the strengthening of international community and its embodiment in the United Nations. This is of one piece with the steps to reduce armaments to rational levels and to withdraw from our presumptuously extended military positions throughout the world. Without such acts of reason, goodwill, and calculated risk for peace, no proposals we can make in the United Nations will encounter a favorable climate for daring response. Such steps, on the other hand, require that in place of our national threatening presence throughout the world there be an international presence much stronger than any now available.

How should the United Nations be changed? No blueprint can be presented here. That will have to be worked out with sustained diplomacy and with the kind of brains, expenditures, and ceaseless effort we have been devoting to military alliances, defense technology, arms making, and explorations of space. We can only outline at this point one specification and several samples of directional goals.

a. Membership Open to All Nations. The exclusion of China, East and West Germany, and the two Koreas from the United Nations weakens its efforts for peace and in no way assists such efforts.[19]

b. Modification of Voting Procedures. The arbitrary definition of exclusive veto power in the Security Council by a short list of great powers (some not actually so large or so strong as others without such veto privilege) is prejudicially discriminatory. A less arbitrary formula must be substituted, but one still preserving substantial weighting for nations which must bear a disproportionately heavy brunt of the cost and labor of implementation.

c. Establishment of a Permanent United Nations Police Force. Eventually, such a force must be stronger than any national force or even any likely alliance of national forces. Eventually, too, it should have powers of inspection and enforcement of U.N. decisions. Such a goal must be approved by degrees.

d. Independent and Reliable Financing. There have been many suggestions for such financing—for example, that the resources under the oceans beyond national limits should be exploited exclusively by the United Nations for the people of the earth. Such plans would not, at least soon, displace financing by national appropriations, but they would increasingly render the U.N. independent of national withdrawal of support in irritation or in times of national economic distress.

The most careful and thought-provoking effort to define changes in the United Nations needed to make it an adequate instrument of world order is in the volume *World Peace Through World Law*, by Grenville Clark and Louis B. Sohn.[20] Both men are distinguished lawyers with unusual training and experience in international law. Clark was initiator of the Selective Service Act of 1940 and consultant to Secretary of War Stimson in 1940–1944. Sohn was formerly legal officer in the United Nations Secretariat.

Even with knowledge of the background of these authors and observance of their learned, persuasive arguments, there is a wide tendency simply to dismiss this, like other studies directed toward world law, as "utopian" or "unrealistic." Any realistic effort for visible world

19. Cf. the eloquent argument for the seating of China by the delegate from Ceylon, Ambassador Gunapala Malalasekera in the U.N. Assembly in 1961, in response to Adlai Stevenson's opposing statement. The text of both statements may be read in *The Strategy of World Order*, Vol. III, pp. 141–58.

20. 2nd ed. (rev.), Cambridge, Mass.: Harvard University Press, 1964.

peace is likely to seem so in the atmosphere created by the multi-billion-dollar preoccupation of Americans with their military establishment and the coordinate obsessively anti-Communist propaganda in which we are continuously submerged.

In response and in closing it must be said that the truly unrealistic and sinful utopianism is to continue in our present course, with only minor modifications. If we do continue in our society to put more money, brains, and effort into sensuous satisfaction, competition, provincial and national power, and the planning of destruction than into faith and education, cooperation for the common good, international law, and making a social and physical environment fit for future generations, then we can be certain of two consequences. First, we shall lose even the form of Christian faith, the substance of which is denied by these choices.[21] Second, we shall leave a heritage of hell on earth for our descendants until the early dismal end of human history.

On the other hand, we have it in our power to turn the corner of human affairs within the decade of the seventies. We can set the world firmly on the path of abolishing poverty, purifying the environment, reaffirming hopeful and wholesome family life, establishing peace and joyful cooperation as the dominant note in local and world society, and regain hope for earth and heaven in a renewal of loving faith which enacts what it affirms in words.

Of course, if we commit ourselves to such faith in action there is no guarantee that the church or nation will adopt any such lifesaving program. We may engage in a lonely struggle and see the world still heading for thermonuclear holocaust or suffocating pollution. In times of such discouragement our faith is placed in God. Our justification is by his grace through faith and not through success in achieving our social goals. To fail in such world-embracing goals for life is better than to succeed in the usual petty and provincial purposes for self and one's own ethnic group. God and current events alike call us to the large vision and the daring effort.

This call to responsible freedom is a summons to faith.

21. Cf. the readable and persuasive book by Jack Corbett, *Christians Awake!* (New York: Harper & Row, 1970).

Index of Personal Names

(Biblical names not included)

Index of Topics
(See also Contents)

———•—◦⟨∞⟩◦—•———

Format by C. Linda Dingler
Set in Janson
Composed, printed and bound by The Haddon Craftsmen, Inc.
HARPER & ROW, PUBLISHERS, INCORPORATED